Borobudur Temple

Author receiving *Bintang Bakti Utama* (Distinguished Service Star) from former Foreign Minister Adam Malik for his contributions to cement relations between Singapore and Indonesia.

A FRAGILE
NATION
THE INDONESIAN CRISIS

LEE KHOON CHOY

World Scientific
Singapore • New Jersey • London • Hong Kong

Published by

World Scientific Publishing Co. Pte. Ltd.
P O Box 128, Farrer Road, Singapore 912805
USA office: Suite 1B, 1060 Main Street, River Edge, NJ 07661
UK office: 57 Shelton Street, Covent Garden, London WC2H 9HE

British Library Cataloguing-in-Publication Data
A catalogue record for this book is available from the British Library.

A FRAGILE NATION — THE INDONESIAN CRISIS

ISBN   981-02-4003-1 (pbk)

Printed in Singapore.

ACKNOWLEDGEMENTS

In the course of writing this book, many Indonesians, some well-known and in positions of authority in the past whilst others just ordinary folks, have helped me along the way. Some have helped me get in touch with people who were not easy to contact, such as the Baduis, the Tenggerese, the Torajans, and the Irianese in Wamena, Sorong and Biak. A word of thanks to Mr Des Alwi for arranging our flight to the island of Banda from Ambon and for taking me and my family on a tour of Banda.

I have also learnt from hundreds of Indonesians from various walks of life in the various regions something about their ways of life, their beliefs, customs and traditions. It is impossible and impracticable for me to mention them all. To each and everyone of them I express my deep appreciation.

I am especially grateful to the late Mas Agung and Drs Harteadji of Idayu, an organisation for research on Indonesian affairs, and Mr Anada Surjono Hamongdarsono of Solo for having kindly arranged to take me on a "spiritual tour" of Central Java which provided me with the opportunity to have a deeper insight into Javanese mysticism.

I want to express especially my deepest appreciation to Associate Professor Leo Suryadinata from the Department of Political Science, National University of Singapore for taking the trouble to read my script, making corrections and giving valuable comments on the book.

I would like also to thank Sharon Siddique for reading the script and giving good suggestions and to Mr Chin Kah Chong of the Pananews Agency and Mr Roberto Z. Coloma, Bureau Chief of Agence France-Presse (AFP) for allowing me to print some of the photographs belonging to them in this book. I am grateful to Mr Dominic Pangborn, President and CEO of Pangborn Design in Detriot for designing the cover of this book.

Last but not least, to my daughter Chuen Ting for her help in making this book possible.

L.K.C.

CONTENTS

A FRAGILE
NATION
THE INDONESIAN CRISIS

INTRODUCTION

Since 1955 when I first visited Bandung to attend the Afro-Asian Conference as a journalist, I have been fascinated by the multi-racial, multi-religious, multi-lingual and multi-cultural society of Indonesia. I returned to Indonesia from time to time as a journalist and visited many provinces. Whilst appreciating the varieties of dishes, dances and music of the people, I also observed the behaviour of the peoples from different provinces.

In 1970, I was posted to Indonesia as Singapore's Ambassador and I took a keener interest in studying the psyche of the people at closer quarters. I spent four-and-a-half years in Indonesia trying to settle differences between the two countries and finally succeeded in cementing the personal friendship between former Prime Minister Lee Kuan Yew and former President Suharto. I came into close contact with various strata of the Indonesian society — from the President, military leaders, ministers, top civil servants down to spiritual leaders, scholars, musicians, dancers, businessmen and other ordinary people of Indonesia. I befriended all of them and developed an affection for them and for Indonesia. I took the opportunity as an ambassador to travel widely in Indonesia and tried to befriend the governors and military leaders of the 26 provinces. When I left the country, Indonesia had not yet annexed East Timor.

Indonesia is an ethnological goldmine. Over the centuries, there has been an influx of people from China, Arabia, Polynesia, Indo-China and, later, Europe into Indonesia. The variety of its human geography is without parallel on earth. It consists of some 336 ethnic groups, living on 13,677 islands, speaking 250 dialects and are religiously and culturally different. The colours of their skins vary from yellow to brown and coal black.

In Indonesia, you can find ways of life which are five thousand years apart — from Jakarta where it is completely modernised to Wamena where I saw the Dhanis who were naked with their men wearing only *kotekas* (the dried skin of a gourd worn as a protection for their private parts), as if they were still living in the stone age. Compared with the Javanese aristocrat, the Irianese are like people from another world. Only a short distance from Bogor in the remote mountains, you can find Baduis who have been isolated from civilisation since the days of the Majapahit Empire in the 13th century.

I have chosen the title "A Fragile Nation — The Indonesian Crisis" because I have reason to agree with Amien Rais, the former leader of the 28-million-strong Muhammadiyah association and the current chairman of the Partai Amanat Rakyat (PAN) of Indonesia, who said in Singapore in July 1998 that Indonesia "was in danger of falling apart" and the "syndrome of Yugoslavia and the former Soviet Union is creeping into Indonesia". He said Indonesia was in danger of "disintegrating with voices of discontent in provinces such as Irian Jaya, Timor and Aceh". Abdurrahman Wahid, the 52-year-old prominent leader of Indonesia's largest Muslim party, the Nadhlatul Ulama (NU), also issued a similar warning.

The riots of May 13-14, 1998 in Jakarta, targetted at ethnic Chinese resulted in 5,000 Chinese-owned buildings being burnt, several thousands of Chinese killed and at least 164 Chinese girls and women raped. There is a serious religious clash between the Muslims and the Christians in Ambon, resulting in at least 1,000 dead and hundreds wounded. The Muslims were burning down Christian churches, and the Christians destroying mosques. Jakarta Muslims are calling for a "jihad" (religious war) in Ambon. If that should happen it will spread

christians vs. Muslims

to other provinces where there are Christians. (These events' showed a serious infringement of the spirit of tolerance as symbolised by the motto *Bhinneka Tunggul Ika* (Unity in Diversity) inscribed on the Indonesian state crest.) The atrocities caused by a minority fanatical group of Indonesians on ethnic Chinese show that this spirit of tolerance is disappearing in the Indonesian society. Let me first explain the meaning of *Bhinneka Tunggul Ika*.

These words appeared in a legend which can be found in a book entitled *Sutasoma*, written in old Javanese by Mpu Tantular around the thirteenth or fourteenth century. An ogre king by the name of *Purushada* (meaning 'eating people') was fond of human flesh for his daily meals. The commonfolk, one after another, became his victims and they were terrified. A knight by the name of *Sutasoma* took pity on the people and offered himself to the king to be devoured instead of the people. Purushada was furious with Sutasoma for trying to interfere with his eating habits which he considered quite normal. He attempted to kill Sutasoma but could not because Sutasoma was equally strong. A bitter struggle took place. Lord Siva entered the body of the king, and Lord Buddha entered that of the knight. It was a long-drawn battle in which supernatural powers were invoked. Neither one could defeat his adversary. Then the Brahmins came, appealed to both warriors to cease fighting, and told them that though their appearances might be different, they were in reality one. In the old Javanese language, the words which the Brahmins used to drop the hint that Siva and Buddha were one in different forms were *Bhinneka Tunggul Ika*. Siva and Buddha, realising the oneness in them, left the bodies of the two warriors. Purushada then gave up his habit of devouring people and began to lead a normal life.

(*Bhinneka Tunggul Ika* means "Unity in Diversity" which describes the flexibility of the Indonesian people to syncretise and to blend the various religious beliefs, traditions and cultures — some of which are conflicting in the eyes of foreigners — into one to suit local conditions.) It reminds the Indonesians of the necessity and virtue of the spirit of tolerance and accommodation in a multi-racial, multi-religious, multi-cultural and multi-lingual society. This spirit of tolerance and syncretism has made intermarriages between persons of different religions a common affair. It is not unusual to find an Indonesian family in which many religions are practised concurrently. I have a friend in high position who is a Muslim. His wife is a Catholic, and his children are either Muslims or Catholics. One of them even practises *kebatinan* (an indigenous Javanese religious movement with a strong element of Buddhism). In this country, nobody tries to force another to adopt his religion, there is mutual respect so that all can live in harmony.

From a religious symbol, *Bhinneka Tunggul Ika* became a political one when former President Sukarno tried to syncretise nationalism, religion and communism into a state ideology under the name of *Nasakom.* Although it might appear to observers that the basic tenets of the three politico-religious concepts contain fundamental contradictions which are irreconcilable, President Sukarno was tempted to give it a trial run. Nasakom ended on the rocks because one of the three components had tried to impose its will on the others by the use of force. It had infringed the spirit of tolerance. Once the rule is broken, the balance of the scale is tipped, and the whole idea collapsed. It was a good lesson to most Indonesians and the spirit of tolerance as symbolised by *Bhinneka Tunggul Ika* has since been institutionalised.

The slogan *Bhinneka Tunggul Ika* may be comparable to the biological term "symbiosis" meaning "relying on one another for survival". The more popular phrase in everyday use is "to live and let live". I remember vividly how the former Minister of Information, Mr Mashuri, explained to me his concept of symbiosis in human relations as opposed to the Western concept of "survival of the fittest". He said the symbiotic approach is to treat one's fellowmen as an interdependent part of the whole human society whose survival is conditional upon mutual help for mutual benefit. On the other hand, the Western concept of "survival of the fittest" makes humans treat one another as separate, antagonistic units. They attempt to eliminate others in order to survive, in the same way as big fish eat small fish and small fish eat the shrimps. Based on this concept, the strong try to dominate the weak and impose their will on them. This is the root of all the trouble in human society.

Mashuri said unless people learn to live with one another instead of following the concept of "survival of the fittest", the world will always be plagued by tension, chaos and friction. The failure of the Nasakom ideology can also be interpreted as a clash between the spirit of "symbiosis" and that of "survival of the fittest". One of the proponents of Nasakom tried to apply the theory of "survival of the fittest" on Indonesian soil, but failed because traditionally the soil had been saturated with the *Bhinneka Tunggul Ika* spirit.

The failure of the Nasakom ideology has brought Indonesia back to the philosophy of *Pancasila* — a philosophy originated by Sukarno but refined by Suharto after he became President. Pancasila means observing the five principles: Belief in one God, Humanity, Sovereignty of the people, Social Justice and Democracy. The Suharto Government has made the first of October (the day after the disastrous Gestapu coup of 30 September 1965) the Pancasila day to remind the people of the disaster of the killing of six generals and one soldier. All seven of them were thrown into the Lubang Buaya (crocodile hole) after their assassination. Blame was put on the Indonesian Communist Party (PKI) for the assasination and about half a million of suspected Communist party members were slaughtered by extreme Muslims after the incident referred to as the *Gestapu* coup.

To revive further the spirit of the 1945 revolution and the struggle for independence, a Pancasila monument was erected at Kalibata where national heroes are buried. The monument comprising five towering pillars representing the five principles of Pancasila was officially declared open by President Suharto on 11 November 1974. The monument was to commemorate the millions of unknown soldiers who had sacrificed their lives for independence.

After the fall of Suharto, even the Pancasila philosophy is facing a serious challenge by some fundamentalist Muslims who are clamouring for an Islamic state for Indonesia. The success of the Islamic revolutions, particularly in Iran and elsewhere, have encouraged them to revive the Islamic dream of enforcing Islamic law in Indonesia. On 30 July, 1998, representatives of Muslim groups slipped into the state secretariat in Jakarta to present a petition to current President Habibie demanding that political parties be freed from the state ideology of Pancasila, and also demanding the establishment of an Islamic state in Indonesia.

The Pancasila spirit is based on the spirit of *Bhinneka Tunggul Ika* and, if weakened, then bloodshed, chaos and disharmony will befall Indonesia. In recent years, there were already many incidents of the Muslim extremists burning down Christian churches and Chinese temples. The May 13 riots demonstrated the intolerance of some people who went on a rampage against the Chinese. If Indonesia is Islamised, several provinces that are non-Muslim will want to split away from Indonesia. That is why I think the country is rather fragile at this moment.

In this book, my first chapter deals with the political and economic situation facing Indonesia after the fall of Suharto and the end of his 32-year-old reign as a "Javanese king". I describe his contribution as the "economic father" of modern Indonesia, but also explain his weakness in not being able to distribute wealth more equally among his people. I give the reasons behind his political collapse, and how he had failed to balance the power between the military forces and Islam. Like Sukarno, who fell because he failed to balance the power between the armed forces and the communists, Suharto also fell because he failed to maintain an equilibrium between the armed forces and Islam. In the first chapter under the title "Why Suharto Fell", I venture into the future of Indonesia and the various problems facing the country if the spirit of *Bhinneka Tunggul Ika* is not observed.

The book describes the diversity of the various peoples, their history, their dialects, their traditions, customs, cultures, their colourful ways of life and their psyche. I have first made an analysis of the Javanese who are the real masters of Indonesia. I became interested in Javanese mysticism after a prominent Sumatran journalist, Mochtar Lubis, had hinted to me that I should first understand Javanese mysticism if I wanted to make headway in Indonesia. Then, even Adam Malik, the former Foreign Minister and Vice-President who was a Batak Muslim, advised me to study Javanese mysticism because he said he himself could not understand the Javanese.

I was made to realise that to understand Indonesia, one must understand Javanese mysticism. An elite of perhaps 2,000 men manipulate Indonesia's politics. Many of them are *abangans* or nominal Muslims who are Muslims and yet not entirely Muslims with their own beliefs. Unlike orthodox Muslims referred to as *santris* who believe only in Mohammed and Allah (God), these abangans believe in kebatinan, that is, the spirits which dwell in the *kris*; they believe in the existence of *Semar*, the guardian spirit of Java; predictions of *Joyoboyo*; and *Lara Kidul*, the Queen of the Indonesian Ocean. The Javanese are addicted to *wayang*, their shadow play. I have written seven sections under the title of Javanese mysticism, describing the wayang, the kris, the *kratons* (Javanese palace), Semar, the Joyoboyo predictions and Lara Kidul. Since the Javanese comprise 45 percent of the population, it is necessary to give more prominence to Javanese mysticism.

The book then deals with the history of the happy-go-lucky Sundanese, who dislike to be called Javanese because historically they hold a grudge against Gajah Mada, the famous Javanese prime minister. Gajah Mada had disgraced a Sundanese princess by putting her in the imperial harem when she should have been officially married to King Hayam Wuruk. The insult led to war between the Javanese and the Sundanese resulting in the killing of the Sundanese king and the princess, who also died in the battle. In the Sundanese city of Bandung, I discovered that there is no street named after Gajah Mada, unlike most other cities.

I next deal with the hot-tempered Madurese, who were also historically hostile to the Javanese kingdom. Then, I deal with the Balinese, who were practitioners of mass suicide and who live in a religious world of their own. I also touched on the Baduis who isolated themselves in the mountains off Bogor, and the Tenggerese who were Hindu devotees living around Mount Bromo. Both these tribes ran away from mainstream Indonesia when Islam came to Java because they refused to be converted.

This book then deals with the Sumatrans who wanted to establish a rebel government with Bukit Tinggi as their headquarters to rival that of Jakarta. There were uprisings in Sumatra engineered by Colonel Simbolon, a famous Sumatran military leader, who, backed by his battalion of Sinta Pohan, went against the Jakarta Government led by Sukarno because they considered him a "wicked and godless man" who got too close with the communists. In Sumatra, I covered the cultures and traditions of the Minangkabaus and their matriarchal system; the Bataks, dynamic people who once practised cannibalism; the Acehnese who are Islamic fundamentalists still trying to establish an Islamic State of Aceh; and the Orang Melayu (Malays) who happen to be the founders of a Buddhist Srivijaya Empire and who now live in the Riau Islands and Palembang. As we know, Melayus are the majority race in Malaysia, but in Indonesia, they are a minority race.

From Sumatra, I turn to Sulawesi, and describe the Bugis (the seafarers) and the Makassarese — both tribes had aspired to set up an "Islamic Republic of South Sulawesi" — and the Torajans, mostly Christians who have their own peculiar customs and traditions and bury their dead in the rock mountains.

I have a special chapter on the Ambonese who were not ashamed to be called "black Dutch" and had been used by the Dutch as professional soldiers just as the Gurkhas were used by the British. These Ambonese were used by the Dutch to suppress the revolutionary movements in Indonesia. They too wanted to secede from Indonesia and form their own republic called "The Republic of Maluku Selatan" when Javanese republican forces came to replace the Dutch colonial army. Their attempt failed and hundreds of thousands of Ambonese and Moluccans were repatriated to Holland where they were stranded and unable to return to Indonesia. Ambon has again hit the newspaper headlines recently when a clash between Muslims and Christians took place causing the death of 200 Ambonese. It is the worst religious riot in history.

I also have a chapter on the Bandanese with a small population in Banda, about an hour's flight from Ambon by a mosquito plane. Although this island is insignificant to modern Indonesia, it was once the centre of the nutmeg trade and an important island because two of Indonesia's leaders, Dr Mohammad Hatta, the Vice-President and Sutan Sjahrir, Indonesia's first Prime Minister — were exiled there by the Dutch colonial authorities.

I have a chapter on the Irianese who, though living in the stone age, are also striving to rid themselves of what they call Javanese colonisation. I describe the primitive way of living in Irian Jaya and also talk about the separatist movement there which considers the moment ripe for a secession after the fall of Suharto. There is another chapter on the East Timorese whom I describe as a "people betrayed" and then discuss how and why Indonesia annexed the country and how the Timorese are still clamouring for independence.

I have a special chapter on the Chinese. They are after all Indonesian citizens and number more than 6.5 million — about three percent of the total population and more than double the population of Singapore. This chapter explains why Indonesians are anti-Chinese, the impact of the economic measures taken by Chinese *cukongs* (economic masters behind the scene) who have aroused feelings of hatred among the other Indonesians. I also discuss the problem of loyalty of the Chinese, their language and cultures. Through the centuries, the Chinese have built up a distribution network that is not easy to replace. Their trustworthiness had helped to draw foreign investments to Indonesia from Japan, America, Europe and overseas Chinese all over the world.

The May 13 riots have caused the Chinese to lose billions of dollars in properties and thousands of lives, and having many of their women raped. This resulted in an exodus of many wealthy Chinese and their capital thereby wrecking Indonesia's economic foundation. Nobody knows whether these Chinese who were essential to the successful functioning of Indonesia's business systems will ever return to Indonesia. Many of them have migrated to Thailand, which offers an easy way of obtaining permanent residency. Some have migrated to Australia which also took the opportunity to draw in new investors. What will happen if all the well-to-do Chinese decide to quit Indonesia? Can Indonesia survive without the Chinese?

I end the book with a chapter on the Dayaks who predominate Kalimantan. Kalimantan occupies three-quarters of Borneo, the third largest island in the world. The Dayaks are notorious for head-hunting and I touch on the culture and traditions of this people and their clash with the Bugis who are also head-hunters.

The aim of this book is to help bring about a better understanding of the Indonesian people who have inherited not only one of the richest natural resources of the world, but also a rich, diverse cultural heritage.

My book was written without scholarly pretensions. I am not afraid, now and then, to introduce my own personal impressions and reflections on the course of events. Nor do I shy away from prying into purely personal relationship. I have deliberately tried to give an account of what I saw or heard in a journalistic style. I realise that the specialists who read my book may discover certain defects. To some extent this is inevitable.

Indonesia is the third largest country in Asia, only smaller than China and India. It is resource-rich. It has large reserves of natural gas, oil, timber, rubber, coffee and other products. It does not need a super genius to run the country. All it needs is a good, lean and credible government, political stability and efficient economic management to restore confidence. With these and the spirit of *Bhinneka Tunggul Ika*, the country has a bright future.

Very little has been written about the colourful cultures of the peoples of Indonesia. As a result, there is much misunderstanding and misconception about the country. The Javanese, for instance, are the most polite and refined people on earth. But, like the volcano, the hidden and suppressed emotions may sometimes burst out and suddenly you find acts of violence such as the Gestapu coup of 1965 and the recent May 13 riots in Jakarta. The Balinese are very charming people, always placid and calm, but there were several occurrences of *puputan* or mass suicide in their modern history. The various races of ethnic peoples in Indonesia have vastly different temperaments and lifestyles. This book makes an attempt to describe them all.

I have always believed that in international relations and human relations, the understanding and appreciation of each other's culture plays a very important role in bringing about peace and harmony in the world today. It is often the cultural barriers and misconceptions of each other's motives and intentions that bring about disputes, chaos and wars. For instance, the Javanese normally speaks softly whereas the Arabs often shout when they speak. There could be misunderstanding when the two races speak to each other. When a Javanese nods his head, it does not mean that he agrees with you but merely that he has heard you. This too could cause misunderstanding if one does not understand Javanese culture. There are many different characteristics and idiosyncracies in the various cultures of the Indonesian peoples and an understanding of them will be useful in dealing with them.

The IMF officials, for instance, recommended that Indonesia should increase petrol prices presumably for economic reasons, at the height of the economic crisis in mid-1998. Apparently, they did not understand the Indonesian culture, thereby precipitating Suharto's fall from office.

It is essential and beneficial for people dealing with the Indonesians or the Indonesian Government, be they IMF officials, foreign tourists or investors, to have a better understanding of the psyche of the Indonesians.

It is my sincere hope and desire that this book will help contribute towards this goal.

1
WHY SUHARTO FELL

With the fall of President Suharto, Indonesia, a country of 200 million people composed of different races, languages, cultures and traditions is facing the danger of falling apart. The cry for independence from Javanese domination has already started in East Timor and Irian Jaya, two provinces which Indonesia annexed during the Suharto regime. There is also an undercurrent of uncertainty in Aceh which has, on several occasions, tried to secede from Indonesia.

At the end of January 1999, Jakarta offered East Timor "wide autonomy" and would propose full independence if it rejects its package of autonomy proposals. Violence erupted again when pro-independence forces clashed with pro-Jakarta forces causing about 30 people to be killed. The pro-Jakarta elements have asked the Indonesian Armed Forces (Abri) to give them arms so that they could protect themselves.

As early as 12 July, 1998, non-East Timorese farmers including ethnic Javanese and Bugis from South Sulawesi who had previously transmigrated to Dili, the East Timorese capital, were fleeing from their home town. Hundreds of cars and buses loaded with these transmigrants, many of whom are civil servants and small traders, were taking them out of East Timor. Most of them have gone to the West Timor capital of Kupang with their household and personal belongings. They fled the town because of rumours that a massive pro-independence rally was about to take place. Ethnic Bugis have long been the focus of attack in East Timor because they are seen as dominating the commercial life of the territory.

In August 1998, Abri soldiers started to pull out of East Timor to appease the Timorese and enable Indonesian Foreign Minister, Ali Alatas, to open negotiations with the Portuguese representatives. This was carried out under the guidance of the United Nation's Secretary-General to give Timor "autonomous" status as promised by the new President B.J. Habibie.

In Wamena, capital of Irian Jaya, there were also demonstrations including the hoisting of an independence flag by pro-independence Irianese. Indonesian soldiers are also withdrawing from Irian Jaya.

In August 1998, Indonesia's Armed Forces Chief and Defence Minister, General Wiranto, announced that Indonesia would end military operations in Aceh and remove its combat troops from the province amid accusations of army atrocities. General Wiranto had gone to North Sumatra to investigate accusations raised since the fall of Suharto about human rights abuses during the military operations with details of abductions, rapes, torture and mass killings. The Legal Aid Foundation in Banda Aceh has said that 190 mass graves had been found at three sites in the province where the armed forces suppressed a separatist insurgency that peaked in the early 1990s. The graves were believed to contain the bodies of hundreds of people killed by soldiers during military operations conducted mainly between 1991 and 1993, to smash the insurgency and flush out its leaders.

When the Abri forces were about to withdraw from Aceh, violence broke out again and General Wiranto had to reinforce his forces to maintain law and order. At the end of last year, mobs believed to be pro-separatist dragged seven soldiers from public transport buses and killed them, an act which local officials attributed to an angry outburst over years of suppression by the military.

Indonesia, a vast archipelago with over 300 ethnic groups spread across 17,000 islands, faces simmering regional tensions which can flare into separatist violence, particularly in the troublesome provinces of East Timor, Irian Jaya and Aceh. Residents from these three provinces have blamed the central government for much of the violence they have experienced over the years, accusing Jakarta of suppressing them so they would not be able to ask for more. They have grown restive as they watched the central government exploit their resources, such as oil and gas and give little in return. Some regional unrest is rooted in centuries-old resistance to central rule.

The fall of Suharto is like the opening of a pandora box and the centre of power is lost. There seems to be a sign of less tolerance on the part of fanatic Islamic elements in the Indonesian population. In the May 13 riots in Jakarta, the brutal rapists were shouting slogans of "Allahu Akbar" meaning "God is the greatest" in Arabic. They were screaming aloud, "'Let's butcher the Chinese', 'Let's kill the pig eaters', 'Let's kill the Chinese pigs'." They even threatened to castrate all Chinese children so that there would be no more Chinese in Indonesia.

The May 13 riots of 1998 in Jakarta targetted at ethnic Chinese resulted in 5,000 Chinese-owned buildings being burnt, several thousands of Chinese killed, and at least 164 Chinese girls and women raped. This caused an exodus of Chinese fleeing the country with just their savings, thus paralysing the Indonesian food distribution system, especially the sundry shops in Jakarta and the countryside which were mostly run by the Chinese. On 17 July, 1998, intimidation and looting and fears of further violence sparked a fresh exodus of ethnic Chinese from Indonesia's second largest city, Surabaya. Around 300 ethnic Chinese crowded the port for ships out of Indonesia. Witnesses in the East Java town of Jember, near Surabaya, said that some shops, warehouses and plantations owned by Chinese had been looted. Hundreds of Indonesians had also plundered rice fields and shrimp farms near Jember, and a large crowd including women and children had stripped clean ten hectares of immature coffee plants. As famine spreads, hungry Indonesians are on the move to grab whatever they can lay their hands on in order to survive.

The spirit of tolerance enshrined in the Indonesian motto *Bhinneka Tunggul Ika* (Unity in Diversity) has suddenly disappeared. The violence which started as racial turned into religious and communal clashes.

There was nothing to stop the violence. There was no more respect for each other's race and religion. There was no rule of law and everyone can take away the life of anyone as he likes. Where is Indonesia heading?

On 6 February, General Wiranto finally issued a stern order to his military commanders that they could shoot rioters on sight to quell the mob violence that had been rippling through the country. He said, "These people are attacking public property and destroying churches and mosques. If this continues, it affects our standing in the international community." Abri was monitoring "hot spots" in Aceh, Medan, Surabaya, Solo, Ujung Pandang and other larger cities which could implode given the sensitive mix of ethnic, religious, labour and economic issues. What will happen if the military commanders really carry out General Wiranto's orders? Will there be more serious repercussions?

General Wiranto's order to shoot received the backing of Gus Dur, the influential Muslim leader who warned that the continued lawlessness in Indonesia might trigger a social revolution which could claim up to three million lives. Gus Dur said, "Considering incidents of lawlessness that have occurred in many parts of the country, Indonesia is now on the brink of a social revolution. And if a social revolution really does happen, it would be a truly racial and national tragedy."

He was speaking in Jakarta at an interactive dialogue on "Preventing Social Revolutions". Gus Dur's estimation on the number of possible casualties was based on a comparison to the 1949 social revolution in China. The upheaval at that time claimed about 12 million lives.

"If the population in Indonesia is a fifth of China's then a social revolution in Indonesia would claim about two to three million lives," he said.

He then voiced support for General Wiranto's order to shoot on sight anybody trying to disrupt security and order.

Speaking to Muslims at a gathering organised by the Centre for Contemporary Islamic Studies at a hotel in Singapore, the leader of Indonesia's 28-million-strong Muhammadiyah Party, Amien Rais, who is standing for election for the Presidency, warned that despite the change in leadership, his country was in danger of falling apart because of worsening economic crisis and continued political uncertainty.

He said, "I find that the syndrome of Yugoslavia and the former Soviet Union is creeping into Indonesia. There is a danger that the country may go the way the two states had gone crumbling into pieces."

Rais said Indonesia was in danger of disintegrating with voices of discontent in provinces such as Irian Jaya, Timor and Aceh. He said such separatist tendencies could be dealt with if there was decentralisation of authority and three provinces were granted a loose form of autonomy.

Rais who was in the forefront in the movement against former Suharto, also noted that the Indonesian economy was getting worse even though Suharto had stepped down in May.

He said, "Our rupiah has been sliding down in value compared to the US dollar. Prices of basic commodities are now beyond the reach of the masses."

In November 1998, Amien Rais even warned that Indonesia might face a civil war and called for urgent talks between student protestors and members of the legislative assembly. He was commenting on the November 1998 riots which demanded the withdrawal of Abri from politics and to hang General Wiranto. The soldiers opened fire on the students causing the death of 11 people.

I tend to agree with Amien Rais when he said Indonesia faces the danger of disintegration and that a civil war is also likely.

In a joint statement by Ms Megawati, daughter of former President Sukarno and leader of the Partai Demokrasi Indonesia (Indonesian Democratic Party), the Bishop of Timor, Carlos Belo, who has been awarded a Nobel Prize, and Abdurrahman Wahid, popularly known as Gus Dur, the 52-year-old leader of Indonesia's largest Muslim Association, the Nadhlatul Ulama (NU), they warned that Indonesia could be in danger of disintegrating if the present crisis facing the country was not overcome quickly.

With the fall of Suharto, there is a power vacuum and the paradigm has changed. Suharto's sudden departure has transformed the political landscape and altered the balance of power in a system that had taken unquestioned leadership for granted. The iron grip of a strong one-man rule is not there anymore. The people's attitude towards authority has changed from fear and cynicism to outright attack and ridicule of his successor.

Suharto's son-in-law General Prabowo has been dismissed by Abri after a military investigation found him directly responsible for the abduction and torture of political activists. There is even suspicion that he had a hand in the May riots. However, there are people who believe that he is only a scapegoat if Abri does not probe deeper into the allegations of past brutalities uncovered in East Timor and Aceh. There is already a strong rumour that factions of Abri led by him have gone underground. There are signs that there is a split within Abri — some pro-Pancasila and others pro-Islamic political parties, and a considerable number still under the influence of Suharto, who stays behind in Jakarta after stepping down, perhaps trying to exert some kind of influence with his wealth.

The man who took over from Suharto by accident was Dr B.J. Habibie, a technocrat and close confidante of Suharto from Sulawesi who was Vice-President when the riots took place. The first thing which President Habibie did when he became President was to visit Chinatown in Jakarta to asssure the Chinese that there would be no more anti-Chinese riots. He was made to realise that without the Chinese, it would be difficult to put Indonesia back economically. Several months back, Habibie had told a Japanese audience that he was not happy with the Chinese who comprise three percent but control 90 percent of Indonesia's economy. On the eve of Indonesia's National Day, Habibie shifted his stand and called on all Indonesians to reaffirm their nationalistic spirit and said the nation had been shamed by those who looted and raped women of ethnic Chinese origin during the May riots. Making his first state-of-the-nation address before Indonesia's 53rd independence day, he promised firmer action against continued looting, which he blamed for slowing down the return of business confidence. He said, "As a civilised and religious nation, we curse these barbaric acts." He added that the spirit of nationalism which led to the proclamation of an independent Indonesia 53 years ago had been challenged by the recent riots and needed to be reaffirmed.

Habibie said he would change the law to remove the differentiation between *pribumi* and non-*pribumi* and the government would give protection to the Chinese.

Will Habibie be able to maintain a grip on Abri now that Suharto is gone? He has never been a soldier and does not have a strong connection with the military. In fact, some military leaders disliked him. He has tried to break away from his past associations with Suharto and to make a difference. He has released political prisoners, allowed new political parties, offered autonomy to East Timor and pulled out troops from Aceh. But, on the economic side, he has done little that matters, despite all that he had said. Even though he is widely seen as a stop-gap president in a time of political transition, he intends to exploit the powers of incumbency to launch his campaigns for the presidential election in December 1999.

Since the fall of President Suharto last May and the collapse of his 32-year regime, more than 200 new political parties have been formed to contest the election for a new Parliament. The Parliament will form the core of the expanded body that will later choose a President to lead the economically devastated country out of its authoritarian past and into the new democratic future. Since Suharto's fall, the Indonesian people seem to be craving for democratic freedom as if democracy will cure all the evils of the country. They seem to think that with democracy, they can do whatever they think is right for their self-interest. The widespread mob violence may be the result of this new-found freedom. With such widespread mob violence, one wonders whether the election will ever take place at all.

There are three major candidates for power. First, Ms Megawati Sukarnoputri. She and her PDI represent the nationalist opposition to the corruption and abuses of the Suharto era. She draws large crowds, primarily due to the power of her family name, particularly for a younger generation with no living memory of Sukarno's chaotic rule in the 1960s. Sukarno used to have more than 100 Cabinet ministers who were good at only shouting political slogans and not solving the economic problems facing the country. I remember he once said, "If we are hungry, we can eat stone."

Ms Megawati's position is bolstered by her tactical alliance with the leader of the country's largest Muslim organisation, Abdurrahman Wahid, nicknamed Gus Dur. It seems that she even got the support of some leading members of Abri.

Gus Dur is the leader of Nadhlatul Ulama (NU) which is the largest and most influential Indonesian Islamic organisation with a membership of 35 million. He is a provocative religious and political thinker and a leading proponent of secular democracy in Indonesia. He is also a figure of considerable international stature, having been honoured with a Ramon Magsaysay Award in 1993 (Asia's equivalent of a Nobel Prize), and since late 1994, has served as a member of the Presidential Board of the prestigious World Council on Religion and Peace. He is leading the organisation founded by his grandfather, Hasyim Asyari and later led by his father, Wahid Hasyim, a national figure and a former Minister of Religion under Sukarno. In 1945, Sukarno consulted him on the implementation of the five principles of Pancasila.

Gus Dur is considered part of a revolutionary generation of Islamic thinkers in Indonesia. He is not afraid to do whatever he thinks is good for the country and for Islam. In October 1994, he travelled to Israel and upon his return home recommended that the Indonesian Government open diplomatic relations with Israel. This caused quite a stir among Muslim circles in Indonesia.

Unfortuntely, Gus Dur is suffering from eye problems and has diabetes. He has to be helped when he moves around. His health is not too good. He has hinted at running for President himself, but most see this as a move to galvanise the 30 million members of his NU to get to the polls. He is running as head of NU's National Awakening Party, but after the election it is rumoured that he may endorse Ms Megawati as President.

Another strong contender is academic Amien Rais, who headed the second largest Muslim organisation, Muhammadiyah, and now chairs the new National Mandate Party. Amien catapulted to national prominence at the forefront of the student-led street demonstrations that ousted Suharto, and he became known as a fiery opponent of the old regime — at a crucial time, when Megawati stayed largely in the background. He may be bolstered if he can form a coalition of urban intellectuals and others looking for an alternative to the PDI leader, who is faulted by many as too cautious, and for failing to articulate a bold vision for Indonesia's future. So far, Megawati has not spelt out her programme for the nation. There is speculation that there may be a tie-up between Amien Rais and Megawati, and if this is true, then Gus Dur may withdraw his support for Megawati. It is a complicated situation.

One thing most Jakarta-based analysts agree on is that President Habibie, the hand-picked Suharto's successor, will have a difficult time remaining in office. His ruling party, Golkar, retains its organisational structure, particularly in the villages, but it has been widely discredited for its unflagging support of Suharto. In January 1999, Golkar chairman, Akbar Tandjung, issued the party's first apology for its "wrongdoings and mistakes in the past".

Golkar has been trying to develop a more reformist image. Some even suggested that the party should drop Habibie as its presidential candidate in a bid for popularity. At the same time, Golkar is also splintering. Several prominent leaders have bolted to form their own Justice and Unity Party, which some predict could siphon votes away from Golkar. With the Parliament passing a law restricting the number of Abri representation to 38 seats and outlawing civil servants from participating in politics, it seems that the wings of Golkar have been clipped. The chances of them winning the majority seats of 75 percent like the old days are gone.

Habibie remains deeply unpopular despite implementing several measures to demonstrate his democratic credentials, such as freeing some political prisoners, unshackling the press, embracing human rights and setting the timetable for new elections. For many Indonesians, he remains the consummate Suharto crony. Political commentator Wimar Witoelar said, "Habibie has lost all support both inside and outside the system." It is precisely because of his perceived weakness that Habibie has become invaluable to those vying to replace him — since he is no longer seen as a serious contender to keep the presidency, his opponents are no longer calling for his resignation, but instead are demanding that he stays on to manage the transition.

Habibie made a few statements which were seen as unfriendly to Singapore. He considered Singapore as just "a red dot" on the world map. His latest remarks about Singapore had angered many Singaporeans, especially the Malay leaders. In an interview with Taiwan journalists in Jakarta, Habibie said, "The little island of Singapore is a country of "real racists" because Malays could never be military officers."

The Singapore minister-in-charge of Muslim Affairs, Abdullah Tarmugi, and other Malay leaders hit back at Habibie and said his remarks were "unfortunate, hurtful and baseless". Tarmugi said that contrary to Habibie's view, there are Malay officers in the Singapore Armed Forces. Singapore newspapers even published the pictures of two Malay officers, one Lieutenant Colonel Ishak Ismail and the other Captain Mohammed Zakir Hamid. Tarmugi said he believed that the Indonesian leader was either misinformed or really did not know what was happening in the Republic.

Yatiman Yusof, a political secretary said he suspected that Habibie's remarks were aimed at "undermining the stability of a multi-racial Singapore". He said, "We do not need outsiders including people like President Habibie to interfere with our internal affairs."

Only Malay Members of Parliament pointed out that all Malay Singaporeans who are physically fit are called up for national service. "Most of them are happy to be in the Singapore Armed Forces (SAF) because they want to contribute like everybody else," they said.

A Malay Member of Parliament, Harun Abdul Ghani, said Dr Habibie "should not insult the Malays in Singapore saying they will never became military officers."

Brigadier-General Lee Hsien Loong, who is Deputy Prime Minister and Second Defence Minister had said that more Malays have qualified to become infantry section leaders and SAF officers.

The Indonesian Education Minister, Dr Juwono Sudarsono, fearing that Habibie's remarks might sour up relations between the two countries, said that Habibie appeared to have been misinformed when he said that Singapore was racist.

He said, "I think Singapore leaders understand that President Habibie has a lot of learning and unlearning to do about Singapore. He may know a lot about technology, but he may not know much about the social and economic context. Since he is in a bubbly person, I think Singapore will understand."

I travelled in a taxi after Habibie's remarks were made and I heard a Chinese taxi-driver saying angrily, "He is not fit to be a President."

The biggest fear now, some people say, is that the Suharto era hard-liners opposed to democracy, might try to remove him between now and June, and then cancel or delay the elections. Some analysts say they are already creating havoc by instigating riots throughout the country in an attempt to divert the energy of the military so that they will have no time to investigate Suharto's alleged wrongdoings.

Whoever wins and takes over as President, he or she will have many giant problems to tackle. With the departure of the Chinese, Indonesia is experiencing not only a serious shortage of rice, but also a shortage of know-how to distribute goods and to develop and run the country economically. The World Bank has predicted that 50 million Indonesians, one in every four, may be unable to afford the food needed to stay healthy. The people of East Nusa Tenggara, one of the poorest and driest provinces which is often affected by drought refer to hunger as *lapar biasa* — the "ordinary hunger". However, they call this latest hardship *lapar luar biasa* or the "extraordinary hunger". In the poor village of East Nusa Tenggara, many families are already preparing a meal of bark for their children once a day. The World Food Mission that visited 26 of Indonesia's 27 provinces estimated that residents of half of them, more than 7 million people, will end up starving. Many villagers in the countryside have committed suicide by drinking poison as they prefer to die than suffer from hunger.

By the end of 1998, 96 million people or 48 percent of the population have sunk below the poverty line, wiping out 30 years of national growth. President Habibie suggested that if all Indonesians fasted twice a week during daylight hours, as the most devout of Muslims do, the country could save three million tons of rice a year. The new President does not need to add that by doing this, he could also save his job. A starving old lady said she did not know whether to laugh or cry over Habibie's fasting call. She said, "How can a man with all the money in the world ask people who can barely afford rice to fast?". Habibie's legacy will depend on how adriotly he answered her question. More to the point, so will his own survival.

In his days as the technology czar, Habibie had diverted billions of dollars in government development funds away from agriculture and into his pet aircraft industry. Now, he has launched a major effort to upgrade farming methods on one-quarter of the nation's cultivated land. This idea is to group small farms into cooperatives and make efficient use of tractors, harvesting machines, and other modern technology, thereby improving yields.

The Central Bureau of Statistics stated that Indonesia's gross domestic product (GDP) for the full year was expected to fall 13.6 percent and per capita gross national product (GNP) was expected to plummet to US$436 in 1998 from US$1,055 in 1997. Indonesia is facing an economic crisis unparalleled since World War II. Indonesia expects its economy to contract about 13 percent in 1998 — the first time the economy has shrunk since 1963.

Nearly all industrial plants in Indonesia have stopped operating, leaving at least 15 million people out of work. No more new foreign investments are forthcoming. All over the world, from Singapore to America, Europe, China, Taiwan, and Hong Kong, ethnic Chinese are demonstrating against the Jakarta's administration for not taking swift action to punish the culprits of the anti-Chinese riots of May 1998.

Nobody envies the new rulers of Indonesia who will be elected in June 1999. The problems they have to solve are tremendous.

Suharto has ruled Indonesia for 32 years like a Javanese king. He adopted Javanese feudalism and administrated Indonesia the same way as a Javanese king would, using the *priyayi* system and trusting only his favourite Chinese *cukongs* to help develop the country's natural resources. He hand-picked the military leaders and governors of all provinces. Unlike Sukarno who depended on balancing power between the military and the Communists to stay in power, Suharto actually tasted power in his tightly-knit administration. His administration whole-heartedly adopted Western development strategies and encouraged foreign investments with major incentives such as tax exemptions and assurances of free transfer of profit. With billions of dollars in Western aid and food imports pouring into the country, Indonesia became a model of successful development.

The trouble with him was that his opponents accuse him of treating the country's resources as belonging to him and his family. They say that while he was successful in bringing in foreign capital and enriching the country, he also enriched his family members who amassed the wealth of the country for private gains. In his eagerness to enrich his children and relatives and cronies, he failed to bring about a fair distribution of wealth among the people. His critics say he has created a society of corruption, nepotism and cronyism with a large proportion of the population remaining poor despite the fast economic growth of the country. The people had tolerated the disparity in wealth distribution for too long and like a volcano, the suppressed feeling suddenly erupted so violently that it took the world by surprise.

It might be due to the nature of those people who live in volcanic countries. Nobody expected the humble-mannered, low-bowing and normally orderly and sheepish Japanese to lose their natural poise and turned into violent people who massacred millions of people in China and Southeast Asia during World War II. Who would have imagine that the normally most polite and well-behaved Javanese would suddenly burst into violence and wreaked havoc in the May riots in Jakarta? Suharto has been ruling Indonesia for over 30 years without realising the strong undercurrent of discontent among the people. To consolidate his political power, he organised the Golkar —

which is his brainchild and he even used the banyan tree whose shade is a place of sacred and mystical importance in Javanese villages as the symbol of Golkar. Abri and the civil servants were the hands and legs of the organisation which dominate the Parliament controlled by the majority seats of Golkar. He was elected for three terms and when he reached 70, there was a suggestion that he should step down. But, how could he do so with so many of his relatives and cronies having vested interests and depending on him for their wealth?

The major problem he faced was the misgivings of Abri in his choice of Vice-President when he was elected President. In 1988, when he was elected President, he chose Sudharmono, his former Executive Secretary and who later became Minister of State as Vice-President. Abri had objected to this appointment, but like a Javanese king, he would not allow anybody or any organisation to dictate terms to him. He, therefore, for the first time counted on the support of the Muslim community to push ahead with his choice.

In 1993, Abri was more successful in putting pressure on Suharto in the choice of Vice-President. Suharto had to give way in the selection of General Try Sutrisno as Vice-President. Suharto did not think General Sutrisno was the right choice because he was only his adjutant, but he would have trouble from Abri if he did not accept their choice. Suharto did not like the idea of Abri dictating what he should do. After all, in his own perception, he was a Javanese king and as king, he should be able to do whatever he thought was right. In his last election when he became President, he chose Habibie as Vice-President and there was strong protest from Abri. To Abri, Habibie was a danger to their influence in politics. Habibie was the Head of the Indonesian Muslim Intellectuals Association (ICMI) started by Suharto, an organisation which was loosely organised and represented by a body of Muslim elites without grassroots. The ICMI was supposed to neutralise the Armed Forces and to split the Islamic movement evident by the late 1980s, particularly in terms of Gus Dur's growing disenchantment with the government's more vis-à-vis Islam. Both Gus Dur and Abri were therefore against the ICMI. But, as Habibie was the Minister of Technology and then confidante of Suharto, many bureacrats have joined ICMI.

It is against this background that we can understand why Suharto had actively courted the Indonesian Muslims as a trump card to balance Abri, and to enhance his Islamic credentials. This move was interpreted as an attempt to diversify his own power base as it became clear by 1988 that Abri was no longer automatically backing him. In the environment of shifting constellation of power and support in elitist politics, Suharto looked to the Muslims to enhance his legitimacy. We heard that it was under Muslim pressure that Suharto got rid of Benny Moerdani, the former Defence Minister who was a Christian and a person the Muslims perceived as hostile to Islam.

After two decades of pushing modernist Muslims into the political wilderness, Suharto became more responsive to Muslim demands. His government relaxed restrictions on the use of *jilbab* (headscarf) at public schools, introduced more Islamic elements into the national schools curriculum, and gave more authority to Islamic courts. On the diplomatic front, the Indonesian Government recognised the state of Palestine. Suharto and his family began increasingly to adopt a more Islamic lifestyle, including a prominently publicised pilgrimage to Mecca in 1991. It was the first time in the history of Java that a "Javanese king" has visited Mecca. It was seen as a step towards reconciliation with Islam. In the same year, he helped established Indonesia's first Islamic-style bank.

One serious problem facing Indonesia is that the extremist Muslims who were behind the student riots are clamouring for an Islamic Indonesia and are against Suharto's Pancasila philosophy. The success of Islamic revolutions particularly in Iran have encouraged Indonesian Muslim extremists to revive the Islamic dream of establishing an Islamic Indonesia based on Islamic law. The Indonesian Armed Forces were worried when they found that Acehnese rebels had been trained in Libya. The Islamic revivalists have made some inroads into the abangan and priyayi elites. Even Suharto himself became more Islamic before he stepped down. During the year before he stepped down, I had noticed some changes in his abangan behaviour and he seemed to be more inclined towards *santri* attitudes. In Indonesia, the nominal Muslims who believe in Javanese mysticism are classifed as abangan and those who are orthodox Muslims are referred to as santri. One wonders whether Suharto is changing his lifestyle because he is aware of the changing mood of the people towards Islam? Or was it a tactical move to pacify the Muslims? Whatever it may be, it is interesting to watch the swing of abangan behaviour towards santricism in Indonesia.

With this change of spirit, government officials are expected to lead prayers and fast during the fasting month of Ramadan. Offices and army buildings have been converted into temporary places for prayers during Ramadan. In recent years, even restaurants in first-class hotels began putting up notices of fasting times for Muslim customers.

Many observers have noted that the Indonesian population has been re-Islamised in the past decade. The Islamisation of the Indonesian society has become palpable. For instance, many abangan Javanese fasted during the fasting month, and abangan children are more aware of Islamic rituals and identity. It is not clear, however, whether or not they have become santri, but Islam as a religion is becoming much more influential in Suharto's Indonesia.

Suharto has given in a lot to the Muslims, but he is against Islam's involvement in politics. As long as Islam is not mixed with politics, he could tolerate it. However, things have changed, and the four Muslim parties which in 1973 merged into one party called the Partai Pesatuan Pembangunan (PPP) — Development Unity Party has become a major challenger to Suharto's administration. The PPP is advocating Islam to replace the nationalist ideology. Its emblem is the *Kaaba*, the most sacred Muslim shrine for worship. This might be interpreted as a political symbol of splitting Indonesian unity.

The potential of Islam as a political force was vividly underlined by the nationwide demonstration organised to protest against the establishment of the state lottery in 1993. During my ambassadorship in Jakarta, there were several casinos but all these were closed down as a result of protests from the Muslims. There is also a feeling in some quarters that the tolerant, pluralistic character of Indonesian

Islam is being eroded by a trend towards "formalism". There has been increasing use of Arabic terms and demands for the implementation of Islamic law, which have the potential to weaken the moderating influence of Indonesian cultural norms and values.

Coming back to Suharto's choice of Habibie as Vice-President, he was strongly opposed by Abri and Gus Dur, but he went ahead to appoint him. The relationship between Abri and Habibie has been strained for some time. Abri saw Habibie as a danger to them because as head of ICMI, he had advocated the democratisation and the eventual reduction of the military's political role in Indonesian politics. As Suharto stubbornly went ahead with his choice, his image diminished in the eyes of Abri.

The conflict of personal and institutional interests between Habibie and Abri partly arose after the responsibility for managing the Indonesian arms industries was transferred to the Ministry of Technology under Habibie. To support Habibie, Suharto reshuffled the Abri leadership in 1994, eliminating those who were against Habibie and elevating those supporting him.

The most serious dispute between Abri and Habibie involved the purchase of 39 ex-East German warships. Abri was highly dissatisfied with the purchase and might have encouraged the press to widely publicise the over-inflated purchase price suggesting that Habibie had badly managed the acquisition. The military hostility towards Habibie was heightened by Abri's perception that Habibie was trying to harness the power of Islam through his leadership of ICMI, and to democratise politics including urging soldiers to return to the barracks.

Even Gus Dur has warned Suharto that a number of prominent intellectuals in ICMI had advocated the establishment of an Islamic society in Indonesia. He felt that the Islamic activities in ICMI would provoke Abri action against the Islamic community. Gus Dur was worried that ICMI would give Abri the excuse to "clamp down" again on Islam. Gus Dur was also disturbed that some of the leaders associated with ICMI have been connected with anti-Chinese and anti-Christian activities since 1990. In a letter to Suharto, Gus Dur warned him that Indonesia might end up like Algeria which saw a clash between the Islamic and non-Islamic elements in society. He saw some Muslims, particularly those associated with ICMI, supporting the democratisation and the demilitarisation of Indonesian politics.

The trouble with Suharto was that he was too confident of himself as a king should be. As the students mounted demonstrations and violent riots, he took time off to attend an Islamic conference in Egypt. In his absence, his son-in-law General Prabowo who was in charge of the security of Jakarta, was trying to fish in troubled waters. He was engineering for a situation when he could emerge as leader under martial law as his main rival was General Wiranto. Something must have happened to the army intelligence that Abri could not cope with the dangerous situation around May 13. There was a devastating riot in Jakarta. Yet, not a bullet was fired by the soldiers and nobody went out to maintain law and order.

When Suharto returned to Jakarta after the conference, he was faced with a situation beyond his control. He was no more in control of Abri. His most trusted confidante, Habibie, was believed to have conspired with the technocrats who were members of the Cabinet who threatened to resign en bloc. He had no alternative, but to turn to the Muslim leaders to whom he had been trying to cultivate. It was his last hope. He summoned them to the Istana and sought their help. He even offered to make them advisers of his cabinet if they would support him. But, to his surprise, they rejected his offer and left him with no alternatives but to announce his resignation and appointed Habibie as the President.

Suharto has failed just as Sukarno had failed because they tried to play an act of balancing. When Sukarno was at the height of power, he discovered that he did not get enough support from Abri, and started to flirt with the Indonesian Communist Party (PKI) and had tried to use their strength to balance Abri. He tried to establish a society where Nationalism, Communism and Religion could exist side by side in the name of Nasakom (Nas represents nationalism, A, religion and Kom, communism). Although it might appear to observers that the basic tenets of the three politico-religious concepts contain fundamental contradictions which are irreconciliable, he was tempted to give it a trial run. Nasakom ended on the rocks. The failure, according to some Javanese leaders, was caused not so much by the irreconciliability of the three concepts, but because one of the three forces tried to impose its will on the others by the use of force. It thus infringed on the spirit of tolerance sacredly inscribed in the Indonesian crest. Once the rule is broken, the balance of the scale is tipped, and the whole idea collapses.

Sukarno even tried to import arms from Communist China for the Communist volunteers, as he was then very friendly with the People's Republic of China. He was then quite ill and both the contenders of power — Abri and the PKI feared that after his death, there was going to be a struggle for power. The Communists feared that Abri would wipe them out after Sukarno's death and Abri was also afraid that the Communists would stage a revolution to overthrow them. Sukarno was already having Chinese medical experts to treat him. The rumours spread that he was about to die. Then, on September 30, 1965 the coup took place when six generals and one soldier was massacred and thrown into a crocodile hole. The incident was known as the "crocodile hole massacre" or "Gestapu coup". Up till today, there is some argument as to who actually instigated the massacre. Some critics even blamed Suharto for masterminding the plot. The coup resulted in a big massacre of Communists and their supporters and a decline in Communist strength and influence. Actions were also taken to take away the rights of ethnic Chinese as they were accused of supporting the Communists. Indonesia even blamed China for trying to ship arms to Indonesia to support the PKI.

Sukarno faulted in his balance of power with Nasakom and was overthrown by Suharto.

Sukarno's main achievement was that he had successfully inculcated national consciousness in the entire Indonesian population. With his oratorical power and dominating "charismatic style", he succeeded in moulding the various peoples who bore great racial, linguistic and cultural differences into a nation, and called themselves

"Indonesians". After Indonesia gained its independence, when you ask any Indonesian for his nationality, he would say "I am Indonesian" irrespective of whether he comes from Java, Sumatra, Sulawesi or Bali.

When Indonesia achieved independence, it had nothing — no teachers, no civil service, and no national income. All mills and factories were closed and destroyed. There was fighting among secessionists, the Communists and the religious fanatics. In the early 1950s, politicians put the interests of their parties above the state and scrambled for power. The new Republic had the biggest turnover of Cabinet ministers, changing almost every six months. There were chaotic bickerings among the military, religious, left-wing and right-wing factions. In 1955, there were 169 political parties fighting for only 257 seats. The only coherent power and strength which Indonesia had was the armed forces and the charisma of Sukarno, plus some business know-how of the Chinese, which unfortunately Sukarno did not utilise.

Sukarno succeeded in welding the people into a nation, but he failed to deliver the fruits of the revolution: better food, better education, better homes and employment. He knew how to create a nation, but did not know how to run it. With his policy of "guided democracy", he banned all political activities but kept a balancing act between the military and the Communists. He squandered billions of dollars on colossal projects, one of which was the Monas, a Russian-built marble obelisk in the centre of Merdeka Square topped by 35 kg of pure gold leaves to symbolise the flame of liberation and freedom. The monument was described as "Sukarno's erection". The inflation rate was running at 65 percent per year and mammoth foreign debts had accumulated. The country went bankrupt and the people still believe in him because the Javanese who were in the majority believe he had the *wahyu* (the spiritual soul of the leader) to rule and that his presence was God-sent.

It was not an easy task to unite a country of so many different races, religions, cultures and traditions. The foundations built by Sukarno led Suharto to initiate the motto *Bhinneka Tunggul Ika* into the Indonesian crest and remind the Indonesians of the spirit of tolerance. But, the foundation may be shaky if all Indonesians do not abide by the spirit.

My fear is that history may repeat itself in Indonesia after the coming general elections on 7 June, 1999. It seems no single political party will win the majority seat and there will be a coalition government. There may be constant political bickerings in the parliament and it will not be easy for any government to bring the country back to its feet. It will be reminiscent of the old Sukarno days. The only difference, of course, is that Indonesia now has a foundation of administrative infrastructure and capable civil servants to help run the country. The only problem is that the country does not have a strong leader and it is not easy for the new government to mobilise the people and to rejuvenate the spirit of *Bhinneka Tunggul Ika*, the spirit of tolerance.

Whilst Sukarno is credited with creating the foundation for a united nation, Suharto is credited with establishing the foundation of Indonesia's economy and in fact was called "Bapak" (father) of Indonesia's development. Suharto ruled with an iron hand. He brought peace and stability to Indonesia for 32 years. He opened up 34 of Indonesia's 60 oil bases for exploitation which will last well into the 21st century. Under Suharto, Sumatra's coal production is expected to reach forty million tons by the year 2000. He succeeded with the help of foreign investment, in exploiting Indonesia's major mineral resources such as tin, copper, bauxite and nickel. He also made Indonesia the largest producer of cloves in the world. Unfortunately, he was accused of corruption, nepotism and cronyism.

Suharto has also done a great deal in consolidating the unity of his people by cementing the philosophy of Pancasila which had replaced Nasakom after the death of Sukarno. He was a strong believer in Pancasila which consists of five principles: Belief in one God, Humanity, Sovereignty of the people, Social Justice and Democracy. The date when the six generals and a soldier were assassinated and thrown into Lubang Buaya (crocodile hole) has officially become Pancasila Day. Thus, every year on the first day of October is a day of national mourning. To revive further the spirit of the 1945 revolution and the struggle for independence, a Pancasila monument was erected at Kalibata where national heroes were buried. The monument comprising five towering pillars representing the five principles of Pancasila was officially declared opened by Suharto on 11 November 1974 and I witnessed the grand ceremony. The monument was to commemorate the millions of unknown Indonesian soldiers who had sacrificed their lives for independence.

Pancasila was also based on the spirit of *Bhinneka Tunggul Ika*, which has become institutionalised. Professor Mukti Ali, who was Minister for Religious Affairs in 1973 and a Muslim, once told me that one of the functions of his Ministry was to preach and implement the spirit of tolerance which is vital to the survival and harmony of a multi-racial, multi-religious and multi-cultural society like Indonesia.

I also remember vividly what the Minister of Information, Mr Mashuri, who is a wise man, had described to me the significance of *Bhinneka Tunggul Ika*. What Mashuri had said 25 years ago is still valid in today's Indonesian situation. Mashuri did not realise that his country and his people would choose the theory of "survival of the fittest" to replace the traditional spirit of "survival for mutual benefit". The fall of Suharto and the May 13 riots of 1998 indicated clearly that the spirit of tolerance or the *Bhinneka Tunggul Ika* spirit was beginning to fade. Not only was there no tolerance, there was also no rule of law.

Indonesia is experiencing a chaotic situation never seen in its history. It is almost comparable to the bloody communist coup of 1965. At least in those dark days, there was no burning of churches and mosques and racial conflicts. Today, there is a sense of weakness all round — a weak President, a tattered economy, and a tainted military. The biggest problem facing Indonesia is that there is no longer a rule of law. People are taking the law into their own hands to attack and kill whoever they think are undesirable.

Now that Indonesia does not have a strong leader like Suharto, and without the spirit of tolerance, can Abri control the security of such a vast country and keep potential rebellions in check? Can the economically weak government feed the 200 million people now that the government is short of funds and reserves? It cannot afford to buy paddy seeds for farmers. Will those who want to be independent take orders from Jakarta? With so many political, economic and social problems in hand, will the government have the time, money and energy to keep the nation as one? From events happening in Indonesia, it appears that there is a danger of the nation breaking up. Nothing could stop the riotings throughout the country. As a result, the Chief of Abri, General Wiranto had to issue orders to his commanders "to shoot at sight" trouble-makers and those who loot properties and destroy churches and mosques.

The government was planning to give its provinces more power to run their own affairs and have more control of their wealth in an effort to ease simmering regional tensions that threaten to tear the diverse nation apart.

Dr Andi Mallarangeng, a member of the law-drafting team, said that the reforms were aimed at reducing regional tensions to prevent the country from disintegrating. He said, "The call for independence by some provinces is a reaction to the centralisation of power under the previous regime. Unless we solve this quickly, we could end up with disintegration."

There is reason why Indonesian leaders are worried that the country might disintegrate. They speak of Yugoslavia, which was once a united people under Tito. But, upon the death of Tito in 1980, there was no longer a final arbitrator for disputes. None of the other major leaders of the Communist Party could be regarded as supra-national in the way Tito was. The disintegration of Yugoslavia was caused by the conflicting interests of the political elites of different nationalities, religions, cultures and traditions. The Serbs' idea of Yugoslavia has been shaped by their people's historical experience as part of Byzantine, including a five-century-long resistance to Turkish Islam, and nurtured by epic poetry and religious festivals. What the Serbs were not aware of was that the other southern Slavic nationalities, especially those who had lived in the former Austria-Hungary, did not share their feelings.

History is perceived as the primary source that supply the required justifications for the actions taken by the Serbs and other Yugoslavian nationalities. Historically speaking, the various nationalities of Yugoslavia have been fighting one another under different flags and for different purposes for a long time. It was Tito who brought the nationalities under one flag.

In Yugoslavia, when Tito was alive, all the nationalities and racial groups happily shared power and lived harmoniously together. I enjoyed the peace and tranquility of Yugoslavia when I was Ambassador to that country. But five years after Tito's death, ugliness appeared when the strongest ethnic group — the Serbs — tried to monopolise political power by imposing its will on the minority groups. The republican Communist elites could no longer agree on how to share power. The Serbians wanted to dominate Yugoslavia politically whilst the Slovenians who were economically more equipped tried to dominate the country economically.

When the Serbian leader, Slobodan Milosevic, succeeded in taking over the leadership of the Serbian Communist Party and thereby the Serbian government, he immediately realised that there was a power vacuum and made a ruthless bid to become Tito's successor. This became obvious to the potentates in the various partners of Yugoslavia who started to press for separation. Then all the latent grievances of the past going back to the long years of historical battles among themselves began to surface. Had Milosevic belonged to any other but Serbian nation, there might have been less resistance to his bid for power. But he is a Serb and the others saw his grip on power as a confirmation of Serbian hegemonistic tendencies.

In the case of Indonesia, the Javanese strongman Suharto, like Tito, was in control of political power for 32 years. During his reign, Indonesia was comparatively peaceful and the peoples of various races and religions lived harmoniously. I really enjoyed myself in Indonesia during my four-and-a-half years stay as Ambassador. I travelled widely throughout the country and met the governors of most provinces, and mayors of most cities. I witnessed how the peoples of various provinces had lived peacefully and happily together. I found the Indonesian people to be the most tolerant on earth. I spoke to Muslims, Christians, Buddhists and even animists. They called themselves "Indonesians" and not as Javanese, Balinese, Minangkabaus, Bataks, Bugis or Torajans. That was the result of Sukarno's nation-building efforts. I witnessed that they had enough food to eat, dressed decently and lived comfortably with a roof above their heads to shelter from the rain or sun. That was the contribution of Suharto as "Bapak Pembangunan Indonesia" (Father of Indonesia's Development).

I found that intermarriages between Muslims and Christians or Buddhists were common. I have Indonesian friends whose family members belong to different religions. The father is a Muslim, mother a Buddhist and the children Christians. They live harmoniously together and never quarrel over religious matters.

The Christians in many areas of Java have been Javanised. I met Indonesian Christians who believe in mysticism and follow Javanese traditions and customs which can be regarded by orthodox Christians as rather unChristian. In the southern part of Jogjakarta, there is a Catholic church where *gamelan* music is played instead of the organ. The hymns are sung in Javanese accompanied by the gamelan to Javanese tunes. Not far away is a *Prambanan* (a temple built by the Buddhist) type of church which is decorated with two statues, one having the image of the King of Madura and the other the face of the wife of Arjuna, one of the five Pandawa heroes of the *Mahabharata*. The King is regarded as the personification of Jesus Christ and the wife of Arjuna that of Mary.

In 1947, somewhere north of Jogjakarta, a Christian priest by the name of Senjaya of Mantilan was killed. Till today, many of his Christian supporters go to his grave to invoke his soul for spiritual guidance. His belongings such as shirts, shoes, and slippers have become *pusaka* (heirloom) and used for curing the sick.

At the Borobudur temple, I met a learned Indonesian official guide who said he was a Buddhist as well as a Muslim. He believed in Prophet Mohammed and Allah, but he also practised the Buddhist way of meditation and the Buddhist way of life, a compromise which is unimaginable anywhere else in the world.

In most parts of Asia, a Buddhist is a Buddhist, a Taoist a Taoist, a Confucianist a Confucianist. But, in Java, the three religions have become one known as the *Sam Kau* (merging the three into one religion called *Sam Kau* in the Fujian dialect). Inside the temple of Sampo Kong (the temple in honour of Admiral Cheng Ho — the Muslim eunuch) in Semarang, Central Java, you will find symbols of Buddhism, the picture of Confucius and the relics of Taoist mysticism. To add to the mystery, the temple was taken care of by Javanese Muslims wearing *pici* (hats) but of Chinese descent.

I have Muslim friends, some in higher society who practise *kebatinan* (a Javanese belief in the soul). One of them was our Indonesian Ambassador to Singapore, Sunarso. He is a Muslim. He once invited me to his house. As I entered the gate, I saw a wooden statue of a Chinese sage. He said to me, "Did you see the statue, he is my spiritual adviser. Whenever I have any problem, he will help me solve it."

The average Indonesian, like the Japanese, believes in the existence of the soul. He believes that death is not the end of everything and that there is such a thing as a soul which can be contacted by well-trained mystics. When a soul is wrongfully treated during his lifetime, it is necessary for the wrong doer to pacify the soul. I remember having to explain the Javanese concept of the soul to Prime Minister Lee Kuan Yew before his official visit to Indonesia. When the time came for him to visit Indonesia, he asked me how he could befriend Suharto. I suggested that he should sprinkle flowers on the graves of the two Indonesian marine saboteurs who were convicted and hanged in Singapore for causing the death of three persons after setting off a bomb at MacDonald House on Orchard Road in 1967. It was during the time of Indonesian confrontation against Malaysia. The hanging of these two Indonesian marines created tension between the two countries. Suharto had appealed to Lee Kuan Yew not to hang the two men. The two were tried and hanged and they were treated as "heroes" and were buried together with other national heroes at Kalibata, the place where all Indonesian heroes were buried. He followed my advice, and when he sprinkled flowers on their graves, I saw tears in the eyes of some generals.

But, soon after Suharto fell, things have changed. In Indonesia, riots and bloodshed seem to be a daily affair. It spreads from Jakarta to other parts of the country. It is beyond the capability of Abri to stop the riotings, killings and burning. The Western theory of "survival of the fittest" has taken over.

In October 1998, a group of mysterious men dressed in black and appearing like Japanese "ninjas" appeared in East Java and went about killing 180 people. The killing started with sorcerers as the primary victims, but later extended to include Muslim clerics and supporters of Nadhlatul Ulama (NU). During that month, mosques in the traditional Muslim stronghold were empty in the evening. At sundown, the streets were deserted, stores closed and roadblocks were manned by youths with swords, knives and sickles. These youths were looking for the "ninjas". They claimed to have arrested one of them, chopped off his head, held it aloof and drank blood dripping from the neck to protect themselves from the evil ninja spirit. They paraded with the severed head impaled on a knife and dragged the body behind a motorcycle for miles in broad daylight without interference from the police. Even three uniformed policemen were slashed to death by the youths.

On 19 January, 1999, violence also broke out in Ambon, a province which had initiated in the early days of Indonesia's independence to establish their own "Republic of South Maluku" but failed in their attempt. Then hundreds of thousands of Ambonese, who had been referred to as "black Dutch" had their loyalty geared to Holland, found their way to the country and are now stranded there. This time, the violence, apparently instigated by unseen forces underground, sparked off a violent clash between the Muslim community and the Christian community. Several churches and mosques were burnt leaving 65 people dead and much of the city destroyed. At least 1,000 people including 219 children had fled the riot-torn Ambon for fear of further unrest and had arrived by ship at Ujung Pandang in South Sulawesi under tight security. Till today, Ambon has become a ghost town with Christian residents hiding under the protection of their churches and the Muslims protected by their mosques. Thousands of

Ambonese are fleeing to safer places in other parts of Indonesia. The situation is complicated by the silent penetration of the Ambonese who came all the way from Amsterdam to support Christian Ambonese not only with supporters but with finance. On the other hand, some Muslim supporters from Jakarta had also infiltrated into Ambon to create havoc.

One of the major reasons of the riots could have been caused by poverty and deteriorating economic condition of the people. Another factor could be that some extreme Muslim leaders saw the introduction of Pancasila as a threat to their political survival. On 30 July 1998, representatives of Muslim groups slipped into the State Secretariat in Jakarta to present a petition to President Habibie, demanding that political parties be freed from the state ideology of Pancasila. Unfurling green banners and posters, the group of 30 petitioners were met by a senior official who took their two-page written petition signed by "The Islamic Committee for Constitutional Reform". The petition stated that "... Therefore, making Pancasila the only ideology for political parties and organisations contradicts the Islamic faith". It argued that Pancasila had failed and was a "source of conflict and division".

There are Muslims in Indonesia who want an Islamic state or at least the 1945 Constitution amended so as to compel Muslims to adhere to Islamic law. The Government's restrictions on political expression by Muslims have given rise to a number of soldiers being killed and several others wounded. There were other incidents such as the Haur Koneng incident in July 1993 and the Pandelglang incident in West Java in late 1994, all involved with attempts to promote an Islamic state.

If Indonesia becomes an Islamic country, what will happen to the other people of Nusa Tenggara, those in Irian Jaya, the Maluku, the people of Toraja and Kalimantan and the Ambonese and the Bataks who are mostly Christians? Will the Balinese, more than 90 percent of whom are Hindu-Buddhists, split away from Java if the Islamic rules are forcefully imposed on them? Since the days of Gajah Mada, they had escaped to Bali because they refused to be Islamised. Will they also ask for autonomous status since such status has already been given to Aceh, and promised to East Timor and Irian Jaya? Will the Balinese do another *puputan* (mass suicide) if they are compelled to follow the Islamic laws? Or will they want to secede from Indonesia?

The Islamisation of Indonesia might encourage a separatist movement in the non-Muslim regions, thereby creating problems for the armed forces who are already handicapped in strength. Is Abri strong enough to suppress the separatist movements which might spread throughout the vast territories of Indonesia?

Gus Dur argues that the formation of an Islamic state would damage the unity of the nation by driving away the non-Muslim populations of the country and encourage the emergence of separatist tendencies.

Historically speaking, several important ethnic groups have had open confrontations with the Javanese. For instance, the Sundanese do not like to be referred to as Javanese even though they live in West Java because one of their kings was killed in a battle by Javanese troops and the insult of their princess by Prime Minister Gajah Mada. The ruling Maduree Cakraningrat family was hostile to the Javanese kingdom during the 18th century, and looted the Javanese royal treasury then. The Sumatrans had attempted to set up *Pemerintah Revolusioner Republik Indonesia* (Indonesian Revolutionary Republic) to challenge Jakarta and they had fought against the central government of Java in the 1950s. The Acehnese had strived for an Islamic State of Aceh and are still fighting for their goal.

There is a danger that such historical grievances of the past would re-emerge if the more predominant group tries to impose its will on the minority. The theory of the "survival of the fittest" has taken over.

In a complex society like Indonesia with so much diversity in race, culture, religion, tradition and customs and lifestyle, the first prerequisite for national survival is for all Indonesians to adhere strictly to the principle of *Bhinneka Tunggul Ika*. If this principle is not observed, the Indonesian society will become fragile and the country may break up. The economic crisis facing Indonesia will make the country even more fragile.

2

THE JAVANESE
No Temper, No Emotion

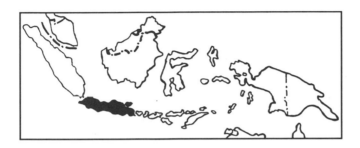

The Javanese comprise about fifty percent of the entire 200 million population of Indonesia but occupy only seven percent of the country's land area — the Greater Sunda islands. Java's total land area is roughly 130,000 square km, one of the most densely populated countries in the world. The Dutch colonial ruler's policy of concentrating their resources on Java for several hundred years has further increased the differences between Java and Indonesia's outer islands.

Java is well developed with processing industries, modern transport and telecommunication facilities. With sixty-five percent of Indonesia's investments concentrated on Java, it is the island of opportunity to which young men flock from rural areas of Indonesia to find jobs.

The Javanese with their light brown skin, straight black hair, high cheekbones, small and slender build belong to the Oceanic branch of the Mongoloid race. However, the Javanese race is actually a blend of many races that have established themselves on the island. Most Javanese belong to four major cultural-linguistic ethnic groups: the Javanese of Central and East Java (about 79 million) whose main cities are Jogjakarta and Solo, the Sundanese of West Java (about 30 million) with Bandung as their capital; the Baduis (2,000-4,000) who live on an isolated mountain off Bogor; the Tenggerese (about 300,000) from the area in East Java around Gunung Bromo; and the Madurese inhabiting the Madura Island. Of these, the Javanese are numerically the largest group and the most influential culturally and politically.

Because of the wealth generated by the huge surplus obtained from wet-rice cultivation throughout its history, Java has attracted many great precolonial inland empires to the island: Majapahit, Singasari, Kediri and Mataram. Ancient Java was a land of cities and temples and peasants and princes, with the peasants producing and working for the *kratons*, thus providing the massive agricultural wealth needed to fuel the empire's maritime trade.

For centuries, Hindu culture dominated Java as the Hindu rulers brought with them their Hindu culture and civilisation. Central Java had been ruled by so many Hindu kingdoms that remnants of Hindu cultural influence still remain. In fact, written history began in Indonesia with the coming of Hinduism. Buddhist and Hindu religious symbols are seen everywhere and even noodles are named after heroes of the Indian epics.

Java's intensely cooperative society gave the Hindu rulers the luxury of building impressive stone monuments to honour their gods. For more than 750 years (732 A.D. to about 1405) temples were built all the way from the Dieng Plateau in Central Java to Candi Kedaton, near Bondowoso in East Java and Borobudur in central Java. Ruins are still being unearthed. All these monuments took decades to build, incurring huge human toil and suffering.

The temple-city concept of the kraton came from India and took root in Indonesia. They became the centres of political power and culture for the Javanese rulers. It was in these kratons that the Javanese preserved their culture and religion.

For centuries, the religion of Java became the most potent political and social force. An estimated 150 *aliran kepercayaan* (religious beliefs) exist in Java. The indigenous religion of Java, *Agama Java*, has evolved into an incredible blending of doctrines and practices quite different from the Islamic religion.

For centuries, Javanese feudalism was the true religion, not the law of the Koran. From its early years, Javanese Islam has been a merger of Sufism, Hinduism and native superstition.

Although Islam penetrated Demak, Cirebon and Gresik in the 14th century, its influence in the hinterland of Central Java became watered down, especially after the arrival of the Europeans in the 16th and 17th centuries. The Dutch colonial policy of economic greed and less interest in culture enabled the Javanese to preserve the Hindu aristocratic culture of the kraton in Jogjakarta and Solo which, in turn, flourished and was scarcely touched by Islam. For a period of 200 years, Java became the key island in the Dutch East Indies empire paying its shareholders in Europe an average financial return of eighteen percent per annum. Under Dutch rule, Java became known as the garden of the tropics, one of the best-governed tropical islands in the world. Batavia (Jakarta) was a paradise for the Dutch where the streets resembled Rotterdam or the Hague with all its Dutch signboards. The whole of Java was a slave camp for the Dutch who profited enormously using cheap Java labour in their plantations for growing cash crops. The Javanese then described the Dutch as "men with good heads but cold hearts".

In Central Java, most of the Javanese are abangans. Although professing themselves to be Muslims, they actually adopt practices and ways of thinking closer to old Javanese mysticism. The widespread abangan cultural awakening was brought about partly because of the aggressiveness of Java's organised politicised Islam, in which hard-line Islamic views and ways of life were imposed upon the majority of the population. Most of the ruling class Javanese including President Suharto and many leading military generals are preoccupied with mystical religious views and metaphysical philosophy. Traditionally, many of Java's kings became hermits when they grew old.

The Dutch colonialist had used the technique of *co-optation* by bringing in the priyayi gentry elite and the abangan as civil servants and administrative personnels and neglected the santri (orthodox

Muslims). During the Sukarno days, the priyayi and abangan too enjoyed privileges in his administration. In the mass massacre after the 1965 Gestapu coup, it was the santris who most aggressively participated in the killings to vent their anger and frustration against the Communists who had received the support of Sukarno. The PKI's followers were almost entirely abangans while traditional Muslims turned more to Masjumi, Mohammadiyah or Nadhlatul Ulama, one of the leading Islamic parties in Indonesia. The main killers, apart from the army itself, were drawn from the orthodox Muslim streams and especially from the youth group Ansor associated with Nadhlatul Ulama.

When Suharto took over, he too adopted Javanese feudalism and controlled Indonesia like a Javanese king. He administered his country the same way as a Javanese king would, using the priyayi system and trusting only his favourite Chinese cukongs to help exploit the country's natural resources. He even used the banyan tree whose shade is a place of sacred and mystical importance in Javanese villages as the symbol of Golkar, a political party that was his brainchild.

The Suharto regime was strong militarily because he had a hand in choosing all his military leaders as well as the governors of all the provinces. Unlike Sukarno, whose power depended on his ability to balance the power between the military and the communists, Suharto had tasted actual power and had it in his grip. But, unfortunately, politically and economically his New Order was considerably more distant from the masses of the population than the Sukarno regime.

After President Suharto took over power, he was still essentially a mystic. He sent his supernatural advisor General Sudjono Humardhani and his personal assistants to Bali to look for Gajah Mada's[a] mask — the possession of which was believed to be one of the requirements of anyone who wanted to control Indonesia. Sudjono went to Bali and, with the help of the *Panglima* (governor) visited a small Balinese temple. In 1973 when I visited Bali, the Panglima received me and took me to the temple to see the Gajah Mada's mask. He opened a

---

[a]Gajah Mada was a prime minister of the Majapahit Empire of Java.

box containing the mask and before he did it, he prayed fervently. I saw the mask which has a red nose and was bundled in cloth. Very few foreigners have had the opportunity to view the mask. It was through the good offices of Sudjono that I was given the rare opportunity to see it.

According to Javanese belief, any ruler of Java needs to possess three things: Gajah Mada's mask, the *wijaya kusuma* — a rare flower found only in Nusa Kembangan in the south of Java and used by ancient Javanese kings when they were crowned, and Gajah Mada's kris.

President Suharto managed to find the first two. He obtained the mask first. Then he sent his troops to the mountains of East Java to search for the flower but he could not find the kris. Nobody knows where the Gajah Mada's kris is. Gajah Mada's mask was ordered by Sudjono to be taken to the Jakarta's Presidential Palace and kept there for a thousand days. It is also rumoured that the officer who took the mask to Jakarta died of a heart attack after performing his duties. This sacred mask was worshipped for a thousand days inside the palace.

The Javanese pride themselves on being one of the most refined, polite and cultivated people on earth. They are brought up to speak softly, behave properly, told never to raise their voice and never to lose their temper even if provoked. They are supposed to behave in a way as described by the Chinese: "Never show your colours whether you are happy or angry". In other words, never to reveal their feelings outwardly and always to be in complete control of themselves. They believe in cultivating their inner energy, and believe that lifting a little finger could figuratively "flick away a heavy-weight champion".

The cultivation of self-control stemmed from the priyayi tradition. Priyayi is the gentry class of Java — the old Hindu-Javanese aristocracy who guarded and upheld such values and ethics as extreme politeness, proper conduct, sophistication, social etiquette, good social graces and the development of arts and artistic skills such as dance, drama, music and verbal eloquence.

It was with this Javanese style of refinement and patience that Suharto took over power from Sukarno in March 1968. In Suharto's

writings on the period between 1965-67, he recalled how he deposed
Sukarno. "If you are too forceful with someone who is out of sorts,
he will only become angrier. But if you face him with wisdom and
an attitude of respect, he will be subdued." He was referring to the
way in which he managed to deal with Sukarno and succeeded to get
Sukarno subdued.

After the Gestapu coup of 1965 when Suharto took over power, he
did not immediately remove Sukarno. Although Suharto was in power,
Sukarno was still president. Sukarno asked Suharto in Javanese "Harto,
just what are you going to do with me?". Suharto replied, "Mr President,
I may have come from a poor farming family but my father always
reminded me to respect my elders." He used two phrases, *mikul
dhuwur* (respect for parents) and *mendhem jero* (not to call attention
to shortcomings), to which Sukarno nodded in approval. Suharto
told Sukarno that he always respected him like he did to his own
parents. He said, "To me, I consider you not only as our national
leader but a parent as well. I would like to regard you highly, but
unfortunately, you do not wish this."

There was a serious split on policy matters between the two leaders.
Suharto wanted to ban the PKI, and Sukarno strongly resisted it. How
did Suharto manage to persuade Sukarno to hand over power to him?
It took him more than a year of wrestling and he did it in beautiful
Javanese style. There is a Javanese proverb which says, *Alon alon asar
kelakon*, meaning, go with the flow as long as you need to achieve
your aim. Suharto adopted this method.

The new order under Suharto adopted the paternalistic and
feudalistic Javanese priyayi political system and ruled the country more
or less like a traditional Javanese kingdom with its elaborate system
of palace-centred patronage. He regarded his cabinet, the civil service
and the Parliament as part of the priyayi political system. Even at the
height of his unpopularity following the economic typhoon and with
Indonesia on the brink of bankruptcy and needing rescue from the
IMF, Suharto still behaved like a Javanese king and ignored public
opinion. He still did things which he thought was best. He appointed
his own daughter as Minister of Social Affairs and Bob Hassan, his

closest confidante and known to be one of the most corrupt business tycoons, as the Minister of Trade and Industry. His new regime was a personalised, bureaucratic form of consensus goverment that had tight control over all avenues of peaceful change and reform. The system only encouraged the belief that only violence could break the mould. Finally, in the middle of May 1998, he was pressured to resign as president following rampaging riots by demonstrating students. Suharto finally lost his kingdom. Even at the last minute when he had to surrender his throne, he wore a bitter smile.

When Suharto resigned as president, he launched the concept of *lengser keprabon* meaning stepping down from the throne in Javanese, or more accurately, "leaving kingship". Suharto had used the expression to indicate his position in the Javanese state and society. Like the old Javanese king, he was *paku-Buwono* — Nail of the Universe. Once the nail which holds the universe in place is taken away, paku-Buwono collapses. In Java, there is no tradition of becoming a Senior Minister like former Prime Minister Lee Kuan Yew in Singapore or becoming a power behind the throne.

Within Suharto's memory, several princes have stepped down from the throne. There was Sultan Hamengkubuwono (1877-1921) who more or less abdicated his kingly duties by living in his pleasure palace, now the four-star Ambarukmo hotel on the outskirts of Jogjakarta. A clearer case of princely abdication was that of Mangkunegara VI in the 1900s because he was disappointed that the Dutch colonial government did not approve of his eldest son as his successor. He ended his life in exile. Mangkunegara VI was, in fact, related to Suharto's late wife Ibu Tien.

Suharto had always regarded himself as a Javanese monarch and felt that his personal control and harmony with the spiritual world was as much a guarantee for the well-being of himself as for the nation and the state. He always thought that his destiny was the same as that of his nation and state. Hence, he always fasted before every August 17th, Indonesia's national independence day, and also on the eve of other important days in his life. He is well-known for associating with various great *pusaka* (sacred heirlooms) like the Gajah Mada's mask and other pusaka from the old royal houses of Java. He believed that such pusaka could transmit their magical power to him.

Suharto also liked to identify himself with *Semar*, the mighty clown figure in the Indian epic, the *Mahabharata*. The Semar was the symbol and embodiment of the people. When Suharto took over power from Sukarno. The phrase *Super Semar*[b] was used to refer to the transfer of power from Sukarno to himself.

On the eve of surrendering his power, Suharto, when confronted with the threat that ten ministers of the cabinet under the leadership of the Coordinating Minister for Economics, Finance and Industry Ginandjar Kartasasmita would resign en bloc if he did not step down, still maintained his royal style in a spiritual and physical way. He was hoping against hope that the leaders of the Muslim parties would back him. He called prominent leaders of the Muslim parties for consultation and support. It was as if he believed that the legendary "Nine Saints" of Java referred to in history as the *Wali Sanga* (the nine saints accredited with bringing the Islamic religion to Java) could pump new magical power into his waning authority. Until the end, Suharto kept his composure as if mastery over his emotions meant continued control over the situation. But it was too late and, partly because of age, a swift *untergang* and *Götterdämmerung* occurred, meaning the "nail" was no longer in place.

By then, he finally discovered that he had lost the support of both the armed forces and the Muslims. He had no alternative but to quit.

Suharto has undoubtedly contributed a great deal to developing Indonesia. He is described as the *Bapak* (father) of Indonesia's development. He has raised the gross national product of the Indonesians and given them a better life. But he manipulated the system so carefully for so long that, towards the end, he personally controlled almost everything — the military, the government and the wealth of the country. The problem with him was that he had become captive to the outrageous demands of his children and their cronies. He

---

[b]In fact, Super Semar is the acronym of <u>Su</u>rat <u>Pe</u>rintah (super) <u>Se</u>belas <u>Mar</u>et (Semar). It means the Letter of Instruction of March 11.

turned a blind eye to his children's avarice in business which tarnished his image. It was this greediness of his children and his cronies that angered the entire population and caused him to lose touch with the feelings of the masses.

The Javanese's refined manners were in a way shaped by the overpopulation of Java. In Java, people would be at one another's throat if they were to be too intimate, too loud, too vulgar or too blunt. The physical environment compelled the Javanese to be polite. It is a virtue to talk "like a Javanese" and not to say what you really mean. Whenever a Javanese suitor goes to the house of his prospective father-in-law to ask for the hand of his daughter, he would immediately know when he is not welcome if he is served a cup of bitter coffee. No Javanese family would chase you away when they dislike you. However, if you are served coffee without sugar, you should know that you are not welcome. Whenever the head of the household finds that his child has not learnt the subtleties of life, he will be told that he is "durung Java" or "not yet Javanese".

Priyayi values still have a strong hold on Javanese of all ages. One is often reminded that one must cultivate "etiquette feelings". Complicated Javanese etiquette dictates eye direction, the positioning of one's hands and the way one sits, stands, points, greets people, laughs, walks and dresses. Javanese even have certain smiles for anger, sorrow, suffering and grief. When I attended official functions as a diplomat, I had many opportunities to watch Javanese dances. Up till today, I find it difficult to know whether the dancers smiled angrily, sorrowfully or in grief. It is not easy to distinguish the niceties of the smile which are built into this discipline with patience. My impression of Javanese dance is that it is always too slow and too dull for me to appreciate. Perhaps I have not developed the skill of refinement needed to appreciate Javanese dancing.

Before Lee Kuan Yew made his first visit to Indonesia to see President Suharto, he sought my advice as to what he should and should not do. I told him that Suharto would consider him *kasar* (uneducated or low class) if he crossed his legs when sitting and that he should never raise his voice. When Lee Kuan Yew met Suharto officially for the first time, his behaviour was *halus* (refined). I remember when I presented credentials to President Suharto in 1970, I could hardly hear his voice for he was speaking very softly.

Whenever a Javanese says "yes", he means he has heard what you said. "Yes" does not mean he agrees with your views. I remember on one occasion when I went to Jakarta with Lee Kuan Yew to see Suharto to discuss the role of Singapore as a financial centre for South East Asia. I remember Lee Kuan Yew suggested some measures which Singapore could take to support Indonesia and Suharto responded "Yes, yes." Lee Kuan Yew took it to mean that Suharto had agreed with his views, but, I told him that Suharto's response only meant that he heard his views. I knew that Suharto would not have accepted his suggestion. This turned out to be true.

In my many years of experience in meeting President Suharto, I have never once seen him lose his temper. Even at the height of the recent student riots, he always smiled and spoke softly. Even at the time when he announced his resignation as President of Indonesia, Suharto did not show his feelings. He did it in true Javanese style. The Javanese have always believed in the ability to exercise stoic self-control because they felt jerkiness and unpredictability are signs of a lack of inner refinement. Loud voices, flamboyant behaviour, bragging, roars of laughter and shows of sorrow are all considered ill-mannered. Passion or anger is expected only of children, wild animals, peasants, the handicapped and foreigners. The Javanese will always maintain a placid exterior and put on a seemingly calm smile.

Whenever a Javanese meets a stranger, he will immediately size him up to see whether he is halus (polite) or kasar (crude). He will judge him up by observing his behaviour, his voice and the way he sits and stands.

The Javanese have the habit of associating someone they know with one of the characters of the Javanese *wayang* or drama. If they meet someone who is fierce with a bad temper, yet loyal and trustworthy, they would say he is like *Bima*, the most feared legendary warrior. If he meets someone who is handsome and romantic but tender-hearted, he would describe him as *Arjuna*, a mythical hero who is iron-willed, has many mistresses and possesses extreme discipline and self-denial.

Someone told me that President Sukarno liked to compare himself to Bima as he was not afraid of the Dutch colonialists. Others, however, say that Sukarno is more like Arjuna because he was romantic and was fond of the opposite sex.

This habit of associating some real personalities with mythical figures because of similarities in character is very much like that of the educated Chinese, who are fond of nicknaming a leader who is loyal and cool-headed as *Liu Pei*, or an upright, just and courageous leader as *Kuan Kong*, or a daring but impulsive personality as *Chang Fei* — the three sworn brothers in the Three Kingdoms period who lived about two thousand years ago. If one is smart and cunning, he is always compared to *Tsao Tsao*, the treacherous character in the *Romance of the Three Kingdoms*, the most popular novel about events in the history of the Three Kingdoms.

The Javanese language is far more complicated than Indonesia's other languages. This is the result of the strong influence of the Indian caste system on Javanese life. The language is the most intricate device ever created to show social rank. Many Javanese prefer to speak Bahasa Indonesia because then they do not have to speak up or down to people. The language also shows the Javanese obsession with politeness. Politeness is an instrument for making others as well as yourself feel peaceful within. For instance, a Javanese would never ask a tailor outright, "How much?". Instead, he would say, "What will be. in exchange for the thread?". "He will refer to his wife as his "friend in the back of the house". As it is considered impolite to point the middle finger at any person, he will use his thumb to point the way for someone asking for directions.

I took an interest in studying Javanese behaviour and thinking in the early part of my assignment in Indonesia because I was advised to do so by Mochtar Lubis, a leading journalist who was imprisoned by Sukarno for many years. He was the first person to draw my attention to the necessity of studying Javanese thinking. Being a Sumatran Batak he could not understand Javanese thinking. He said the Javanese had allowed Sukarno who was "only good at shouting slogans" to rule them for seventeen years because they believed that he had been sent down by God to rule them. When the economy finally turned bad, even though Sukarno asked the people to eat "stones" they still tolerated him until they believed his *wahyu* (soul of the leader) had left him. Similarly, when Suharto lost his power and was forced to resign, the Javanese, especially the students, said he had no more wahyu in him.

Javanese, being fatalists, believe that their leaders are destined by heaven to rule.

I was also motivated to study the Javanese mind by Adam Malik, the former Indonesian Foreign Minister who is a Batak Muslim. Adam Malik admitted to me that he too could not understand the Javanese. In the earlier part of my diplomatic assignment, he helped me a great deal in planning Lee Kuan Yew's visit to Indonesia. He had thought that it would be a simple affair and had promised he could pull it together without realizing the many hurdles he would have to overcome simply because the men who were really in charge were Javanese. He finally gave me a clue as to who had caused the hindrances and asked me to work on them. It was from this clue that I managed to concentrate on cultivating relations firstly with General Sudjono Humardhani, the spiritual adviser of Suharto, then with General Ali Murtopo, one of the most powerful *Aspri* (Presidential Assistant) in charge of political affairs, and finally with General Sumitro, Head of Kopkamtib (the Security Body) and the most powerful man in security matters. It took a great deal of work, patience and diplomacy but I finally succeeded in arranging for Lee Kuan Yew to visit Indonesia.

After developing friendship with these three important Javanese military leaders, I finally saw a light at the end of the tunnel. The success of my mission was mostly due to my studying and learning to understand Javanese thinking and feelings. One such issue was the importance of pacifying the soul with flowers, which I mentioned earlier. When Lee Kuan Yew visited Kalibata and put flowers on the tombs of the two marines who were hanged in Singapore, I saw tears flowing from the eyes of the Indonesian ambassador to Singapore,

General Rukminto. When I conveyed the event to General Ali Murtopo, Suharto's right-hand man, he felt really happy. Since then, Suharto has been very friendly with Lee Kuan Yew and the two countries have enjoyed many years of good relations and friendship.

There are two hundred million Indonesians. How do we know who are Javanese, who are Sumatrans, Balinese, Torajans or of the other races? There is a simple way. Just ask for his name and if his name ends with an "o", such as Sukarno, Suharto, Ali Murtopo or Sumitro, then he is a Javanese. This is, however, just an indication as there are also other Javanese whose names do not end with an "o". Another clue is to see how they behave. Most Javanese behave very politely or in a way which they consider as halus and often speak softly. A Javanese, for instance, will consider an Arab kasar because Arabs, Bataks, Ambonese or Madurese tend to speak loudly and the Javanese consider this behaviour rather offensive.

To enable readers to further understand the Javanese, I have made a deeper study into the various aspects of Javanese mysticism and have divided them into different sections such as the kraton culture, Javanese wayang kulit, Semar — the guardian spirit of Java, Gajah Mada's kris, Joyoboyo predictions, kebatinan, Lara Kidul and Javanese legends.

In West Java, there is a tribe of about two to four thousand Sunda-speaking people known as the mysterious "Amish of West Java" who live in 27 villages in a fifty-square-kilometre forest territory around Gunung Kendang, southeast of Rangkasbitung. They are called the Baduis. For four hundred years, the Baduis have maintained almost complete isolation from the outside world, preserving their way of life. They not only speak Sundanese but live in houses which are traditionally Sundanese. One theory maintains that they could be the survivors of the aristocracy of the Sunda kingdom of Pajajaran who lived near Batutulis in the hills around Boar. The Baduis went into the mountains to escape invading Muslims in the sixteenth century. They still pay respects to Siliwangi, the last of the Hindu kings.

In West Java, too, there are about sixty thousand mountain people with almost Tibetan features who lived in some forty villages ranging from 1,500-2,745 metres above sea level around Gunung Bromo.

Speaking an archaic dialect of Javanese, the Tenggerese are highly regarded by other Javanese as being intelligent, peace-keeping, hard-working, possessing high moral values and have a history of opposition to foreign influences.

When armed conflict broke out between the Islamised coastal districts and the Majapahit Empire of East Java in the 1400s, the nobles, priests and artisans fled to Bali but the ordinary people withdrew to the Tengger highlands to keep their Hindu faith. Today, the Tenggerese are the only people in all of East Java who practise Hinduism openly.

I will give my impression of the Baduis and the Tenggerese in separate chapters.

Today, however, the character of the Muslim abangan is also changing. The santris seem to be making some inroads in their attempt to 'Islamise' the Javanese population including the abangans. The success of the fundamentalists in Iran in overthrowing the Shah of Iran with an uprising has encouraged some of them to try to do the same thing in Indonesia.

Even Suharto himself has become more Islamic as he becomes older. In 1991, he helped establish Indonesia's first Islamic-style bank. Even the Golkar have stepped up its efforts to project a more accommodating front to Islam and highlighted government efforts to build mosques and other Islamic facilities. Perhaps Suharto needed Islamic support to counterbalance the armed forces just as Sukarno had tried to maintain a balance between the armed forces and communism.

In culture, nothing is static. Neither are abangans forever abangans. With the influence of aggressive Islam from Iran, the characteristics of abangans have also changed. A close friend of mine, Mas Agung, was an ethnic Chinese who did not speak Chinese and was very much Javanised. Although he was the person responsible for introducing me to Javanese mysticism, he then suddenly converted to Orthodox Islam and became a Muslim. Similarly, Suharto, who originally believed in Javanese mysticism, has recently also become very Islamic in his lifestyle. I have also noticed many others who were previously abangans changing their attitude as they grow older.

The impact of Islamic influence is growing among abangans in Java. Will there be a santricisation of abangans? Will Javanese mysticism and its belief in the spirit of the kris, trees, rocks, mountains and rivers disappear? With the influx and influence of Western cinemas and entertainment, will the popularity for the wayang kulit decline? Will the Javanese stop believing in the spirit and strength of Semar? Will the influence of kraton culture ever disappear? What about kebatinan (belief in the soul)? Can it survive the onslaught of Islam? Many of my Indonesian friends still talk about the Joyoboyo predictions. Some even predicted that their *Ratu Adil* will come when all the Chinese have left Indonesia.

Habits and beliefs die hard. I do not believe that Javanese mysticism will disappear with the arrival of Islam. It is not easy for the Javanese to change their habits and beliefs overnight. They will remain intact and be a part of their lifestyle for some time to come.

I think that the biggest impact on the Javanese is that the country now has a President who is not a Javanese. This is the first time Indonesia does not have a Javanese president. Habibie is from a small village in Sulawesi. Both Sukarno and Suharto were Javanese. Will the Javanese who comprise sixty percent of the population allow a non-Javanese to run the country? Will the next President be a Javanese? That would be interesting to find out.

JAVANESE MYSTICISM

a) The wayang

A good leader has to be:
like the Earth, bearing the burden of the planet;
like the Sun, giving warmth without expecting anything in return;
like the Moon, giving joy and comfort to all;
like the Stars, maintaining high ideals to serve mankind;
like the Ocean, great and therefore broad-minded;

like the Fire, fierce but just;
like the Wind, knowing the aspiration of the people,
like the Water, giving knowledge to all who thirst for it.

Verse by a *dalang* (puppeteer)

The Javanese word "wayang" means "shadow" or "ghost". Wayang is a theatrical performance of living actors, three-dimensional puppets or shadow images held on a back-lit screen. A *dalang* (the operator) sits behind the screen and relates the story as he manipulates the puppets, normally in the Javanese or Sundanese language. Most often, the stories are told in *Kawi* (old Javanese), as archaic a language of Java today as Shakespearean English is in English-speaking countries. Nowadays, it is also done in the Indonesian national language — *Bahasa.*

Wayang is staged when some traditional event occurs in a person's life: birthdays, weddings, important religious occasions or as ritual entertainment during family feasts. While providing entertainment, wayang also teaches the meaning and purpose of life: the contradictions and anomalies of modern life. The Indonesian Government uses wayang as a means of transmitting its policies because it has become one of the most popular means of entertainment and leisure in Indonesia.

The wayang plays do not just show the direct victory of good over evil, but also the weaknesses as well as the strengths in all its characters and, by implication, in society as a whole.

Wayang dates back to the 9th century B.C. before the arrival of Hinduism from India. In ancient pre-Hindu days, wayang puppets were perhaps portraits of deceased ancestors who came down to earth to visit and communicate with their descendents during the performance. The function of wayang was to placate and please the gods so as to increase fertility or to exorcise ghosts and evil spirits. Since the moving, flickering silhouettes were regarded as the souls of the dead, the dalang (puppeteer) was esteemed as a shaman, a medium between the dead and the living.

With the arrival of Hinduism from India sometime after the 1st century A.D. India's dramatic *Ramayana* and *Mahabharata* epics were incorporated into wayang performances. During this intensive period of Hindu influence, Hindu teachers used wayang to popularise their religion. Indian heroes, gods, demons and giants eventually replaced all the ancient ancestoral figures as the characters of wayang performances.

When Hinduism gave way to Islam in the 13th century, Muslims made heroes of the Islamic literary figures and turned them into puppet characters. The Islamic Sultans used wayang to flatter themselves and to glorify their feudalistic courts. Because Islam banned the depiction of the human form, both good and evil puppets were made to appear ugly and grotesque so as not to resemble living beings, and the puppets' faces, colours, hair-dos, costumes and jewellery became more symbolic than representative of actual human figures.

The first time I saw a Javanese *wayang kulit* (leather) was in Jogjakarta in 1955 during my holidays after a hectic week in Bandung covering the Afro-Asian Conference. It was my first experience with the wayang, and I must confess my impression was that of a jumble of leather puppets casting mysterious shadows on a white screen.

The performance was in a dimly-lit village near an old kraton. The reverberating sound of the gamelan, accompanied by dreamy sounds of the Javanese violin and a potpourri of other unfamiliar sounds, attracted me to the place. A single oil-lamp flickered overhead, casting a hemisphere of pale yellowish light. It drew darting reflections from the gongs and the lacquered stands of the gamelan orchestra. The soothing, harmonious rhythm of the gamelan music was interrupted by the harsh and soft voices of the spectators who milled around. Vendors of sweets, balloons, pin-wheels, cigarettes, ice-cream, and vile-coloured soft-drinks circulated among the spectators, screeching their wares. Beyond the gamelan, at the base of the white screen, the *dalang*, whose magic touch brings shadows to life, sat cross-legged on the stone floor of the pavilion. To the left and right of him was an array of lacy, coloured buffalo-skin puppets, some taller and others shorter, some handsome with slim and refined bodies whilst others ugly and gigantic. There were some funny-looking clowns with distorted features.

The dalang, who was an old man dressed in sarong and wearing a headgear, started to chant his recital in Javanese, first wishing the people a prosperous and peaceful state. He turned up the oil-lamp, a symbol of eternal life, and raised a large triangular leather puppet to the middle of the screen to indicate that the performance was about to begin. This figure, which is called *gunungan*, is an intricately cut, beautiful sheet of leather. Its upper half shows the branches of the tree of life. Monkeys climb about the branches and cat-like creatures sharpen their claws. Snakes crawl about and fight with other animals. Surrounding the branches are blossoms, birds spreading their wings, peacocks displaying their tails, and insects flying.

My Javanese friend explained to me that the tree of life represented the world of nature created by God. He then went on to point out the lower parts of the gunungan and their significance. Below the red-faced demon is a house with a pyramid-shaped roof and curved eaves. The elaborately decorated doors are locked and guarded on both sides by two ferocious-looking dwarfed giants holding huge clubs. On the roof-tops are two connons guarding the house which represents the personal life of man. The two weapon-carrying dwarfed giants symbolise punishment for wrong doings and evil thoughts.

As a whole, the theme of the gunungan depicts man having to master his aspiration for good and his carnal desires before he is able to attain perfection of the soul. The distractions and obstacles to perfection are symbolised by monkeys and other animals which obstruct the way in the search for inner peace of mind, which is hidden away behind closed doors. It is not easy to get there because of the many distractions, obstacles and temptations. The gunungan as a whole is somewhat like a tapestry of life, interweaving the real and mythical, with God Almighty determining all activities in the Universe.

As I sat enthralled listening to the explanation of the significance of the gunungan, the flame of the oil-lamp flickered in the breeze and the punched-out leather puppets cast their shadows in a quivering manner across the screen. The voice of the dalang floated through the thin muslin screen, narrating the introduction of the Mahabharata, the great Hindu epic which for centuries has championed the victory of good over evil in India and then in Indonesia. Adapted to a Javanese setting with Javanese characters, the Hindu Mahabharata relates the story of the war and intrigues that went on between the *Pandawas* and the *Kurawas*, two families in conflict over the throne.

The story of the Mahabharata goes something like this: Once upon a time, *Prabu Adjasa* ruled the great Kingdom of *Ngastina* with justice, peace and prosperity. Yet the king had a secret sorrow. His three sons were invalids. The eldest son *Drestarata* was blind; the second, *Pandu*, was an albino and the third, *Widura*, was incurably lame. When the King abdicated due to old age, he named Pandu his successor because it would be difficult for Drestarata, the blind elder brother to rule. The throne was handed over, however, on the condition that it would later revert to Drestarata's line. However, Pandu, once crowned sovereign King, was entitled to nominate his own successor and it was feared that he would not abide by the condition. This was the origin of the bitter feud between the sons of Drestarata who were referred to as the Kurawas and the sons of Pandu, called the Pandawas. The Kurawas consisted of 99 boys and one girl and the Pandawas, only five in number, all boys. Most the plot centres around the five Pandawas and their feuds with their Kurawa cousins.

The eldest of the five Pandawas was *Prabu Judistira*, a humble aristocrat, who never raised his voice in anger and never said no to anyone, a passionless inward-looking intellectual who spent most of his time in meditation. The second Pandawa, *Wrekudawa*, more popularly known as *Bima*, was a greatly feared warrior, hot-headed and impulsively brave, who created havoc with his terrible club and atrocious fingernails (*pancanaka*). But he was honest, loyal and truthful. The third was handsome, romantic *Arjuna*, who was tender-hearted, yet iron-willed, a hero whose romantic episodes with his wives and mistresses filled the many pages of the Mahabharata. And yet he was capable of extreme discipline and self-denial, and had a deep feeling of loyalty for his family. The other two brothers, who were the twins *Nangkula* and *Sadewa*, born to Pandu's second wife, were less popular and less known.

On the death of their father, the Pandawas were still little children and were left in the care of their blind uncle Drestarata, who became regent till their maturity. Both the Kurawas and Pandawas were brought up together at Ngastina, and from the very beginning the cousins were in constant bitter rivalry. Through trickery, the Kurawas usurped their position and forced the Pandawas to flee. For many years, they roamed the forests, befriending all creatures and spent their time acquiring strength and spiritual power through meditation and self-denial. In the cultivation of their land, the Pandawas were helped by the monkey *Hanuman*, the elephant *Lakubanda*, the griffin *Waneya*, the serpent *Basuki* and the giant *Jayah Sweka*. They built a magnificent palace and crowned Jusdistira King and called their kingdom *Ngamarta*.

The Pandawas attracted many people to settle in their kingdom. This incurred the jealousy of the Kurawas, who tricked Judistira into gambling away his kingdom. Once again, the Pandawas were forced to roam in lonely poverty through the woods and mountains, attended as always by their faithful servant clowns called *panakawan*, such as Semar, Gareng and Petruk. Whenever the Pandawas were in trouble, Semar and the others were around to give them comfort and assistance. When the Pandawas became strong again with the help of one of their cousins, *Kresna*, who was the reincarnation of the mighty Vishnu, they negotiated for a partition of the Kingdom of Ngamarta into two on the basis of peaceful co-existence. The Kurawas not only turned down the request but also tried to assassinate Kresna who was sent as the envoy of the Pandawas. This led to frequent confrontation and ultimately, a settlement by the last war known as the *Bharatajudha Jayabinagun*, or the *Bharatajudha* war.

The war ended in pure slaughter. The Kurawas — Suyudana, their leader together with his 98 brothers — fled from Arjuna's magic arrows and Bima's club. In the last episode Bima tore to pieces the slanderous mouth of *Sakuni*, the cunning Chief Minister of the Kurawa regime, with his thumbnail. The war was over. The Pandawas regained their kingdom of Ngamarta but their splendour was short-lived. The Pandawas were tired of war as their sons had been killed in the battles.

After a long and beneficent reign, the Pandawas abdicated and wandered about in search of truth.

It was a long philosophical story which went on until the early hours of the morning. The dalang imparted so much life into the puppets that we forgot that we were watching only shadows.

The Javanese spectators were well-acquainted with the story of the Mahabharata. They liked to hear the jokes of Semar, see the mighty warrior Bima using his thumbnail to tear the cunning Sukuni into pieces, and they were always fascinated by the romantic adventures of the refined Arjuna. Apart from the excitement, the people went to the wayang to gain wisdom, insight and peace of mind.

When Arjuna was being groomed to be a good leader, the dalang, imitating the low voice of a *Guru* (teacher) said, "To be a knight or a good leader, one must have a strong mind and character to bear troubles and sorrows, just as the earth has to bear everything which exists on the surface of the planet. A good leader must be like the sun, giving warmth and life to all creatures without expecting anything in return; like the moon, giving peace and joy to all; and like the stars twinkling in the sky, maintaining high ideals to serve mankind. He must also be like the ocean, vast and broad-minded; like the fire, fierce but just; like the wind, intelligently knowing the aspirations of the people; and like water, giving knowledge to all who thirst for it."

It was good advice to all leaders who want to rule Java or Indonesia. As millions of Javanese are watching the wayang every night, this concept of fairness of their leaders are always in their mind. They expect their leaders to follow the rules and requirements of leadership as depicted in the wayang. Although the wayang is only a form of entertainment, the spectators learn a lot about how a country should be run and how their leaders are expected to behave.

This was how the Javanese had expected Suharto to behave when he became President. They found him wanting in fulfilling the requirements of a real and just Javanese king and therefore decided to get rid of him.

I saw the dalang placed the gunungan back at the centre of the screen to indicate that the show was over. The thirst of some spectators apparently unquenched; they still stared blankly at the screen where the shadows had faded away and as the rays of the morning sun seeped in. Some were fast asleep. Many stretched their arms and legs and dragged their feet to go home.

After the show, I talked to the dalang who did not seem to show any sign of tiredness. Against the morning sun, his face looked more wrinkled. He wore a moustache. I wanted to know what it was like to be a dalang. His answer was a quotation from a poem called "Serat Centini":

"The dalang has to be proficient in four ways: Firstly, he has to be able to tell the story. Secondly, he must know the music and the art of chanting. Thirdly, he must have a sense of humour and lastly, he must be able to handle the wayang puppets skilfully throughout the performance." A dalang is an expert only after long years of practice and experience. He said the younger generation nowadays was luckier, for courses in this art were now conducted in both Solo and Jogjakarta. Some of the students of Gajah Mada University attend such courses because it is compulsory for those in the Faculty of Letters to know the art of the wayang.

The dalang told me that there were altogether some six hundred puppet figures, half of them kept on his right and the other half on his left. I asked him how he could remember the faces of the different puppets. With usual Javanese politeness, the dalang said the puppets on his right were the Pandawa family and those on the left were the Kurawas. Roughly speaking, the puppets are divided into various groups. The giants called *Rhakasa* or *Buta*, are easily recognised by their huge size and the fangs protruding from the corners of their mouths. The servants like Semar, Gareng and Petruk have extraordinary, ugly faces and distorted figures and are painted black and white. The deities, like Sanghiang Batara, or Dewa and priest wear cloaks and shoes. There remains the larger group made up of kings called *Prabu*, princes called *Raden* and ministers call *Patih*. The upper part of their bodies is unclothed, but they wear the *dodot*, a long piece of cloth wrapped round the hips. The headgear worn by the figures also indicates the rank and social status of the characters.

As for the leaders of the Pandawas and the Kurawas, they were easily recognisable and he has become familiar with them.

I asked the dalang which characters he liked best in the Mahabharata epic. With a soft voice, he said: "As a dalang, I should not favour either the Pandawas or the Kurawas. Every character has a role to play just as every man has a place under the sun. It would be a mistake for me to make a king dance like a clown or a clown behave like a king."

During the performance, I noticed the dalang tapping a stick against a box from time to time. This puzzled me, so I asked the dalang what it meant. He explained that each tap was to signal that he was about to start talking so the audience would listen attentively. He would also puncture his speech with a gentle tap.

"What about the clinking sound which I hear from time to time?", I asked. He said it was a signal for the gamelan orchestra to start playing or was simply done to add colour to create the mood of excitement during a violent battle. Although the gamelan orchestra has its own conductor who normally plays the *kandang* or *rebab* (the Javanese violin) he takes his cue from the dalang.

Every dalang has a handbook, called the *pakem*, which contains certain rules on what he should do and say. The pakem varies from place to place, but the pakem of Solo and Jogjakarta are regarded as the most outstanding and refined, and dalangs from most regions usually adhere to one of them. Basically, there are two kinds of pakem, one with detailed rules specifying exactly what a dalang should do and say. This is meant for the beginners in order for them to acquire a good foundation. The other, the incomplete one which contains only the outline of a story, gives the more experienced dalang room for improvisations which often appeals more to the audience.

The mysterious shadows of the wayang that I saw in Jogjakarta in 1955 left a mixed impression on my mind. I was re-introduced to the shadow play when I returned to Indonesia as a diplomat in 1970. The four and a half years gave me time to see more wayang kulit performances and I decided to make a closer study of the subject.

I have enjoyed watching many stories of the wayang kulit and have talked to people who have a similar interest. There are so many *lakons* (stories) in the Mahabharata and the Ramayana epics that it is impossible for most people to view all of them. On the rise and fall of the Pandawas and the Kurawas alone there are more than two hundred lakons. But of all the lakons that I have seen, only a few have left a lasting impression on my mind. One of them is the "lakon Dewaruci" which relates the adventures of Bima through dangerous mountains and treacherous oceans in search of the holy spring, *Tritapawitra*, which could give him eternal youth and wisdom. This lakon also happens to be one of the most popular among the ordinary Javanese folk.

One day, Bima heard about a holy spring from his old teacher *Durna*, in the Ngastina Palace. Durna was under the influence of the Kurawas who wanted to eliminate Bima, the strongest and most daring of the *Pandawas*. He told Bima that the holy spring was hidden in the Candramujka Grotto, at the foot of Mount Gadamadana. Little did Bima know that it was a trap to kill him. When he reached the place after much difficulty, the giants, Rakmaka and Rukmakala, were waiting to devour him. Bima caught them by their "hippie" hair and whirled them one by one against the rocks till they died. He uprooted trees and looked high and low but found no holy spring. In desperation, he gave up and returned to the palace, only to be told by Durna that it was meant as a test of his bravery, determination and patience. Durna then told him that he had to go into the ocean where the holy spring was really hidden. Bima, who had strength but not wisdom, left immediately for the ocean and again encountered many obstacles.

He met a gigantic sea-serpent with flames darting from its protruding eyes and poisonous venom pouring from its huge mouth. It was exciting to watch the fight between Bima and the sea-serpent. Bima nearly gave up when suddenly he remembered the strength of his kuku pancanaka. He stuck it into the monster's jaw and blood spurted in all directions, turning the ocean red. Having disposed of the most dangerous demon of the oceans, he went on searching for the holy spring *Tritapawitra*, but in vain.

Finally, he met *Dewaruci*, a tiny unknown creature the size of a small child who appeared from nowhere. Bima was surprised that Dewaruci knew all about him, including his ancestors, where he came from and what he was looking for. The tiny creature asked him to enter into its body. At first it appeared to Bima that this was impossible, for he was huge and the creature tiny. He was finally persuaded and found no difficulty entering Dewaruci's body through its little ear. Through Dewaruci's eyes he saw the whole universe in its real perspective. All sorts of symbols, colours and patterns appeared before him. Dewaruci explained their significance. Through the soft-spoken voice of Dewaruci, Bima discovered himself and the meaning of life. The giant-sized hero, Bima found himself bowing humbly to Dewaruci who, though so tiny, knew the secrets of life, wisdom, strength, peace of mind and everlasting happiness. After imparting to *Bima* truth and wisdom, Dewaruci disappeared leaving an enlightened Bima.

It was through the conversation between Bima and Dewaruci that a dalang imparted to the audience the Javanese philosopy of life. Bima's search for the holy spring, Tritapawitra represents man's search for eternal life, immortality and happiness. Man looks for them high and low without realizing that they are all hidden in the holy pramana (inner soul) within him. Once he is able to reach his soul, he will be able to communicate with God. To do so, he has to learn how to subdue smell, hearing, sight, feeling and taste. He must suppress these senses so that the physical world ceases to exist. Only then can the physical body conform to the spiritual, a union of which would enable him to receive impulses from God and attain peace of mind. This is the purpose of meditation which helps to subdue human sensual desires and leads him to better self-control, so that he may be the master of his own destiny.

The necessity of exercising self-control over one's sensual gratifications and carnal desires was stressed over and over again in all the themes of the stories in the Mahabharata. Arjuna was known for his romantic episodes. His largest weakness was the opposite sex. Yet he was capable of extreme self-control and self-denial after long moments of meditation.

On another occasion in Solo, I saw a wayang kulit performance called the "Lakon Arjuna Mintaraga" which showed how Arjuna's self-control was tested. When he was doing penance one day, seven beautiful nymphs were sent to tempt him. One of them was the wife of *Sujudana* (the eldest of the Kurawas) with whom he was secretly in love. But he was unmoved. A priest was also sent to arouse his temper by passing sarcastic and insulting remarks. Arjuna was so absorbed in his meditation that he did not even notice the presence of the priest nor did he hear the remarks.

Other Javanese values in moral and social matters, such as loyalty and dedication, were subtly imparted to the audience by the dalang through conversations between one personality and another in many lakons of the Mahabharata and Ramayana.

The most touching story about loyalty and dedication to duty that I saw was a lakon called "Semar Papa". Semar, the most powerful but loyal servant of the Pandawas, was always associated with hilarious jokes and laughter. But there were moments when his selfless loyalty to his masters made him so pitiful that the audience burst into tears. The Pandawa kingdom of Ngamarta was visited by an inexplicable plague and a seer warned that the disaster could only be averted by the death of Semar. Despite the fact that Semar was the one who had waited on them from birth and rescued them from innumerable troubles and crises, the Pandawas, being Sastriya (warriors) did not shy from their duties to society. They decided to do away with Semar.

Judistira, the eldest of the Pandawas ordered his nephew *Abimanju*, the eldest son of Arjuna, to carry out the unpleasant task. Abimanju took Semar to the forest. The audience was tense and one could hear sobbing from the crowd when Semar blew his nose and cried like a child. He did not resist Abimanju, but was ready to accept his fate. The tender-hearted Abimanju could not bring himself to carry out his uncle's orders. He released Semar, who hurried away with profound gratitude and started again to crack jokes. The audience, with a sigh of relief, broke into laughter again.

In the Javanese sense of moral code, the Pandawas did the right thing in ordering the sacrifice of Semar for the sake of the community.

Abimanju's behaviour was considered an act of cowardice for he acted like a woman and not like a warrior. Semar's willingness to die was interpreted as moral courage and a great sense of loyalty.

Besides the Mahabharata the Ramayana is another world-renowned Hindu epic which originated in India, and is also exceedingly popular among the Javanese and Balinese wayang fans. I have enjoyed the Ramayana stories on many occasions in Jogjakarta, Surabaya and Bali. The story tells of King *Desarata* in the state of *Nyayoga* in the northern part of India who wanted to abdicate his throne in favour of Crown Prince *Rama*. This was opposed by his second wife, *Dewi Kekayi*, who reminded the king that he had once promised to make her son *Barata* his successor. So she plotted to banish Rama from the country. The noble Barata, however, did not approve of the ambitious plan of his mother, and went into exile for fourteen years with his faithful wife, *Dewi Sita*, and his brother *Lesmono*.

Rama went to the Dandaka forest and fought with Barsasas (giants) who created havoc there and *Raksasa* who resided in the *Nyalanka* (Sri Lanka) was afraid of Rama and did not dare fight him. Instead, he abducted Rama's beloved wife, Dewi Sita. In order to free her, Rama sought the help of the white monkeys in the jungle, whose king was *Ssugriswas* and their general, Hanuman. After defeating *Raksasa* and rescuing his wife, Rama returned to the palace of Nyayoga and assisted his brother Barata to rule the country.

The Ramayana stories are depicted on the walls of the Siva temple of Prambanan in Central Java. The history of the old Javanese *Ramayana Kekawin* was already popular during the peak periods of power of kingdoms such as Kediri, Singasari and Majapahit (eleventh to sixteenth centuries). In the court of Jogjakarta, the Javanese developed a new choreography for the Ramayana, using huge crowds of people imitating monkeys. This perhaps was the origin of the now famous *kecak* monkey dance of Bali, which is one of the main attractions for tourists to Bali.

The Ramayana epic, though originally from India, has always had a tremendous impact on Indonesians. The Government of Indonesia, inspired by the Ramayana stories, chose the image of Rama — in a pose bending the bow of Sita — as the emblem for the 1962 Asian Games. The pose was taken from one of the reliefs of the Siva temple at Prambanan. In 1972, the Indonesian Government also organised an Asian Ramayana festival in Pandaan East Java. Nearly all the Asian countries including India, Burma, Sri Lanka, Thailand and Malaysia participated in this great festival.

The story of Rama and Sita contains important lessons on morality and good conduct, especially on how to be a good and wise leader.

I became more and more interested in the wayang kulit because I found that nothing has influenced the Javanese mind more than wayang. To understand the wayang is the first step towards understanding the Javanese. There is at least one wayang group which performs regularly for viewers of all ages in every village throughout Java. It has become a way of life — not so much a form of entertainment as part of social education.

From a tender age, the Javanese mind is moulded not only by the strict Javanese home discipline, but also by direct exposure to the wayang performances. Through the screen and the mythical characters of the Mahabharata and Ramayana, the dalang conveys to the viewers and listeners the Javanese concept of the universe. As he relates and captivates the crowd with interesting stories, he also expounds poetically on the existential position of the Javanese personality, his relationship with the natural and supernatural order, and the importance of maintaining harmony and stability in a world of conflict. By frequenting wayang performances, a boy soon becomes familiar with characters like Arjuna, the frail-looking, tender-hearted romantic but well-disciplined hero, or Bima, the ill-tempered, courageous dare-devil fighter, or Semar, the clown with supernatural powers. The young Javanese audiences have so many characters to choose from for a role model. These diverse characters also provide mental guidelines for them to interpret any personalities they happen to meet.

Perhaps nowhere in the world has mythology and mysticism made such an impact on the minds of the people than in Java through the wayang. Mythological stories of war between the Pandawas and the Kurawas, between right and wrong, and stories of the supernatural powers of the warriors derived from their *alat* (instrument), as well as stories of reincarnation, cannot but influence the Javanese minds, particularly the younger ones. Apart from conveying mythical tales and mysticism, the wayang has also more serious philosophical connotations. The wayang, in fact, represents the whole Javanese philosophy of vagueness and their idea of man and God. The use of the shadow to project one's philosophy is typical of Javanese genius. The shadow itself is a vague thing. It is perhaps the only thing in the world that one can see but cannot touch and feel. It is real and yet intangible. It has two dimensions. The Javanese have chosen the shadow to illustrate their concept of the invisible world. Through the shadow, they project the spirits of their ancestor. Through the shadow, the dalang tries to convey the meaning of life and the destiny of man. He tries to teach man his place in the universal order, the cosmos as well as his relationship to the Divine. The wayang implants in the Javanese mind the philosopy that everyone has a different role to play in society, and everyone must know his own role. In other words, a king must behave like a king and a clown a clown. A king could never behave like a clown and a clown, a king.

The Javanese like to compare real personalities that they come across with wayang personalities. They read personalities with the knowledge of the images of the wayang. During my stay in Indonesia, I often heard Javanese friends commenting that so and so was like Arjuna or like Bima. Someone told me that the former President Sukarno liked to compare himself to Bima as he was not afraid of the Dutch colonialists. Some however felt that Sukarno was like Arjuna because he was very romantic.

Suharto is said to identify strongly with the clown god Semar, who in the traditional wayang plays often steps in to save the situation when more refined characters have failed. It is also said that Suharto is much more a Javanese king than an "elected president", and that Indonesia is much more like a Javanese kingdom than a republic. Admirers of Suharto compare him to the wise kings of the wayang puppet shows, who turn chaos into order and bring prosperity to the kingdom. But critics of the Suharto regime also retort that he rules the country more like a Javanese king or sultan with systems of palace-centred patronage, favouritism and officially-sponsored corruption, particularly involving his own family. As Suharto failed to cope with the economic typhoon presently sweeping Southeast Asia and particularly Indonesia, student riots erupted in all corners of Indonesia calling for the "king" to step down. The student riots have finally succeeded. Suharto has relinquished his presidency and for the first time, a non-Javanese has taken over as president.

From the point of Javanese spectators, Suharto failed to fulfilled his role as "king" of Java. He has not fulfilled his role as the sun, which gives warmth without expecting anything in return. Yes, he had helped to develop the rich resources of the country, but he failed to distribute the wealth derived from such resources more equally among the people. He treated all the wealth as belonging to his family. He was not like the wind, which knew the aspiration of the people. He became a little isolated and aloof and did not keep in touch with the ground. He was over-confident and went to Cairo to attend an Islamic conference at the peak of the student riots and never dreamt that his closest supporters would betray him.

I personally have the impression that Suharto was the dalang who has been pulling the strings of his puppets for 32 years. He has put nearly all his adjutants into positions of commanders-in-chief of the army, navy and air force, and had picked all his favourites to be governors of the provinces. He moved his fingers and the puppets followed his motion. This time, however, when he tried to move the puppets, some of the puppets got entangled and did not move. Things have changed. His role as the dalang has ended.

I watched the political wayang play that enacted behind the scene in the struggle for power, the student riots and the final collapse of the Suharto regime. For some years, I felt that Suharto was losing the confidence and trust of the people. I saw how his closest lieutenants — the Speaker of the House, Harmoko, the Chief of the Armed Forces and Defence Minister General Wiranto, and even his successor Habibie and the entire cabinet — let him down. Because of the heavy pressure of the student riots, they withdrew their support and Suharto fell.

In philosophical terms, the illuminated screen of the wayang kulit is the visible world and the puppets represent varieties of God's creations. The *gedebok*, the banana trunk used to support puppets by sticking them into it, represents the surface of the world; the *blencong*, the lamp over the head of the dalang is the light of life and the gamelan orchestra is a symbol of harmony of all worldly activities. The dalang, who manipulates the puppets and gives them life is the personification of God. Without the dalang, no puppet can come to life. Thus, the Javanese feel that it is wrong for humans to think that they can decide things by themselves or to act as they wish. The dalang and the wayang serve as an external expression of the various ways in which God acts and works in the world. He holds in his hands the fate of every single human being as He orders and guides all events. Fortune or misfortune, a short or long life, success or failure are all in the hands of the dalang of the Universe — God.

This is to my mind another philosophical aspect to the wayang. It concerns the two categories of the audience present at each wayang performance — one group sits in front of the screen, and the other group behind the screen. Those in front see only the shadows and are not aware of what goes on behind the screen. Perhaps the few behind the screen can be considered privileged, having a deeper understanding of the feelings, behaviour and aspirations of the manipulator.

Wayang puppets are very colourful. Their faces are painted according to their characters and their different roles. They also wear colourful clothing to match their status. I sometimes wonder why colours are necesssary at all for puppets, since colours are not visible through the screen. What is the idea of having the puppets painted when the audience can only see their shadows? But such colours are not meant to be seen by the common audience, or shall I say, the masses. Only the audience behind the stage, those who are closer to the dalang have the privilege of seeing the true colours of the faces and costumes of the puppets.

When a warrior like Arjuna or Bima is about to appear, the dalang places on that puppet a golden mask. The audience close to the dalang behind the stage knows in advance that a war is about to begin before the front audience sees it over the screen. Moreover, the audience in front has no means of knowng when the hero has changed masks. Perhaps it is meant to be that the dual personality of a puppet should be hidden from ordinary eyes. After all, vagueness is the essence of a wayang culture. The leather puppet is real, but its shadow a myth. A wayang performance is therefore an interplay between myth and reality.

The term wayang has the same etymological root as the Javanese word for "shadow". However, the term may also have another origin connected with ancient traditions of remembering one's ancestors. One legend says that the Hindu King *Joyoboyo* in the year 861 A.D. ordered his artists to make drawings of the stone figures of his ancestors on palm leaves called *lontar*. He named the lontar images *wayang puruwa*. It is said that the present word wayang was borrowed from this word, which originally referred to the images of Javanese ancestors.

The real origin of the word wayang, however is still a matter of debate among scholars concerned with the subject. Some of them believe that the wayang originated in Indonesia because as early as the seventh century A.D. there was already a *prasasti* (inscription) which contained the word *angringgit* which means "to perform the shadow play". Other scholars argue that India was the place of origin of the wayang because of a kind of shadow play called *chayanataka* which was performed in India in ancient times but which is now extinct. Whatever it may be, nobody can deny the fact that in Indonesia the development of the wayang has reached a high standard of perfection and popularity unparalled in any other country in the world. And indeed, the wayang has not lost its grip on the Indonesian audiences despite the introduction of modern types of entertainment such as the cinema.

In the old days there were no schools in the rural areas in which general education could be given. The teaching of morality and standards of human behaviour could only be done through the wayang. It became so deeply rooted that even the *Wali* (Muslim saints) found it necessary to decree later that the wayang was, in fact, an invention of *Sunan Kalijaga*, one of the most celebrated and honoured saints of Islam in Indonesia. The powerful clown Semar in the Mahabharata was so popular that the Wali had to use wooden figures of Semar patterned out of Arabic scripts to preach Islam in the hinterland of Java. They have also introduced stories of Amir Hamzah, the heroic uncle of the Prophet Mohammed into wayang performances. Such stories were later known as *wayang menak*.

Historically, the wayang was first introduced in the inscription of Kedu dated 907 A.D. The first mention of the leather puppets of a wayang was made in the *Arjun Wiwala* (which is about the marriage of *Arjun*, one the first heroes, to *Dewi Surpabha*) written by *Mou Kanwe* in the eleventh century. Since olden times, the Javanese kings were protectors and patrons of culture and thus took great pains in the development of the wayang until it reached the present standard. The Dutch rulers allowed the wayang to flourish and when the Indonesian people gained their independence, it received the support and encouragement of the government. This explains the uninterrupted development and continuity in the art of the wayang.

Besides the wayang kulit, there are also other kinds of wayang. In the wayang golek, for instance, the puppets are made of wood, three-dimensional and resemble human figures. For the wayang golek no screen is necessary, as it is not actually a shadow play. Apparently, it was created by *Sunan Kudus*, one of the Islamic priests in 1583. The wayang golek is very popular in Cirebon, a town on the border of Central Java and West Java, where both the Javanese and Sundanese languages are spoken. (It is a common mistake among foreigners to think that all the people who live in Java speak Javanese. The residents in West Java speak Sundanese and many of them do not understand Javanese. Neither can the average Javanese speak Sundanese.)

The wayang golek has three variants differentiated by the stories they perform. The one that performs stories from the Ramayana and Mahabharata is called *wayang golek purwa;* the one that shows the Panji stories is called *wayang golek gedog;* and the third kind called *wayang golek nemak* gets its stories from Persian and Arabic sources, mostly about Amir Hamzah, who was considered the uncle of Prophet Mohammed and whose Javanese name is *wong agung nemak joyegrana*.

Another type of wayang created at the beginning of the nineteenth century by Mangkunegara IV in Surakarta is called *wayang madya*. The repertoire is taken from the Book of Hajipamasa, a book of mythical stories, whose central figure is Aji Saka. It tells of the coming of the Hindus to Indonesia.

The *wayang topeng* of Malang in East Java is also known throughout Java. It is a dance drama based on the stories of the Panji cycle. The wayang topeng is performed by human actors wearing wooden masks. (The word topeng means "mask".) As the human actors dance with masks on, the dalang who in this case does not manipulate them physically narrates the story. This type of mask dancing is also popular throughout Asia, particularly in Japan and Thailand. In Indonesia, different regions have different types of topeng, costumes and styles of dancing. Malang is the centre of topeng culture.

The latest invention of the twentieth century is the *wayang suluh*. It is used by the Ministry of Information to relate the contemporary history of Indonesia and to disseminate propaganda. The dalang uses Bahasa Indonesia instead of Javanese. The puppets are also made of leather, but have human profiles. The figure Arjuna, for instance, wears a military cap and carries a modern pistol, symbolising a revolutionary hero, and Bima is often depicted as a guerrilla fighting against the Dutch colonialists. The modern figure of Arjuna has the new name of Nusantara Putra. The wayang suluh, which utilises the shapes and figures of the wayang puruwa heroes and characters built with variations, is used to convey new standards of social behaviour and modern concepts. For example, experiments are being made to use the wayang suluh to teach the people the importance of family planning, with Semar cracking jokes about those having too many children. Modern social values are put across through the subtle mingling of old and new stories. It is also being used as a useful weapon during elections to publicise party platforms or to poke fun at political opponents.

It seems to me that the wayang tradition is here to stay. In olden times, wayang was only performed at night until the early hours of the morning, as this was the appropriate time for the ancestral spirits to attend. Nowadays, the shadow play is intended mostly for entertainment. A great deal of religious significance has been lost in the course of history. The wayang is performed these days in Indonesia to celebrate the birth of a child, a wedding, an anniversary, or the so-called *tumbukan* — when someone reaches the age of 48, 56 or 64 years old according to the Javanese eight-year cycle. The wayang performances which are still reminiscent of ancient type of religious festivals can still be seen in Java during the month of *Ruwah* (the eighth month of the Muslim calendar) or during the big harvest. The first is a kind of ancestor worship celebration, the latter, a thanksgiving party.

The wayang culture is taken very seriously in Indonesia. It is treated not merely as a form of entertainment but as one important stream of Indonesian education. Children in primary and secondary schools are taught the stories on which the wayang is based and learn to recognise the various characters which appear on the screen. They also learn to appreciate and play gamelan music.

Indeed, the wayang has become an important part of the Indonesian cultural heritage.

b) Kraton culture

A *kraton* is a fortified palace of Javanese rulers in the olden days of Javanese empires. It became the centre of political power and culture. The building of kraton was inspired by India when Hindu culture and civilisation was introduced to Java. As in India, the kraton incorporated all the needs of the surrounding region such as commerce, art, and religion. In this city within a city were found banks, shops, temples, meditation chambers, schools, workshops and quarters for scribes and concubines: everything, for both body and soul, that the royalty had a use for.

In ancient times, kraton became the home of leisurely aristrocrats with wealth who could use the kraton to cultivate and develop the arts and crafts, dances and dramas. Other forms of indigenous customs and animism held sway among the rural population. During the colonial period, when the colonial masters left cultural matters in the hands of Javanese aristocrats, much money was spent on pompous ceremonial occasions to give free rein to artistic expressions. The finest wayang puppets and masks were produced in and for the kraton.

The kratons have always been regarded as the centre of the world for the masses, the reservoirs of spiritual power. They were even built in such a way as to represent a microcosm of the universe.

One of the most important factors influencing the minds of the Javanese is the kraton culture, which still lingers in commonfolk Javanese who had lived in the shadows of the kraton for centuries. However, when Indonesia gained her independence and declared herself a Republic in 1945, the people did away with feudalism. Political power is no more decided by inheritance. Sultans lost their political grip as the system of feudalism and aristocracy was phased out. The kratons of Surakarta and Jogjakarta have now become symbols of ancient Javanese feudalism and aristocracy. The same applies to the kratons in Cirebon, Siak, Kota Waringin in Langkat and Goa in Sulawesi.

Was it not a fact that, in the past, Javanese aristocrats have always regarded Central Java as the centre of the universe? The names of the Javanese kings throw light on this concept. *Hamengkubuwono* literally means "the universe (*buwono*) is on the lap (*mengku*) of the king". Thus, Sultan Hamengkubuwono, the former Vice-President of Indonesia was supposed to be the descendent of the king who had the whole universe on his lap. Similarly, *mangkunegera* means "the whole country on the lap of the prince", and *Paku Alam*, the title held by another Sultan of Jogjakarta, means "nailing (*paku*) the universe (*alam*)". In other words, Jogjakarta was seen to be the centre of the universe at which the nail was pinned, and was thus the centre seat of power in the universe.

In the 16th century, there was only one kraton in the capital of the Mataram Empire — also known as Solo in Surakarta. Later, a land dispute between the *Susuhanan* (Prince) of Surakarta, *Pakubowono II*, and his younger brother, the Prince of *Mangkubumi*, brought about a partition of the realm into two self-governing principalities in 1755.

The Sultanate of Jogjakarta thus came into being and *Mangkubumi* assumed the title of Sultan of Jogjakarta. A further dispute followed between Susuhanan of Surakarta and a *Raden Mas Sahid* (a member of the Surakarta aristocracy) resulting in a further split of the Surakarta realm. This was the birth of the small self-governing principality called *Mangkunegara* in 1757, headed by Sahid, who took the title of Prince Mangkunegara.

In the Sultanate of Jogjakarta, a similar divide-and-rule tactic was adopted by the British when they took over control during the interregnum around 1816. They created a small enclave within the Jogjakarta Sultanate and appointed Prince *Notosusumo*, a brother of Sultan Hamengkubuwono II, as its ruler. Sultan Hamengkubuwono II was then exiled by the British Government. The new principality, which was smaller in size, took the name of Paku Alam, and its ruler became known as Prince Paku Alam.

By 1816 the former Mataram Empire had been split into four self-governing principalities and each had its own kraton, which remained until this day. Under the colonial period, the ruler of each of these realms was no longer a monarch with absolute political, military and religious powers. In theory, the rulers held sway over all lands within their borders, but in practice, they were left only with the right to continue with their traditional ways of administration, culture and ceremonies. With considerable means at their disposal, they were able to devote themselves to the cultivation of courtly art forms and the maintenance of the kraton culture.

Many of the art forms in the traditional kraton dances, such as those we see today in the Jogjakarta and Surakarta kratons, were refined during this period. Despite the 350 years of Dutch rule, nothing much has changed in the field of cultural tradition and court ceremonies, for there was little interference in such activities.

It is not an exaggeration to say that to understand the Javanese, it is necessary to make frequent visits to Central Java, particularly the kraton. These kraton in Jogjakarta and Surakarta were once the centres of political intrigues and cultural activities of old Java.

Whenever time permitted, I would visit the kraton which never failed to stimulate my imagination. I always tried to imagine what had happened in those palaces during the days of the Sultanates. I never missed an opportunity to examine the array of pusaka, the former rulers' collections of kris, spears, sacred musical instruments, carriages and other objects which formed an integral part of every kraton. It is no longer easy to find people such as the albinos, clowns, dwarfs and soothsayers who once wandered about in the kraton compounds. It was believed that these extraordinary people provided an additional source of spiritual energy for the rulers who were able to absorb their powers. Their disappearance was considered a diminution of the king's power and a sign of the impending collapse of a dynasty. The customs and traditions that originated from the kratons are most fascinating and still make an impact on the Javanese way of life.

When I was Ambassador to Indonesia, I had the privilege to visit the Surakarta kraton to witness a royal wedding. The whole ceremony gave me a glimpse of the past grandeur of Javanese aristocracy. It was a traditional Javanese wedding, one of the most interesting and elaborate that I have ever seen. It was the wedding of the second daughter of the Susuhunan (Sultan) of Java and the Governor of Central Kalimantan, who happend to be a friend of mine. The hosts were General Sudjono Humardhani, then Presidential Assistant for Economic Affairs, and General Surono, then Deputy Commander of the Indonesian Armed Forces. My wife and I were their guests. It was a rare opportunity for me. The bridegroom was a Christian Dayak and the bride, an abangan Muslim Javanese. It was one of the grandest weddings ever performed in Solo in recent years and the first ever held inside the palace since Indonesia's independence.

The bridegroom arrived from Kalimantan three days before the wedding. He reported to the Susuhunan and was immediately confined by the guards to a small room inside the compound of the palace. For three days and three nights, he was kept there with only one companion — a small chicken — and offerings, such as flowers and Javanese rice-cakes. Among the offerings was a pair of human figurines — a bridal couple — made of rice cake. The bridegroom had his meals brought to him as he was not supposed to leave the room until the third day when the grand wedding ceremony was to take place. On the third morning, he was escorted to the palace hall for the initiation ceremony. The official conducting the ceremony was an *imam* (a Muslim preacher). Can an imam bless a marriage between a Christian and a Muslim? With the traditional Javanese spirit of compromise and tolerance, nothing is impossible. The imam just had to bless the marriage contract and everything was happily settled.

The real show began at twilight. The bridegroom, bare-chested and wearing a silvery *pici* (hat) and a pair of loose trousers, arrived to fetch the bride from the inner chamber of the palace, called the *dalem*. He was ushered all the way by two older female court dancers with painted faces, apparently meant to be clowns to attract attention. The beating of drums accompanied them all the way. At the *pringgitan* (outer chamber) of the palace, the Susuhunan gave away the bride. Together, the bridal couple emerged from the pringgitan, followed by relatives and friends. The bride had a hair-do similar to that of an actress in the traditional Chinese opera. The style of wearing her hair in undulating curls above her forehead was exactly the same. The bride was beautifully powdered and wore the sparkling, traditional off-shoulder Javanese dress. A pagoda-like carriage called *tandu*, with wooden handles on both sides, was lowered for the bride to take her seat accompanied by a bridesmaid. Eight muscular men in kraton costume then lifted the tandu onto their strong shoulders. I noticed that a colourful dragon and phoenix decorated the pagoda-like carriage. It reminded me of the ancient Chinese wooden palanquin known as *Riao Tze* in one of the imperial palaces of the Forbidden City in Beijing during my visit there in March 1975. It was used to carry the Empress Dowager of the Ching dynasty around the Forbidden City.

The Javanese wedding entourage was preceded by an army of spear-carrying soldiers in traditional military uniform. The bridegroom had to walk beside the carriage until he reached the entrance of the palace where a horse was waiting. He was assisted onto the horse and the journey to another ceremony began. All the way, the bridegroom was escorted by another army of soldiers carrying bows and arrows. The whole procession was a spectacle of colour and pomp. The crowd milled along to watch the fun.

On arrival at the house where the bridegroom was staying, the bride alighted from the carriage. The bridegroom dismounted and performed the most symbolic part of the wedding ceremony. An egg was placed in front of the bridegroom. He stepped on it, causing it to crack under his foot. It was a vow that he would be faithful to her for as long as the broken egg could not turn back into a chick — that is, forever. With a smile on her sweet face, the bride washed his foot with water taken from a basin as a token of gratitude. The washing of his feet was also a symbol of her willingness to obey.

The ceremony entered its third phase when he carried her in his arms to the chamber. When the two were seated at the *springgintan* (wedding chair), the bridegroom fed the bride with some *klimah* (rice balls). This gesture signified that she would take anything that might be offered to her by the bridegroom, symbolising her willingness to go through life with him for better or for worse and through thick and thin. This traditional wedding ceremony is being revived throughout Java in what seems to be a conscious effort to uphold tradition.

The bride and bridegroom spent the rest of the evening seated at the springgitan of the kraton facing the *pendopo* (a front open hall) where a royal dance was performed to entertain the dignitaries. When the soft tones of the *paleton* (Javanese musical instrument) and the melodious *suluk* (flute) were heard accompanied by the reverberating gamelan, nine dancers appeared from inside the palace to perform the *Bedaya* (Javanese dance). Slowly and stately, they advanced in single file towards the stage surrounded by pillars. Two female attendants crouched on their knees all the way to see that their feet did not step on the wine-red *cinde* cloth which trailed at their ankles. The dancers wore dark blue, gold embossed dodot, heavy gold armlets and bracelets, and crescent-shaped gold medallions hanging from their slender necks. Again, their faces and hairstyle reminded me of Teochew opera actresses. However, it was the Surakarta court style of bridal make-up.

The costumes were esoterically designed with patterns symbolising animals of the forest, mountains and oceans. The dancers' hair was coiled into buns with centerpieces of *garuda* birds, surrounded by quivering gold butterflies, flowers and metal spirals. Moving slowly and languidly with eyes downcast, the dancers occasionally flicked their long sashes and gently kicked their swirling trains.

The hypnotic bell-like sound of the *kamandak* (an archaic instrument played loudly on royal occasions) and the dreamy chanting gave added charm to the tranquil atmosphere. When the last heavy gong struck, the dancers stopped. The nine dancers rose slowly and gracefully to return to the inner chambers followed by the two crouching attendants.

It was a rare and unforgettable sight. This dance was originally ordered by Sultan Agung to commemorate the Queen of the Indonesian Ocean, Lara Kidul. It was really a dance befitting the Queen. Sultan Agung was the last of the great kings whose lives and miraculous exploits were the subject of tales connecting them with spirits and ancestors. He was also accredited with supernatural powers.

The kraton of Jogjakarta is one of the finest examples of Javanese palace architecture in existence. The greater kraton is enclosed on four sides by high brick walls within which some 26,000 people live. There is a market, some shops, cottage industries making batik and silverware, schools, and mosques. A large section of the kraton also houses the medical college of the Gajah Mada University.

Outside the entrance is a rectangular cage with wire fencing above a wooden stage. It was used in ancient times to confine a convict who had been sentenced to death. This was to give everybody a chance to look at the convict before he was brought to the gallows.

The basic concept of most Javanese palace architecture is to provide open pavilions and spacious courtyards. The two large northern courtyards — *Pagelag* and *Sitihinggil* — were used until very recently (1949-1973) by the Gajah Mada University as classrooms and an administrative centre.

The gateway to the inner courtyard is guarded by two giant demons — *lindoroboro* on the right representing the goodness of man, and *Bolokukoto* on the left symbolising evil. The significance is that both good and evil spirits dwell in the heart of every man and the fight goes on eternally to possess the soul.

I was always enchanted by the sweet, unpunctuated chirps of thousands of little sparrows from the *sawo* (a juicy fruit called *chiku* in Malay) trees which gave the spacious inner compound of the kraton an atmosphere of mellow calm. The blue and white Ming and Ching porcelains here and there surrounding the edges of the compound adds to the beauty and grandeur of the palace. They also remind us of the close historical connection between Java and China.

Admiral Cheng Ho, the Muslim eunuch of the Ming dynasty, had been to Java on many occasions and his treasure ships were always filled with Chinese treasures including porcelains.

I was also tempted to pause a little whenever I put my feet on the "sacred square". I felt silently guilty for having my shoes on, for I could visualise the sanctity of the place when large numbers of leafpickers were employed in the old days to pick leaves with their sharp-pointed spears to clean up the garden. In those days, the compound was considered sacred and no brooms were allowed. At least a hundred or more servants were employed to pick the leaves daily with pointed spears. Times have changed and the traditional way of keeping the place clean has now given way to brooms.

The subtle and indirect Javanese approach has been applied in hinting at the year of construction of the kraton which was completed in 1853. The date is depicted by a chronogram of crown *candrasang kala* (meaning one) and curled snake in the figure of 8 and giants which look like the numbers 5 and 3. The four figures are all inter-woven into a harmonious design reading from right to left, the way Arabic characters are read.

In another section of the kraton, there are separate entrances for the opposite sexes. This was indicated, not by means of characters in terms of "ladies" and "gentleman", but by two giant sized dragons one a "he" dragon and the other a "she" dragon. To me, the two dragons look alike and I may have gone through the wrong entrance. But perhaps it was meant to be that way. Unlike the Chinese dragon, a Javanese dragon has no horns and has the tail of a snake. It looked very fearful.

At another entrance, I saw an old Javanese in traditional dress sitting cross-legged, reading an old Javanese script of the Mahabharata which contained wayang puppet figures. While killing time this way, he occasionally glanced at an antique grandfather clock to see that he did not neglect his duty of striking the drum every half an hour to keep inmates of the kraton informed of the time of the day. This tradition goes on despite the invention of watches. Perhaps the grandfather clock was more reliable. It is yet another example of Javanese conservatism. Perhaps the tradition is meant to bring home the Javanese philosophical approach to time and space.

Time is important (shown by keeping everyone informed of the correct time) and yet unimportant (by wasting manpower just to strike the drum every half hour). At the corner, leading to the rooms is a huge, bottle-shaped wooden gong. This used to be struck as an alarm in case of fire, disasters or accidents of God.

The most interesting section of the kraton is the room where old photographs showing the royal family tree are kept. In this room are also the personal belongings of past Sultans, their wives and children, including precious dowries of past royal weddings. Among the photographs are some showing the grandest mass royal wedding of the century which took place about thirty years ago. There were seven couples including the two brothers and five sisters of Sri Sultan Hamengkubuwono. Some of the pictures show the brides and bridegrooms walking together with their little fingers interwined to indicate that the bride was a commoner. Other pictures show the bridegrooms carrying the brides in their arms — an indication that the brides were from another royal family.

The dowries of olden days consisted of gold in the shape of different types of animals. There were the dragon (*dardowaliko*), the cock (*sawung*), the duck (*banyak*), the deer (*dalang*) and the peacock (*galing*), *each* having its own mystical meaning. The rice bed, called *demisori* which resembles a bed, is still being used at royal weddings for the bride and bridegroom to sit on. It is meant to bring fertility to the married couple to produce as many children as the harvests of rice produced on a fertile farm.

History repeated itself on a smaller scale in the Jogjakarta kraton sometime in May 1974 when Sultan Hamengkubuwono gave away four of his daughters in a mass royal wedding ceremony. It was less spectacular compared to that of thirty years ago for the Sultan, who was also Vice-President of Indonesia, and wanted to set an example for austerity which was being propagated throughout the country.

The Jogjakarta kraton also has a special room which houses the wayang puppets. They are kept like sacred humans. Every Thursday, they are brought out to the garden one by one to breathe some fresh air. Once a year, they are given a holy bath together with other royal articles when a special ceremony is held.

About two minutes drive from the kraton is a large royal godown where all the royal carriages are kept. One made in England has a British crown embossed on it and the others were either specially ordered or locally made. When I visited the royal garage on a Friday, I found fresh flowers sprinkled round it. Offerings of this nature are made by many Javanese every Friday. Some believers even sleep in the carriages overnight, hoping that the souls of past kings might descend on them to provide spiritual guidance.

In Solo, not very far from the Surakarta kraton, is the Mangkunegara kraton. Occupying an area of more than 900 square metres, the Mangkunegara kraton dates back to 1757, built by Raden Mas Sahid, the founder of the House, one of whose descendents was Ibu Tien Suharto. Like all kratons, it is divided into three sections consisting of the pendopo (front), the pringgitan (middle) and the dalem (inner court). In the Mangkunegara kraton, old Javanese traditions and practices such as hitting the time drum every half hour are less often adhered to. In fact, the Mangkunegara kraton has become a tourist attraction and at times important visitors are allowed to view the inner bedrooms and bathrooms of the princesses.

The first thing that struck me when I entered the pendopo was the four beautifully-carved *soko guru* (pillars) in *joglo* architectural style, and the rounded ceiling composed of hundreds of *sirap* (wooden tiles) lined with copper for preservation. The four *soko guru*, made of solid teak, represent the four elements of nature — earth, water, fire and wind. The ceiling, which is 11 metres from the ground, is intricately ornamented with figures of the zodiac signs harmoniously draped in Javanese style with eye-catching colours.

The main motif of the painting on the ceiling is the sparkling flame inspired by the prince's collection of old Javanese miniatures called *Kunudhowati*. In the centre of the ceiling are painted the eight points of the zodiac compass, each in its own mystical colour. Yellow signifies a preventive against sleepiness; blue, a preventive against disease; black, against hunger; green, against desire; white, against lust; rose, against fear; red, against evil; and purple, against wicked thoughts. All the zodiac decorations symbolically reflect the meanings of Javanese philosophical life. The two-century-old pendopo is probably the largest ever constructed in the country. It was enlarged by the late Mangkunegara VII and is being carefully maintained.

On the right-hand side of the pendopo is the *kyai kanyut mesem*, one of the oldest sets of gamelan. In Javanese, *kyai* means "reverence" and *kanyut mesem* means "drifting in smile". Thus, this complete set of classical instruments, "drifting in smile", brings back memories of past glories of the Mangkunegara Kingdom when they are performed every Wednesday.

A few steps up from the pendopo is the pringgitan, the front part of the dalem. This is where the royal family receives guests. Sometimes wayang kulit is performed in this part of the building with the screen facing inwards so that woman attendants in the dalem can view the performance from inside, while the other guests have the privilege of seeing the dalang operating the puppets from behind. The wall of the pringgitan is decorated with paintings by Basuki Abdullah, Indonesia's world-famous artist.

It was a rare privilege in the past to be invited into the privacy of the dalem, beautiful with its ancient Javanese architecture and eight soko guru — the eight pillars of wisdom. This part of the palace is used for traditional ceremonies such as royal weddings and other important festivities. Upon entering the hall, one is immediately attracted by two figures made of stone and seated on the floor. They represent the bride and bridegroom, called *Loro Blonyo* in Javanese. Both are dressed in traditional Javanese wedding costumes. At traditional ceremonies the guests also have to sit on the floor.

Being interested in antiques, I was captivated by the rich collection of ancient articles of cultural value arranged systematically inside the various cupboards and glass showcases. This was a collection by Mangkunegara VII half a century ago. It includes old coins, bronze Hindu-Javanese statues, and gold jewellery from the Hindu *Majapahit* and *Mataram* periods. What really stirred my imagination was the unusually big and heavy-looking gold Buddhistic rings with mantra inscriptions. Were they designed for giant fingers? One wonders.

There is also a complete collection of masks from various areas of Indonesia including Bali, Madura, Bandung, Jogjakarta and Solo. An old library contains classical literary works of the late Mangkunegara, a rich source of wisdom.

The bathroom next door is even more interesting. It is built for the traditional way of bathing that is practised in the village. One has to descend a few steps to a well, hold a bucket of water with the right hand, squats down a little and pours the water over the head and body. The European long bath has not yet caught up with even the royal families of Central Java.

Both the prince and princess were very hospitable. Explaining the spread of Islam to Java, they showed me a heavy wooden plaque on which is carved the figure of Semar. This figure was composed of a combination of Arabic characters showing that in the early days even the Muslims respected Semar and had to use his mystical personality to spread the teaching of Islam.

Times have changed, but many old traditional ceremonies of the kraton are still being performed. As mentioned earlier, once a year in the month of *Susro*, on Friday as the fifth day of the five days is considered to be auspicious, the ceremony of *Siraman* is performed. It is the time when all the heirlooms inside the palace are given a holy bath. The objects, which include the golden cart used by the Prince on ceremonial occasions, the many kris, the gamelan and the wayang kulit puppets which are kept individually in separate boxes are all taken to the bathing site. There, before thousands of spectators, these objects are gently bathed as a mother would bathe her baby. The officers who perform the ceremony are *kraton pungawa* who have fasted for one week before this holy undertaking. The ceremony is carried out solemnly and seriously. The spectators bring with them bottles and cans, ready to take away with them the water that was used to bathe the objects. They believe that the water has magical powers. They would pour the water in their homes, or over their domestic animals to free them from misfortune or disease. Some pour the water over their rice fields for better harvest.

At almost the same time, court officers filled the *encer* (water basin) in the graveyard of the ancestors with water. The people in the surrounding village believe that if the water in the basin does not dry up, the people of Java will have ample food. If the water dries up, it is a sign of approaching famine.

Another *kraton* tradition is the beating of the gamelan placed on the left kraton and right wings facing the great mosque in Mecca. Called *Sekaten*, it is held for a week in the month of Maulud, Prophet Mohammed's birthday. Kraton officers play on the gamelan in turn, day and night. Only on Fridays do they take a rest for their prayers. This ceremony originated during the spread of Islam when it was a means to summon people to the mosque to listen to the imam. But now Sekaten has become more of a form of entertainment.

When an epidemic hits a village, a special ceremony is performed to ward off the evil spirit which is believed to be responsible for the epidemic. The villagers will gather and, led by court officers, will walk barefooted in strict silence round the fortress surrounding the kraton. Participants have to walk throughout the night until the next morning.

When I was in Jogjakarta, I attended a Javanese funeral. It was the burial ceremony of a prominent person in the community. The deceased was a Muslim, perhaps a nominal one. However, I found the customs practised at this particular ceremony different from the usual Muslim funeral. Unlike Muslim funerals held in the Middle East or in Singapore and Malaysia, the ladies were allowed to attend the funeral procession to the graveyard. The orthodox Muslim burials which I have seen usually end with a body returning to Mother Earth naked, the mouth kissing the soil facing Mecca. In the burial which I saw in Jogjakarta, the body was lowered into the ground in a wooden coffin. There was a sweet smell of *kemayan* prevading the air as the Muslim imam read the relevant passages of the Koran. This Javanese funeral ceremony was a combination of Islamic customs and Javanese traditions. Yet another example of the spirit of tolerance and compromise, I thought.

c) The Gajah Mada's kris

Java is a land of mysticism. It is common belief that when a person has passed away, his spirit, whether good or evil, will *numpang* (take a ride or seek temporary accommodation) in corporeal objects such as a banyan tree, a kris, a gem or other heirlooms. Such materials inhabited by spirits are called *pusaka.*

Of all the pusaka, the most popular is the *kris*, or dagger. It is rare for a Javanese man not to possess a kris. On ceremonial occasions, a Javanese always wears a kris tucked into his belt. A person who has studied the kris would know at a glance the status of the person wearing it, for there are krises symbolising higher status which can be worn only by people of high standing. It is believed that the kris knows where to look for its master. A sacred kris, for instance, will never fall into the hands of a common man. If a person gets a kris which is not *cocok* (befitting) to him, he will feel uneasy, and sometimes misfortune may befall him.

I was told that since Suharto came into power, he has been searching for the Gajah Mada's kris previously worn by the Prime Minister of Majapahit (1320-1364), Gajah Mada, the famous and most powerful Javanese leader in Javanese history. It is believed that his soul has entered into a kris, and whoever possesses that kris would lead Indonesia. When Sukarno came into power, he had possession of the kris. But since the death of Sukarno, nobody knows where the kris had gone. It had just disappeared and has been haunting the mind of Suharto since he took office as President of Indonesia. How could anyone who does not possess Gajah Mada's kris rule Indonesia?

The Javanese believe that whoever wants to rule Indonesia must possess three things: First, Gajah Mada's mask; second, the *wijaya kusuma*, a flowering plant found in Nusa Kembangan; and third, Gajah Mada's kris, which would give the possessor spiritual authority to rule the country. It is therefore natural for a new president of Indonesia to want to own Gajah Mada's kris.

The Javanese kris is a slender dagger with a fine blade. It is mounted preferably in a handle made of gold, ivory and precious stones, and encased in a sheath of beautifully carved and polished wood. The blade is either straight or wavy and is sharp along both edges. When the blade is being forged, the steel is first made white hot before being hammered and shaped. It is then tempered in water to blacken the metal so the delicate and fine engraving on the blade can be seen.

The finest krises are made in Central Java on the outskirts of Jogjakarta. The master craftsmen, who flourished during the Majapahit period, were not only expert metal workers but also *kyai* (a Muslim scholar). On completion of a kris, the craftsman would mumble magical words into the kris to give it mystical powers. In the past, some *dukun* (medicine man) even resorted to sacrificing a beautiful maiden so that her soul could enter the kris. The kris is said to have added mystical powers if it has tasted the blood of an enemy.

When I visited a Javanese friend, he took his kris down from the wall and showed it to me. When I attempted to pull the kris out of the sheath, he stopped me.

"Please don't do that," he said, "for if the blade leaves the sheath, it will look for blood to satisfy its need." The kris he possessed had been in many battle fields during the Indonesian revolution. Now he has to tend to it every week by burning *kemayan* (smelly kind of wood), otherwise the kris will lose its power and may even bring bad luck.

The kris is designed to inflict maximum injury to an enemy. The wavy blade opens a wound that is wider than the blade itself, and can even pierce through the bones of the body. In fact, mystics believe that the kris need not even touch an enemy to cause harm. They believe that a powerful kris needs only to be pointed at the enemy from a distance and the man would die of an incurable illness. They also believe that a magical kris can move, speak, swim in deep seas or fly over mountains to attack the enemy. Sometimes a kris would vanish, later to return to the owner after performing its job.

Is there such a thing as a flying kris? I wanted to know as I have heard of this phenomena so often from my friend Anada Surjono, whenever I visited Wonogiri, a village in central Java. There I met a police officer named Pak Musnadi who claimed that he could invoke the spirit of his dead father to make a kris fly. Out of curiosity, my wife, my friend Mas Agung and I requested a demonstration.

The demonstration took place at night in a Muslim cemetery about 30 kilometres from Wonogiri. When we arrived, we had to use a torchlight to find the way to the grave where Pak Musnadi's father was buried. As I sat down with the others on a mat in front of the grave, watching the necessary offerings being made to the spirit, my eyes wandered around and saw nothing but the stars twinkling in the dark sky. The atmosphere was rather eerie. As usual, kemayan was burnt and everyone had to sprinkle flowers over the grave.

Musnadi meditated and prayed, then mumbled some words in Javanese to invoke the soul of his dead father. Then there was a long wait. As mosquitoes hummed about our ears and our feet felt numb, Musnadi explained to us how his deceased father had given him the power of making a kris fly. Before his father died several years ago, he willed that his most precious pusaka be buried beside him in the grave. He also instructed that someone in the family should watch over the grave for at least 40 days and 40 nights. Musnadi was the only son who took the trouble to carry out his father's will.

As he was watching over the grave one night, he begged the deceased father to bestow on him some magical powers. It was then that he was inspired with the idea of making a kris fly and indeed, found that he was able to cause his kris to fly. However, he explained that it was not actually his power that would make the kris fly but the power of the soul of his father.

A sudden spark of green light from the darkness of the woods interrupted Musnadi's story and he asked everyone to be silent for the spirit had arrived. He proceeded to perform the ceremony of circling a sacred spot to the accompaniment of tape-recorded Javanese music. Musnadi explained that the sacred spot was a demarcated cosmic sphere where the spirits hovered, although not visible to the human eye.

At the ceremony, a kris was placed within the cosmic sphere and Musnadi asked everyone to examine it. He explained that the invoked soul of his father would make his kris fly to his garden some 30 kilometres away. To ensure that it would be the same kris that would land in his garden, I suggested that a piece of paper with my signature on it be stuck to the tip of the kris. Musnadi agreed to my suggestion. Everyone waited with excitement when suddenly white and greenish lights began to flicker from the dark spot where the kris had been. We scrutinised the spot and found the kris missing. I asked Musnadi why were we not allowed to see the kris flying. He replied that the glare of the beam of light radiating from the kris would be so strong that it might blind us. He claimed that once, when he was experimenting with the art, a chicken walked past and was instantly killed by the rays.

Some time was wasted chatting at the graveyard about the kris that had disappeared. Then Musnadi decided to repeat the feat with another kris before going back to his house. When we finally got to Musnadi's house, we saw the two kris stuck into a banana tree. I examined the one which I had marked with paper and found the paper missing. It was later found inside a cupboard in Musnadi's bedroom.

I asked Musnadi how the paper got into his cupboard and he explained apologetically that the kris was confused by the piece of paper and went into his bedroom first and then went out through the window to the banana tree.

It had indeed been a most interesting experience for me. My friend Mas Agung who accompanied me was convinced that the kris actually flew, for he later took the trouble to have the piece of paper examined by a medium in Solo who said the piece of paper contained radiation.

Did the kris actually fly? How could it be scientifically speaking? At the time when the kris flickered, I noticed the noise of a motor cycle nearby starting off. Could it be its rider who had taken the kris to Musnadi's house? It was only a guess.

There are many legendary tales about the kris. The most popular one is that of the *Pasopati kris*. King *Kajamojoyo*, who was kind and brave, possessed a kris that had extraordinary powers of conquest. During battles, he always led his people to the frontline and his kris never failed him. News about his magic kris soon reached an evil monster. One day, when the King was taking a nap under a tree, the monster kidnapped and imprisoned him, and stole his magic kris. As the King had lost his kris, his entire kingdom fell. One night in his prison cell, the King had a dream. A voice from above told him that he would one day obtain a kris more powerful than the one he had lost. Soon after, he heard another voice, the voice of a lady giving him the same message. The King recalled his dream so often that he became ill. Seeing that the King was about to die, the evil monster took pity on him and agreed to release him on the condition that the people in his kingdom surrendered all their weapons. The people agreed, their King was released and soon recovered from his illness.

One day, when the King was conducting a meeting with his ministers, an old man by the name of *Pasopati* came along and sought audience with the King. He looked like the person whom the King saw in his dream. Pasopati told the King and his Cabinet members not to worry, for the King would soon receive a more powerful kris to defeat the enemy. The ministers laughed at him and in fact, put him in jail for spreading false information.

Not long afterwards, the Queen gave birth to a son who had a golden kris tied to his left hand. The King realized that the old man had spoken the truth and ordered that he be brought before him. When Pasopati was brought to the King, he was about to die. His last words were that the King should believe in Islam and that the kris should only be used for protection. The King was very worried and named the kris Pasopati. He eventually used the kris, which was invincible to defeat the evil monster.

Pasopati happened to be the first man who embraced Islam in the country. The Pasopati kris has therefore helped to spread the teaching of Islam in Indonesia.

Another story told by Sunan Giri was about a kris belonging to a Muslim king whose kingdom was surrounded by the powerful forces of Majapahit. The King was writing when the news came and he became so angry that he threw the pen to the floor. The pen turned into a kris, went flying to the battlefield, killed the enemies and returned to the King.

Stories of magic kris are numerous and are passed down from generation to generation. They may seem incomprehensible to some, but are not taken lightly by the Indonesians.

My friend, a Javanese by the name of RT.T. Hardjonegoro, who was a Chinese descendent and had a Chinese name Go Tek Suan, was the *bupati* (village head) of the kraton of Surakarta. He showed me several precious and historical kris when I visited his home in Solo. In fact, many leading Javanese leaders were descendents of the Chinese.

Although Hardjonegoro has Chinese blood, he does not speak any Chinese dialects and speaks only Javanese. He had been completely assimilated into the Javanese culture and way of life and has become related to the Indonesian royal family. He showed me one of his kris possessions which belonged to Pakubuwono VII, carved like a dragon with seven curves along its blades. The carving is etched in gold and the seven curves signified that Pakubuwono was the seventh descendent of the throne. It took the craftsman twenty-eight years to finish this magnificent kris. The King was so impressed that he ordered seven more of the same design to be made. According to Hardjonegoro, there are only three left in Indonesia. The other four were presented to foreign dignitaries, one was presented to Emperor Hirohito of Japan, the second is with a descendent of Mussolini, the dictator of Italy during World War II, the third is with the King of Sweden, and the fourth is in the treasury of the Queen of Holland. It was a tradition in the past for kings and noblemen to order a number of kris to be made with specific designs to commemorate their reign and to acquire magical powers. There are many shops all over Indonesia selling kris, but it is believed that a kris bought from a shop loses its magical power. To be pusaka a kris must be given by someone and not bought.

I was presented with an unusually beautiful kris when I visited Bali. Nobody knows the history of the kris but I am sure it once belonged to someone powerful. It has become a pusaka of my family. The sheath is made of ivory, embedded with red and green precious stones. The kris itself is curvy and graceful. It is now a treasure in my collection.

The second time I was presented with a kris was at the last stage of preparation for Lee Kuan Yew's visit to Indonesia. I had gone to consult mystic gurus as recommended by Sudjono Humardhani, the spiritual adviser of Suharto. I wanted to know whether my mission to bring Lee Kuan Yew to Indonesia would be successful. The guru was a wise old man, and I was told Suharto used to consult him before making an important decision. He predicted that my mission would be successful and gave me a kris without a sheath. Before handing it over to me, he mumbled some Javanese words into it. He said the kris would bring about closer and better understanding between Indonesia and Singapore and that the two countries would work as *adek bradek* (brothers).

I brought the kris back to Jakarta and left it outside my bedroom on a table. One night in 1974, several months before I completed my mission in Indonesia, a thief entered my house after midnight when I was asleep. I knew nothing about the attempted theft. The next morning, my butler, an Indonesian called Nordin woke me up early in the morning and said there has been a thief in the house. I got up and saw my porcelain antiques lying about the garden and found the house in a mess. I discovered the kris was in the bathtub, apparently thrown there by the thief. He must have attempted to steal the kris and was so frightened after he touched the kris that he threw it away in the bathtub and ran away from my house. Was it the magic of the kris that had prevented the thief from stealing my belongings? It is still a mystery to me.

It later dawned on me that the thief had first stolen the kris and was so frightened that he threw the kris in the bathtub. There must have been some magic in the kris that made the thief do that.

It had been the last night of my 50th birthday and I had locked my bedroom. All along, I had not locked my bedroom because I found it unnecessary. But, on that particular night, a thought came into my mind, "Why not lock the room? My father died at 49 years of age and surely I must live longer than my father." If I had not locked the room, the thief, after stealing my kris, might have entered it and I would have to confront him and endanger my life. What a coincidence that I had decided to lock the room that night.

I had lost nothing, but the thought of the thief coming into my room with the kris, had really made me shiver.

Apart from the kris, the other pusaka popular among the Javanese are precious stones. They also believe that in every precious stone there dwells a spirit which may be good or bad for the person wearing it. In any market place in Jakarta or Central Java, there are stall-keepers and itinerant peddlars displaying an assortment of polished and unpolished stones of little or no intrinsic value. They are mounted on the spot into rings which may cost the buyer only a few hundred or a few thousand rupiahs. It is not the value of the stone that matters, but its mystical and spiritual connotations which the Javanese believe in. Most Javanese wear rings with stones of a variety of shapes and colours. It is not uncommon to see *becak* (trishaw) drivers, waiters and ordinary workmen wearing rings displaying their favourite stones.

Even ethnic Chinese who have lived in Java for a long period of time are influenced by this Javanese custom of wearing rings. My old friend Chen Tse Hsing alias Hendra, a multi-millionaire banker who once owned six hotels in Singapore, used to wear rings on his left and right hands, each costing more than S$500,000. They were huge accessories and he had the habit of showing them to me and my wife.

Another professor friend of mine Dr Kenneth Hidayat, a graduate of Harvard University who was Chinese-educated, is also fond of rings. He possesses natural stones of different colours, each with a different kind of animal images inside the stone. He showed me stones which contained images such as the dragon, elephant, tiger, lion, bird and other symbols of good fortune.

Gemstones are generally appreciated for their beauty and value, but rarely are they treated with such reverence as they are in Java. Like the kris, a gemstone is preferably acquired as a gift. Elderly people warn that if the spirit that dwells in a stone is incompatible with a person owning it, it may bring bad luck, illness and even harm to him. Some people consult the mystics for advice before wearing a certain stone. They believe that each stone has its own *dzin* or spirit dwelling in it and therefore must be examined for its suitability to the new owner.

Modern science confirms that each mineral has its specific radiation which can affect one's skin or even endanger one's health. Some stones have become famous or infamous in the course of history. The fortune of a certain stone may last only a limited period of time. For instance, Hendra may possess many precious stones but they did not protect him from having to run away when the economic typhoon swept Indonesia and many banks away, including his own which had to close down.

The jewels from the Russian Imperial Crown, scattered throughout the world, also seemed to bring disaster. The Black Prince's ruby in the British Imperial State Crown is second to none for its romantic history. Other stones have become famous for having peculiar or mystical properties. The amethyst is said to prevent nervous tension and drunkenness; the black opal is said to cause tragedy to certain wearers; and jade is said to darken its colour if worn continuously.

In Java, belief in the mystical properties of gems and stones is still very strong. There are so many beliefs related to specific stones that it is impossible to list them all. So I shall confine myself to the more popular ones.

The *tapak jalak* is a stone with the design of a bird's footprint which looks like a cross. (*Tapak* means 'footprint' and *jalak* is a kind of bird.) This stone is much sought after by policemen and soldiers who believe that wearing the tapak jalak will make one strong and powerful and will help attain one's goals.

The *kendit*, a stone with one or more circles, helps to protect the wearer against danger, especially from attack by enemies.

The *suleiman* has an eye-like design which is supposed to be King Solomon's eye. Wearing this stone on your finger helps you think clearly and justly. It is believed that the stone will bring the wearer better prospects of promotion.

The *benteng* has a square-like design resembling a fort. It is supposed to give protection against almost anything.

The *cempaka* is a stone with the colour of the *cempaka* flower, the *michelia champaca* in Latin. The Javanese believe that the wearer of cempaka will lead a happy, romantic life.

The *jahman* is a brownish black stone. It is an extraordinary stone which is always in great demand, for it is believed to contain special magical powers to protect the wearer from danger. It also brings good luck.

The *krong buntut* looks like an unopened clam and is said to bring success in business.

The *mustika* is pink and resembles the seed of the pomegranate fruit. It is said to provide eternal youth and protection from evil spirits. The Tenggerese of Bali consider it a sacred stone which they insert into the mouth of a corpse to help preserve the body and ensure the soul's smooth passage to heaven.

The *krisna dana* is a family of colourful stones in shades of blue, black, grey and violet. They help to fulfill one's wishes.

The *ngagah satru* is a rare stone and therefore more expensive. It keeps away enemies.

The *mirah pingaseh* is another expensive stone, keenly sought after by Don Juans who wish to attract young ladies. This stone is also known as the Ruby of Love.

In the higher circles of society, one often hears stories about expensive stones. The stone which is most talked about and sought after is the *buntut mustika* — a big, black magical stone obtained from

the anus of a special breed of insect in Banjarmasin, Kalimantan. It
is found in one out of a million of such insects. The *buntut mustika*
protects the wearer from evil spirits, brings him good luck, fortune
and status. It is also used for its medicinal properties by dipping the
stone in a glass of water for the sick to drink.

I also learnt of the huge sacred black stone found in a village
called Cibinong close to Bogor in West Java. The stone is consulted
on matters of mythology, astrology and the weather, such as will
there be rain or sunshine tomorrow. One gets the answer by lifting
the stone. If it is light there will be sunshine. But if it is heavy there
will be rain. Many people still go to Cibinong to consult the stone
on various mystical matters.

Yet, no stone could predict the onslaught of the economic typhoon
which swept Indonesia in early 1998 and many of those wearing
powerful stones have disappeared from the country.

d) *Semar* — The guardian spirit of Java

Of all the characters in the Javanese wayang, none fascinates me more
than *Semar*. It is not because he looks funny and ugly or because he
is the most popular clown. It is a character not found in the Hindu-
inspired Mahabharata epics. It is a creation indigenous to Java.

The ugliest features that can be found on the human anatomy are
ascribed to Semar. He has a peculiar forehead with a pear-like crown
above his "third eye". His other two eyes are slanting, his nose is
curled, and his ears look like butterflies. His large mouth displays
uneven teeth and his chin droops down. Semar has a big round
stomach and huge buttocks. His arms are long and flexible, but his
left hand usually points to the ground while his right hand rests on
his buttock. His short legs and flat feet make him look like a duck.
However, despite his ugly and ungainly features, Semar is the most
popular clown on the wayang kulit screen. His appearance alone is
amusing enough to provoke laughter from the audience — even more
so when the old clown laughs like a baby or cries with a running
nose. To make people laugh he sometimes takes off his golden ear

studs and replaces them with red chillies. Semar is especially humble to children but readily pokes fun at adults.

In wayang performances, Semar is the servant of the five Pandawas, especially of Arjuna. Semar's instruction from the God Sanghiang Tunggal is to see that his masters keep a good balance of their senses and are not swayed by their emotions. Semar's role is also to expose the evil in the human character. He looks ugly but is kind-hearted, powerful but humble, brave but faithful. He appears stupid but is often brilliant and wise. Endowed with supernatural powers, Semar never once misuses them, but always comes to the rescue of the helpless. Whenever a good kingdom is about to fall, he is there to save the day.

However, Semar is a controversial figure among the Indonesians. He has a multi-faceted character and means different things to different people. As a clown, he is known as Semar. As a guru, he is called *Batara Manikmaya*. And as a saint, he is known as *Sanghiang Ismaya*. It is commonly believed that Semar is the brother of Siva, a god of many attributes and various functions. Javanese Hindus, on the one hand believe that Siva was sent as a guardian to the Indian continent, whereas Semar was sent to the South Pacific and is thus regarded as the guardian spirit of Java. Balinese Hindus on the other hand regard Semar as simply an old, clumsy clown, whom they call *Twalan*.

"Do you know why *Twalan* looks so ugly and disfigured?", a Balinese friend once asked me. He then went on to give me the Balinese version of how Twalan became so ugly. It is acknowledged that Twalan is the son of *Tintiya*, the original God, and is thus brother of Siva. However, Twalan has another brother, *Togog*, known to the Balinese as *Delam*, who is as ugly as Twalan. Delam is bald-headed, has huge round eyes and the mouth of a toothless crocodile. He, too, has as big a belly and buttocks as Twalan. At one time, however, both Twalan and Delam had handsome and attractive features. They were always quarrelling and fighting for supremacy, until one day both challenged each other over the superiority of their supernatural powers. Siva stood aloof and watched the two fight it out. The first challenge was to swallow a huge mountain facing them. Twalan transformed his mouth and belly as large as he could so that he could swallow the mountain. He failed and became disfigured because he could not regain his original appearance. Delam followed suit and also met with the same fate. This explains how the two brothers acquired such gross features.

As mentioned earlier, although Balinese Hindus acknowledge Semar as the brother of Lord Siva, they do not regard him as their guardian spirit. To them, Semar and his brother, Togog were both given to worldly pleasures and did not care to become gods. They preferred to remain as servants so that they could indulge in eating and drinking. However, the Balinese do concede that Semar has exorcising powers and can defend a good prince and his country from evil.

The Javanese Hindus, however, place Semar high in the hierarchy of the cosmic world, guiding the destiny of *Nusantara* (the Indonesian archipelago). Romo Hardjanta, a Javanese Hindu and founder of *Majapahit Pancasila* — now officially recognised as a branch of the Hindu-Dharma religion — is of the opinion that as Semar has the *Louna* or *Dohi*, the crown on his forehead, he is even more powerful than Siva, who does not have this. The image of Semar is also used as the emblem of one of the major schools of *Kebatinan-Sapta Darma*, a Javanese spiritual organisation. Although Semar is venerated mainly by Javanese Hindus, you can ask any Javanese either in the streets of the big cities or in the villages in the countryside, and it would be rare if he has not heard of Semar. It was because of Semar's widespread popularity that I was spurred on to find out more about this interesting character and his religious significance.

Although Semar is only a symbolic clown figure in Javanese Mahabharata wayang play, it is hard to believe that most Javanese believe that Semar is a deity and is real. They believe that Semar exists in the cosmic world and have given him a title Sanghiang Ismaya (God of Ismoyo), and that he can be contacted and consulted whenever his advice is needed. Some claim that they have heard his voice and others, that they have seen him. In order to communicate with him, one should visit either of the two holy caves of Semar — the Guwa Ratu cave on Gunung Srendang near the village of Adipolo or the Guwa Ratu on the Dieng Plateau, both in central Java. To these famous caves many Indonesians go for meditation. President Suharto had been known to spend a night here when things became tricky. The fate of Portuguese Timor may have been sealed in this cave when Suharto and the Australian Prime Minister Gough Whitlam conferred within its dark walls in 1974. The cave is said to be the physical centre of Java.

The Dieng Plateau where the *Guwa Semar* is situated is surrounded by live volcanoes including Mount Perahu to the north and Mount Sundoro to the south. One can even see the heat rise from the volcanic inferno and hear the lava bubbling. But the cave itself is set in idyllic, cool Guwa Semar surroundings, quite unaffected by the volcanic heat. Semar is a natural cave, the entrance of which is identified by a hugh rock resembling Semar himself.

As I was interested in Semar, I took the trouble to visit the caves. When I visited the cave Guwar Semar in Gunung Srendang, the small entrance gate was locked. The assistant caretaker inside the cave was meditating and did not want to be disturbed. He explained that from time to time very important persons would come incognito. He mentioned the visit of the former Australian Prime Minister Gough Whitlam accompanied by President Suharto sometime in August 1974. Some visitors would spend days fasting and meditating inside the cave in order to make contact with the spirit of Sanghiang Ismaya for spiritual guidance.

The Guwa Ratu where Semar is supposed to dwell is situated on a treacherous mountain, Gunung Srendang. My wife and I were invited to visit the cave through our friend Mas Agung, once the proprietor of the MPH Bookshops in Singapore, a Chinese who believed in Javanese mysticism. We went by car to Gunung Srendang and met the caretaker of the cave Nyoman. When we reached the river near the cave, it was already dusk and darkness was approaching. The caretaker suggested that we should take a boat because the distance would be shorter and less tedious. I looked at the small canoe which twelve of us were supposed to squeeze into. The moon and stars were hidden by thick clouds and there was complete darkness. There was not even a life-saver. What should we do if the boat should capsize?

Where could we swim to and in which direction? I was apprehensive and told him that we would prefer to go by car over the mountain.

To reach Guwa Ratu by land, one must first go to the foot of Gunung Srendang by car along a remote jungle track covered with *lalang* (tall wild grass). We alighted from the car and climbed the mountain by foot along steep and dangerous cliffs. We had to hold hands during our journey. My wife began to complain that we were taking too much risk. What would happen if we should misjudge the rocky steps? We would fall into the deep valley below. The sky was pitch dark and we could hardly see the path. Only the fire flies gave some flickers of light. Frogs were croaking in the swamps, owls hooting in the forest and crickets chorusing in a loud, monotonous dirge, which only helped to make the bleak dark night more eerie. I told my wife to have confidence in me as I held her hand for there was no way we could turn back. We did not carry any torchlight then.

"Where is the cave?", I asked Nyoman rather impatiently. "We're not there yet. This way please," he replied. Walking through lalang taller than ourselves, we groped down a slope in darkness. About half an hour, we came to a halt. Nyoman called out, "Be careful. We have reached the end of the path and now have to climb down the rocky cliff face." Imagine my feeling of alarm as we stood in darkness on the edge of the cliff with valleys far below. But, that was not the time to panic for we had already come so far. What was needed were calm nerves and courage. With the help of a torchlight, which we bought in a shop in Adipolo, we started to move downwards, one careful foot after another, step by step, our hands fumbling to cling to any hold for support. I can't remember how many steps there were, or how long we took. But, we finally made it. There was a sigh of relief all round. Our clothes were wet and dirty and we saw a stream flowed at the entrance to the cave. Bathing was symbolic of cleansing one's soul before entering a sacred place. We went for a bath and it was cooling.

After the bath, we approached the entrance of the cave by torchlight, passed through the big, iron gates and soon found ourselves inside the cave. We lit a few candles which revealed a small guest room partitioned off by carved wooden pillars. Walking barefooted on the blackish, volcanic sand, we entered the guest room and found mats made of bamboo leaves scattered over the floor. We sat down on the mats to wait for the arrival of Sanghiang Ismaya as it was nearing midnight.

As I entered the Semar cave, I found nothing inside. It was cool, quiet and serene. It was so dark that I could not see my own hands. In this complete darkness, I was asked to sit cross-legged and wait for the spirit of Sanghiang Ismaya to descend.

It was my curiosity and a burning desire to know more about the spiritual significance of Sanghiang Ismaya that prompted me to make this risky trip. I was travelling incognito. The arrangements were made by a Javanese friend of Mas Agung, Ananda Suyono, who played an active role in the development of the spiritual life of the people of Solo. Nyoman, our guide and medium, had earlier outlined a little history of the cave. He said leaders of the past had always gone to the cave to seek spiritual guidance from Semar. Before the Indonesian revolution, the young Sukarno often went there for inspiration and meditation. During the Dutch colonial days, Guwa Ratu was a prohibited area, for the Dutch rulers were afraid that the cave would be used by revolutionaries as a place for plotting against them. During the Japanese occupation, the Indonesian people were again barred from visiting the cave. It was only during the last few years that the place was properly refurbished and made accessible for anyone wishing to go there.

At about one o'clock in the morning, Nyoman called for me. According to him, the spirit of the God had descended. Leaving our candles behind, we passed through a small wooden gate carved in the shape of an Islamic dome and reached the inner chamber of the cave. We then walked along the bleak, dark tunnel until we reached the end where Nyoman beckoned me to sit down and wait quietly. It was there that we soon heard a low voice speaking in classical Javanese. The tone of soberness was occasionally interrupted by a jovial roar of laughter. It was somewhat similar to the voice of Semar which I had heard during a Javanese shadow play. The dalang would speak in a low and sober tone when Semar was defending a good general against evil, then suddenly burst into laughter when poking fun at people. It was remarkable that the voice echoing within the cave so closely resembled that uttered by the dalang. Some Javanese wayang fans believe that when the dalang speaks for Semar, it is not the dalang expressing himself but Semar who had entered the soul of the dalang.

The voice in the cave was accompanied by three other voices, one sounding like a lady's. I was later informed that she was *Lara Kidul*, Queen of the Indonesian Ocean. The other two voice were those of *Ki Bondoyudo*, the spiritual knight and *Noyoginggong*, his companion, both guardians of Sanghiang Ismaya. The four voices spoke for about twenty minutes, and all the time I was recording them on my tape recorder.

When we returned to Cilacap, my friend tried to interpret the utterances, which seemed to concern mainly the world situation and warned of imminent changes. It was not so much the message that interested me, but the satisfaction of having visited the cave where few foreigners have been. It was indeed an unforgettable and rewarding experience, for it enable me to have a deeper understanding of the spiritual life of the Javanese people.

During my stay in Indonesia, I was honoured to have met several gurus (spiritual teachers) who were highly respected as prominent spiritual leaders of Java. According to them, Semar created the ancestors of the Javanese, long before the advent of Hinduism, Buddhism or Islam. Chatting together in his home one evening, Romo Budi told me how, from time to time, the spirit of Sanghiang Ismaya would enter his soul. He explained how the spirit even spoke through him in Chinese. At that moment in the conversation, Romo Budi suddenly went into a trance and later came out of the trance, claiming that he had just been visited by the spirit and asked me whether I understood the message. I regretted I was unable to catch the meaning, perhaps because of the unfamiliar Chinese dialect which was spoken.

Romo Budi then went on to tell me a fantastic but interesting story about Sanghiang Ismaya. He said about 15 years ago, the spirit of Semar told him that he would receive a photograph that he should treasure. Soon afterwards, a Dutch friend sent him a picture thinking that it belonged to him. The photography was taken when a group of twenty-three junior high school students went to the Guwa Ratu area for a picnic. When one of them was about to take a picture of the group, he heard a voice calling out "Wait for me, Wait for me." He looked around, but saw nothing amiss. So he took the picture. When the film was developed, none of the twenty-two schoolmates was in the photograph. Instead, there appeared the image of Semar.

Romo Budi paused, then went to his bedroom to fetch the photograph. The picture clearly showed *Semar* with his plump figure and a human face with a long nose curling upwards. Romo Budi was kind enough to let me borrow the photograph to have it reproduced.

All this time, the same questions kept passing through my mind — was the photograph a true image of Semar? Did the incident actually happen? Although it sounded scientifically impossible, people believe that it may well be one of those rare phenomena that are not easily explained by modern science. My meeting with Romo Budi was a valuable one, as it gave me another glimpse of the spiritual significance of Semar which intrigued me.

Through an introduction by Ananda Suyono, I met Pak Parno, who, like Romo Budi, claims to be able to communicate with Sanghiang Ismaya. Although Pak Parno was an executive in an Indonesian Bank, he was also a guru capable of conducting group meditation. Besides communicating with Semar, he could also communicate with the spirit of Mangkunegara I, the deceased Sultan of Solo. Pak Parno related how he spent his childhood days in adventures in caves and on mountains, and later in meditation in these solitary places, thereby gaining much experience in being able to communicate with the spirits. It was Pak Parno who got the blessing of Sanghiang Ismaya for us to visit the Guwa Ratu cave.

I had often wondered what Javanese Muslims thought of Semar and whether belief in Semar would conflict with their belief in the Prophet Mohammed. So I sought the views of Javanese Muslim leaders. It was interesting to learn that in the early days of the Islamisation of Central Java, the imam (preacher) had used the puppet Semar to help propagate the religion. When I visited the kraton of Mangkunegara, my host Sultan Mangkunegara VIII showed me several wooden carvings of Semar, inscribed with Arabic characters. These were once used to help convince the commonfolk that even Semar had been converted to Islam.

I also met Pak Daryatomokan, 82-year old Muslim leader of the community of Wonogiri, as he was receiving villagers who had come to him for advice. They considered him doctor, teacher, preacher and wise man, who could cure many illnesses whether physical, spiritual or emotional. Pak Daryatmo has already been mentioned in another book *The Smiling General* (meaning Suharto) by the German author Roeder, who tells how President Suharto in his youth stayed with Pak Daryatmo for three years. When I asked Pak Daryatmo, a staunch Muslim, what he thought of Semar, his reply summed up the views of many Muslim leaders, "Semar is the spiritual guardian of Java." The answer was short but firm. He found it unnecessary to elaborate. The Javanese, like all other Indonesians, have an extraordinary capacity for syncretism and an unusual sense of tolerance for all religions.

The more scientifically-minded scholars and historians regard Semar as an imaginary figure introduced into the Javanese wayang performances. Historically, Semar first appeared on the relief of *Sudamala* at *Candi Tigamangi* in 1358. Later Semar was found on the relief of *Candi Sukuh*, completed in 1439. The story of Sudamala was copied from the original during the Majapahit period. Before that, there was no Semar in the wayang performances. In the Kediri period, the clownish servants of the Pandawas, known as *panakawan*, were *Pinta*, *Juru Deh* and *Prasanta*. These were the first panakawan in Javanese literature created by *Mpu Panuloh* in the *Ghaatokacasraya* (a Javanese tale). However, these panakawan had no appeal to the wayang audience and were not popular. It was only after panakawan like Semar and his family were invented that they immediately captured the imagination of the Javanese audiences. The earlier panakawan faded from the scene.

Semar's popularity grew to such dimensions that he became more than just a legendary figure in wayang performances. The Javanese like someone who is powerful and yet humble and generous who always likes to joke but at the same time is clever, faithful and wise. The Semar personality has created in the minds of the Javanese a belief that whatever he says must be the truth. Both the preachers of Hinduism and Islam had exploited this belief in spreading their religions in Java. The philosophical justification was that without the support of the native population, neither territories could have flourished in Java. Another philosophical aspect of the Semar myth was that without the support of Semar the Pandawas would not have won their feud with the Kurawas.

The lesson to all in modern terms is that without the support of the masses, no ruler can succeed in staying in power. Can Suharto who wants to be identified as Semar, be gradually losing the support of the masses because he is not carrying out his role of Semar as a protector of the people in providing them with sufficient food, shelter, contentment and happiness?

e) *Kebatinan* — A new trend in the spiritual horizon

God is within you
God is everywhere
But do not think that you are God

a *Kebatinan* commandment

In Java today, there is a large number of Javanese who follow the Islamic faith very similar to that of the Middle East. However, there are also many who will admit quite frankly and openly that they are just "nominal" Muslims, known as abangan. Dr H.M. Rasjidi, a well-known and outspoken Islamic scholar, commented in his book on Islam and kebatinan that the population of Java generally only profess Islam but many of them are in fact practising kebatinan, an attempt at reversion to the concepts of Buddhism and Hinduism.

What is kebatinan, a term which has come into prominence only during the past few years, although the principles have existed for a long time? The word *batin* means "inner self" in Arabic. It is difficult to understand how and why an Arabic word was used to describe something which is entirely Javanese in origin. Kebatinan means "to search for the inner self". It is not a religion in the true sense of the word, like Islam, Buddhism, Hinduism or Christianity. It has no church, which it considers unnecessary. There are no scriptures, like the Bible or Koran, no prophets in the same sense as Jesus, Mohammed or Buddha. It is not concerned so much with life after death, heaven and hell, or devils and angels.

Kebatinan is a metaphysical search for harmony within one's inner self, harmony between one's inner self and one's fellow-men and nature, and harmony with the universe, and Almighty God. It is a combination of occultism, metaphysics, mysticism and other esoteric doctrines — a typical product of the Javanese genius for synthesis. It has a touch of Confucianism in trying to harmonise one's behaviour to bring about an orderly society and in the practice of ancestor worship; a little bit of Taoism in the belief in supernatural powers and communication with the soul of the deceased; a little of Buddhism in the philosophy of contentment, and renunciation of one's ego and ambitions; a pinch of Hinduism in the mystic belief in reincarnation; as well as a little of the Islam faith in surrendering oneself to God. The essential, however, is a peace of mind.

The Javanese mind is so flexible that nothing on earth seems uncompromisable and, given a will, everything, however contraditory, can be harmonised and syncretised.

Javanese spiritualism is a never-ending source of wonder and surprise to foreign visitors, who are often puzzled by numerous apparent contradictions. Most Javanese see nothing wrong or unusual in having a dukun exorcise evil spirits from their homes, then go to the mosque, the church or the temple to pray to their respective gods. The Javanese mind is essentially a flexible and pragmatic one as far as a person's spiritual life is concerned. This complexity is perhaps the result of its complicated cultural background and influences. But basically, Javanese spiritualism is individualistic in approach, something very Javanese, a person-to-person or person-to-guru relationship. Through he influence of the wayang, a Javanese becomes familiar with the relationship between a warrior and his guru, he is aware of the mystical power of communicating with the supernatural and realises the philosophical value of self-discipline in relation to society and the universe.

The Javanese traditional spirit of tolerance allows free play for all religions. But the Javanese latent desire in wanting to be fundamentally a Javanese provides a natural filter for the Javanese mind to accept only qualities in "imported" religions that can be absorbed into the Javanese culture, character and personality. One thing that hurts the feelings of a Javanese is to be called *durung ngerti*, meaning "not able to understand". In other words, there is no point in arguing or punishing such a person since he has not yet grown up. Like the Japanese, the Javanese mother takes care not to allow her child to be excited or frightened by lightning and thunder, or to be frustrated. She makes every effort to educate the child to be a real Javanese, someone who is obedient, polite, respectful to his parents and elders and has self-discipline and self-control over his emotions. Thus, a Javanese will always try to absorb whatever religion or culture that comes into the country and then Javanise it, accepting only those aspects that are in keeping with the Javanese character. In this respect, they are very similar to the Japanese who absorbs Chinese culture and other cultures into their own and Japanise them into something which they can call their own.

For instance, Ramayana and Mahabharata epics have become so Javanised in the wayang that Hindus from India would find it difficult to recognise their Indian origin.

One of the major reasons why Javanese nominal Muslims generally profess themselves as Muslims but in fact practise kebatinan was that the Islamic scholars in Java have mostly been trained in religious schools whose curricula were geared to social conditions of two or three centuries ago. They lack the ability to impart the spirit and sense of Islam and for that reason lay undue stress on its formalities.

Two other reasons, according to another well-known scholar Professor M.M. Dajadiguna, for many Javanese straying away from Islamic practice and adopting kebatinan are: firstly, some religious leaders were either incompetent or reluctant to summarise the principles of their religion into simple basic points which the ordinary Javanese could understand and determine their position in relation to their fellow-men and to God when facing problems of life. Secondly, kebatinan provides no language problem. Followers need not have to struggle with a difficult language, such as Arabic, the medium of Islam. Sometimes, the pedantry of Islamic scholars unwittingly hurts the sensitive feelings of the people when they are forced to learn Arabic.

I have met a large number of Javanese who practise kebatinan; they represent a cross section of the various schools. Normally a person who practises kebatinan is rather reluctant to disclose that he is doing so if you do not know him well enough. Once the ice is broken, he will not hesitate to discuss the subject in great detail. Those who practise kebatinan include intellectuals who have been educated in Western universities. A large number of them take up this belief as a means of releasing physical, mental and emotional tensions which they believe are the cause of ill health. Others are more esoteric and seek to strengthen their spiritual powers to communicate with souls of ancestors, spirits of deities and the cosmic world.

General speaking, kebatinan followers believe in the existence of a super-consciousness in the cosmic world which is beyond man's comprehension, and which controls and guides man's affairs and destiny. The super-consciousness, it is believed, can be contacted through meditation. I came across a guru who got his disciples to demonstrate to me and a group of interested persons how they communicated with the soul of Sultan Mangkunegara. I also met a middle-aged Javanese who demonstrated the validity of the theory of mind over matter. He caused a cigarette to rise from a table and drop into a cup without even touching it. It was not magic but the result of years of training in meditation.

In Solo, many people have heard of a 71-year-old woman by the name of Bu Isrini, in Karang Talon. She is a well-known Javanese astrologer and a follower of kebatinan. Few people have actually seen her, she hides herself in her own dark room to avoid seeing sunlight. She leaves the room only once a year, on the first day of the first full moon, to receive relatives who normally come to pay their respects for the New Year. One of those who have seen her is Go Tek Suan, a friend of mine who was the *bupati* (district officer) of the Surakarta kraton. He says she is bald-headed and very pale. She cures people by giving prescriptions even without seeing the patients.

Another well-known kebatinan follower in Central Java was Tay Chin Pock, a Chinese who could cure people when he was in a trance. He passed away about 20 years ago. His grandson told me that whenever the old man went into a trance, his body would give off a rich perfume. It took more than twenty-five years of continuous meditation for his grandfather to acquire this mystical power.

In Malang, a young Chinese named Go Boon Bee, went to Gunung Lawu and meditated for ten years after he was separated from his wife at the age of nineteen. He learnt the art of *tapa kalong*, a method of meditation in the posture of a bat. He later became a guru (teacher). Gunung Lawu is a mountain where many people — including high officials — still go to practise kebatinan. The highest point of the mountain is called Ti Ling, which in the Chinese language means "the peak of the king". A place near Ti Ling is Suk Moh, again in Chinese, meaning "the ripened touch". Suk Moh is situated in a dangerously dark passage, and a sensitive touch is necessary to cross safely. I have heard that some meditators fell to their death when visiting the spot. Nobody has yet discovered the origin of the names of these two vital spots in Gunung Lawu. Could it be that, in ancient days, Chinese Buddhists have visited the spot and named it Ti Ling?

Many Chinese in Java have been Javanised. They carry Javanese names, behaved like Javanese and are completely assimilated. Many of them have become *gurus* of Javanese mysticism.

There are as many ways of *tapa* (fasting) as there are schools of meditation. Besides *tapa kalong* there are also *tapa geni* (fire), *tapa seneb* (Monday), *tapa ngableng* (darkness) and many other techniques. In Java, *tapa mutih* (white means abstention from eating anything that is salted). This practise resembles the Taoist *ku-hung* of abstaining from grains. Through *ku-hung* the Taoists try to survive on air and dew, absolutely renouncing rice and other grains. Some Taoist masters are believed to have lived on this diet for two, three even ten years without growing pale or weak.

Fasting is one of the common methods used by the spiritualists to attain discipline of the mind and body and to be rid of material and emotional desires. Many kebatinan followers still keep their professed religion but they meditate in their own way to seek spiritual and emotional relief — not in churches or mosques, but at home, in caves or on mountains.

Most Javanese abangan (the nominal Muslims) do not mind being just Muslims as long as the religion does not force them to take political sides or interfere with their kebatinan. There are however other more militant types of kebatinan followers who feel that the time has come for them to tell the world what they really believe in. This group has come out publicly to demand that kebatinan be recognised legally as a separate religion. They argue that kebatinan, which is an indigenous form of religious expression, is in no way inferior to any "imported" religion, and that it should enjoy equal status as other religions like Islam, Catholicism, Protestantism, Hinduism and Buddhism.

Owing to pressure from orthodox Muslims, kebatinan not only failed to be recognised as a religion, but was withdrawn from the jurisdiction of the Ministry of Religion and incorporated into that of the Ministry of Education and Culture. It is now termed *Kepercayaan Terhadap Tuhan yang Maha Esa* (Belief in One Mighty God). This was interpreted by *Tempo* newspaper as acknowledging that kebatinan is not a religion. It is now associated more with Pancasila than Islam.

During my visits to Central Java, I toured a number of places where kebatinan practices were being taught and collectively practised. Most of these gatherings were held very informally in private homes. One of the homes I visited was that a Javanese Buddhist, Anada Surjono, a middle-aged gentleman who is quite knowledgeable on spiritual matters and who is in frequent contact with those involved with similar movements throughout the country. Almost every night the hall next to his study was crowded with disciples of all races including hippies from Australia and sometimes from Europe. When I visited the kebatinan class one evening, I saw a number of hippies, two of whom were obviously suffering from some sort of nervous breakdown and needing peace of mind. The guru was Pak Darno, an old man who belongs to the Sumarah school, one of the major schools of kebatinan in Java. In the Javanese language, a guru who guides a recruit in seeking peace of mind is called *pamong* (guardian). Pak Darno is a rather shy and reserved personality. He speaks only Javanese. When all the visitors had taken their places, Surjono, who spoke English, warned that the exercise was about to begin. I noticed a sudden silence. Everyone cast his eyes downwards and relaxed. Fifteen minutes later, Pak Darno broke the silence and pointed out that the atmosphere in the class was still tense and started to give a lecture on how to relax and to seek peace of mind and harmony with nature.

According to one of Pak Darno's disciples, Dr Hatachi of Idayu (an institute to promote research on Indonesia and named after the name of former President Sukarno, Ida) who had arranged for me to witness the group meditation, is known to be able to diagnose from a distance whether a person is suffering from physical illness, emotional tension or mental disturbances. He is able to assist the patient to cure himself through meditation.

In these sessions, the pamong will know the internal meditative state of each group member and is in a position to inform the member whether his meditation is right or not. The extent to which a pamong is capable of analysing the state of a person's meditation differs considerably. Some are only capable of saying whether it is right or wrong, whilst others can be more specific by pointing out to the person concerned where too much attention is concentrated. The principle at work is communication through vibrations called getaran in Javanese. The experienced pamong has developed the capacity of feeling the other person's vibrations like a radio receiver.

Pak Darno is a Buddhist and yet a pamong of the Sumarah school. He has read a lot about Confucianism, Taoism, Hinduism and other religions. He works as a peon in the Perkumpulan Masharakat Ming Kong Hui, which helps the poor in burial matters. He is a simple man and leads a simple life. When we sent a car to fetch him, he preferred to ride a bicycle. Because of his devotion to the task of helping others to find inner peace without expecting anything in return, he has become a very popular figure in Solo.

According to the metaphysics of Sumarah, man is in misery the moment he is born — somewhat similar to Buddhist teaching. He is at the mercy of his passions. So long as he is unable to be rid of these passions, he has to suffer misery after misery through the process of reincarnation. The reincarnation is explained this way: when one dies, the soul (*jiwa*) wanders about in the form of a spirit, carrying with it its passions. The wandering spirit with passions is alway attracted towards worldly life. When such a wandering spirit meets a worldly couple having an affair, he is tempted to enter the womb of the woman and mingle with the union of semen and egg. In this way, he is reincarnated. This is by far the most interesting version of the theory of reincarnation I have come across.

According to the Sumarah school, man and his physical and spiritual world are divided into three parts: the physical body and brain, an invisible world and a more elusive and sublime world. In the brain, the faculty of thinking has two functions — one to record memories and the other to serve as a means of communion with God. One section, which is called *sukusma*, governs the passions. The jiwa provides a driving force for the faculty of thinking. The invisible world which is situated somewhere near the chest is the jiwa, the unsubstantial soul, and the deeper feelings (*rasa*). The more elusive and sublime world is hidden somewhere near the Masjid Al Haram — the holy Mosque. It is interesting to note that although this belief is contrary to the doctrine of the Koran, Arabic names are used.

In brief, the whole spiritual exercise of Sumarah is to help its students liberate himself from his passions so that he will reach his final destination to be one with God. Sumarah's concept of God is quite different from that of Islam. It considers God as being in all living things — plants, animals and men — as it is visualised in the Hindu-Javanese and Sumatran-Islamic mystical literature. The Sumarah theology says that man's soul is like the Holy Spirit, a spark from the Divine Essence similar to God. In other words, man can find God within himself, similar to the "I, God" theory found in Hindu-

Javanese literature. The way of liberation is *sujud* or thought-concentration, which is reminiscent of the Hindu yoga exercise.

Two of the three founder members of the Sumarah were humble folks. One of them, Pak Hardo, was a barber and the other, Pak Sukina, a minor employee of the Jogja (Jogjakarta) Court; both were from Jogja. Only Pak Sutadi from Solo was a highly educated member of the Colonial Parliament. Sumarah is the short form for Pagujuban Sumarah, or the Society of the Self-Surrenderers. During the early stages of Sumarah's development in 1935, it was a loose organisation. The activity of the group was tied in with Indonesia's revolutionary struggle.

In the early days, meditation sessions of the Sumarah school involved magical practices, and the participants were divided into groups according to sex and age. The youth group was taught the *kanoman*, which involved a wide range of occultism such as invulnerabilty to knives and guns. This was regarded as essential for youths in the struggle for independence against the Dutch. The mystical circles then were geared to fighting the Dutch, who possessed weapons. The other group was taught the *kesepuhan* which instilled the spirit of surrender to the independence struggle. At that time, there was no formal organisation of these groups.

During the revolutionary struggle around 1950, a young medical practitioner from Jogja, Dr Surono, streamlined the Sumarah movement and took over the organisations. There was a shift of emphasis from kanoman and magic to the spirit of 'surrender to God', an attitude similar to that of Christ's "Thy will be done". From 1957 internal squabbles took place within the organisation between Dr Surono on the one hand and Pak Sukino and Pak Hardo on the other, culminating in an open conflict in 1966 over a statement that only Dr Surono could receive true instructions from God. The conflict led to a vote of "no confidence" at a meeting against Dr Surono. Dr Ary Muthy, an economist, became the new leader. The seat of the organisation was then transferred from Jogja to Jakarta. Later however, it was moved back to Jogja.

I was told that one of the factors that led to the split was that one of the leaders was trying to carry the message of Sumarah not only to those now living but also to the ancestral kingdom associated with sacred coastlines, volcanoes, caves, temples and graveyards.

Sumarah is only one of the streams of kebatinan. There are other major kebatinan schools such as the Sapta Darma, Pangestu, Subud and Majapahit Pancasila.

Sapta Darma was founded by Harjosapura, a barber from a village called Para in East Java. Believers of Sapta Darma say that the concept of Sapta Darma was revealed to the founder on the night of 27 December 1952. They even remember the time, which was one o'clock in the morning. According to Sri Pawenang, the present leader, Sapta Darma kebatinan was a product of the Indonesian revolution. It was God's wish to provide the Indonesian people with a new spiritual approach in their search for peace of mind and happiness at a time when they were undergoing a mental and spiritual crisis. Sapta Darma believers are convinced that one of these days, kebatinan will become a recognised religion in Indonesia. In December 1955, the founder of the movement was consecrated and was given the name of Sri Gotama. He was further bestowed the title of *Panuntun Agung* (the exalted Leader), so that the official title of the leader has now become Panuntun Agung Sri Gotama. When he died in December 1964, Sri Gotama was succeeded by a woman then studying law at the Gajah Mada University in Jogjakarta.

Like Sumarah, Sapta Darma is also a training school for *sujud* (meditation). The origin of Sapta Darma is described in a small booklet entitled *Wwarah Agama Sapta Darma*, written by Sri Pawenang. A retired journalist by the name of Bratakesawa has also written a book *Kunji Swarge* (key of heaven) in the form of a dialogue between a teacher and his disciple, which propounded further the theory of Sapta Darma. It was an attempt by the author to have Javanese mysticism founded on the Koran. It deals with God, death, the way to search for God and other esoteric matters.

A significant aspect of the Sapta Darma doctrine is the use of Semar, the guardian spirit of Java, as its main symbol. Semar is seen carrying in his left hand a symbol of his exalted feeling. In his right hand he holds a weapon signifying that he possesses magical powers. Semar wears a five-pleated gown symbolising Pancasila, the five principles of the Indonesian State. The idea is that constant meditation should bring one in touch with Semar. But to get in touch with Semar is not easy as indicated in the Sapta Darma symbol. Semar is seen surrounded by various hues of colour — starting outermost from a green square, inwards to a brown triangle, then a layer of black, red, yellow and finally white, where Semar is seated. One has to pierce through the different layers or obstacles through meditation before one can reach Semar to find peace and tranquility of mind.

The theory and practice of Sapta Darma meditation resembles that of the Indian Kundalini, the awakening of the serpent power in man, practised very widely in Southern India. It involves generating vibrations in the twelve *chakras* (centres of power in the human body). The chakra that controls passion is situated in the navel and is termed Majandara, representing the bestial monkey characteristic in man-mischieviousness and *hanuman* (monkey) desire for teasing and seducing. The power that is situated in the vertebral column just as in Kundalini yoga is called Nagatuhun, the dragon of the soul. It has the characteristics of the serpent for it is poisonous and complicated, but extremely powerful when awakened. It seems to me that Sapta Darma is a combination of Hindu yoga, the Islamic Koran and Javanese mysticism. The aim of Sapta Darma is the same as that of Sumarah, that is, to liberate men from the grip of his passions.

I first learnt about Pangestu from a general when he visited my office in Jakarta. We were talking generally about kebatinan and he admitted that he belonged to the Pangestu school. He was General Sudjono Humardhani, Presidential Assistant to Suharto. He introduced me to many of his friend who practised kebatinan in Java.

Pangestu was founded in Surakarta sometime in May 1949. The doctrine in its "holy scripture" called the *Serat Sasangka Djati* is believed to have been revealed to one Sunarto Mertowarjoyo in 1932. Later it was put into writing by R.T. Harjoparakowo and R. Trihardono Sumodiharjo Pangestu. It describes the way to attain wahyu, the blessing of God. It is a general belief of the Javanese that only people with wahyu can become rulers. When Sukarno's power was gone, the Javanese said he had lost his wahyu. Similarly, when Suharto fell from power, the people also said he had lost his wahyu.

The Pangestu scripture consists of seven parts: (1) the *Hasta sila* (the eight forms of good behaviour); (2) *Paliwara* (the great prohibitions); (3) *Guymelaring Dumadi* (the unfolding of creations); (4) *Sangkan Paran* (origin and destination); (5) *Panembah* (adoration); (6) *Tunggal Sabda Dalan Rahayu* (the way of salvation); and (7) *Panembah* (adoration). Pangestu is indeed a modern, organised, mystical school and has many followers among the intellectuals. In 1956, Dr Sumantri Hardjoprakoso wrote a dissertation in Dutch on this mystical school entitled *The Indonesian Concept of Man Based on Psychotherapeutics*. In it, he attempted to give scientific meaning to its mystical doctrines.

Another school which is also practised among Europeans is the *Suhud*, which has branches all over the world. It has a more pragmatic approach to modern problems, for the organisation also indulges in business enterprises to increase its funds. It has its meditation centre in the form of a huge housing complex on the outskirts of Jakarta. Many Europeans and Americans from abroad stay in the Suhud centre when they are in Jakarta. They are often members of similar organisations in their respective countries. During their stay, they undergo training in meditation under a panel of gurus who were trained by Pak Suhud, the founder of the school who has since passed away.

The name Suhud was formed from the words *susila*, *budhi*, and *Dharama*. *Susila* refers to the good character of man. *Budhi* means "the force of the inner self". *Dharma* means "trust in God".

Suhud is someone who has the inner feeling and who is able to establish contact with the Great Holy Life Force. The aim of Suhud is to attain perfection of character according to the will of God. Suhud does not consider itself a religion or teaching in itself, but merely the spiritual experience of awakening by the power of God, leading to spiritual reality, freedom from the influence of passion, heart and mind.

According to Suhud theory, unless passion, heart and mind are separated from the inner feeling, it is impossible for the inner feeling to establish contact with the Great Life Force which permeates everywhere. By separating passion, heart and mind from the inner feeling, one is able to distinguish between the various kinds of life forces in man. This will eventually lead to the realisation of one's true self and the elimination of the false one. The Suhud school believes that as chemistry can extract iron, tin, gold, silver and other materials from the earth, man's mind and heart can draw out similar vital forces, the chemistry in the spiritual realm, through God whose power reaches far beyond the powers and abilities of man.

The latest entry into the kebatinan mystic world was a school called Majapahit Pancasila founded by a Javanese mystic W. Hardjanta Pardjapangarsa, when he was 50 years old. When I visited him in 1974, he was living in a dilapidated shop-house in a back lane behind the Surakarta *kraton*. It was a sunny day and I found him discussing his theory and method of practising Kundalini yoga with some of his disciples, some of whom came from Australia and others from as far as Bonn. Wearing a *blangkon* (headgear) and the traditional Javanese sarong, he sat in a squatting position on a rickety chair. Piles of books and files filled his simple wooden cupboards in a rather disorderly fashion. The old junk-store look of his house only helped to strengthen my impression of Hardjanta's simplicity and humble way of life. He went around barefooted and helped anyone who came in search of the secret path of *Kundalini*, the serpent power which makes one permanently young and strong, physically and spiritually.

I was interested in Kundalini because I had taken up Kundalini since 1963 from an Indian guru from Madras. He initiated me with his magic fingers and brought the power from my spine to the top chakra of my head. I was physically weak when I became Parliamentary Secretary of the Ministry of Culture. Everyday after lunch I had to take a long nap before I could carry on working. After the initiation, however, I became stronger and stronger, physically and mentally, and I believed in Kundalini. My teacher was Paranjothi Mahan, who was over 70 with silvery hair, had big eyes and was always smiling. He taught me a great deal about Kundalini and that was why I was interested in Kundalini yoga. Paranjothi Mahan started his Universal Peace Sanctuary all over India and has a branch in Singapore. It was in this Sanctuary in Upper Serangoon Road that I was initiated.

Hardjanta was supposed to be a Kundalini expert and wanted to compare the type of Kundalini that I knew with his method.

Hardjanta had never stepped into a university nor did he claim to be a scholar. He was an autodidact — a self-taught person. He had never been to an English school and yet he wrote beautiful English and was able to expound his theory clearly in that foreign language. He was popular among the European and Australian seekers of mystical knowledge, probably because he was conversant with the English language.

Hardjanta's emblem for Majapahit Pancasila reflects a syncretism of many sources of wisdom. At its base curled two serpents — one *ying* (female) and the other *yang* (male) — and above the serpents stands the *garuda* bird. The bird represents power arising from the awakening of the serpent power of the Kundalini practice. Above this stands the figure of Vishnu representing eternal wisdom. This emblem is carved in cement and prominently displayed outside Hardjanta's humble dwelling.

Originally, it was the intention of Hardjanta to proclaim Majapahit Pancasila a new religion. However, under certain rules promulgated in Indonesia in 1967, when the Pancasila Democracy was implemented, one of the principles of which was "Belief in God", no new religion would be tolerated apart from the official religions already in existence, such as Islam, Hinduism, Christianity, Buddhism, Confucianism, Taoism and other world-recognised religions. So Hardjanta finally got his school registered under the Hindu-Dharma religion.

Hardjanta's Majapahit Pancasila is pehaps the only school of kebatinan which uses Kundalini yoga as the means of attaining spiritual enlightenment and mystical powers. It is one of the highest forms of yoga, with a strong influence of Tantrism from Tibet.

Kundalini is a sort of mystical force, in the form of mercury, coiled like a serpent and hidden in a tiny spot at the end of the vertebral column of the human spine. Through meditation or other methods, the power is awakened and is brought through the spinal canal to the "third eye" (between the two eyebrows) and the top of the head called the "wisdom eye". As it rises to the top, it vitalises the seven centres of power called chakra along its invisible course to the brain. Those who have mastered Kundalini yoga possess special energy beyond the reach of ordinary souls.

There are many esoteric methods of awakening the Kundalini power in a person. In ancient time, the secrets were carefully guarded, and disciples had to undergo years of apprenticeship before the guru would divulge the secrets. Kundalini was also practised by ancient Egyptians in the temple of Luxor. All Egytian Pharaohs had a serpent headgear above their heads indicating that they had Kundalini power like the serpent. In India, there are hundreds of Kundalini schools under different names and using different methods of awakening the serpent power.

In Solo, where Hardjanta's Kundalini practice is becoming popular, particularly among Westerners, the method of initiation is rather different from that of my Indian guru. Hardjanta uses the power of the sun to initiate his disciples. At the back of a compound of sawo (a kind of tropical fruit called chiku in Malay) trees I saw a number of disciples, with their eyes blindfolded with black cloth, lying on the ground with their faces to the sky. It was midday and the blazing sun pierced through the sawo trees casting menacing rays on the disciples who were supposed to keep their blindfolded eyes on the sun between 11.30 a.m. and 1.30 p.m. The exercise was supposed to go on for 40 days in order to awaken the serpent power of the spine.

In the presence of Hardjanta, I interviewed a young Australian Air Force man who had taken leave from Butterworth (my hometown, off Penang) airfield in Malaysia, where he worked as a pilot, to come to Solo to look for the secret knowledge of Kundalini. He had become interested in Indian mysticism because he had fallen in love with an Indian girl from Kedah. Seemingly excited and agitated, the frank and outspoken Australian told us of his six-day experience in the sun-gazing Kundalini initiation.

"I cannot stand it any longer. I will go mad if I continue," he said. "What is the reason?", asked the guru, who was taken aback by the comments of the Australian.

The young man replied that there were many ants crawling on his head and legs during the meditation and he could not bear it any more.

"Why not put some kerosene around you to keep away the ants if they are the only obstacles?", suggested the guru. The young Australian appeared rather flabbergasted and went on to tell of his other frightful experiences. He said he could not sleep at night. Whenever he closed his eyes even in the daytime, he could see little blue devils about the size of one's thumb dancing in front of him and coming towards him. He said as the devils approach him they became bigger and bigger. He also mentioned the fantastic visions that had haunted him during his sleep.

Hardjanta explained that these were the effective result of the meditation and that they were the cosmic visions which were hidden from the ordinary eye. He tried to persuade the Australian pilot to complete the forty-day meditation for it would mean better achievement than what other pupils did.

According to Hardjanta, anyone who had mastered the sun meditation would be invulnerable to external attacks by knives, daggers and other weapons, and nobody could harm him. He would also have supernatural powers and wisdom. But to complete the intiation required patience, faith and perseverance. Not everyone could succeed.

Hardjanta had several young Javanese disciples who were undergoing Kundalini initiation which was not confined to sun meditation only. Each disciple had to soak himself inside a bathtub filled with cold water up to his neck. He had to hold his navel with his left hand and touch the back of his shoulder with his right hand. This method of meditation was called moon meditation. It would result in clarity of mind and the development of extra-sensory perception.

While we were discussing mysticism, a Polish couple hurried in and were whisked away by a young tutor. I was told that the couple wanted to get their "third eye" opened within three days as they were in a hurry to leave. For such emergency cases, Hardjanta said, special intensive methods had to be used. I did not press him to explain the method.

The word "Majapahit" is used for his philosophy and religion because it was the name of the strongest and most famous empire in the history of Nusantara (Indonesia). Hardjanta said one of his aims was to revive Hinduism in its true form and to bring back the glory of Hindu practices.

There are hundreds of other *kebatinan* schools of which a complete discussion would require a separate book. The ones that I have mentioned are those with large followings. Owing to the mushrooming of kebatinan schools and practices, the Office of the Public Prosecutor had set up Pakem, a body in charge of supervising religious schools in order to keep them under control. The Pakem — *Pengawasan Aliran Kepercayaan Masjarakat* meaning literally, "Authority for the Supervision of Social Beliefs" — sees to it that *kebatinan* schools or Islamic mystical brotherhood (*tarakat*) minority religions, soothsayers and traditional healers do not abuse their powers or carry out undesirable activities. Undesirable practices, which are commonly known as klenik, are those that lead people astray by inciting them to break the law and disturb social order, by ridiculing or insulting other established religions, or by involvement with the communists. The fear is that some of these schools may be exploited by political adventurers which may endanger peace and security. There was an incident in March 1967 in Central Java, where the Mbah Suro Incident resulted in the death of more than 80 people and the near-obliteration of the hamlet of Nginggil. It was caused by the outlawed Indonesian Communist Party (PKI) which had infiltrated and subverted a fanatical pseudo-religious sect. The incident was precipitated by the defiance of the mystical adherents of Mbah Suro who believed in their invulnerability to guns and pistols. At the time of his death, Mbah Suro was identified as both a *dukun klenik* and a dupe of the PKI.

Meanwhile, the leaders of the different kebatinan groups such as Sumarah, Sapta Darma and Pangestu have been active since 1965 to bring together all the assorted contemporary mystical groups into a congress called the BKKI (*Badan Kongress Kebatinan Indonesia*) or The People's Congress of Kebatinan of Indonesia. This congress has held several meetings and seminars since its formation. The Congress, under the leadership of Mr Wong-Sonegoro, a lawyer, has been striving hard to get kebatinan recognised as one of the official religions of the country. Since the conference of mystical groups held in Jogja in December 1970, a Secretariat called *Kerjasama Kepercajaan Kebatinan Kejiwaan* (Joint Secretariat for the Promotion of Kebatinan) has been formed with this aim. As a result, the recent parliamentary session has given recognition to the practice of kebatinan. This newly gained status has given its leader the impetus to come to grips with some fundamental problems of properly defining their objectives and practices to the public. In the process of adjusting to changing conditions, each group is seriously examining itself in relation to the larger group as a whole and in relation to society. For instance, there is increasing emphasis on meditation in daily life as opposed to the esoteric aspects of the movement. The implications of "surrender through meditation" is being more clearly defined as a comprehensive philosophy of life and action.

Another aspect of the changes in theory and practice involves an attempt to synthesise the adaptable concepts of other religions such as Buddhism, Hinduism, Islam and Christianity. Meanwhile, the BKKI has yet to develop into an effective organisation. It has so far gathered more than 85 *aliran* (schools) and a number of individual mystics at its Congress, whilst there are some 1,000 *alirans* in Java alone.

The struggle for recognition marks the beginning of an era in the history of religious beliefs in Indonesia and will have far-reaching effects on the future development of the country. But the extreme Islamic fanatics are strongly against the expansion of the kebatinan movement. But it is also not easy to do away with the kebatinan movement.

After the fall of Suharto, there was a revival of kebatinan in the name of worshipping the past president Sukarno. At the 28th anniversary of his death, tens of thousands of Javanese flocked to his cemetery to put flowers and a new kebatinan movement is being created in his name. It is not easy for the Javanese to give up their belief which for centuries has been influenced by Hindu-Buddhism.

f) The Joyoboyo predictions of the arrival of *Ratu Adil*

M Besulk yen wusana jago wiring kuning
Saka lor witan lekani
Iku bakal ilangi kekbo bule
wiwer natand

Tomorrow the yellow peacock from the
northeast will come to drive away the
white buffalo with blue eyes — meaning
the Japanese from the northeast will
come to drive away the Dutch colonialists

Europe has its French astrologer Nostradamus (1503-1566) who predicted that the end of the world would come at the end of the 20th century, and China has its astrologer Liu Pai Un who predicted China's history from ancient days in a book called "Tsui Pei Do". Indonesia too has a astrologer — a King Prabu Joyoboyo who predicted Indonesia's history. Nostradamus predicted that the end of the world would be preceded by natural disasters, war, famine and death, and the arrival of a King of Terror. The Chinese astrologer Liu Pai Un predicted that the Mongolians and later the Manchurians would conquer China. The Indonesia astrologer King Prabu Joyoboyo predicted the defeat of the Dutch described as "white buffalo" by the Japanese who were described as the "yellow peacock". He also predicted the arrival of several Javanese kings, the arrival of Islam in Java and also the emergence of Sukarno and finally the arrival of the *Ratu Adil* (the just King) in Indonesia who would bring prosperity and happiness to the people.

Prabu Joyoboyo was a Javanese King who lived in Kendiri around 1157 or 1079 according to the Javanese calendar (during the period when Mongolians ruled China) His full name was Sang Mapani

Jayabaya Sri Dharmaishwara Petera Makhota Sri Erlangger Raja. He was an unusual king in that he was not only a good warrior and administrator, but also a gifted poet and astrologer.

King Joyoboyo was responsible for the revised version of *Baharatajudha*, the popular theme of the wayang play depicting the bitter war between the Pandawa and Kurawa families. Like a prophet, he received inspiration from God and predicted the whole history of Java including the birth of the Indonesian nation, all beautifully written in old Javanese *pantun*. His predictions were considered so accurate by his followers that both the Dutch and later the Japanese colonialists banned the Joyoboyo predictions for fear that they might inspire the people to revolt.

It is claimed that Joyoboyo had predicted hundreds of years ago that a "yellow peacock" from the northeast would come to drive away the "white buffalo with blue eyes" from the Indonesian soil. When events unfolded believers of Joyoboyo's predictions interpreted "yellow peacock" to mean the Japanese and the "white buffalo" the Dutch colonialists. The prediction later added that "the black ants will lay eggs on fine ashes" which was interpreted to mean that the Indonesian people would achieve their independence by revolution.

Another Joyoboyo prediction, *Ana merak bandrek lawar haja* meaning a peacock commits adultery with a crocodile, was interpreted to mean that the red men, the British, conspired with the crocodile, the Dutch, to regain their colonial possessions.

The Joyoboyo predictions also give advice such as *kuching gering ingkang nunggonni* meaning "the sick cat is unable to guard against rats". A cat is a symbol of a guardian or an administrator. If it is sick or lazy, the rat which represents the villains will be free to run around it in circles.

Si percil ingkang and jaga (a little frog guards the well) means that there is hope in the younger generations who will safeguard the nation.

Since Joyoboyo is believed to have predicted very accurately the past history of Indonesia, the people are waiting for the last phase of his prediction, the arrival of Ratu Adil, a just king who will bring peace, justice, stability and prosperity to the nation.

Joyoboyo never anticipated the arrival of democracy or that the Indonesians would elect their own leaders. Whoever was elected or ruled over Java or Indonesia will be regarded as "king".

Having heard a lot about the coming of the Ratu Adil, I was naturally curious to know more about him. According to the *Badab Diponegoro* which described the most famous revolt against the Dutch (1825-1830), Diponegoro (the hero who fought against the Dutch) himself claimed to have seen Ratu Adil at the foot of a mountain situated south-east of Rasamuni in Central Java. The following are excerpts from the long chronicle: "Ratu Adil was standing on the top of the mountain viewing the sun's splendour, so that he paled for a time," and spoke to the Prince Diponegoro, "I have summoned you to tell you that you must lead my whole army into battle. Conquer Java with it."

In the history of Java, several leaders had tried to claim that they were the Ratu Adil or were instructed by Ratu Adil to save the nation. Gajah Mada, the most powerful prime minister of the Majapahit Empire, had claimed that he was the Ratu Adil. So had Diponegoro, the Javanese hero who fought against the Dutch and was captured and died in jail. Sukarno who liberated Indonesia from the Dutch claimed that he was Ratu Adil, so had Suharto. Events have shown that they were not the real Ratu Adil. The real Ratu Adil has yet to appear.

The most worrying part of the prediction which some mystics described as the Joyoboyo prediction is about what will happen in Indonesia before and after the fall of Suharto. Thousands of multi-storey buildings, shops and homes belonging to ethnic Chinese were burnt down on May 13, 1998 and thousands of women were openly raped. There was in fact a massacre of the Chinese. Mystics claim that the "Joyoboyo prediction" had predicted this "mad period" for Indonesia Chinese would leave only a minority of Chinese remaining in the country. This is the time when the Ratu Adil will arrive. I do not know whether this is the true prediction of Joyoboyo. If that is a true prediction of Joyoboyo, then something must be wrong somewhere. How can the Ratu Adil bring about peace and prosperity to Indonesians when all ethnic Chinese have left the country? Who is to manage the economy of the country and with what capital? Is it not true that the new President of Indonesia Dr Habibie, who did not have a good feeling towards the Chinese, had to appeal to the Chinese who have left the country to return with the promise to grant them equal status as the *pribumi*, and not to discriminate against the non-*pribumi* any more?

Was the massacre of the Chinese on May 13 inspired by the Joyoboyo prediction? Or was it a conspiracy by some group to do away with the Chinese by making use of an alleged Joyoboyo prediction? Or was it a deliberate misinterpretation of the Joyobobyo prediction to make the people believe that the presence of the Chinese was obstructing the arrival of Ratu Adil? Or was it because someone is not happy with the Chinese whom he thought were "exploiting" the resources of the country and the people and must be got rid off?

One mystic in Indonesia told me that Joyoboyo even predicted who would become the presidents of Indonesia after independence. He said the prediction was coined in a phrase "No-to-ne-go-ro". These were the last two characters of the names of Indonesia's leaders. "No" may refer to Sukar<u>no</u> and "to" Suhar<u>to</u>. That is to say that he had rightly predicted that Sukarno and Suharto would be presidents of Indonesia a thousand years ago. What about "ne"? It does not fit into the name of the present president Habibie, because Habibie's name does not end with a "ne". Can it be that Habibie is only a temporary president and someone with a name ending with "ne" would be the next president, and that the president that follows will have "go" and "ro" endings in their names? Only time will tell.

Since the Joyoboyo predictions, many more predictions have been made by mystics from generation to generation. They form part of the pattern of life in Javanese society. Those who are in close touch with mystical predictions sometimes have an advantage over others. Some of the predictions have, somehow or other, turned out to be true.

In 1965, just before the Gestapu coup on 30 September, a young mystic made a prediction in a letter to General Yani. I read a photocopy of the letter dated March 1965, written by the mystic who called himself Sjah. General Yani was then Chief of Staff of the Army under former President Sukarno.

Sjah's letter predicted a big change in the Indonesian Government, involving chaos and bloodshed. Sjah predicted that after the upheaval, a new leader would emerge to lead the Indonesian nation towards peace and stability, for the better. The letter warned General Yani, repeatedly using the word *berhati-hati* (be careful) in the months of August, September and October. General Yani received this warning six months before he was murdered. He died in the early hours of the first of October 1965 when six generals and a soldier were assassinated and thrown into a crocodile hole called Lubang Buaya. Suharto who was in charge of military movements in Jakarta under the name of "Kostrad" took over power and at least one million communists were massacred. It was said that the Communists had committed the crime of murdering the six generals and a soldier. But, there were others who claimed that Suharto had engineered the whole affair. Whatever it may be, a new mystical element has been added to the death of General Yani and the other generals.

At Lubang Buaya, there stands a massive monument to commemorate the seven Indonesian officers who were tortured and killed on 30 September 1965. The official name of the monument is *Pancasila Sakti*. Replicas of the six murdered generals and one army officer stand on top of a wall. Ironically, a brother of one of the six senior officers, Lt. Gen. S. Parman was a high-ranking communist ideologue.

I was told that before the riots of 15 January 1974, a well-known mystic received messages of warning that dark clouds would loom over Jakarta and that the fate of the country would be decided in January that year. That was the day when there was a serious riot in Jakarta against the visit of the Japanese Prime Minister Kakuei Tanaka because the Indonesians were angry that the Japanese investors had chosen ethnic Chinese as their business partners instead of Indonesians.

Rioters burnt down the display-windows of shops owned by agents of Japanese cars. On the arrival of Tanaka, I went to the airport to receive the Prime Minister but Tanaka had to be flown out in a helicopter from the airport to the Istana. On my way back to Jakarta wihout having met Tanaka, my car was stopped by student rioters because they mistook me for Tanaka as in profile I resembled Tanaka. Then some students noticed the Singapore flag and realised that I was not and I sighed in great relief. Tanaka was flown by helicopter to the Istana because the Indonesians would not have allowed him to take the risk of travelling by road.

Sometime in 1972, through an Indonesian friend, I met a young mystic who claimed to have supernatural powers. He had five hundred needles stuck all over his body and asked me to touch a needle to convince me that the needle was real. He said the needles helped him to communicate with the supernatural beings in the cosmos.

In order to convince me that he could contact the supernatural powers, he immediately went into a trance with his eyes closed for about ten minutes. He said he had contacted the spirit of Joyoboyo after he opened his eyes. I asked: "You mean you have contacted the spirit of King Joyoboyo, the poet king and astrologer who was supposed to have existed some nine hundred years ago?". He replied, "Yes."

"What did he tell you?", I asked.

He said King Joyoboyo predicted that there would be further trouble in the country and one had to be on one's guard. That was sometime in the middle of 1972. Incidentally, there were riots in Bandung in August 1973 and further riots in Jakarta in January 1974.

The young mystic often went to the mountains with his guru to communicate with the supernatural. I asked him how he managed to get the five hundred needles into his body, thinking that it had something to do with methods used in Chinese acupuncture. He replied, "It was quite easy. My guru put the needles in his mouth, said some mantra and blew them into my body without feeling of any pain."

If the mystic can contact the soul of Joyoboyo, surely he can also contact the souls of Gajah Mada, or the spirit of Prince Diponegoro.

In Java, each empire had its heroes who were worshipped religiously
as a mystical source of guidance. These heroes were buried in sacred
places, which became places of worship or meditation for mystics or
their believers.

The tomb of Diponegoro, the revolutionary hero who rose against
the Dutch colonialists, is in Makassar. Mystics still frequent mountains,
caves or landmarks known for their connection with past heroes and
gods. To Muslims, the sacred graves of holy men of Islam in Cirebon,
Demak, Tuban, Gresik, Surabaya and Denpasar are places for religious
pilgrimage. The visit to these graves is considered equal to that of
performing the obligatory pilgrimage to Mecca, which is one of the
pillars of Islam.

The custom and tradition of paying respect to dead heroes has
almost become institutionalised in present-day official functions. Once
a year, on the first of October, the armed forces and the whole cabinet
led by the President pay homage to the seven *pahlawan* (heroes) who
were massacred in the Gestapu coup and buried in Lubang Buaya on
the outskirts of Jakarta. There is also a touch of mysticism about the
Lubang Buaya affair, for the day the six generals and a soldier was
found massacred, an extraordinary *durian* (a fruit with a thorny shell
and a strong smell) with seven seeds was found about a foot away
from the hole. During the Sukarno regime, Heroes Day was officially
celebrated on the tenth of October. Even at the opening session of the
Indonesian parliament there is always a silent pause of three minutes
to remember the dead heroes called *mengheningkan cipta kepada para
pahlawan*.

It is interesting to note that in the ancient history of Java, whenever
a new king emerged to succeed the old one, the poet of the court,
known as the king's *pujangga*, would write about the new king's divine
descent. The new king would therefore be justified to be the leader
of his people, who would then regard him as having been endowed
with supernatural powers. Historical facts interwoven with popular
beliefs and mystical phenomena therefore dominate the historical
records of Java. The old Javanese writers perhaps had to strengthen the
king's image and legitimacy by emphasising his mystical powers, for

this was the main pillar upon which his kingdom and the well-being of his people rested.

In later Javanese history, whenever a new leader emerged to lead the people to revolt against oppression or against foreign colonial domination, one would come across stories that the leader had heard a voice from above giving him inspiration or instruction. Most mystics believe that rulers are chosen by the Almighty God, and that they are given *wahyu cakraningrat* (the blessing for ruling the country) which ordinary people do not possess. When Sukarno emerged as Indonesia's leader, the people said he had the wahyu and the people trusted and supported him. Apart from playing with the balance of power between the communists and the armed forces, he did a lot of slogan shouting and indulged in great oratory, which did not benefit the people economically speaking. He was a good revolutionary hero, but a poor nation builder. He asked the people to eat stone and they would do so. But when he fell, they said he had lost his wahyu. When Suharto took over, he was supposed to be endowed with the wahyu and he did bring some economic benefit to the people, but the Suharto family had benefited most because they controlled almost all the natural resources and wealth of the country. For 32 years, he had the wahyu, but it began to fade away in May 1998 when riots rocked the country before his return from Egypt attending an Islamic conference. Students demonstrators and opposition leaders all demanded that he stepped down. They accused him of encouraging corruption, mal-administration and bringing the country down the drain.

This talk of wahyu existed in the days of Gajah Mada, the greatest Prime Minister of the Majapahit Empire. Mystery surrounds the birth of Gajah Mada. The Balinese believe that he was born in Bali Agung and later moved to the Kingdom of Majapahit. The Balinese also believe that Gajah Mada had no father and no mother, and that he was found in a coconut — the reincarnation of Sanghiang Narajana or Vishnu. Even Chinese chronicles added a touch of mystery to the birth of Gajah Mada. According to the Chinese source on Java entitled *Ying Ya Sheng Lan* written in 1415, the Chinese who visited Java heard a legend that went something like this:

It is told that in olden times, a king of devils (Mararaja) with a green face, a red body and brown hair, who lived in this country, united himself with a bad spirit in the shape of an elephant and ate more than a hundred children, living on human flesh and blood. One day, a flash of thunder and lightning split open a rock. Inside, a man was sitting cross-legged. The people were greatly astonished at this and at once took him for their leader. He then led the people against the ghostly elephant and drove it away. The scourge was thus ridded and the people multiplied again in peace. Gajah Mada's name strangely has some connection with the elephant for the word *gajah* means elephant.

Gajah Mada was a Buddhist and often went to the mountains to meditate for inner strength and to contact Vishnu for spiritual guidance. In 1355, at the height of his victories, King Hayam Wuruk gave him a piece of land near Purbalingga, in East Java. This place, which was name Madakaripura by King Hayam Wuruk to honour his distinguished Prime Minister, became the spiritual retreat for Gajah Mada to meditate. According to a legend, sometime in 1365 when Gajah Mada was 60 years old, he took his wives and a group of beautiful maidens, all of them enchantingly dressed, to Madakaripura one evening. When they were there, they saw Gajah Mada vanished into thin air, never to be seen again.

Gajah Mada had done a *moksa* — a Javanese term to describe the mystical skill of making oneself disappear from this earth. King Hayam Wuruk went hunting high and low for him, but in vain. Since then, mystics have believed that Gajah Mada's soul and spirit can be contacted in Madakaripura. Some still go there to meditate, to get in touch with his soul.

It was Gajah Mada, the dynamic Prime Minister, who did most to glorify the Kingdom of Majapahit. He believed then that he was the Ratu Adil. He became an inspiring hero after his death, with historical writings and legends perpetuating his image. Some things which he used during his lifetime, such as his kris, his mask and other alat or pusaka, are believed to possess mystical powers. The most sought after pusaka of Gajah Mada were his wooden mask and his magic kris.

Gajah Mada's mask is now carefully preserved in a temple called Pura Penopengan in the village of Belah Batu in Bali. Being interested in Javanese mysticism, I sought the help of General Sudjono Humardhani, then Presidential Assistant to Suharto on spiritual matters, to help arrange for a visit to this temple. With the help of the Panglima (military commander) of Bali, B.-G. Pranoto, I was taken by a special convoy to this temple when I was Ambassador to Indonesia. It was sometime in 1973.

It was about half an hour's drive from Denpasar, the capital of Bali, to the village of Belah Batu. We arrived at an inconspicuous temple called Pura Penopengan. Nobody could believe that the mask of Gajah Mada was hidden in this little temple. The keeper of the mask was a 60-year-old Balinese of royal descent, I. Gusti Ngurah Mantra, a collector of Indonesian masks. Gusti's family has been the keeper of Gajah Mada's mask for six hundred years. It was given to his great great grandfather Aria Rohaya, Commander of War of the Vassal State, by King Hayam Wuruk. Aria Rohaya had served under Gajah Mada when the latter conquered Bali.

During a revolt in East Java, Commander Aria was sent to subdue the rebels. When he had accomplished his mission, King Hayam Wuruk asked him what he wanted as a reward. Aria knew about Gajah Mada's mask and took a liking for it, as he was a collector of masks. So he asked for the mask and a set of antique leather puppets used in the wayang kulit. He got them.

For six centuries, the mask and wayang kulit were kept in a small dilapidated temple and nobody except the keepers took much notice of them. Then one day, sometime in 1967, someone from Jakarta came to borrow the mask. The man was Sudjono Humardhani, Presidential Assistant to President Suharto on supernatural affairs. Suharto had just come into power and was looking for Gajah Mada's mask as he himself was a mystic. When Gusti opened the box containing the mask to Sudjono, a sudden thunderstorm struck the whole of Bali. Gusti said it was a good omen, and that it was a manifestation of the mask's tremendous supernatural power.

Sudjono told me that the officer who took the mask to Jakarta died of a heart attack. The mask stayed at the Istana for one thousand days to give Suharto blessing. Every night special praying was performed facing the mask.

Word soon spread that Gajah Mada's mask had been removed from the Belah Batu temple in Bali and sent on loan to Jakarta. One prominent Balinese was annoyed and upset that he himself had not had the privilege of seeing the mask. His mental torment was so great that one night, Gajah Mada came to him in a dream, appearing in the form of a gigantic shadow image. The spirit had apparently come to console him and told him to look out for a gift. For three successive days, on his return from work, he would ask his wife whether anyone had brought a gift. The answer was negative. On the fourth day, when he had almost given up hope, a parcel in banana leaves was mysteriously delivered to his house. He opened it and found a stone image of Gajah Mada, similar to that kept in the Belah Batu temple. The owner of this stone image of Gajah Mada has a B.A. degree, holding an important job, and is highly respected in the Balinese community. He showed me that stone image.

When I arrived at the Belah Batu temple, Gusti asked me to rest in the lounge, then he took me to an inner chamber where the mask was kept. A priest uttered mantras and sprinkled holy water to purify the temple. Barefooted and with a piece of cloth tied round our waists, my companions and I stepped into the temple which was the home of Gajah Mada's mask. The priest again sprinkled holy water and *komkom* (fresh flowers in water) and said his prayers. The box containing the mask was put on the altar, and another ritual of seeking permission to open it was performed.

I could feel the tense atmosphere and excitement as the box was opened, for it was indeed a rare moment. The mask was wrapped in the *merah puteh* (Indonesian national flag colour), a sign of official recognition. Gajah Mada's mask was handsome with its high forehead, dynamically piercing eyes, large nose, high cheekbones, broad mouth, long ears and well-formed chin. The most conspicuous part of the reddish-brown mask was the third eye between the brows which signified his possession of mystical powers. The Indian Kundalini Yogi believes that when the third eye of a person is initiated, he will have supernatural powers and could foresee events.

Gajah Mada was not at all handsome when he was alive. He had a flat nose and a pair of uneven teeth. When he conquered Bali, he fell in love with a Balinese girl Gunti Ayu Bebet, and asked for her hand in marriage. She refused because Gajah Mada's face did not appeal to her. So Gajah Mada prayed to God for supernatural power to make himself more presentable. His prayer was answered. When Gunti Ayu saw him next, he appeared rather handsome with a high nose and a charming, broad smile. The mask apparently was made to commemorate the successful romance. The story of Gajah Mada's mask therefore hangs between myth and reality.

Today, the image of Gajah Mada, made of stone, is used by mystics in their reading rooms for spiritual communications. Every morning and evening, the owners place flowers below the statue and hope that on one day the soul of Gajah Mada can be invoked. In same homes, there are huge paintings of Gajah Mada standing triumphantly riding an elephant conquering his enemies at the height of his battle victories. This is a common theme for artists, particularly those from East Java.

I visited an artist's studio in Surabaya and on the wall were at least ten paintings of Gajah Mada riding on an elephant or holding his magic kris. There was also a scene where Gajah Mada bowed before King Hayam Wuruk to demonstrate his loyalty. The artist told me that these Gajah Mada paintings were in great demand. This clearly indicates the respect and veneration that the Indonesian people still have for Gajah Mada today. It is not uncommon, therefore, to find streets named after him in many towns and cities of Java.

A great deal of mysticism also surrounds Prince Diponegoro, the anti-colonial hero who fought against the Dutch. Many streets all over Indonesia are named after him. One of them is in Jakarta where the Singapore Embassy is situated. In the Presidential Square, next to the National Monument, stands a bronze statue of Diponegoro on horseback. In the Presidential Palace hangs a beautiful oil painting of Diponegoro by Basuki Abdullah, one of Indonesia's famous painters.

The hero's name will invariably pass through he lips of all Indonesians when they relate the anti-colonial struggle of the past.

Diponegoro was born in November 1785, the eldest son of Sultan Hamengkubuwono II, also known as Sultan Raja. He grew up during a turbulent period that witnessed the decline and fall of the Dutch East Indies Company, the subsequent occupation of Java by the British, and then the return of the Dutch colonial administration.

In his youthful days, Diponegoro was more interested in spiritual matters and lived in Tegalejo in Central Java where he was educated by his grandmother. He soon led a life of seclusion and meditation in the mountains, interrupted occasionally by distasteful news of the court and of his brother Sultan Hamengkubuwono IV, who was indulging in a life of pleasure and ignoring his state duties. The Queen mother was equally corrupt and was more interested in court intrigue than anything else. The situation in the court was described in a poem composed by a famous Javanese society poet, R. Ng Ranggamarsita. It was a satire on-Javanese society of that period which was marked by moral decline. A stanza in the *Kalatida* (the age of darkness) reads as follows:

We have witnessed a time of madness,
In which everyone is confused in his mind.
One cannot bear to join in the madness,
But if he does not do so, he will not share in its spoils
And will starve as a result.
Indeed, it is the will of Allah
Those who are careful and vigilant
Are much happier than those who are careless.

Diponegoro wanted to change the situation. So one day he sent his servant, Jaya Mustapa, to the tomb of Sultan Agung, the great ruler of the Mataram Empire in the seventeenth century, to wait for a mystical sign. Jaya Mustapa was admitted to the tomb and spent the night in meditation. The next morning, after finishing his prayers, he saw on the curtain covering the entrance of the tomb a bloodstain as big as a plate. He asked the caretaker what it was and the latter replied that there was bloodstain there the night before. The caretaker Kyay Ballad then remarked, "It is God's will that much blood must be shed in Java; it is a sign that war will come. The will of God is absolute, his decision cannot be changed."

When Diponegoro heard about this, he went further into meditation and contemplation until one day, as he sat dreaming, he heard a voice from heaven asking him to change his name to Ngabdul-kamid, Servant of God. The voice told him that he was destined to be the man of action who would bring Java back to its original splendour and prestige. In order to do that he would soon receive Sasutana, a magic arrow. When the Prince woke up, he saw a flash of lightning hit the ground before him. When he lifted his head, he was surprised to see an arrow-head, Sasutana, stuck in the rock. The voice he heard was believed to be that of Queen Lara Kidul.

The news of Diponegoro's mystical experience spread like wildfire. Soon after, Diponegoro led a rebellion against the Dutch, but failed as the time was not ripe for a revolution. However, an uprising finally ousted the Dutch in 1945. When Diponegoro's insurrection failed, he was arrested by the Dutch and exiled to Manado on the island of Celebes, where he wrote his autobiography. Later he was brought to more habitable quarters in Makassar. His last years were spent in ascetic practices, in meditation and writing. In 1855 he died in Makassar. His grave became a shrine and has attracted many visitors and worshippers from all over Indonesia.

In Jogjakarta, the authorities made a Diponegoro Museum of the old residence of the hero. The museum has a big hall for theatrical performances and another smaller compound house where all the belongings and pusaka of Diponegoro are kept. An old painting by the Dutch attracted my attention. The scene was the place where the museum is now situated. In that painting, the houses were ablaze, having been set on fire by the Dutch, and Diponegoro was directing his relatives and supporters to escape through a hole in a solid brick wall. My guide, who was the caretaker of the museum, took me to the broken wall. He told me that Diponegoro had shattered the thick wall with his bare fists. Of course, it was not so much his magical powers but his courage to fight the Dutch colonialists that had won him the respect of the Indonesian people.

The Diponegoro Museum is also the meeting place for the Rumpum Diponegoro, the unit of all members of the Diponegoro Division headed by President Suharto. I was told that President Suharto himself grew up in a village very near the residence of Diponegoro.

Visiting the graves of heroes and kings is now common practice in Java. They go to these places to contact the souls of the heroes. In Solo, I met a guru called Pak Parno, who could teach people how to contact the souls of past heroes and kings. I witnessed how his disciples gathered together to contact the soul of King Mangkunegara I. The disciples pressed their left hands to their necks and their right hands to their left armpits and meditated. After fifteen minutes, one of them reported that he had established contact with the spirit of the King. Through him, the King said that he was pleased with our visit and that when I was at the grave, the King had touched my forehead and had provided me with a yellow umbrella over my head as a sign of welcome. This was of course myth to me but to them, they were real.

According to Pak Parno, the Javanese believe that spirits are like humans except for the physical body — they have thoughts, desires and feelings. Therefore, the ancestors continue to take an interest in their descendents so that the latter could gratify their desires through them. From the mystical point of view, the contact between the living and the dead was a matter of sending and receiving vibrations. Those who have been properly trained and have acquired mystical powers have stronger perception or more powerful "transmitters" to enable them to transmit and receive messages from the spiritual world. This was briefly the theory of mystics as explained to me by Pak Parno.

The spirits of past Javanese kings and heroes, as well as presidents and prime ministers are there for those who have strong mystical power to contact and consult. The Joyoboyo predictions still make an impact on the psyche of the Javanese today.

g) *Lara Kidul* and other Javanese legends

*"Come, Dewi Srengenge, A kingdom
awaits you. You will regain your beauty
and live forever" a voice from the watery
depths beckoned to the princess who was
to become Queen of the Indian Ocean."*

from *A Voice From Heaven*

In Indonesia, especially in Java, there are many myths and legends. The Javanese believe in myths and legends which influence the psyche of the Javanese and those who live in Java. Most Javanese legends are mystical and many concern the ocean, the volcanoes, rivers and the straits.

The most popular myth is that of Queen *Lara Kidul*, Queen of the Indonesian Ocean. It would be an exception if someone had not heard of Lara Kidul. Queen Lara Kidul is not only a legend or a myth. To most Javanese she is real. She dwells in the rough seas off the southern coast of Java. The legend tells of the relationship of the Queen to the royal family of Jogjakarta and Surakarta. This legend still influences the thinking of many Indonesian Javanese today.

I had a glimpse of the angry sea where Queen Lara Kidul is said to reside. The rocky cliffs that surround the winding coastline and the luxuriant vegetation are a feast for the artist's eye. The constant murmur of the sea and the roar of the rolling waves, now and then interrupted by the shrieks of giant birds, are an inspiration for the composer. The atmosphere is full of excitement and mystery, particularly for those who know the legend of Queen Lara Kidul.

Nyai Lara Kidul's maiden name was Dewi Srengenge, or Sun Maiden. Her beauty was unsurpassed. The King of Banyumas in Central Java fell in love with her and made her his favourite wife. This made one of his other wives, Dewi Kundati, jealous. So she employed an old wizard to use magical powers to turn Dewi Srengenge into an ugly and frightening creature. Dewi Srengenge was so distressed that she ran away.

As she wandered, she met a kind-hearted old man who listened to her story and took pity on her. The old man reported her story to the King, who immediately sentenced Dewi Kundati and the wizard to death. But no one could give back Dewi's beauty. In her sadness, she roamed from village to village until she finally reached the southern coast of West Java. At the beach near Samudra, she heard a voice calling, "Come, Dewi Srengenge. A kingdom awaits you. You will regain your beauty and live forever. Come." Lured by the voice, Dewi entered the sea and from then on was known as Lara Kidul, Queen of the Indian Ocean.

It happened that Nyai Lara Kidul had a beloved sister who had been searching for her. It was not long before her search led her to the same spot where Lara Kidul entered the sea. Grieving over the loss of her sister, she stood there sobbing when suddenly a voice made itself heard.

"You need a fish's tail if you wish to join your sister." Thereupon, Kidul's sister was transformed into a mermaid and she swam into the ocean to join her sister the queen in her watery palace.

This legend also serves to explain the etymology of the mermaid called *air mata duyong*, meaning "longing tears". Today, there is a kind of fish called *ikan duyung* which appears like a fish with tears.

However, the story of Lara Kidul does not end here. It is said that Senopati, King of the Mataram Empire, once went to the southern beach to meditate. Nyai Lara Kidul came to know of it and appeared before the King. A romantic version of the legend says that he was at once struck by her beauty, fell in love, and married her. Thus was established the tie between Queen Lara Kidul and the great royal house of Mataram. Another more prosaic version says that Lara Kidul promised to come to the aid of King Senopati and his royal descendents whenever they needed her service.

The deep spiritual significance of the union of Queen Lara Kidul and the King of Mataram can be witnessed during the Labuhan Ceremony still celebrated annually at the waters edge. The ceremony, which takes place one day after the birthday of the Sultan of Jogja, is to honour Queen Lara Kidul and to ask for her blessing on the

Sultan, his court and his people. Offerings are brought from the Sultan's palace to Parangsumo on the southern coast facing the Indonesian Ocean. The offerings include money, petals and female garments such as shawls and lengths of batik. There are also cuttings of the Sultan's hair and clippings of his fingernails. The offerings are first brought to the village of Kretek on the western bank of the river Opak early in the morning. They are then carried across the river and down to the village of Parangtritis at the waters edge. This is where Senopati, the sixteenth century Maratam ruler, was said to have met Lara Kidul. The offerings are then placed on a bamboo raft and cast out to sea by kraton officers. An enthusiastic crowd watches as the raft is tossed by the waves, throwing the offerings into the sea. When the offerings are eventually washed back to shore, spectators scramble to collect them, believing that they contain supernatural powers. The Sultan's hair and fingernail clippings however are buried in the sand in a special walled-in spot on the beach. These too are eventually dug up by spectators and kept as sacred souvenirs.

A ceremony of this nature was held on 21 June 1971 in conjunction with the celebration of the 61st birthday of Sultan Hamengkubuwono IX, who became Vice-President of the Republic of Indonesia when I was ambassador to the country. The offerings included a complete set of clothing for a princess — a *sarong*, a *kebaya* (blouse), *a selendang* (shawl) and an umbrella, in addition to food. Some people are prepared to pay high prices for these items of clothing or other offerings retrieved from the sea if the finders are willing to part with them. It is commonly believed that possession of these objects brings material as well as spiritual good fortune.

Today, the legend of Queen Lara Kidul is still very much a part of local traditions and beliefs. Whenever a swimmer is swept away by the treacherous waves along the Samudra Beach resort at Labuhan Ratu in West Java, local folklore has it that the Queen has taken another to join her entourage. Some years back an ambassador from an East-European country went for a swim there and never returned. During violent thunderstorms, villagers of nearby Sukabumi locked their windows, as they feared Queen Lara Kidul's display of her temper. On special occasions during court festivals, Queen Lara Kidul is again venerated in a palace dance called *Bedoyo Ketawang*.

East Java also has many legends. One of them concerns a perfumed river called *Banyuwangi*. There is a little town in East Java called Banyuwangi. This town becomes well-known because of its name, which is derived from this legend. I visited the town and found nothing very special about it except for its name.

The legend says that the Prime Minister to King Sindwaja, named Sidapaksa, once lived here. Sidapaksa married a beautiful woman whom he loved so much that even his own mother became jealous. She was determined to break up the marriage because her daughter-in-law was a commoner and she wanted her son to marry into royalty.

The Queen of Sindwaja was looking for a magic flower that could give her eternal youth and beauty. When Sidapaksa's mother heard about this, she saw it as an opportunity to break up her son's marriage. She convinced her son that, as Prime Minister, he should try to please the Queen by offering to go to Mount Ijen to look for the magic flower. At first Sidapaksa was reluctant to leave his wife, who was then pregnant, but finally he departed.

In his absence, his wife gave birth to a son. When the baby was only three days old, the mother-in-law quietly snatched him away and threw him into the river. When Sidapaksa's wife discovered her son missing, she rushed about the village searching for him in vain. She soon fell seriously ill. Meanwhile, Sidapaksa had succeeded in finding the magic flower for the Queen and was highly commended for his noble deed. He rushed home to share his happiness and success with his wife and new baby. But before he reached home, his mother had poisoned his mind with rumours that his wife had been unfaithful to him and that she had thrown the baby into the river. In a mad fury, he went to the sick wife and drew his kris, ready to stab her. Denying the allegations, she pleaded with him to bring her to the river to witness the truth for himself.

When she reached the river, she jumped into it and disappeared. Sidapaksa was shocked yet disappointed that he had still not learnt the truth. At that moment, two pure white lotus flowers — one large and one small — appeared on the surface of the water. The bigger lotus spoke, "Let your own son tells you the truth." The smaller lotus said, "Pak, it was your mother, my grandmother, who threw me into the river." The two flowers then disappeared into the waters of the river, leaving behind a fragrance which permeated the air throughout the village. And this explains the origin of the name of the river Banyuwangi.

It is strange that, like the Chinese, the Javanese also regard lotus as symbolising purity and cleanliness. Perhaps, like the Chinese, Javanese were also influenced by Buddhism which associates the lotus with purity.

There is also a legend about the strait that separates Java from Bali. Long long ago, there was a wealthy man called Sadimandara, who lived in Kediri in Java. Although he was rich, he was sad because he had no children. He went to the temple to pray for a son. Soon after, his wife gave birth to a boy and naturally the parents pampered the child and gave him whatever he wanted. The child grew up to be a hot-tempered man devoting his energy and time to gambling. He became a habitual gambler and spent all the savings of his parents and they became poor.

The father Sadimandara went to a cave in Gunung Agung, the biggest volcano in Java and worshipped by the people who pray for good luck. Inside the cave was a huge dragon with fiery eyes and a diamond in its tail. He prayed to the dragon and wished that his son would give up the gambling habit. The dragon took pity on Sadimandara and spat out a few pieces of gold from his mouth.

Sadimandara went back with the gold and gave one piece to his son making him promise that he would not gamble again. The son agreed, but soon he not only lost that piece of gold but went on to steal his father's gold hidden under his bed. His son then gambled away the fortune in a cock-fight. Out of desperation, Sadimandara went to ask the dragon for another favour. The dragon, as usual being kind-hearted, gave him a few more pieces of gold and asked him to be strict with his son. Again, he warned his son not to gamble, but the son could not change his habit. Sadimandara had no alternative but to chase the son out of the house.

The son, who became poor, went to the cave to pray to the dragon. When he saw the dragon had a diamond in its tail, he became greedy and wanted to steal the diamond. When the dragon asked him what he wanted, he said quite impolitely, "I come to collect some gold." The dragon replied, "Please wait". When the dragon turned away from him, he took out his kris and wanted to chop off the diamond in the tail of the dragon. The dragon attacked him and crushed him to pieces.

Sadimandara knew that his son might have gone to the cave and went there to look for him. When he arrived, he saw his son in a pool of blood and apparently dead. He cried over the corpse and begged the dragon to give his son a chance. The dragon, again out of a good heart, licked his son and he was alive again. Sadimandara and his son thanked the dragon whole-heartedly and the son finally gave up his gambling habit. He left the family and went to work with his own hands.

Sadimandara was feeling lonely and went about looking for his son and finally found him. He was trying to earn his living by farming. He was happy to see his son a changed man. He took a *changkul* (shovel) and started to dig a hole near his farm and prayed that water would flow into the farm. The hole soon widened and became the Straits of Bali, dividing Java from Bali.

There is another legend about the imperial flower called *wijaya kusuma* — which was a requirement for the crowning of a king on his coronation day. This was the flower which Suharto was looking for when he became President of Indonesia.

This is the origin of the wijaya kusuma:

There was once a cruel king of Java who had a dream just before he was crowned. He dreamt that there was an imperial flower called wijaya kusuma guarded by huge giants, which could only be found on an island off Nusa Kembangan, south of Java. He instructed his soldiers to organise a team to look for this flower. He told them that they would be killed if they could not bring back the flower. The soldiers took off for the island, but no one would dare approach the island. Then, a fisherman came along and said that he could help them if the King would reward him with a fishing boat and fishing nets, his having been eaten up by the giants who lived on the island. The soldiers promised that it would be done.

The fisherman daringly swam to the island and succeeded in stealing the flower. When the giants saw what he did, they threatened to kill him. He ignored their threat and dived deep into the sea to escape from them. The giants caught him and threw him into the ocean. Yet, he held tightly unto the flower. His body was swept to the shore with his hands still holding the flower. He told the soldiers to advise the king not to use the flower and not to eat it. With those words, he fell unconscious.

The soldiers brought the wijaya kusuma to the king, and conveyed to him the fisherman's warning not to use the flower. The king ignored the advice. In fact, he adorned his crown with the flower and the Queen stepped on it and asked his cook to prepare a dish for the coronation day. The Queen after taking the flower suddenly died of poisoning. The King asked the soldiers to look for the fisherman but he could not be found after 40 days of searching.

From then on, all Javanese kings dare not send troops to Nusa Kembangan in search of the wijaya kusuma.

Another legend tells the story of how a prince was turned into stone. The prince was Pajajaran. His stone image is in Gunung Sawal. The prince fell in love with a princess of the Langkakalin kingdom, who was a much-sought after beauty in those days. Her father wanted her to marry the king of Cirebon, but dared not offend Pajajaran because he was heir to a powerful kingdom.

In the palace of the princess was a seat of honour made of jade known as the "jade chair". Whoever sat on that seat would meet with disaster. The princess's father conceived a plot to spoil the marriage of her daughter to Pajajaran. When Pajajaran came to the palace with his rich dowries and slaves, he was asked to sit on that chair. When Pajajaran was about to sit on it, his advisers warned him not to do that because disaster would befall him. Then, he told his future father-in-law that he would sit on it after the marriage.

On the wedding day, Panjajaran forgot what his adviser had said and sat on the chair. That very moment, the princess was kidnapped and she was missing from the wedding. Panjajaran rode on a horse and went to Gunung Tjereme to look for her. At the foot of the mountain he met an old magician and asked for his flying horse. The old man told him that all his horses had been borrowed to fight a war. Panjajaran pleaded desperately and finally the old man asked him to close his eyes. With his magical power, he turned Panjajaran's horse into a flying horse. Panjajaran rode the flying horse to look for his bride. At the foot of the hill, he found six men lazing there. He asked one of them, "Have you seen the princess?". The man said, "She has been turned into a white pigeon and has flown away." He asked the others and they said she has become an angel, or a deer, or a female tiger eating a lamb, or that she had become an old and ugly woman and was already killed and thrown into the valley. Panjajaran was furious and slaughtered all the six men.

After he had done the killing, he began to regret what he had done and was about to ride his horse to continue the search when an old and ugly lady approached him and embraced him saying, "I am your wife, the princess." He could not believe his eyes and asked, "How can you be my wife? My wife is beautiful and you are so ugly." She jumped unto the horse and rode off with Panjajaran. On the way, she kicked him off the horse. His body became stiff and later turned into a stone. She wept over his dead body for 40 days. All the weaving thread she was holding became wet. She reached Telaga and appeared in day-time and continued weaving at night.

Till today, whenever there is moonlight, villagers in Telaga would hear the sound of weaving.

3
THE SUNDANESE
Pioneers of Islam in Java

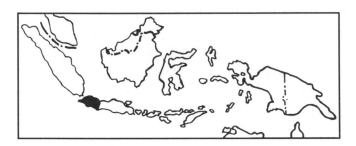

Indonesia's 39 million Sundanese comprising about 20 percent of the population live in a province with an area of about 44,118 square km stretching from Krakatoa to Cirebon. This area is historically and culturally rich with beautiful mountains, deep-green tea plantations, rugged wildlife reserves, lush botanical gardens, fertile rice paddies and the royal courts of Cirebon.

West Java is noticeably more mountainous than the rest of Java. The volcanic peaks of the region are tightly packed here, producing fragmented series of narrow upland valleys and plateaus that are difficult to access.

The province was historically named Sunda meaning "white". This referred to the white ash from volcanic eruptions which covers the land and renders the soil rich and fertile. West Java's volcanoes are exceedingly active. In 1982, there was an eruption in Galunggung causing the death of 20 people with damage estimated at US$25 million.

Sunda made its name in history when the Krakatoa volcano erupted on 27 August 1883 spewing up 20 cubic kilometres of rock and causing the island to collapse and disappear. The name Krakatoa comes from an old Sanskrit word *karkata* meaning "crab" (perhaps referring to the shape of the atolls once formed by the volcano's caldera). It lies in the middle of the Sunda Strait, right on the unstable "elbow" where the range of volcanic mountains forming Sumatra turns abruptly eastward to form Java. The resulting explosion of the volcano was catastrophic. Tons and tons of rocks and debris were hurled into the sky and some landed on Madagascar on the other side of the Indian Ocean. The blast was heard in Brisbane over 4,000 km away in Australia. The eruption wiped out 163 villages along the coast of western Java and southern Sumatra and rocked vessels as far away as the English Channel. No one knows the exact toll of the explosion in human lives, though the figure commonly cited is 35,000. Eyewitnesses described a wall of water "taller than a palm tree" sweeping away everything in its path. Renewed seismic activity was detected in 1979.

Although the metropolitan capital enclave of Jakarta is situated within the province, Sunda's capital is Bandung, situated in a cool mountain pleateau 180 km to the southeast. Large factories ring the cities and produce everything from textiles to computers. More than half of all the electricity produced in Indonesia is consumed here. The province also houses Indonesia's only aircraft factory and atomic reactor, along with a prestigious technological institute (ITB).

The first half of the 16th century saw the military expansion of the Muslim state of Demak and in 1524 Muslim power first made itself felt in West Java. During that year, Demak's leader, Sunan Gunung Jati, occupied the port of Banten and later Sunda Kelapa. Sunda Kelapa changed its name to Jakarta after the Indonesian independence. Gunung Jati became the first of the kings of Cirebon. He was a powerful figure, one of the nine *walis* or saints who spread Islam to Java and was closely associated with the rise of Cirebon to greatness and glory. As legend has it, he was the son of a Middle Eastern sultan by Cakrabuana's younger sister while going on a pilgrimage to Mecca with her brother. Born in Sumatra, as a young boy he was placed on the throne in Cirebon the moment he set foot on the soil. He was so pious that he developed a formidable following and became a respectable holy man. During the 16th century, which was the Golden Age of Islam in Java, Gunung Jati allied himself with powerful Demak and conquered the Hindu ports of Sunda and Banten which are on the western tip of Java. Gunung Jati died in 1568 leaving behind the Astana Gunung Jati which is the most famous Cirebon's attraction there. Sunan Gunung Jati was one of the original missionaries who brought Islam to Java and destroyed the Hindu Panjajaran Kingdom in Sunda by conquering Jakarta. He died after ruling the kingdom of Cirebon. His tomb is still one of the holiest places in Java. A series of courtyards are full of gravestones, all surrounding the holy tomb. This site is visited by both Indonesian and Chinese pilgrims.

Demak was the most powerful Muslim kingdom situated about 26 km east of Semarang and was instrumental in bringing Islam to the rest of Java. Its rise to importance was partly due to a ready supply of teakwood from nearby forests and the great skill of its shipwrights. The kingdom was founded during the end of the 15th century by a Chinese Muslim known in history as Raden Patah. His son, Raden Trenggana, ascended the throne around 1505 and succeeded in subjugating not only the inland kingdoms of Kediri/Majapahit, but all the major ports on the coast. Trenggana was killed around 1546 during a military campaign, and Demak's hegemony waned and did not outlive him.

Legendary accounts of Demak's rise and "Islamisation" of the inland kingdoms was attributed to the role played by the court's spiritual adviser, Sunan Kalijaga. He is said to have used *wayang kulit* performances to teach Islam to the masses, and to have played gamelan music in the mosque to attract their attendance. In those days, some Muslims felt that he was doing something heretical. Sunan Kalijaga was also accredited with developing the Islamic court festivals of Grebeg and Sekaten, both of which incorporate elements of earlier Hindu-Buddhist court rites. These are today major events in the ritual calendars of the Jogja, Solo and Cirebon palaces. Grebeg is still celebrated in Demak on Muslim festival occasions when mountains of food are carried from the Kabupaten district offices to the mosque. After being blessed, the food morsels are eagerly snatched up for their putative talismanic powers. This belief is entirely Hindu-Buddhistic and not Islamic. Sunan Kalijaga's grave lies in Kadilangu, 2 km southeast of Demak, and is visited by thousands of pilgrims each year.

Although Demak is Java's first great Islamic kingdom, the people still pay great emphasis on its links with the earlier kingdom of Majapahit. Raden Patah is conventionally described as the son of Majapahit's last king by a Chinese princess, while Sunan Kalijaga is said to be the son of a Majapahit nobleman.

These links can be seen in the Grand Mosque, situated in the square of the city and regarded as the holiest mosque in Java. Muslims who pay homage to this mosque seven times is equivalent to pay respect to Mecca once.

Sunan Gunung Jati's marriage to a Chinese must have taken place after the visit to Cirebon and Demak by the famous Chinese Admiral Cheng Ho, a Muslim eunuch. Admiral Cheng Ho brought some Chinese brides from China as "gifts" and married them to Javanese sultans.

For those interested in Chinese influence in Indonesia, Cirebon is also an interesting place to visit, for Chinese legacy is embodied in the elaborate designs found here of phoenixes, cranes and peonies. I visited Kraton Kasepuhan, a palace which was built by the founder of Cirebon, Sunan Gunung Jati. The palace was decrepit over the centuries until 1928, when it was restored by a Dutch archeologist. I walked through the split red-brick candi bentar into the kraton (palace), and saw ornate Chinese carved tigers guarding the kraton's front gateway.

Cirebon is perhaps the only major port in Indonesia which has survived until today with its palaces and royal buildings intact. Indeed, these are the oldest surviving courts on the island of Java, founded some three centuries before Jogjakarta or Solo. It is located in a strategic position, providing a crossroad between Hinduism and Islam. During the Hindu times, Cirebon was the principal port of the powerful Sundanese kingdom of Galuh, whose capital lies to the south in the fertile Citanduy River valley around present-day Citamis. The word Cirebon is translated as "Shrimp River" and the town has adopted the name "Prawn City". According to historical record, however, the name Cirebon derives from the word *caruban*, meaning "mixing" or "mingling" — a testament to Cirebon's highly heterogeneous heritage. Cirebon has a deep Hindu past. It became a major power only after the arrival of Islam. In fact, it was the first Islamic state in Java, even before Gresik and Demak.

To understand the rise of Islam and the gradual fall of the Hindu empire, one must visit Cirebon, an ancient precolonial port town near the border of West and Central Java. Cirebon is the meeting point of the Sundanese and Javanese cultures with a local dialect which is a blend of the two.

The Chinese influence came about because Sunan Gunung Jati took a Chinese bride named Ong Tien who died three years after arriving in Java. She stayed with Sunan in a three-storey red brick and concrete grotto which was called Taman Sunyaragi. This house is still referred to locally as "the pleasure gardens of the Chinese Princess". At that time, the building was adorned with cascading waterfalls and the area landscaped with small lakes and gardens.

The name Gua Sunyaragi means "Place of Isolation". In Hindu-Javanese history, remote sites were traditionally used by royalty for seeking inner knowledge and strength or as testing places where believers practised a form of spiritual discipline. In these secret chambers practitioners were taught such ascetic pursuits as meditation and military science.

Sunyaragi later became the site of a weapons workshop and armoury. Legend has it that partisans against the Dutch regime operated out of Sunyaragi during and after the Diponegoro war (1825-30) when the whole structure was turned into a guerrilla post. When the Dutch learned of their plans, they destroyed all the decorations and statues. In 1853, Sunyaragi was restored and redesigned by a Chinese architect in a curious Chinese architectural style.

Banten was then a state independent from the control of the great Javanese power Mataram. Banten, located 80 km to the west of Jakarta on Java's northwestern shore was the largest and most important spice trading entrepot in all of Southeast Asia during the 16th and early 17th century — rivaling even Amsterdam in size and importance in its heyday. Today, it remains a small fishing village.

Banten is well-known in the world for its short-legged bantam hen called ayam katik, and a historical relic of the advent of Islam in Java. Banten was one of Java's two dominant states in the 17th century. Ruins of the once great Islamic kingdom can still be seen in the town. I visited the Istana Kaibon — the royal palace with a heavily fortified compound and archways. There is a main gate and massive four-metre-high crumbing walls built around what is now a completely pastoral setting. I saw ruins of Chinese temples and an old minaret inside the grounds.

Banten was powerful and wealthy in the 16th century when it became the centre of the pepper trade between India and the spice islands. It was a prominent city in West Java's history. As early as 1300 A.D. Banten was the site of a seaport belonging to the ancient kingdom of Sunda, whose capital, Pajajaran, lay in the interior near present-day Bogor. When the Portuguese arrived in Banten at the beginning of the 16th century, Sunda was still a Buddhist country. A commonality of interest led the Portuguese and the ruler of Panjajaran to forge an alliance against the encroaching forces of Islam. However, a Muslim army from Denmak invaded Sunda in 1525 and quickly subdued the ports, though the inland capital was not conquered until 1578. Banten then became the capital of a new Islamic trading kingdom, and soon became the principal spice trading port in Java.

How was West Java Islamised? This is a controversial question. Many conclude that the coastal region of West Java was Islamised by people from the Middle East. There is however another theory that it was Admiral Cheng Ho, the Muslim eunuch who visited Cirebon and Banten during his seven voyages to Southeast Asia and the Middle East that brought Islam to Java. During Cheng Ho's early expeditions, his 63 treasure ships carried among others, Cheng Ho as the imperial eunuch, six grand eunuchs, ten high ranking eunuchs and 53 minor eunuchs. All of them were Muslims. Some of the crews took their wives, concubines and children with them. The impact of so many Muslim eunuchs in West Java could have been great. They might have gone down to the shores to preach the Islamic religion. For instance, when they arrived, it was puasa (fasting) month, and when the local people discovered that they were not eating during the day, they started asking for the reason. They were told of the significance of fasting and the essense of the Islamic religion.

Recently, there have been publication of articles and books producing controversial evidence about the spread of Islam to West Java. Some even said some of the nine *walis* and rulers of Demak were actually Muslim Chinese. Among the leaders of the *santri* (orthodox) community, this theory would not be acceptable. But the impact of the Chinese influence in West Java can be seen both in the architecture, in the old *kelenteng* (temple) and the various Chinese antiques found in the Cirebon palace, as well as the notable Sam Po (Cheng Ho's honorific name) temple in Semarang with the syncreticism of Chinese and Javanese cult figures.

Before the demise of the Demak in the early 17th century, two powers arrived in the Java political scene to compete for supremacy. One was the inland Kingdom of Mataram founded by Senopati which rapidly conquered under the leadership of its ruler Agung. He introduced the Javanese Islamic calendar and obtained from Mecca the title of sultan. The other was the Dutch who founded the Dutch East Indies Company (VOC) in 1602 and established a trading post on the northwest coast of Java at Banten in 1603.

The Dutchmen came in 1602 and later in 1603 the British appeared. There was much rivalry between the Dutch and the British. The Dutch finally expelled the British in 1683. In 1684, the Dutch destroyed the sultan's forces in Banten and consolidated their power. By the 19th century, Banten became a backwater fishing village.

The sultanate of Banten was so rebellious toward the Dutch that it became known as "The Aceh of Java". The Bantenese are still a proud and culturally distinct people. They are real orthodox Muslims and practise strict Islamic rules. When I visited the place, I saw the schoolgirls veiled in white shawls. Many men in Banten claim to have special magical powers that protect them from cuts and slashes. They also claim to be able to perform feats of emerging unscathed after being buried alive. They also show their invulnerability by eating glass fragments, cutting their tongues, rolling over barbed wires and other magical stunts. They can control fear, pain, the heat of fire and sharpness of weapons. They peform a sort of dance by religious ascetics known as *nayaga*.

In Banten, I also visited a newly renovated *kelenteng* (Chinese temple) which is 200 years old. It was a gift from the sultan to the Chinese community in gratitude for their help in supplying medicine to curb a malaria epidemic.

Because of their proximity to the Dutch capital of Batavia (present Jakarta), the Sundanese are more influenced by Western culture though more Islamic than their Javanese neighbours. They are a proud people, more jovial, more relaxed, more outspoken, cheerful and happy-go-lucky. They do not share the same cultural values or act the same way as the Javanese. They speak a different language from the Javanese, Madurese or Jakarta Malay spoken on the rest of the island, and have artistic traditions — including some of the most intricate drumming heard anywhere in the traditional world. Ancient Sundanese kingdoms flourished in West Java from the 5th century, but left behind few stone monuments due to the isolation and sparse population of the region in the old days.

The Sundanese capital, Bandung, is Indonesia's third largest metropolis. It is the administrative and commercial centre of West Java, easily the most Europeanised of all Indonesian towns. It has over 2 million to 4 million population if the surrounding towns are taken into consideration. The city is situated on a high plateau at an altitude of 768 metres (2,500 feet) surrounded on all sides by brooding volcanoes and lofty mountain ridges. It boasts of many universities and academies including the prestigious Bandung Institute of Technology. A centre for monitoring Indonesia's volcanoes and a nuclear research station are also situated there. Bandung rivals Jakarta as the home of artists, writers and academics. The most daring artistic and political movements germinate among Bandung's progressive student population. The Siliwangi division based there has always been regarded as Indonesia's most technically skilled and best disciplined army unit.

The Dutch found Bandung an ideal place for relaxation and made the town the holiday resort for the colonial masters. Therefore, the region is well endowed with old colonial estates and buildings — now dilapidated. West Java remained under more direct Dutch colonial control, right up till independence in 1949, than the rest of Indonesia.

Several racial groups of Indonesia are indigenous to this part of Java. The interior plateau of West Java is called the Prinagan, heartland of the Sundanese who make up the majority of the province's population of 39 million. Of all the peoples of Java, the Sundanese are closest to the Malays. Bandung is acclaimed for the beauty of its women. Because of the cool climate, they have a lighter complexion than the other Indonesians, and the Sundanese diet featuring raw vegetables, is said to confer them soft skin. Bandung ladies are fashion conscious and the city is known as "Paris of the East".

In Bandung, the authorities have erected a Museum Konperensi (Conference Museum) in the Merdeka Building on Jalan Asia Afrika to commemorate the Afro-Asian Conference of 1955. Whenever I visit Bandung, I always try to visit the Museum to remember the days when I covered the conference. The pictures on the wall of Sukarno, Chou En-lai of China, Nehru of India, U Nu of Burma, Ho Chi Ming of Vietnam and Nasser of Egypt, remind me of my contacts with them. The building itself dates from 1879 and was originally the "Concordia Societeit" a meeting hall of Dutch associations and the centre of high society.

The Savoy Hofmann Hotel where the Afro-Asian delegates stayed were classic art-deco confections. The tree-lined neighbourhoods of Jalan Juanda and Jalan Cipanganti were showcases of colonial suburban life. Bandung has been the cultural and intellectual centre since the end of the last century. I stayed at Savoy after the Afro-Asian delegates had left.

During World War II, Bandung was the main defence position of the Dutch government. The Japanese captured the Allied headquaters here on 7 March 1942. During the struggle for independence, Sukarno first emerged as a nationalist leader at the Bandung Institute of Technology.

Because of the numerous universities and colleges, Bandung attracts some of Indonesia's brighest students It is a youthful city and a haven for academics and intellectuals. Bandung student leaders pride themselves on being the most radical in all of Indonesia, claiming to be the catalyst for nationwide student protests and strikes. Youth groups are constantly agitating for social and political changes, regularly disseminating their progaganda in vituperative underground print and broadcast media. Even in the struggle to bring down the Suharto regime in 1998, Bandung students also staged demonstrations in May to echo the student riots in Jakarta.

As the Sundanese are more influenced by Islam, there are more Muslim fundamentalists in West Java. West Java was therefore the base of extreme Muslim fundamentalists. At the inception of the Indonesian army to fight the Dutch in 1945, the Japanese trained Pembela Tanah Air (Beta) or the Motherland Defence Force, which comprised soldiers recruited predominantly from the youth with priyayi and the abangan backgrounds. Both the Japanese and the Javanese shared a distrust of the santri Muslim militancy. The Japanese, however, also built up an army consisting of the santri known as Hizubullah — the army of the Allah. The Hizubullah also fought against the Dutch from 1945 to 1949. In 1947, sections of the guerrilla movement took on a new name, Darul Islam, or House of Islam, and established their own armed faction called the Indonesian Islamic Army.

Sometime in 1949, the Darul Islam based in West Java and headed by Sekar Madji Kartosuwiryo refused to submit to the control of the regular army and proclaimed a separate Islamic state. Kartosuwiryo was unhappy with the central government led by Sukarno because he thought it violated the principle of Islam to declare Indonesia a secular state. The Darul Islam insurgency received the support of rebels in Aceh and later South Sulawesi and other areas. The insurgency went on until 1962 when Kartosuwiryo was captured and executed. However, the Darul Islam movement reappeared with the establishment of the Islamic State of Indonesia. Their activities were concentrated in both Aceh and South Sulawesi. It opened the eyes of Indonesian abangan leaders to the danger of the modernist Muslim's aspiration The fanatical *Darul Islam* was based on the hills south of Bandung, from which it waged its Holy War against the unfortunate peasants in the name of an Islamic Republic. Hardly a day passed without reports in the papers of villages being looted, houses burnt and men killed by these ideological "revolutionaries".

Although Sunda is within Java, the Sundanese do not like to be called Javanese. Even though there are still traces of Hindu-Buddhist remains and scattered relics in Sunda, the Hindu-Buddhist influence is not so strong among the Sundanese.

The Sundanese are different from the Javanese. They have their own distinct non-Javanese culture. The Sundanese tend to be easier-going and more enlightened than the more refined, hierarchical and aloof Javanese. They are also more strongly Islamised. They have their own form of dreamy melancholic music and evocative poetic imagery literature. They have their own language and writing, with numerous levels of formal address — a legacy of the Hindu kingdoms which held sway here from the 8th to 16th centuries.

A Sundanese generally does not want to be called a Javanese. There is a historical reason behind this. When I attended the Afro-Asian Conference, I was surprised to discover that there is not a single street named after Gajah Mada, the famous Prime Minister of the Majapahit Empire. My Sundanese friend explained to me why they had refused to name a street after Gajah Mada. It seems there was an unfortunate incident involving Gajah Mada and the Sundanese royal family. The young King Hayam Wuruk of East Java wished to marry the daughter of the King of Sunda. After negotiations were conducted by Gajah Mada, an invitation was extended to the Sundanese King to visit the Majapahit capital with his daughter. The Sundanese were proud that the daughter of their King was to become the official queen of the mighty Majapahit Empire. The wedding would have meant an alliance between the two kingdoms, whereby the poor state of Sunda might share some of the wealth of its eastern neighbour. But Gajah Mada wanted the King of Sunda to deliver his princess to the royal harem as a tribute from a vassal to his overlord. The Sundanese, being a proud people, refused and a battle ensued in which the Sudanese King was killed. According to the story, the princess killed herself on the battlefield beside her father's body. After that massacre, rancour and hostility existed between the Javanese and the Sundanese, and the latter never submitted to Gajah Mada's authority.

The highland of Bandung is the Prinagan or Parahyangan (from *para* — meaning many and *hyang* meaning "god") which may be roughly translated as "Abode of the Gods". This is the sacred Sundanese homeland — a tangled and cone-isolated series of peaks and valleys stretching from Bogor in the west to Ciamis in the east.

Thousands of years ago, a cataclysmic eruption of Mt. Tangkuban Perahu dammed the Citarum River, forming a vast lake where Bandung's central square now is, to a depth of 30 metres of water. Two millennia later, an earthquake opened a crack in the side of the valley and allowed the lake to slowly drain, leaving behind fertile alluvial deposits and swampy ponds that have since been filled in. Ringing the valley is an array of dramatic volcanoes, many of them sputtering and boiling with sulphurous hot springs, solfataras and fumaroles. This is where Tangkuban Perahu is situated.

Tangkuban Perahu carries a Sundanese legend. Long, long ago, the country of Prinagan in West Java was covered with forest where wild animals were free to roam. There was a powerful king called Raden Sungging Perbangkara. This king had an unusual relationship with a wild boar which gave birth to a beautiful daughter named Dewi Rara Sati. Dewi loved to sit in the mountainous forest knitting while admiring the scenery of lush valleys below. One hot day, as she was knitting at the top of a mountain, she dozed off and one of her knitting needles fell into the valley. As she treasured her knitting, Dewi Rara Sati promised to marry whoever could retrieve the needle. A dog by the name of Si Tumang heard Dewi's pledge and rushed into the valley to look for the needle. After a long search, he found it and returned it to her. In order to keep her promise, Dewi was obliged to marry Si Tumang. A year later, she gave birth to a son who was named Sangkuriang. Mother and son lived happily together, and Sangkuriang never knew the identity of his father, Si Tumang, the dog or his grandmother, the boar.

Dewi was very proud of the boy because he was a good hunter and often brought home the hearts of mouse deer for dinner. One evening, Sangkuriang could not get a deer, but instead wounded a wild-boar which happend to be the mother of Dewi. Fortunately for Dewi, her boar-mother escaped into the forest. Sangkuriang then asked the dog Si Tumang to chase after the wild-boar, but Tumang stubbornly refused. In great anger and desperation, he shot Tumang instead and brought Dewi Tumang's heart and lied to his mother that it was the heart of a deer. His mother soon discovered that it was the heart of Si Tumang, her husband and the father of Sangkuriang. She went into a fit of rage, took a *tongkat* (walking stick) and hit her son on the forehead. He left the house with a bleeding wound, not to return for many years.

Sangkuriang grew into a fine young man. One day he happened to come by a mountain and did not recognise that it was his birthplace. There he saw a beautiful woman and fell in love with her. It was Dewi Rara Sati, his mother, who had managed to keep her youth all these years. When they were about to marry, Dewi accidentally discovered the wound on the forehead of the young man and immediately realised that he was her son. She did not disclose her identity but secretly determined not to marry him. She told him she would marry him only if he could fulfill one condition to prove his worth. She gave him an impossible task of digging a lake out of the mountain and building a boat before sunset so that they could sail on their honeymoon.

Love worked wonders and when Sangkuriang had almost accomplished the task, Dewi became alarmed. She used her magical powers to change the colour of the sky from blue to crimson, and sunset soon turned to twilight before Sangkuriang could finish the boat. He, in turn, was so angry that he turned the half-completed boat upside down. As he did that, the earth shook and trembled and the mountain erupted fiery lava which swept both Dewi and Sangkuriang away in the volcanic streams. Today, the live volcano looks like a capsized boat.

Whenever I visited Bandung, I never miss the opportunity to view Tangkuban Perahu which is also known as Sangkuriang. My first visit there was in 1955 as a journalist to the Bandung Conference. It is one of the places I like to visit, not because I like the smell of sulphur which pervades the atmosphere, but because it is cool, pleasant and gives one a feeling of calm despite the hot, bubbling lava in the volcano below.

I often think of the legend of Sangkuriang and ponder over its significance — the relationship between a king and a wild boar, then that between a beautiful princess and a dog, and later between mother and son, a remarkably strange but interesting legend which seems to have a theme. There is throughout the story a conflict between fulfilment of desire and keeping it a secret. The king keeps a secret about his wife who was a wild boar, the princess about her relationship with her dog-husband, and finally the mother tries to keep the secret of her identity from her son. Secret relationships and hidden truths lead to human tragedy.

Another place which was chosen by the Dutch colonialists for an excellent retreat was Bogor, 60 km south of Jakarta situated between the Ciliwung and Cisadane rivers. In 1745, while the Dutch Governor-General for the Dutch East Indies Company, Baron Gustaf Willem van Imhoff, was making a duty tour of the upper interior territories, he became fascinated by the peaceful village of Bogor. He built a small resthouse there and named it *Buiternzog* (Without A Care). He used it as a retreat from his busy social life and government responsibility in Batavia (Jakarta). Over the years, the humble resthouse has developed into a splendid colonial palace. Huge glamorous parties were held there attended by the elite from all over Indonesia. Whenever I visited the palace, I was always attracted by spotted deer herd roaming the undulating lawns under big shady trees. Experts say the womb of young deer makes good aphrodisiac. This was an item which was well sought after by Sukarno.

In 1950, the palace was taken over by the Indonesian Government. Sukarno used it as his retreat. The palace interior covers an area of about 14,000 square metres and the grounds cover 24 hectares. Inside the mansion are sumptuously-appointed rooms, lavish reception chambers and a fabulous international collection of art all belonging to and collected by Sukarno during his political career. Being half Balinese, Sukarno fancied himself an art connoisseur. He had collected many incredible paintings by some of Indonesia's most renowned painters, a few of which were said to have been "improved" by him to suit his taste. There are about 219 paintings and 136 sculptures, many of voluptuous nudes representing different races. Sukarno's private collection of erotic paintings and sculptures is locked in a special room.

Sukarno signed away his power to his successor Suharto in this palace. Suharto called the handover of power the *Super Semar* act. Suharto had always wanted to regard himself as "Semar", the ugly but powerful clown of the Mahabharata epic.

During Suharto's 32-year reign of Indonesia, he never stayed a single night in this palace because Sukarno's ghost is said to haunt the corridors at night.

The Kebun Raya Botanical Garden in Bogor is another pride of West Java. The 87-hectare garden is one of the world's leading botanical institutions and has been an important scientific research centre for over 170 years. This world famous garden was the inspiration of the Dutch Governor-General Van Der Capellan, who expanded a garden established in 1911 by Sir Stamford Raffles, an avid botanist. Today, one of the garden's main task is to continue to collect and maintain living plants, with special interest in those that have economic potential. The very first specimen of oil palm introduced into Indonesia in 1848 is still growing in the gardens. This is the ancestor of the high-grade oil palms now cultivated throughout Indonesia and Malaysia, a crop which is to this day one of Indonesia's main exports. This was an item well sought after by Sukarno.

The first Sundanese leader I met when I became Ambassador to Indonesia was the governor of Jakarta, Ali Sadikin. Tall and handsome,

Ali Sadikin was bold and daring, rather outspoken and frequently took unpleasant measures to improve the city. Jakarta was then only a big sprawling village. With his dynamic and charismatic personality, he pushed ahead to make Jakarta into a modern city. I remembered the days when he took steps to drive away the trishaw riders from the city and force the attap dwellers to move to highrise buildings. Once noisy and foul-smelling with overcrowded streets and open sewers, today it has been transformed into a rapidly modernised mega-city with tall skyscrapers.

Another prominent Sundanese is the present "czar" of economics and finance in Indonesia, Ginandjar Kartasasmita, who was one of those who got the cabinet to oust Suharto.

Sundanese have a rich tradition of performing arts. With an orchestra comprising the *angklung* (bamboo percussion instrument) and the mournful *kecapi suling* (lute and flute music), the music played is very soothing and dreamy. The *kecapi* is a type of lute which is plucked and the *suling* is a soft-toned bamboo flute which fades in and out of the long vibrating notes of the *kecapi*.

The *angklung* was first introduced to Singapore by Pak Kasur, the leader of a cultural delegation which came to Singapore in 1960 when Singapore first achieved independence. I was then Parliamentary Secretary to the Ministry of Culture and I went to Clifford Pier to welcome the delegation. Pak Kasur's visit was the result of an earlier delegation led by Lee Kuan Yew to pay respect to President Sukarno who was then at the height of his power after we gained self-government. I remember Pak Kasur brought the orchestra to the Prime Minister's office at the City Hall and there played a new tune *Geylang si paku Geylang* with the *angklung*. The angklung later became popular in Singapore schools.

Another traditional Sundanese music form is the *gamelan degung*. It is played by a small ensemble similar to the Javanese gamelan with the addition of the degung, which is a set of small suspended gongs, and the suling. It is found only in Sunda. It is less soporific but more rhythmic than the Javanese gamelan but not as dramatic as the Balinese gamelan. It has a wider range, spanning some three octaves.

The ensemble includes a short, four-holed bamboo flute called the suling degung. The purely instrumental repertoire from the courts is now rarely played.

Like the degung, the *kecapi* (zither) is unique to Sunda. There are two types. One is more "classical"; the instrument resembles a boat and is called *kecapi perahu* (boat) with an elegantly curled prow and stern. The other type which is less refined is called *kecapi kawih*, which looks like a regular rectangular box. It is less expensive and normally used by buskers, many of whom are blind.

The Sundanese are also well-known for their *Jaipongan* which is modern music and dance. It is popular in Bandung and Jakarta. Jaipongan features dynamic drumming coupled with *erotic* and sometimes combined with dance movements of *pencak silat* (Indonesian martial arts). Jaipongan was derived from a more traditional Sundanese dance called *ketuktilu*, previously performed by female dancers (sometimes prostitutes) to entertain male spectators. *Jaipongan* songs are always interspersed with the older ketuktilu.

The Sundanese also have their wayang kulit called wayang golek. The Sundanese prefer their own shadow play to that of the Javanese. It was first used for Muslim propaganda. In the early 19th century, a Sundanese prince of Sumedang had a set of wooden puppets made to correspond exactly to the wayang kulit puppets of the Javanese courts. With these, he was able to perform the Hindu epics with the traditional splendour of his rivals but at the same time preserve his regional identity by using puppets long associated with anti-Javanese art.

The Sundanese also perform the Ramayana and Mahabharata, but their favourite clown is the red-faced *Cepot*, who always put on slapstick comic relief and social commentary. Cepot often has a cigarette drooping from his mouth.

Just as Bali is well-known for its cockfighting, Madura for its bull racing, Toraja for its bull-fighting and Central Java for its *jangkrik* fighting, West Java is a land well-known for its ram fighting called *adu domba*. Ram fighting has been a tradition in West Java for hundreds of years. It has become so popular as a folk game that every village has its own ram fighting society. The societies are so well organised that their influence extends from the grassroots level to the provincial level.

The West Java provincial administration now has a provincial Federation of Ram Fighting Societies called the Persadom (Persatuan Dombak Adu Domba). Visitors can easily see a ram fight on Sundays in any one of the villages of West Java. Once a fortnight, a tournament is held at the village level. The best rams are chosen for the grand show of the provincial ram fighting tournament which the Governor attends. I was told that the West Java Governor himself owns a strong ram of which he is very proud of.

I saw a ram fight one afternoon in Cikalong, a village about two hours drive from Jakarta. Like other villages, Cikalong has a community ram fight shed constructed of wooden poles and a roof thatched with palm leaves. There are no walls, only pillars. The sound of drums and gongs played by little children attracted us. A small crowd had gathered to watch the show. It was a weekly affair. I saw two rams, one brown and one white, being dragged to the centre of the shed. The rams seemed to nod at each other and then retreated simultaneously to a distance of about ten feet apart. They stared at each other for a few seconds, lowered their horns, charged and then there was literally a head-on clash. The horns banged, followed by the sound of the gong. A second retreat took place, then another clash, accompanied by drums, gongs and hand clapping. At the end of the third bang, the white ram appeared dazed and stayed motionless, apparently unable to back off for another charge.

The crowd booed and shouted the name of the ram, provoking it to continue the fight. The owner went forward, took hold of the ram and started to massage it from head to tail, including its testicles. He lifted its front legs and then the hindlegs. Minutes later, the fight continued, but the white ram was too weak to carry on any more clashes and ran away.

Although I saw no betting at the Cikalong ram fight, I was told that betting was more rampant at the district and provincial ram fights. When a ram is killed in the fight, the earnings from the bets go to buy the owner another ram. This, the organiser explained, was in the spirit of *gotong royong* (mutual help). After all, it was more for fun than for gambling. The objective was to encourage farmers to rear a better and stronger breed of ram.

The West Javanese ram is an unusual type of animal. It has the face of a timid sheep with long curling horns. The body and hips resemble an Alsatian dog. It has woolly fur on its head but its coat is well-cropped at the back. A good fighting ram can fetch a price as high as half a million rupiahs (then about US$1,000). Like the heroes of the bull races of Madura and other game fights, the champion ram also becomes the pet of the village, especially the children. At the time I saw the fight, the village of Cigarut was producing the best breed of rams. Once a year, handsome prizes are presented to the village which produces the best ram. This is judged by the Provincial Ram Fight Federation.

The well-organised ram fights of West Java reflect the thriving spirit of *gotong royong* in the tightly-knit village community. Ram fights are always held in an atmosphere of fun and gaiety, truly revealing the temperament of the Sundanese.

4

THE BADUIS
The Isolationists

Touch not the dirty hands of civilisation
Be pure and loyal to nature's salvation

a Badui saying

Whilst I was driving through the outskirts of a town called Banten which was considered the centre of Islam one evening, I saw an old man walking alone. It was getting dark as the sun had set and the road was quiet and isolated. I stopped to ask the old man whether I could give him a lift. With a polite smile, he answered, "No, thank you." He was wearing a peculiar black costume rarely seen in Jakarta. He had a white turban on his head quite similar to that worn by the Sikhs and was barefooted. As he walked along, he held on firmly to a parcel wrapped in black cloth.

I asked my Indonesian friend who was travelling with me, "Why did he refuse to take a lift from me? Don't you think it is rather late for an old man to be walking alone on this deserted road?". My friend said, "He is a Badui and it is taboo for a Badui to ride in a car, on a bicycle or use any other means of transportation invented by modern civilisation. The Baduis are anti-civilisation. He is on his way to the mountain range of Kendeng in the mountains off West Java where the Baduis live." All Baduis have to travel on foot and be barefooted as well.

My friend told me that the Baduis are also prohibited by their tribal laws from touching anything that is associated with modern civilisation. Consequently, they have no furniture in their homes — no chairs, no tables, not even a toothbrush, comb or mirror. The Baduis are also against the "civilised" methods of irrigation for farming as they believe that the process of irrigation would harm the soil. They depend entirely on God-sent rain. Most surprising, however, is that education itself is also taboo to the Baduis.

Yet, the Baduis are by no means uncivilised. They have inherited from their ancestors very austere laws of behaviour and moral standards. For instance, a Badui does not normally remarry after his wife dies and will always cherish the memory of her. The Baduis must adhere to a rigid code of ethics somewhat similar to the Ten Commandments. They are one of the most puritanical peoples still living in this world and try truly to make peace with nature. They believe that their God is the only true God.

That was the first time I came to know about the Baduis. I began to take an interest in this minority group which have lived in isolation since the advent of Islam to Indonesia. Sometime in 1523, when the Muslim religion swept into West Java, a group of people who are believed to be the descendents of the old Kingdom of Pajajaran refused to be converted to Islam. Now commonly referred to as the Baduis, these people escaped to the mountains, taking with them their own well-preserved religion and way of life.

The Baduis, then numbering about 800, were pursued by Sultan Yusof, who became the successful leader of the religious war, and later by his son, Pangeran Yusuf. The Muslim victors would pardon no one who refused to embrace Islam. So the Baduis retreated to the hills and finally settled down in an area on a mountain called Gunung Badui. Perhaps the name "Badui", came from the name of the mountain or the nearby river. The Baduis, however, do not like that name, and prefer to be called Orang Kanekes, or Orang Rawajan after the names of the villages where they now live.

From the time the Baduis settled down in Rawajan Village, they have isolated themselves from civilisation as we know it. As far as they are concerned, life is the same as it was in 1523. The Islamisation of Java, followed by the three hundred years of Dutch colonisation and then the fervent Indonesian revolution, did not affect the Baduis. They seemed to show little concern over matters of the outside world. To them, the most important thing was to be left alone to live their own way of life and to ensure that their sacred boundary was not infringed upon. Their zone was officially recognised through treaties with the Sultan of Banten and was later acknowledged by the Dutch Government for more than one hundred years.

Since 1822, Dutch scholars, colonial officials, missisonaries, and later Indonesian Government officials have from time to time tried to do research on the Baduis. Various reports have been submitted together with recommendations to improve the lot of the Baduis or persuade them to accept certain benefits offered by modern civilisation. But the Baduis prefer to remain where they are and be what they are.

So far, only very few people from the outside world have had the privilege of being allowed into Badui Dalam, the inner zone of Badui territory, which is still sacredly guarded. And only a handful of outsiders, including former President Suharto, have come face to face with any of the three top chieftains of the Baduis, known as pu'uns, who have not left the soil of Badui Dalam since they were born. The ardent desire of the Baduis to live in isolation and the strict rules guarding entry into their sacred land, therefore, make the task of research workers immensely difficult.

Most researchers have managed to get only to the outer area of Badui land. Badui Dalam is strictly guarded — not so much by armed guards or vigilante corps but by natural obstacles. The inner zone, or zone forbidden to outsiders, is surrounded by such dense jungle that it is almost impossible to get even near it. It is commonly believed that the Baduis, particularly the pu'uns and their dukuns, have magical powers as well as such keen instincts that they would know immediately whenever a stranger sets foot on the soil of their sacred land. Without first seeking their permission and blessing, it would be dangerous to venture into this zone.

The shyness and reticent nature of the Baduis concerning contact with the outside world also contribute to the obstacles encountered by researchers. I myself tried to arrange a visit with the help of several contacts, one who had blood ties with the Baduis and even held high positions in the government. He was then the Secretary General of the Ministry of Foreign Affairs. But, after some effort, he gave up the attempt to arrange the visit. I, however, managed to gather some useful information regarding the Baduis by visiting the outer zone of Badui and interviewing Baduis who had grown up in the inner zone. Those I interviewed were allowed to go to the outside world as couriers. I have also spoken to Reverend Geise, a Dutch priest, who spent two years living on the border of Badui Dalam and who has lived the best part of his life in Indonesia.

One Badui I met was brought to my Jakarta residence in Imam Bondjol by some friends who were distantly related to the Badui people. I felt honoured to have met Yakmin, an aged Badui who had lived most of his life in Badui Dalam and who claimed to be 170 years old. If appearances are true indicators of age, I was inclined to believe that Yakmin was 170 years old because I had never seen such a wrinked face before. He had a white turban round his forehead leaving his long, curly hair visible from the top. His tiny eyes were always cast downwards but his occasional glances were sharp and piercing, though friendly. Yakmin spoke in a soft voice. He spoke in Sundanese and I had an interpreter. As he sipped a glass of soft cold beer, he told me of his younger days, of the living conditions of Badui Dalam and of how he had decided to leave the "sacred place meant only for pure souls".

When it came to sensitive issues relating to the Badui religion and supernatural practices, Yakmin would say with a polite smile, "I am sorry, we are not allowed to disclose such matters."

Yakmin was born in the inner Badui zone. He did not attend school for there was no school. The Baduis believe in developing their intuition and acquiring knowledge through natural instincts. Thus no education was considered necessary. In Badui Dalam, there are no shops, no marketplaces, no cinemas, no clinics or anything that is related to modern civilisation. There are no churches, no mosques, no temples or any buildings for worship for they do not need any. The Baduis only worship their ancestors in a sacred place called Araca Domas where, they believe, their ancestors were buried. Through constant meditation, they communicate with the souls of their ancestors to seek inspiration, guidance and advice.

The forbidden land of Badui Dalam consists of three kampongs: Cikeusik, the most sacred in hierarchy, then Cibeo and Cikartawan. There must be only 40 families in the three kampongs at any one time. Whenever the number of families exceeds 40, one of them will have to leave the inner Badui zone. It is the pu'un who decides which family should leave. No arbitration or argument is allowed for the pu'un's decision is final.

When someone in the inner zone commits a crime, such as murder, theft or adultery, or violates serious *buyut* (taboos or prohibitions), he is exiled to a place just within or just outside the Badui Dalam. Each pu'un has his own place to keep his exiles: the pu'un of Cikeusik's place of exile is Cibengkung; and the pu'un of Cikartawan's place of exile is Cilenggor. In other words, the exiles are entirely excommunicated from the inner community but are normally allowed to go through some form of purification to redeem them from their sins.

In the purification rituals, the sinner seeks the forgiveness of the eternal Sun God. A tub containing *sirih* (betel leaves) is offered when asking for pardon. It is also a symbol of purification. This tub is transported through the three sacred villages, finally reaching the most sacred village of Cikeusik. The sinner therefore receives pardon just before he is exiled to the outer zones.

As one would expect, the pu'un of Cikeusik is considered the highest ranked among the three chieftains. However, each pu'un is regarded as a descendent of the Badui ancestors who can be traced ultimately to their God Almighty called Batara Tunggal. The pu'uns, being the descendents of the most sacred God, must not be seen by non-Baduis. As a sign of humility, even ordinary Baduis should not look at the pu'un when speaking to him. Whenever a pu'un dies, he is succeeded by his own son or, if this is not possible, by a member of the closest family such as a younger brother or a nephew. When a pu'un becomes a widower, he has to resign. When he is too old to perform his duties, he can retire but has to abide by certain strict rules, one of which is that he cannot leave the village. On retirement, the pu'un acquires the privilege of enjoying his rice ration from the *huma serang* (a sacred plot of land where rice is grown and the produce is consumed only during harvest festivals).

All Baduis believe that their pu'uns possess supernatural powers. There are many strange stories about the mystical powers of the pu'uns and the dukuns who work under them. One source says the Badui dukuns and pu'uns can make themselves disappear like evaporating gas and go to any part of the world. Thus the invention of modern jet planes means nothing to them. This may sound rather ridiculous but the Baduis firmly believe that their leaders possess such miraculous powers and therefore have a fearful respect for the pu'uns and their decisions. They believe that their chieftains know what is happening all over the world without leaving the village. That means they can see the world without radio or television. The pu'uns know when it will rain and can even bring rain when a drought threatens their rice harvest. That is why they do not need irrigation.

Yakmin, the 170-year-old Badui, still believed in the mystical powers of his pu'un. He believed that when a visitor arrived at the border of the forbidden land, he need only tie a knot in the grass of the sacred soil and the pu'un would get the message of the visitor's arrival.

Yakmin thought that to live a puritanical life was noble. He confessed very humbly that it was too difficult a task for him. There are just too many *buyut* (restrictions) which Yakmin found impossible to observe. For him, these included not being allowed to touch money, to smoke a cigarette, to drink wine or to look at a woman with covetous intentions. And above all, there is no entertainment in the modern sense. Thus, some years back, Yakmin decided to quit the forbidden land. How did he manage to do it? It was a difficult decision especially as Yakmin was married to a pu'un's daughter. Being a law-abiding citizen by Badui standards, he discussed the matter with the pu'un and they finally came to a compromise. Yakmin would accept the job of a courier despite his old age. He would be sent out from time to time to get rations and to act as a liaison officer between the outside world and Badui land. It was an honourable job of trust. As Yakmin described his job, I could not help wondering how he managed to keep up at his age. As a courier, he walked barefooted and at a lively pace by any standard. When I asked him the secret of his strength, he replied with a smile, "There is no secret. It is God's wish. I lead a very simple life." Yakmin had two sons and lived on the outskirts of Badui land.

Many Baduis today live outside the forbidden zone in 24 villagers mostly on the western and northern sides of the inner zone. The small villages are under the administrative control of three heads of *jaro* appointed by the Indonesian Government to preside over the areas of Cisement, Cibungar, and Karangcombong.

Speaking more on entertainment, Yakmin said that it was not entirely true to say that there was no form of relaxation in Badui Dalam. He told me about his friend who was deputy pu'un in the forbidden land and who played a kind of string instrument called *kecapi* (harp) of Sundanese origin. It is like the Chinese *ch'in* which is plucked with one's fingers. Whenever his friend played this instrument, the villagers would gather round and entertain themselves with *pantun* (short verses) accompanied by the melodious tone of the kecapi. Before the deputy pu'un played the instrument, he would meditate for a short while. *Kemayan* (a sweet scented joss stick) was often burnt to invoke the Goddess of Music to enter his soul and he would go into a trance. With his eyes closed and in a trance, he would relate the history of the 25 Badui kingdoms for two or sometimes three hours in the old Sundanese language whilst playing the kecapi. According to Yakmin, there were originally 25 kingdoms but as time went on they were gradually reduced to three. The stories of these kingdoms, normally referred to as *Selawi Negara*, explain the origin of the Baduis or Orang Rawayan. I asked Yakmin whether the Orang Rawayan had a written record of the Selawi Negara. The answer was negative for the Baduis prohibit the use of writing materials, especially paper which is a product of modern civilisation.

To me it seemed a pity that the Badui version of the origin of Orang Rawayan was still unrecorded. So I asked whether it was possible for me to have the music and pantun tape-recorded. Yakmin promised to invite me to his house on the outskirts of the forbidden land where he would ask the deputy pu'un to play for me. He also promised to try to seek permission to get the whole thing recorded. I waited for several months in vain, as it seems that the pu'un would not allow outside visitors even to enter the outer areas of the forbidden land during the months of April and August.

So far there is still no record of any kind about the history of the Baduis, their origin, religion, customs and traditions. In my conversations with Yakmin and others, I learnt that the Baduis are neither followers of Buddha, nor are they Hindus. Like animists, the Baduis believe in the spirits of their ancestors whom they can contact through meditation. Their supreme God is Batara Tunggal, their original ancestor. Batara means "God" and Tunggal means "the Only". They believe that when a Badui from Badui Dalam dies, the soul leaves the body and goes straight to Arca Domas, the holy place where their ancestors were buried and where all souls reunite with Batara Tunggal. In the case of the Baduis from the outer zone of Badui land, their souls must obtain purification before they can be reunited with Batara Tunggal. To be united with Batara Tunggal in the next world is the ultimate aim of every Badui, for it means eternal peace and happiness. Unlike the Balinese, the Torajans or the Egyptians, who believe that the body should be preserved for the return of its soul, the Baduis do not care for the corpse. The burial customs of the Baduis are therefore very simple. The bodies are buried without coffins or tombstones and are forgotten after seven days. In fact, the Baduis purposely bury the dead in obscure places without markings so that they cannot be easily identified later. Anyway, it would be difficult to find the grave later because they are soon overgrown by thick forest.

To the Baduis, Arca Domas which is located very near the source of the Ciudung River, is the sacred home of all souls. It consists of thirteen terraces arranged like rocky beds facing south. It is interesting to note that the Torojans also regard the south as the place where the spirits of the dead are found. The first terrace resembles a grave which is considered the spiritual home of Batara Tunggal. It is about two and a half metres high and three-quarters of a metre square. The second terrace is the Lemah Bodasa, so named because of the white sand which covers sit. (*Lemah* means "sand" and *bodasa* "white".) This is the resting place for the spirits of the Baduis from the inner zone. Another terrace is for the spirits of the Baduis from the outer zone whose souls have undergone purification. Thus, each terrace is classified according to the different categories of spirits. The terraces look like a stepped rice field.

The name "Arca Domas" may have some historical significance. The translation of two words *Arca* and *Domas* means "eight hundred", perhaps referring to the 800 staunch Badui ancestors who fled from Islamisation and eventually chose Arca Domas as their burial ground. The Baduis today consider it an act of courage to preserve their own religion, culture and way of life as well as a means of purifying their souls.

In order to lead a noble life and die with a pure soul, the Baduis have a strict code of behaviour to maintain high moral standards. As I mentioned earlier, the Baduis have a list of *buyut* or taboos somewhat similar to the Ten Commandments. It is taboo to kill one's fellow-man, to steal, to lie, to commit adultery or to be violent. It is also sinful to receive presents or touch money or ride on vehicles. A Badui may not smoke or get drunk. He should never have dinner before dark. He should not wear clothing with colours other than white, blue or black. It is also a sin to sleep on anything except a mat on top of Mother Earth. A Badui should resist the temptation to sing or dance to the accompaniment of music which is considered "vulgar".

The number of things which are considered buyut runs into many pages. Apart from the buyut commmandments, which are fundamental, any temptation to enjoy the fruits of modern civilisation is also classified as buyut. For instance, it is buyut to use an iron plough, to cut a tree with a steel saw or to tend the ground with a *cangkul* (hoe).

Strange as it may seem, Badui laws prohibit the rearing of cows, pigs, horses, goats, ducks or even fish in a pond. The breeding of chickens, dogs and cats is however, permissible. In the inner forbidden land, one can find hardly any of the domestic animals which are so common in the outer Badui zones. They probably have their own reasons for not allowing domestic animals to be reared in the sacred zone.

Of all the buyut, the ones that are most disturbing to those who want to help raise the standard of living of the Baduis are the buyut against reading and writing and the buyut against the use of irrigation for farming. The Baduis would rather develop their instincts and intuitive power through meditation. Education to them means corrupting the mind and contaminating the soul. Reading and writing are unnecessary as folklore, songs and buyut are passed down from generation to generation by word of mouth.

Despite the lack of medicine as we know it, the Baduis have great faith in the healing powers of the pu'un and the dukun. A Badui friend of mine told me about the time he went back to the Badui land to visit his relatives and took with him a first-aid kit in case of mishap during the long and tedious trek through the dense jungle. Fortunately he did not have cause to use it. But, when he was staying with his relatives, one of his neighbours accidentally cut his leg whilst chopping wood. My friend rushed to the rescue with the first-aid kit but was prevented from helping. Instead, a dukun was summoned. The dukun stood by the patient, mumbled words and then applied herbs to the gaping wound. According to my friend, the injured man was back at work as usual the next day.

The Baduis have, however, suffered a lot from contagious diseases such as smallpox and tuberculosis. In every family at least half the children die of one of these diseases. The Baduis, nevertheless, continue to fight the diseases with prayers and local medication. They believe that Batara Tunggal decides on life and death and therefore decides on the fate of each man. Smallpox is, in fact, considered a favour of Batara Tunggal because the Lord himself has a pock-marked face.

The buyut on irrigation is a major problem facing the bupati who controls the land adjoining the territories of the inner Badui zone. He is naturally eager to see an improvement in the yield of rice at harvest time. But engineers find it difficult to implement any irrigation scheme where the water supply must cut across the inner zone of Badui land. Until today, the jurisdiction over the territories of the inner zone of the Badui land is entirely in the hands of the pu'un and the Indonesian authorities have chosen to leave the Baduis alone to lead their own way of life. This, once again, is characteristic of the Indonesian spirit of cultural and religious tolerance.

Because of the buyut against irrigation, the Badui rice fields are dry, yielding a type of dry climate rice. The staple diet of the Baduis consists mainly of natural foods — rice, vegetables, eggs, wild honey and coconuts. The rice-planting and harvesting times, therefore, call for special rituals to express thanksgiving for their continued food supply and their survival.

Rice is always planted first in the huma serang of the pu'un as ordinary Baduis are not allowed to plant their rice before the pu'un. Preparations start around the nineteenth day of the seventh moon when the field is cleared. The actual planting begins when the constellation *kidang* (Orion) appears in the late evening sky. All members of the village sit cross-legged in the field while the *tukang melak* (master of ceremonies) chants "nyi pohti Sang Hiang Sri Laksmi" (May the young seeds survive and thrive, Goddess of Fertility). At day break, angklung (West Javanese bamboo musical instrument) players accompany the tukang melak to the huma (field for dry rice cultivation). When they reach the plot, the music stops as the group solemnly approaches the *pungpuhanam*, a small bamboo cottage where the goddess Dewi Sari dwells. The tukang melak then takes one betel nut to chew and spits the juice at the sticks to be used for rice-planting. To mark the start of the planting session, the tukang melak finally takes a stained stick, digs a hole and plants two seeds of rice. After this ceremony, called *mitembej melak*, a representative from each Badui family assists in sowing the field.

The harvest festival is celebrated during the so-called *kawalu* month but before the fasting festival. The pu'un retires to Ci Simut, a cave near the source of the Ciudung River and meditates for three days and three nights, waiting for a message from Batara Tunggal, the Supreme God. When he has received the message, he will go hunting, taking along just one arrow. Invariably he comes across a deer. When the pu'un aims his arrow, the deer will remain spellbound so that the arrow is shot straight through its heart. The deer is slaughtered and the feast begins. The festive food includes varieties of *ketan* (glutinous rice). The festive ketan is served with venison, carp, squirrel meat, scorpion and cricket. During the feast, the Baduis rejoice and shout gaily as a sign that Batara Tunggal has given his blessing for them to enjoy the fruits of their labour. In the evening, they relax and sing to the accompaniment of the kecapi.

Following the *kawalu* festival is another named *laksa* — a kind of compressed rice-flour. The laksa is distributed to everyone who has helped with cultivating the crop. The festival is started off by women who pound the rice contained in big *dangkak* (square wooden containers) and make it into flour. Seven women are specially selected to knead and compress the flour in the laksa cottage.

In Badui Dalam, no one is allowed to own land or accumulate wealth. The urge to accumulate wealth and money is taboo. Everyone's reward is measured by his or her contribution. To a certain extent, the Badui philosophy of distributing wealth according to each individual's contribution rather resembles the socialist philosophy. In a society which has to depend on dry rice cultivation, idleness cannot be tolerated. This is another aspect of Badui society and its economy which is worthy of proper research.

Researchers are still puzzling over the mystery of the origin of the Baduis and trying to predict the future of these people. The Baduis themselves, however, are quite content with the following legend explaining their origin and the founding of the three villages of Badui Dalam.

"At the time of the coming of Islam, the King of Pajajaran and his followers, who refused to be converted, fled to the hills. The king was looking for a safe place to resettle his people. In his search, the king turned himself into a bird called *beo* and flew into the sky. When the bird flew over the Kendeng Mountain Range, he looked down and found the water in the Ciudung River, sparkling and clear; the sand was white; and the land fertile. The bird went down to the river's edge, took off its wings, and started to drink from the stream. As soon as the bird's beak touched the water, the king of Pajajaran was transformed back to his original self. He decided to settle down there, naming the place Cibeo. Later he looked for another favourable site for his followers. He chose a site with white sand and called it Cikeusik. Then he found another site fertile enough for farming and called it Cikartawan which means "a forest which is rich and fertile".

I had an interesting talk wih Romo Budi, a prominent mystic in Central Java who had been to Badui Dalam. He thought the Baduis were the original Javanese before the arrival of any religion from outside Java. I found the comments made by Reverend Guise rather convincing. In his opinion, the Baduis were the original Sundanese before the arrival of Islam. One sound argument is that the Baduis still use the old Sundanese language. He felt that a study of the Badui way of life, their religious beliefs, and so on would enable one to have a deeper understanding of the old ways of life and beliefs of the ancient Sundanese.

Whatever research unfolds in connection with the origin of the Baduis, it is equally interesting to keep track of their future. One naturally wonders how long the Baduis of Badui Dalam can resist the influence of modern civilisation or how long this small group of people will survive in isolation. According to a census conducted by Pennings, a Dutchman, there were 184 Baduis in the inner zone in 1888. This number was reduced to 156 in 1908 and to 140 by 1928. As tradition dictates, the number of families in Badui Dalam must not exceed 40. As more Baduis are slowly lured by modern civilisation to the outer zone, it is inevitable that they will gradually mix freely with people of other races, cultures and religions, just as Yakmin has.

I asked Yakmin what he treasured most in his long life of 170 years. Surprisingly, his reply was "money". But, he went on to explain,

"I need money to provide education, proper sanitation and welfare facilities for my people." Despite Yakmin's noble intentions, it seems unlikely that the Baduis of the inner zone would appreciate his efforts at this stage. Former President Suharto once made an offer, as a sincere gesture, to upgrade their standard of living and to provide educational facilities. For the first time in history, the pu'un ventured out to meet the President when he visited the outer zone. The visit was well received by both sides but the Baduis have still not taken up the offer of assistance. As the authorities have no intention of interfering with the traditional way of life of the Baduis, the pu'uns are still permitted to rule their sacred territory as they wish.

5

THE TENGGERESE
The Staunch Hindu Devotees

When I was Singapore's Ambassador to Indonesia I have heard that there were some 60,000 mountain people with almost Tibetan features living in some 40 villages at an altitude ranging from 1,500-2,745 metres elevation around Gunung Bromo which is one of the most popular travel destinations in East Java. It is a 2,392-metre high active volcano situated 112 km southeast of Surabaya.

Bromo means "fire" and Gunung Bromo means the mountain of fire. It is one of the three mountains within the 2,200 metre-high "sand sea". There are three small crater lakes inside the larger crater and the area offers an excellent locale for hiking.

Through the help of the Foreign Ministry, a visit to Gunung Bromo was arranged. A guide took us (my wife and myself) from Surabaya to Probolinggo and from there to Ngadisari. At Probolinggo, there was nothing much to see. We saw crowds of hawkers, hecklers and harassers who attacked us more quickly than flies when we stepped off our bus. From Ngadisari we went by horseback and reached Cemoro Lawang. From here, we started the ascent to the Bromo crater. It took about two hours by foot. As it was cold up the crater, we borrowed some blankets from the motel. We also took flashlights. When we reached the foot of Gunung Bromo, we saw a steep 256-step concrete staircase leading up to the rim.

It was really a tiring journey but it was worthwhile and unforgettable. My purpose was to find out how the Tenggerese lived.

The sight of the Bromo crater was really exciting. The whole crater is said to have been dug out by an ogre with half a coconut shell in a single night to win the hands of a princess. When the king feared that the ogre would succeed, he ordered all his servants to pound rice. At that, the cocks started to crow thinking that dawn had broken. The ogre could not finish the job and he died of grief and exhaustion.

Inside the Widodaren in the Bromo crater complex are buried the legendary ancestors of the Tengger, Roro Ateng (wife) and Joko Seger (husband). They were childless and prayed for offspring, vowing to sacrifice one of their children to the gods if their prayers were granted. The couple went on to produce 25 children, but never lived up to their end of the bargain. Joko Seger was finally reminded of his pledge when pestilence and death swept through the village. Finally, the sacred couple had to take their last child, Kusuma, into the sand sea to appease the gods. Immediately, a volcano erupted and Gunung Bromo was born. The Tenggerese believe that Roro Ateng and Joko Seger still live in a cave on Widodaren, Gua Adam, where the Tenggerese go to pray and are granted wishes. The name "Tengger" is said to be derived from the last syllables of their names.

We witnessed the "Karo Feast" which is held once a year. It is usually held in February. This annual ceremony to commemorate deceased ancestors and relatives goes back to Majapahit times. We saw thousands of torch-carrying worshippers climbing to the top of Gunung Bromo on foot and on horseback. Hundreds of people at a time perched along the razor-thin edge overlooking roaring jets of steam 2,100 metres below. They asked for special favours of Bromo and bowed their heads in front of their village priest and made their wishes. The priest uttered mantras and prayers and then threw their offerings of fruits, flowers, goats and chickens into the crater. There was an atmosphere of unreality, like a black mass, until the sun came up, dispelling the magic and fear.

Unlike the Baduis, who had to flee in order to preserve their religion when Islam came, the Tenggerese in East Java were left alone to practise their Hindu-Brahma religion, unaffected by the advent of Islam. After Islam swept Java in the early 16th century, Majapahit's aristrocrats and priests took flight to the small Hindu principality of Blambangan at Java's far eastern tip nearing Bali. The other commoners are said to have sought refuge in the Tengger highlands. In Tengger today, there are some 40 villages scattered along the valleys between the famous volcano Gunung Bromo, which rises 2,392 metres above sea level, and Gunung Semeru, which rises to a height of 3,680 metres.

The Tengger highlanders are not archaic 'lost tribe'. They are ethnically Javanese and physically indistinguishable from their East Javanese neighbours. Although they are Hindus, there is no caste system; their kinship and social patterns are essentially the same as the Javanese Muslims. In some respects, the Tengger do differ. They speak a dialect related to that of the Osing Javanese of Blambangan — lacking the "levels" which are required by Javanese to distinguish their status when speaking to one another. They speak to each other as equal partners with no status differentiation.

The Tenggerese are hospitable. When we visited them, they invited us to see their kitchen, offered us some drinks and if we stayed a little longer, might even offer some food. It was polite to accept their hospitality.

During the rule of the Hindu Majapahit Empire, believers of Lord Brahma worshipped on the famous volcanic mountain Bromo and went there to meditate. They believed that it was a sacred place where Lord Brahma dwelt and where he could be contacted through meditation. The word "Bromo" sounds like "Brahma" and it could therefore be a corrupted version of "Brahma". The worship of Mount Bromo is recorded in the inscription of King Hayam Wuruk of the Majapahit Empire. The Hindu Kings encouraged their supporters to settle down on Gunung Bromo and gave them special privileges such as exemption from taxes. The idea was to make Gunung Bromo the centre of worship of Lord Brahma. It was perhaps due to their harmless, self-imposed isolation and the dangerous terrain that the Muslim invaders decided to leave the Tenggerese alone.

For centuries the Tenggerese went about their own way of life, worshipping their own gods and showing little interest in what was going on in the outside world. However, unlike the Baduis, the Tenggerese do not isolate themselves completely from civilisation. Instead, they welcome outsiders to visit their villages and are willing to share the wonderful experiences provided by their breathtaking mountain scenery, especially when one views the surroundings from the top of Gunung Bromo.

When armed conflict broke out between the Islamised coastal districts and the Majapahit Empire in East Java during the 1400s, the nobles, priests, and artisans fled to Bali, but the ordinary people withdrew to the Tengger highlands to keep their Hindu faith. Today, the Tengger are the only people in East Java who practise the Hindu religion openly. The Tenggerese call their religion Buddha Mahayana. Their belief system incorporates traces of Buddhism, but their caste system and calendar are similar to those of the Hindu Balinese. They have their own priests but no temples, and an altar is maintained in each home. A place of worship, usually located on a hill overlooking the village, consists of a smooth, flat rock or a neatly fenced area of one or two flowers and is usually crowded with people uttering prayers and performing religious duties.

Myth has proved to have a stronger influence than historical reality. Like the Baduis, the Tenggerese are proud of their own religion which is a mixture of both Hinduism and Buddhism plus elements peculiar to their own culture. They call their god Bumi Truka Sanghiang Dewata Batur and they are followers of the original religion of Java. Unlike the Balinese, who also fled from Islamisation of Java, the Tenggerese do not practise cremation of their dead. Their wedding customs are also more similar to those of the Javanese. Generally, the Tenggerese way of life is similar to that of the Samins, who are advocates of kebatinan.

The head of the village is called *petinggi* (the word *tinggi* means high) and is assisted by a *kabayan*. Both of them are elected by the villagers. A village has four priests, or dukuns, who look after the archives and sacred tribal writings inscribed on *lontar* (paper made of bamboo). They describe the Tenggerese concept of the world, the attributes of their deity, and the forms of worship to be observed on religious occasions. The petinggi and dukun have lost track of the origin of the Tenggerese, but consider it their duty to pass on to their children and grandchildren the sacred books in order to perpetuate the traditions and culture of their ancestors.

The customs and rituals of the Tenggerese relating to events of life such as birth, marriage and death are different from those of the Balinese, the Baduis or the Trugunese, all of whom shared a common fate when Islam came to Java. When a wedding takes place, the bride and the bridegroom are brought before the dukun. They first bow to the south, then to the fire place, then to the earth and lastly upwards to the first floor of the building where tools for farming are kept. After bowing to the dukun and the elders, the bride washes the feet of the bridegroom. An exchange of gifts takes place when the ceremony ends.

The gifts can include krises, buffaloes, farm tools or betel leaves. The marriage is not consummated until the fifth day after the ceremony. This interval is called *undang mantu* (inviting a son-in-law), a custom which is still observed in many parts of Java. It is interesting to note that in present-day Javanese weddings, the bride also washes the feet of the bridegroom but he first breaks an egg with his right foot.

The burial ceremony of the Tenggerese has special features of its own. The corpse is lowerd into the grave with the head facing south. This is contrary to the direction observed by Muslims. The corpse is covered with bamboo and planks and does not come into contact with earth at all. When the grave is finally covered with sand, two posts are placed upright over the body. Resting horizontally on the posts is a length of hollow bamboo. For seven successive days, this bamboo is watered with clean water which is considered to be holy. Offerings of two dishes are made to the deceased. At the end of the seventh day, a feast is held for relatives and friends and a fully-clothed dummy of the deceased, adorned with a garland, is erected in a prominent place. The dukun chants mantras and sprinkles water over the feast. After the ceremony, the clothes of the deceased are distributed to the relatives and friends who then gather around to eat. No more rites are observed until a thousand days later.

There is no stipulation of punishment against crimes such as adultery, theft or cheating, for such sins do not exist in the peaceful land of Tengger. However when a man commits a sin, a subtle reproach by the petinggi, the village chief, is sufficient embarrassment and punishment. The Tenggerese are an honest, industrious and happy people with high moral standards. One can leave one's doors open day and night without fear. Theft, gambling or drug abuse is unheard of.

6
THE MADURESE
The Eternal Fire

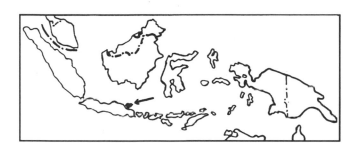

Madura is a large and rugged island about 160 km long and 35 km wide, separated from Surabaya by a narrow strait. Madurese who comprise about 14 million or 7.5 percent of the Indonesian population are different from the Javanese although they live very near to Java. The dry, sun-baked island of Madura bears little resemblance to its luxuriant neighbour Java. Culturally too, Madura is distinct from the mainland. They are pious Muslims who show great respect for their religious leaders.

The Madurese men claim that the name Madura is derived from the words *madu* (honey) and *dara* (girl). Madura's "honey girls" are famous throughout Java for their sexual skills although Madura is a devoutly Islamic society.

The petty states of Madura were first united under the prince of Arosbaya in the 15th century, they are recorded as being loyal vassals of the rulers of Majapahit.

In 1528, the son of the Prince of Arosbaya became the first Madurese ruler to convert the people to Islam. He established a rigorous Islamic state first in West Madura and later extended his power to the East. Since then, Islam has been the single most influential factor in Madurese politics.

Madura has always been heavily involved in Java's wars; indeed princes of each island have constantly tried to subjugate one another. Initially, Madura was a major source of colonial troops, for the Dutch were able to exploit the sentiments of the Madurese, who were historically hostile to the Javanese rulers. In 1624, the island was conquered by Sultan Agung of Mataram, the Hindu ruler of the Mataram Empire, and its government came under one Madurese princely line called the Cakraningrats. Until the middle of the 18th century, the Cakraningrat family fiercely opposed the Central Javanese rule and, from time to time, harassed the Kingdom of Mataram, often conquering large parts of the kingdom. Prince Raden Trunojoyo even succeeded in looting the royal treasury of Mataram in 1677.

The Cakraningrats had helped the Dutch put down a rebellion that broke out in Central Java after the notorious Chinese massacre in 1740. Thousands of Chinese were killed in Batavia in what was later called "the red river massacre". Cakraningrat IV tried to go against the Dutch but finally a treaty was signed in 1743 in which Pakubuwono II ceded full sovereignty of Madura to the Dutch. Cakraningrat fled to Banjarmasin and took refuge on an English ship but was robbed, betrayed by the sultan, finally captured by the Dutch and exiled to the Cape of Good Hope (South Africa).

The Dutch had to intervene in several internal conflicts between the Madurese and the Javanese resulting in Mataram having to cede several coastal districts, including Madura, to the Dutch East Indies Company. Later on, realising the hostility of the Madura towards the Javanese, the Dutch recruited many Madurese to fight their war with Java. The Dutch found the Madurese very good soldiers and exploited them in their attempt to control Java.

When the Japanese invaded Indonesia, the Madurese suffered a great deal. Many Madurese starved or were rounded up to do forced labour, never to be seen again.

Since independence, there has been much migration of Madurese to other parts of Indonesia including Jakarta. The positive consequence has been that today, the culinary delights of Madurese *sate* and *soto Madura* can be enjoyed throughout Indonesia.

Madura is famous for its bull races called the *kerapan sapi*. I had heard of the Madura bull race since my arrival in Indonesia and longed to see one. However, my time-consuming job of arranging for Lee Kuan Yew's visit to Indonesia prevented me from going to Madura earlier. Soon after I fulfilled my duty in 1974 and successfully arranged the visit when I received an invitation from the then Governor of Madura, Mohamed Noor. It was very timely as I was in a mood to relax.

The trip to Madura was a tedious four-hour drive from Surabaya. The soothing music emanating from the cool air-conditioned luxury bus, however, made the long journey less uncomfortable. The bus, belonging to the East Java provincial administration, was evidence of the slow but steady progress made by the authorities in rural communication. Overloaded lorries, cars, bicycles and passengers jammed the old-fashioned ferry-boat which took us across the narrow Straits of Madura. All the traffic seemed to be heading in the same direction — the village of Pamekasan where the bull race was to be held.

Madura's capital, Pamekasan, is a slow-moving city, very easy-going, quiet and undeveloped. The town centre is lined with casuarina trees. When we arrived, the whole city seemed to be deserted. The Madura people had gone to see the *kerapan sapi* held in a field about one km from the city centre.

When we arrived at the stadium, the villagers had packed it and it was a spectacle of colours. The air was filled with excitement and festivity. The buzzing voices intermingling with tinkling ice-cream bells conspired to gear the bulls into a frenzy. About a hundred of them, pairs yoked in tandem, were snorting at the crowd in the open field. Wearing fancy halters, each pair of bulls trailed a long narrow rig meant for the jockey to ride on. They were made to parade the arena to the blare of flutes, drums, gongs and gamelan music. Proudly, they displayed their dazzling gilt and tinselled leather bibs, tasselled horn-sheaths and golden studded harnesses, all gaily bedecked with fresh flowers. Above each pair of bull was perched either a colourful tasselled parasol or flag. Each bull also had a large bell dangling from its yoke, making sharp jangling sounds that seemed to compete with the gamelan music.

The bull parade ended and the crowd's excitement mounted. Racing fans began to bet. Suddenly a trumpet sounded. The first race was about to begin. The handlers prodded two pairs of bulls into position. Several strong-armed youths used all their might to hold back the bulls which were apparently feeling the effect of the rum, beer and raw eggs which they had been fed with earlier. The jockeys bent low on their rigs waiting for the signal. The crowd roared. Fans shouted the names of their favourite bulls as the jockeys prodded the animals from behind with pointed sticks.

Suddenly the noise rose in crescendo as one pair of bulls made a zigzag and plunged headlong into the yelling crowd which scrambled in all directions. The other pair of bulls headed straight for the finishing line and the audience screamed with excitement. The race was over for the first four bulls and two jockeys but not for the young spectators who often gathered near the winning post. For them, the excitement was not so much in seeing which bulls won but to get the thrill of scampering away from charging bulls, very much like the younger Spanish bull fans. Some even tried to climb onto charging bulls after the race. Gambling with death is the surest way to gain real excitement. Sometimes death triumphed, for on several occasions, one or two of the spectators were stampeded or gored to death.

Unlike conventional horse-racing and greyhound-racing where there are proper race tracks, the Madura bull race is held in a stadium where there is no clear dividing line between the racing area and the spectators' area. There is no enclosure or fence to separate the two. The only line visible in the field is the finishing line marked with a white line.

The grassy turf area which holds both the bull race and the spectators is about 130 metres by 40 metres. The best time recorded so far is nine seconds, faster than any man's world track record. The winners are always the pet and pride of the village. When the victorious bulls parade back to their home-town, there is great rejoicing and a feast is usually thrown to celebrate the occasion. All members of the village feel a sense of pride when their bulls win a race. The love for bulls has given rise to a tradition not to kill any bulls that have won a bull race. It has, therefore, become a superstition that if champion bulls are slaughtered, bad luck would befall the village.

The village of Sumenep is reputed for its champion bulls well known for their stamina and swiftness. Nowadays, bull races are becoming increasingly popular in Madura. The sport reflects the general ruggedness and impulsive character of the Madurese.

The idea of racing bulls started originally from racing plowing teams. The island's small sturdy breed of cattle is descended from the wild banteng that once roamed freely over western Indonesia. Only the strongest and most handsome bulls are chosen for competition.

After a series of regional competitions which begin in April, the grand finale — the all-Madura championship race, is then held at the end of the dry session in the stadium of Pamekasan. The championship cup was sometimes handed over by President Suharto himself. During the week prior to the race, traditional games, ceremonies, parades of decorated bulls, gamelan orchestras and night bazaars take place in all the towns.

Each day the bulls are given herbs, raw eggs, honey and even beer. The night before the big race, cattle raisers sing their best bulls to sleep. The next morning they are bathed, brushed and tenderly massaged.

Apart from the bull race, there is nothing to attract tourists. Madura is famous for three things: its women, its salt and its bull race.

Madura belongs geographically to East Java and was split off when the strait between the two islands was flooded over during the last ice age. Madura is a generally flat and dry island of treeless, infertile and rocky limestone slopes. There are rambling fruit gardens and endless tobacco estates. Bougainvillea bushes overhang the roads and brighten lanes. Fishing villages stretch along the whole southern coastline and the island's cemeteries with their mossy gravestones and craggy trees are supposed to be the most haunted graveyards in Indonesia making them excellent horror-movie sets.

The Madurese are active seafaring people with their cargo boats taking whole forests of timber out of Sumatra. In the fishing villages along the south coast, double outrigger canoes with huge triangular sails are used.

The Madurese wear the *pici* but the older ones still tend to wear the *destar* (headcovering). Even though tens of thousands of Madurese have moved to Java, they still retain their own language. Their language is quite different from that of the Javanese.

The Madurese are known for their tenacity and are regarded as a people of independent spirit. They are also known for their exuberant energy, thrift and hot-temperedness. The Madurese men usually spot black moustaches and have high cheekbones and narrow faces. The mere sight of one is enough to strike fear in the hearts of effete Surabayans. They carry knives and practise a mystic form of *pencak silat* (martial arts) which is fierce and swift. It is said that it is better not to quarrel or argue with the Madurese because when they lose their temper, they would often use their knives and start killing before they talk. It is strange that this impression is created because the ordinary peasants appear cool and even aloof. They are a proud people but have a keen sense of humour and enjoy the good things in life.

The Madurese women are small and dark with very fine features. They walk with a sensual grace carrying heavy enamel wash basins or trays over their heads. The Madura women are famous because of the special techniques of massage during love-making which makes the partner happy and excited. This massage is called *goyang madura.* Men fiercely protect the honour of their wives and daughters, yet boast about the sexual skills of their women. In the streets of Madura, many girls are selling *jamu* (a kind of aphrodisiac tonic) both for men and women.

There is a good reason why Madurese are so hot-tempered and fiery. In the vicinity of Pamekasan where the bull race is held there is a natural gas field where fire sprouts out of the earth. It is called "the eternal fire". Legend says that it comes from the mouth of a giant who was punished by the gods. There is a signboard which says: "Tak Kunjung Padam" meaning "it will never go out". The site lies 800 metres from the highway and is surrounded by a metal fence. We went there one night when there was a full moon and we witnessed a remarkable sight of fire sprouting out from the earth at night. It was a magnificent sight. We could even cook satay with the fire. The Madurese even divide the site into two distinct sides — the male side and the female side.

Madura is known for salt because one of its products is salt. Madura's economy thrives on salt, tobacco, cattle, fishing, poultry and goats. Recently, oil exploration has been taking place. Ever since the Dutch colonial government held a monopoly on salt, Madura has produced much of Indonesia's domestic supply. Tides wash in the sea water where the salt then collects in pools, notably in the region of Manbakor and around Kalianget. Madura is still the center for the spice trade and superb jamus are made here.

Madurese craftsmen were inspired by Chinese and European imports and the island is perhaps best known for its fine beds, screens, chests and cupboards. Madura's batik uses rich, bold mengkudu red, red-brown or indigo colouring incorporating vigorous winged naga-snakes, sharks, airborne horses with fish and other strange animal representations associated with the ocean. In the shade of late afternoon, women sit in their compounds drawing motifs of birds and flowers on the cloth.

Madurese crafts are much sought after in other parts of Indonesia and abroad, especially the carved wooden furniture and chests with wheels. The rooster motif plays an important role in both the wood carvings and batiks.

The Madura *soto buntut* is famous throughout Indonesia, and whenever I went for Indonesian food, I would always asked for Madura soto buntut.

At the eastern end of Madura is Sumenep, the island's most interesting town. It is centred on the kraton, mosque and market and is considered to be the most halus (refined) area of Madura. Sumenep's decaying villas with white-washed walls, high ceilings and cool porches resemble a Mediterranean town which has some Arabic influence. It is the town that produces the best racing bulls.

We visited the kraton and the *taman sari* (pleasure garden) built in the 18th century by Panembahan Sumolo, son of Queen Raden Ayu Tirtonegoro, who was a descendent of a Muslim scholar. The architect who built the kraton is believed to have been the grandson of one of the first Chinese to settle down in Sumenep after the 1740 massacre in Batavia. It is presently occupied by the *bupati* (district officer) of Sumenep. Part of the building is a museum which has an interesting collection of royal possessions including Madurese furniture, stone sculptures and *binggels* — heavy silver anklets worn by Madurese women.

We also visited the Mesjid Jamik Mosque which was built in the 18th century. It is notable for its three-tiered Meru-style roof and Chinese porcelain tiles and ceramics. Admiral Cheng Ho or his followers must have visited Sumenep for there is also a Chinese temple there.

Madura's oldest and most beautiful cemetery is on a hill near Arasbaya about two km from Ketapang. It is called *Air Mata* meaning tears. It is the resting place of the families of the Cakraningrat royal line. It is a vast complex of very old graves. The *juru kunci* (guide) explained to us the connection between those buried and their connections with the Sultan Agung and the Mataram rulers.

It is interesting to note that the Madurese called the royal tomb *Air Mata* (tears).

One interesting place to visit was the northern side of Madura which is more picturesque than the southern part. In the north, it is more agriculture-oriented, not fishing. We saw banyan trees, cactus, volcanic rocks, dense coconut groves, rolling dunes, sandy yellow beaches and more vegetation and varied crops.

The north is more isolated than the south and we saw more signs of poverty. This part of the island seemed rather neglected by the authorities. There was not much social development. We saw many children with swollen eyes. There were more ox-carts and less hotels. The women wore colourful traditional sarong kebayas and turbans. It is hard to imagine that life is so different and difficult in north Madura even though it is only a few hours from Surabaya.

7

THE BALINESE
Face Death with a Smile

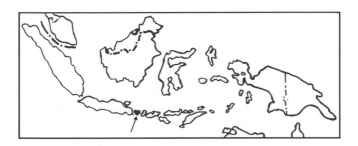

The world has perhaps heard more about Bali, the beauty of the island and the exotic culture of its people, than about the rest of Indonesia. Although the first Dutch war-yacht found this heaven on earth in 1597, it was only in the 1930s that the world got to know about Bali after several popular documentaries were produced. Today, the unbelievably complex social and religious fabric is gradually breaking down with the onslaught of tourists from all over the world.

The three million Balinese now inhabiting Bali were descendents of the cream of Java's Gajah Mada's scholars, dancers, rulers and elites from East Java who escaped to Bali after the invasion of Islam. The mass exodus to Bali came when the Majapahit kingdom fell apart. This exodus was led by the priest, Niratha, who is credited with introducing many of the complexities of Balinese religion to the island.

Gajah Mada took over the island in 1343 and brought it under Javanese influence. He conquered Bali when Java was in turmoil and Bali regained its autonomy and the Pejeng dynasty, which was centred near modern-day Ubud, rose to power.

Prior to 1815 Bali had a bigger population density than Java, which suggests that the Bali-Hindu civilisation was even more successful than that of Java. The Indian cultural influence started as early as the 9th century and Balinese writing is derived from the Palawa script of southern India. Today, Bali provides clues for scholars about India's past religious life and old sacred texts that have long since vanished in India.

When the Dutch war-yacht pulled into Bali on 22 February 1597, Bali was at the height of prosperity and artistry. The royal king had 200 wives, a chariot pulled by two white buffalos and 50 dwarves whose bodies were bent to resemble kris handles. The Dutch who came to Bali were interested in commercial profits and not culture. The island remained obscure for a long time because of its lack of spices and ivory and because it was surrounded by steep cliffs, deep straits and treacherous tidal currents. In 1906 when a wrecked Dutch cargo ship was looted by the Balinese, the Dutch took it as an excuse to bombard Denpasar, the capital of Bali.

When the Balinese found that they were outnumbered and outgunned, as fatalists, they took an honourable path of suicidal *puputan* — a fight to death. The rajas, dressed in their finest jewellery and golden krises, confronted the Dutch invaders who came with modern weapons. Wave after wave of Balinese nobility marched forward to their death. They preferred to commit suicide rather than face the disgrace of exile.

Dutch rule of Bali was however short-lived when it fell to the Japanese during World World II.

On 17 August, 1945 when Sukarno proclaimed Indonesia's independence, the Dutch tried to get Bali back. However, the fatalist Balinese repeated their *puputan* and resisted the Dutch who wiped out the resistance on 20 December 1946 in the battle of Marga. It was not until 1949 that the Dutch finally recognised Indonesia's independence.

When the Gestapu coup occurred in 1965, Bali became the scene of bloody anti-Communist killings. 50,000 Balinese who themselves claimed to be members of the Communist Party of Indonesia dressed themselves up in spotless white ceremonial attire and were led away for execution. Those executed believed that the communist devils had invaded their souls and their deaths were necessary to cleanse the island of evil. They believed that they were going to heaven.

I mentioned the Gestapu coup because the Balinese mystics seem to link this second great national disaster with the wrong date for performing the Great Ceremonial offering of mass cremation. The first disaster was the eruption of Gunung Agung which resulted in great damages to the Balinese countryside. When the volcano erupted, many Hindu and Buddhist priests went to Gunung Semeru, the highest mountain in Java, to pray. It is difficult to understand why they chose to pray to Gunung Semeru which is far way and not Gunung Agung in Bali which had erupted. Apparently, Gunung Semeru is regarded as the father of Gunung Agung and is therefore more powerful and sacred. The mystics explained that when Gunung Semeru was angry, its anger was expressed through its son in Bali. But why did Gunung Semeru get angry? Perhaps it was because it had been neglected for too long. Before the Hindus in Java escaped to Bali when the Muslims came, they must have prayed to Gunung Semeru, and since then their attention had shifted to Gunung Agung. However, the Balinese Hindus still believe that all souls ultimately return to Mahameru in Central Java mainland — the most sacred mountain.

When the coup of September 30 (Gestapu) came to ravage Bali, some mystics said the gods were angry because they had been disturbed before the time was ripe for the Grand Cremation held earlier. The gods thus demanded human sacrifices as compensation. Other mystics believe that when Bali was cleared of its graves, the goddess Durga felt lonely and needed company. These graves were soon filled up with new tenants — victims of the coup. This explains why the Balinese never resisted when time came for them to die. They believe in fate and punishment of their wrong doings.

The Balinese seem to have a mystical explanation for every worldly incident. When the Pan-American Airways aeroplane crashed in Bali in the late 1970s, they believed that the plane had landed on a ghost airstrip. Incidentally, the Dutch had planned to build an airport at the site of the air crash, but the plan was shelved. The mystics say that the underworld nevertheless helped to complete the airport and the pilot at the time of landing had, in fact, received clearance from the airport officials to land at the "devil's airstrip".

The Balinese are a small handsome people with round delicate features. They have long sweeping eye-lashes and heart-shaped lips. Unlike the Javanese who are refined in their manners and have complete control over their emotions both in life and art, the Balinese are expressionists who believe in dramaticism and in releasing their emotions. Their music is explosive and dramatic and the dances jerky with frequent rolling of the eyes.

I have visited Bali many times, the first was in 1955 when I went there for a holiday after the conclusion of the Bandung Conference. The Balinese culture fascinated me so much that when I became Ambassador to Indonesia in 1970, I made Bali my retreat and took a special interest in Balinese culture.

My general impression of the Balinese is that they live in a world of their own. They are fatalists by nature. They go about their daily life in harmony and with poise, never distracted by what happens in the world outside. They attend to their farms from sunrise to sunset, but when evening approaches, they transform themselves into dramatic dancers and musicians. They are also good artists.

The Balinese have a traditional caste system which resembles the Indian Hindu system but they do not have the untouchables. They do not have an intricate division of labour based on caste except for the Brahmana priesthood who have the Ida title. The second ranked caste is the Kshatriyas with the title of Deva and the Vashiyas with the title of Gusti. About 90 percent of Bali's population practise Bali-Hinduism. There is a sprinkling of Muslims in the coastal areas, Buddhists in the mountains and Christians in the western part of Bali. In Denpasar, there are about 500 Arabs and Indians and 10,000 Chinese running the majority of the businesses.

The life of the Balinese follows a rhythmic pattern. Their main purpose in life is to appease their ancestors and their gods by prayers and offerings. In return, the Balinese will be rewarded with abundant harvests and be assured of a safe passage to heaven. To the Balinese, the afterlife is more important than the present life. Consequently, it is the ambition of each Balinese to have a temple which they call *pura*. If this is not possible, they will make use of the village pura. Their whole life is linked up with the *pura*.

There are puras everywhere — in houses, courtyards, marketplaces, cemeteries, rice paddies, beaches, on barren rocks offshore, on deserted hilltops, deep inside the caves and high mountains and also in shady banyan trees. The biggest pura — the mother of pura — is in Basakih which is the state temple. It is situated on the slopes of Gunung Agung, also known as "the navel of the world", the holiest mountain in Bali where all the gods and goddesses are believed to dwell.

There are about 20,000 puras in Bali. These are the centres of life for the Balinese. Since every Balinese belongs to so many temples, their frequent visits to these temples consume much of their time. The Balinese always remember the birthdays of their temples, the birthdays of their ancestors and their gods. On each of these birthdays, they offer prayers and offerings and sometimes dancing and feasting. They believe that on those birthdays, their ancestors and gods would descend from heaven and enter the places of worship. They also celebrate on the birthdays of their childen, their first cutting of nails and hair, the filing of their teeth, piercing of earlobes, marriages and finally death.

There is an unending chain of festivals — over 60 religious holidays a year. The basic belief of a Balinese is that the island is owned by their supreme God Sanghiang Widhi. Balinese devote their entire waking hours to an endless series of offerings, purifications, temples festivities, processions, dances, cremations and dozens of other religious rites. They are forever busy with these festivals, offerings and prayers. Gods are often invited down to visit the Earth and are gorged with offerings and entertained with music and dances.

Balinese society is held together by a sense of collective responsibility. Women are not allowed to enter a pura during menstruation. It is an insult to the god when such an offence is committed by a woman. Not only the transgressor is punished but so also will the whole village and community. This collective responsibility produces considerable pressure on the individual Balinese to conform to traditional values and custom, called *adat*.

When I was in Bali, I noticed that the traditional Balinese house is always surrounded by a high wall and the compound is usually entered through a gateway backed by a small wall known as the *aling aling*. It serves a practical and spiritual purpose — both preventing passsers-by from seeing the inside of the temple and stopping evil spirits from entering. The Balinese believe that evil spirits cannot easily turn corners and so the aling aling stops them from entering straight in through the gate. Inside the pura is a family temple in one corner, a garden and a separate small building for each household function: cooking, sleeping, washing and the toilet.

Each Balinese village is a little self-contained republic, which is independently run like town councils by leaders of the *banjars*. These *banjars* have kept intact the Balinese way of life after the decline of the local adats. Each family pays a subscription fee and it is compulsory for every man to be a member when he marries. If he does not, he is considered spiritually dead. The head of each household has to attend regular banjar meetings and will be fined if he is absent.

The banjar runs its own communal bank from which villagers may borrow to buy farm equipment, cattle or other necessary items. The banjar supports and maintains village temples, owns a gamelan, handles taxation, divorces, cockfighting, and helps to finance weddings, family celebrations, festivals and cremations. Each banjar has its own meeting house for people to get together in the evenings to sip *tuak* (liquor), talk and gamble. Everyone takes turn to cook or serve as waiters. The leader of the banjar is democratically elected and approved by the gods through a medium.

The Balinese believe that each part of the house corresponds to a part of the human anatomy: the bedrooms and the social parlour are the arms, the courtyard the navel, the gates the sexual organs, the garbage pit in the backyard the anus, the kitchen and granary, the legs and feet, and the family pura the head.

I was also always fascinated by the way Balinese women and girls carry heavy loads on their heads. I saw a girl carrying 30 kg and more than one metre high of articles on her head. She walked steadily and nothing happened to the load. A young Balinese girl can train herself to carry up to 40 coconuts, stacks of fruits as well as a great jar of water without using her hands while riding a bicycle down a bumpy road. The Balinese women wear bras like European women's bikini tops. Unmarried girls always have a loose lock of hair hanging down the back over her shoulder with a *gonjer* (flower) dangling from it.

The life of Balinese women is tough. Whilst they work in the paddy fields and do all the cooking and household affairs, their husbands are smoothening the feathers of fighting cocks getting ready for the cockfights. They treat the cock as if it is a new wife.

Bali is well-known for its cockfights. I went several times to watch cockfights in a village. One early morning at a village near Ubud, I was attracted by the hysterical screams and gesticulations of the spectators. They made bets by exchanging money by hand with their opponents. The fight was first blessed. Then the owners of the cock teased their birds, pulled their tails, ruffled their feathers and then spit palm wine down their throats to arouse their fighting spirit. They then strapped sharp spurs onto the bird's legs. The game started when the cocks were in a fighting mood. The referee signalled the owners to let the birds loose. The fight was over in less than 20 seconds. I saw the wounded cock display an amazing ferocity even though it had been crippled by wounds received. Then the successful bettors collect their pay-offs and disappear.

Cockfights are a regular part of temple ceremonies. Men keep fighting cocks as prized pets. Whenever they are free, they would carefully groom and massage their pets. They put them in bell-shaped cages and place them at roadsides to amuse passers-by so that the birds are not lonely.

Another thing that always enchanted me was Balinese music and dancing. Whenever I arrived at Bali, the first thing that attracted me was the sound of echoing xylophones, drums, clashing cymbals and Balinese gamelan music. They can be heard at all hours of the day and night throughout Bali. The Balinese gamelan is played more vigorously and passionately than the slow and rambling Javanese gamelan music. Unlike the Javanese gamelan music which is slow and soporific, Balinese like their music electrifying and extremely loud with sharp changes in tempo and volume.

I was always fascinated by Balinese dancing and the dancers who wear dazzling costumes swathed in cocoons of gold-plaited fabric, their hands fluttering and their eyes flashing. They dance to rapid staccato rhythms with wide-open eyes, hips swaying and backs arched, all of their movements executed in perfect unison.

I have seen the barong dance, the legong dance and the gambuh dance. But the dance that had the most impact on me was the kecak (monkey) dance because the dance has no instrumental music — no gamelan, no drums or anything instrumental. The music comes from the vocal sounds of savage apes made by 100 performers, all bare-chested and wearing only sarongs. The dance takes place in a big shadow-filled area, usually under a banyan tree at night with only burning torches around the all-male choir. While they dance, the performers chatter, hiss and moan in perfect unison, passionate and fearful, all voicing shock, despair or panic. Fierce bellows and other weird primeval sounds pierce the night air. All the bodies appear black and they keep throwing their arms out all at once and shaking their fingers wildly.

Kecak tells the tale of Ramayana, the quest of Prince Rama to rescue his wife Sita after she had been kidnapped by Rawana, the King of Lanka. Rama is accompanied by Sugriwa to Lanka, the king of the monkeys with an army of monkeys. They dance in circles and provide a non-stop accompaniment of voices rising to a crescendo when Rama fights it out with Rawana.

The other dance that intrigued me was the barong dance. In Bali, barong is also known as barong sai. To the Balinese, barong represents good and righteousness. The Barong is a mythical animal which has the features of a lion and also resembles a dragon. The Barong is the sun, the male element in the cosmic world, referred to as yang in Chinese cosmology. He is the defender of everything good. Randa is the female, the ying, representing everything evil. The Balinese say Barong and Randa had an ancient feud which has not yet been settled to this day. The feud is depicted in the various Balinese dances, the most popular to the tourists being the barong and kris dance where Barong and Randa demonstrate their magical powers. Randa makes krises stab their owners whereas Barong uses his power to protect them from being hurt.

The introduction of barong into Balinese culture and religion presents a most intriguing problem to anthropologists. A great deal of speculation still revolves around the significance of the word "barong" for which there appears to be no satisfactory explanation. Some suggest that the word may have been derived from the Malay word *baruang* which means "bear". But the Malay language is a comparatively modern language and there were never bears in Bali. Evidently, "barong" is not a native word of the Balinese. So how and where did the word come from and how did the barong sai dance originate? The sight of the barong invariably brings to my mind the various Chinese lion dances I have seen in Singapore and Hong Kong. It is worth noting that the word "sai" attached to the Balinese barong is a Chinese word which means "lion" in the Hokkien dialect, one of the major Chinese dialects spoken in Southern China and the predominant dialect of the Chinese in most Southeast Asian ports. In Singapore, the lion dance is called "boo sai" meaning "dance" and "lion". Considering the fact that large quantities of ancient Chinese coins are still being found and used for ceremonial purposes in Bali, I am inclined to believe that the barong was also introduced from China. Having been educated in Chinese, I also venture to suggest as a layman that the second syllable "rong" in the word "barong" came from the Chinese word *"long"* which means "dragon" . The first syllable "ba" may be a short form of Bali or maybe "ba" means "crawl". Thus, the "Balinese dragon" or the "crawling dragon". But one might ask why a lion should be called a dragon? To explain the possible confusion, we have to return to the Chinese mythical animal, *chi-ling*, which appeared on the wooden door of the Jagat shrine of Trungen.

My wife and I visited Trungen, an island across Lake Batur facing Kintamani which is the cradle of Balinese culture. We went down the valley of Kintamani on horseback, followed by an hour's boat ride across Lake Batur. We discovered two chi-lings, a mythical animal which was well-known throughout China's countless centuries but became famous only during the Ming dynasty. The chi-ling was associated with ancestor worship and fertility. During the Ming dynasty in the 15th century, Admiral Cheng Ho the famous eunuch visited Indonesia many times. The Cheng Ho mission could have landed in Trungen. Could it be that the ancestors of the Trungen had some knowledge of this Chinese mythical beast and adopted it as a symbol of their king and ancestor for whom the shrine was dedicated?

The chi-ling, which belongs to the family of the dragon, is also called a lion-dog. In appearance, the face of the Barong does resemble the chi-ling. In any case, the Balinese themselves have chosen the words "barong sai" to describe the mythical animal, which could mean "Bali dragon lion".

I met an anthropologist Walter Spies who had made a study of Trungen. According to him, the boys of Trungen performed a dance in ancient days semi-naked. They wore a sort of primitive mask and ran around the temple grounds whipping savagely anyone they came across. These fierce, little monsters were called *barong berutuk*, a term for which there was no interpretation. Could it be that *barong berutuk* was the name given for chi-ling? Could this be the origin of the Balinese barong?

I have seen the barong dance many times and cannot help noticing the remarkable similarities between the barong sai of Bali and the boo sai of Singapore and Hong Kong. Both lions have large bulging eyes, big noses and wide mouths with snapping jaws. Both also have long beards and large ears. One difference is that the Balinese lion has a pair of Dracula-like teeth protruding from the sides of its mouth whereas the Chinese lion seen in Singapore has a set of properly filed even teeth, ironically befitting the traditional Balinese requirement for all who wish to gain entry to heaven.

I had often wished that the Balinese barong would meet the Singapore lion and dance together. My wish came true in early November 1974 when a Singapore cultural and goodwill mission visited Bali as a result of the two countries becoming closer after Lee

Kuan Yew's visit to Indonesia. The Singapore lion and the Balinese barong met significantly in a village called Singapadu, which when translated literally means "the lion fight". It was not a fight but a happy encounter of the two, which, in my opinion may have originated from the same source. Excitement gripped the Balinese and Singaporeans spectators when the Singapore lion tried to flirt with the more timid Balinese barong against a background of Balinese gamelan music accompanied by Chinese drums. It was great fun and the crowd roared with laughter. It was the first time that the Balinese had seen a Singapore "barong". They were greatly amused by the acrobatic stunts of the Singapore "barong" which sometimes rolled and sometimes stood on its hind legs. The Balinese barong, in comparison, appeared rather shy and would hardly venture to make such wild moves. As the first performance was so well received, the Singapore sponsors suggested that the same act be repeated on stage at the Bali Beach Hotel theatre where the Singaporeans were to perform again. However, the priest of the Singapadu temple politely declined the offer and explained that the Balinese barong was sacred and could not perform in any place other than a holy temple.

The Balinese barong dance is the most violent of Balinese dances and is often used as a means to exorcise evils. It is a dance representing a fight between good and evil. Barong personifies good and protects the village against Randa the evil. He is always surrounded by a group of men with krises. When Randa, with her long tongues lolling, her pendulous breasts quivering, fangs protruding from her mouth and sabre-like finger nails clawing the air, appears on the stage, the men with krises started to attack her. My first contact with Randa was in the hotel where I stayed. It was a wooden carving of an ugly witch with bulging eyes, Dracula-like teeth, tongue hanging out, untidy loose hair and long sharp fingernails. It was so frightening a sight that I had to remove it from the wall of my bedroom. On stage, Randa uses her magical powers to put the kris-carrying men into a trance and they start to stab themselves with their krises. Barong also uses his magical powers to protect the men from hurting themselves. At this dramatic moment, the gamelan sounds crazily whilst the men rush back and forth, waving their krises — foaming from their mouths, sometimes even rolling on the ground in a desperate attempt to stab themselves. Finally, Randa is defeated and retires from the stage — good has triumphed over evil.

Bali is perhaps best known for its cremation ceremonies. Few tourists, however, have the opportunity to see one because it is expensive to organise. It involves the construction of a large wooden cow which holds the body of the deceased and a multi-tiered pagoda which is the cremation tower. A gamelan orchestra has to be engaged and a feast prepared big enough for all the relatives, friends and helpers. This type of funeral is beyond the means of the average Balinese farmer. Most Balinese must, therefore, temporarily bury the corpse while they save up for a cremation, or await the mass cremation held once a hundred years. However, cremation is essential because only in that way can the soul be released to go to *nirwana* (heaven) or be reincarnated. It is the wish and ambition of every Hindu or Buddhist that his soul will reach the stage of nirwana that he need not be reborn again. Only when the soul is still imperfect must it be reincarnated, sometimes in the form of animals, sometimes as geniuses, depending on one's past life. Balinese believe that only after the body is cremated can the soul be released for reincarnation or to attain the stage of nirwana.

According to Balinese metaphysics, human beings are made of three essential elements: fire, representing Lord Brahma; water representing Lord Vishnu; and wind, representing Lord Siva. When one dies, one has to return to nature and this happens through cremation. When the body is cremated, it is fire. The ashes of the human body and bones are crushed into powder and thrown into the sea where it dissolves in water. When the water evaporates, it turns into wind in the form of vapour and ascends as the soul.

For the living to contact the soul, it is necessary to erect an altar in the temple complex. Some of the altars are just ordinary boxes supported by wooden pillars resembling cages for pigeons. Others, which are more elaborate, are in the shape of pagodas. These are called *meru*, derived from the word Mahameru or Semeru, the name of the highest mountain in East Java where, according to Javanese Hinduism, all souls will ultimately rest. The altars, whether in the form of boxes or meru, are "contact points" for dialogue with the souls of ancestors. Before contact can be made, a purification ceremony has to be performed. This involves calling in both a Hindu priest and a Buddhist priest to make offerings and chant *mantras*, and to sprinkle holy water on all the relatives and friends. The holy water is brought from eleven sources including the Besakih, which is the supreme temple where the souls of the earliest Balinese ancestors are housed. Once the temple is purified, one can invite the souls of the deceased to enter the meru. If desired, a medium can be employed to go into a trance to have a dialogue with the dead.

The Balinese have adopted certain aspects of the feudal and caste systems of Hinduism from India. In the past, the cremation of a king involved the construction of a wooden dragon, called *naga banda*, which had a long tail. The corpse of the king was placed inside the dragon for burning. In the case of heroes, the coffin takes the form of a flying lion called *Singa-kaang*. A prominent person such as a priest, a rich trader or a community leader is cremated in a coffin shaped like a cow. The cows are again divided into three colours — black, white and yellow. The black cow is meant for a deceased who had married, the yellow cow for a bachelor and the white cow for a holy man. The towers built for cremations are also differentiated according to the social status of the deceased. Only the tower of a king can have eleven tiers, a priest's can have nine and that of other classes of people seven. During the cremation ceremony, bearers of the cremation tower zig-zag their way along so that the soul of the deceased cannot trace its way back. Everyone rejoices for the dead as a cremation means ambitions fulfilled.

In order that all Balinese can fulfill their ambition of having a cremation, the Bali-Hindu religion provides an outlet for the less fortunate who cannot afford to pay for their own ceremonies. Once in every one hundred years, all the temporary graves in Bali, with the exception of those in Trungen and other Bali-Aga villages, are cleared and the remains cremated in one grand ceremony. This communal cremation is held on a *gotong-royong* basis, with everyone lending a helping hand. This grand festival is called *Karia Tour Agung Ekadasa Rudra*, "The great ceremonial offering to the Eleven Rudras". The eleven rudras are the guardian spirits of the eleven points of the Balinese compass. The last great offering was held in 1963, a few months before the beginning of the Balinese century. This ceremony should rightly have been held at the start of the new century. However, the Balinese were apparently too anxious to perform the great offering because for three centuries this festival had been neglected and this neglect, they believed, had brought about many calamities to befall Bali.

The great temple of Besakih, the central temple for all Balinese Hindus, was chosen as the right place to perform the purification ceremony for the whole island. This ceremony was sponsored by the Bali Provincial Government and took place during the Sukarno regime, less than two years before the Gestapu coup on September 30. It was an historic and very happy occasion for all Balinese as their ancestors, who could not afford the expense of cremation, were finally able to have their souls released. The only expense that the poorer descendents had to pay towards the ceremony was the price of a small wood-carving of an elephant fish to contain the ashes of their ancestors. These little ash-containers were assembled at the Besakih Temple to join the cremation towers built by more affluent participants of the festival.

As I have said, the Balinese live in a world of their own. They are not very much bothered with the world outside. Nor are they interested in what the world outside thinks of them. To them, Bali is the centre of the world and Gunung Agung is its navel. As revealed by old manuscripts, in the beginning there was nothing in the universe except a magnet. Then the world serpent, *Antaboga*, through meditation, created the earth in the form of a turtle which floated on the ocean with the island of Bali resting on it. The Balinese concept divides the universe into the underworld, the middle world and the upper world. The upper world is divided into different levels again: the level of the clouds where the god of love dwells, the middle level of the atmosphere and the dark blue sky where the sun and moon are and the upper perfumed sky where the bird, *Tjak*, and the serpent, *Takasaka*, dwell with the stars. Higher still is the *gringsing wayang*, the flaming heaven of the ancestors. Above all the skies live the great gods who watch over the heavenly nymphs.

The underworld is ruled by *Batara Kala* and his goddess *Satesuyara*. *Kala* was an offspring from Siva's sperm which fell to the ground while Siva made love to his wife, *Uma*, when she was in an angry mood. Siva wanted to destroy the sperm and ordered the lesser gods to shoot at it with their magic arrows. However, Kala managed to grow into a mighty, fearful giant who demanded food to fill his insatiable stomach. Siva sent him down to earth to teach the human creatures a lesson for they went about naked and behaved like savages. But Kala came down to earth only to devour the human race. Alarmed, Siva recalled Kala and sent down gods to teach the human race how to behave, to grow food and to follow a religion. Today, Kala is seen in every corner of Bali and in most parts of Indonesia. In Bali, particularly large stone images of Kala are common at the entrance of houses, temples and also hotels. He is no more the man-eating demon but a guard and protector against evil. However, some Balinese still believe in the legend which says that once a year, three days before the Balinese New Year, Batara Kala, also known as *Galunggan Kala*, would come down to earth in the form of *Sanghiang Tiga Wisesa* to eat people. It is therefore dangerous and sinful not to make special offerings to him.

The Balinese live in a world of gods and demons. They spend their whole life trying to contact their gods, seeking the blessing of the souls of their ancestors and at the same time pacifying the anger of the demons. Thus, at the corner of every street, stone images of Vishnu, Siva, Brahma and other gods make their presence felt and there are temples and small shrines everywhere. In the modern world of rationality, the Balinese may appear to be living in a world of myths. To them, however, the myths are realities. It will take some time for the Balinese to change their way of life. But then, is there any reason why it cannot withstand modernisation? They are obviously much more contented than the tourists who flock to see them. Is the increasing flow of Western hippies not an indication that the Balinese have something to offer those who appear to have lost their way in the intricate cobweb of modern civilisation?

8
THE TIMORESE
A People Betrayed

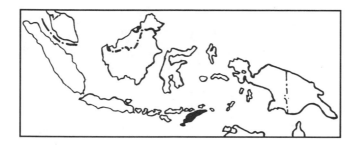

From July 1998, hundreds of troops of the Indonesian Armed Forces started to pull out of East Timor to appease the Timorese. This move was to enable the Indonesian Foreign Minister Ali Alatas to open negotiations with the Portuguese representative under the guidance of the United Nations Secretary-General. The subject of the talk was on Timor's "autonomous" status promised by the new President Habibie. The withdrawal of Indonesian troops coincided with the mass exodus of some 50,000 non-Timorese including ethnic Javanese and Bugis who were in fear of insecurity following the fall of President Suharto in May 1998.

The Timorese, whose land was colonised by the Indonesians since 1975, renewed their fight for independence. On 17 June, 1998, about 200 East Timorese students rallied outside Jakarta's Ministry of Justice and demanded a referendum for self-determination in their territory. Nine students presented officials with their demands, which included the release of their leader Xanana Gusmao, scrapping the subversive law and nullification of the 1976 presidential decree which annexed

East Timor as Indonesia's 27th province. The Indonesian military authorities had to apologise publicly for the shooting of an East Timorese youth to death which took place in Manatujto, 60 km east of Dili, capital of East Timor. A soldier shot the 21-year-old Herman Dasdores Soars on 16 June 1998 as he was loading wood on to a truck with his cousin. He died while being taken to Dili for treatment.

The military apology said: "There was no reason for shots to be fired, since the soldier only suspected the victim of stealing wood. The soldier in quesion, Agus Medi of the Battalion 315, has immediately been summoned along with witnesses and is now under military police questioning. We will take action against him according to the law."

The death was reported to Dili Bishop and Nobel prize winner Carlos Belo by the parents of the victim. The death came as the Indonesian authorities face mounting pressure to launch an initiative over East Timor. They have released 15 East Timor political detainees but have rejected calls for the release of jailed rebel leader Xanana Gusmao.

On 22 June 1998, President Habibie offered a form of "special status" for Timor and said that Xanana Gusmao could be freed in return for international recognition of Indonesian sovereignty over the territory.

The Portuguese, who were the former colonial master of East Timor, however, were not happy with Habibie's statement. A Portuguese spokesman of the Foreign Ministry said, "If Indonesia wants to move towards democracy, its principal aim must be to ensure that the East Timorese have the right to choose how they want to live."

Although Indonesia has annexed East Timor, the United Nations does not recognise Jakarta's sovereignty over it.

Gusmao, who has served six years in Indonesian prison for his 20-year term for armed rebellion, said on his 52th birthday celebrated in gaol that only a referendum on self-determination would settle the issue that has bedevilled Indonesian foreign policy for 20 years. He also dismissed Habibie's proposal as unacceptable.

The East Timorese, who live in the eastern half of the Timor Archipelago, number 650,000. The population of West Timor, formerly colonised by the Dutch, was 1.2 million. When Indonesia achieved independence, they took over the Dutch-controlled Timor, leaving the Portuguese still in the hands of the Portuguese. After the military coup in Portugal which toppled the dictatorship in April 1974, Portugal rid themselves of all colonial possessions in Southeast Asia. In 1975, Lisbon granted independence to East Timor. The Indonesian authorities, fearing that an independent East Timor would inspire separatism in other parts of Indonesia, and that the new Government of East Timor would be under the influence of the communists, launched an invasion and annexed the territory. Today, the whole island of Timor, West Timor which is called Timor Barat and East Timor referred to as Timor Timur or "Tim Tim" comes under Indonesian control.

Historically speaking, there may be a reason for Indonesia to take over West Timor because it was part of the Dutch territories, but Portuguese East Timor had little to do with Indonesia. It had never been within the boundaries of colonial or post-colonial Indonesia and the peoples are very different from Javanese or other people of Java, Sumatra, Sulawesi or Kalimantan. The Timorese had always wanted independence and freedom. In fact, when Lisbon granted them independence, the East Timorese zealously formed three main political parties in readiness for a general election to elect their own government. The first political party formed was the Timorese Democratic Union (UDT) on 11 May 1974. It was inaugurated little more than a fortnight after the Lisbon coup. The founding president was Mario Carrascalao, a 37-year-old forestry engineer whose father had been deported to Timor in the early 1930s because of his activities as a Communist youth leader and whose mother was Timorese. The leadership of the UDT, that is the 14 central executive members, were generally conservative, representing as they did the more prosperous citizens, the administrative officials and the wealthier planters. The party which was rather anti-communist started off as the largest of the three political parties in the province, but it soon began to lose ground to the Association of Timorese Social Democrats (*Associacao*

Social Democrata Timorese) generally referred to as the Fretilin Party, founded on 20 May 1974. In its communiqué, the Fretilin described itself as "being based on the universal doctrines of socialism and democracy" and as being committed to "the right to independence and to the rejection of colonialism and to counter measures against neo-colonialism". Its leader was Francisco Xavier do Amaral, a 37-year-old former official in the Customs Department, who was a soft-spoken, humble intellectual. His charisma and ability to speak soon made him a popular figure among the Timorese. His leadership was however taken over by a younger full-blooded Timorese. A third leader who preferred to work behind the scene was Jose Manujel Ramos Horta, a *mestico* (mixed blood of European and Timorese) who was exiled to Mozambique by the Portuguese for his student activity but came back as a journalist. Soon after the formation of the party, Horta was sent to see Indonesia's foreign minister, Adam Malik and Presidential Assistant to Suharto, General Ali Murtopo, both of whom then approved of Timor's independence.

The third party, the Timorese Popular Democratic Association or Apodeti, was formed on 27 May 1974. This party advocated integration of Timor with Indonesia. The leaders of Apodeti belonged to the older generation, one of whom was connected with the former royal family and another having collaborated with the Japanese. The real man behind Apodeti's early activities and organisation was Jose Osorio Soares, a 37-year-old former schoolteacher and official in the administration. Originally he operated behind the scene but soon became the movement's secretary-general. The political goals proclaimed by Apodeti proved to be no match for the independence programs of Fretilin and UDT.

The most popular party was the Fretilin which is translated to mean "Revolutionary Front for the Independence of East Timor", which unfortunately gave the wrong impression to the Indonesians that they were communist inspired.

In the struggle for power between the UDT and Fretilin in August 1975 civil war broke out. For several days, fighting raged in the streets of Dili, sending a flood of refugees to the wharf area where they anxiously waited for evacuation. Two vessels took some 2,000 Portuguese, Chinese and Timorese (most of the whom were families of UDT supporters) to Darwin, while an Indonesian frigate slipped into Dili and evacuated the staff of the Indonesian consulate. The struggle for control of Dili was bitter. About 400 people died in the streets of the capital, while damage to buildings and houses from mortar and light artillery fire was surprisingly light. The main UDT force was forced out of Dili and withdrew to Liquica, a town some 25 km to the west in the direction of Indonesian Timor. The bulk of the fighting was already over, and the UDT remnants were already heading for the Indonesian border — the only possible sanctuary open to them.

In the upheaval of the civil war, the fragile economy of East Timor ground to a halt. Most shops were closed, farms were untended or abandoned, and in most cases town services were no longer operating. Dili was teeming with refugees, many of whom were Chinese who had come to the capital from towns and villages where fighting had disrupted their business operation.

One of the consequences of the Fretilin victory was that the victors had to look after a large number of prisoners, most of them UDT leaders and their followers. Altogether there were some 2,000 of these prisoners in several detention centres.

Meanwhile, the Portuguese administrators withdrew from Dili after 206 years of rule, never to return, only after 16 months of the civil war. They were humiliated and demoralized as they were ignored by both the Fretilin and UDT.

When the UDT left, Fretilin became the *de facto* government of East Timor. Under the pretext of restoring law and order, Indonesian troops invaded East Timor 24 hours after President Ford and U.S. Secretary of State Henry Kissinger had left Jakarta after their brief visit in December 1975. This was to spare the American leaders the embarrassment. The Indonesian soldiers entered Dili and massacred an estimated 100,000 Timorese. The planning of the assault was done under the guidance of Major-General Moerdani, the Christian general in Indonesia, who later became Indonesia's Defence Minister. It was the biggest military operation since Indonesia's independence involving 10,000 troops plus battalions from *Siliwangi* from West Java and *Brawijaya* division. The invasion was staged from several bases, among them Ambon, Kupang and bases set up on the nearby islands of Timor. It was a brutal case of genocide — the most massive since Cambodia's Pol Pot regime. Not much publicity was given in the local and world press. The Indonesians also lost about 1,800 soldiers and thousands of them were wounded and found their way to Jakarta hospitals. The Fretilin guerrilla fighters, described by the Indonesians as "Marxist terrorists" were defeated and run into the hills that cover two-thirds of East Timor to wage protracted and bloody guerrila warfare against the Indonesian troops.

Initially, Suharto was reluctant to invade East Timor, but by the end of September a few months after the Fretilin victory, he was persuaded by General Panggabean, the then Minister of Defence, Yoga Sugama, Chief of Bakin (intelligence), Ali Murtopo and Benny Moerdani (also of Indonesian intelligence) to agree to intervene in East Timor. Meanwhile, Harry Tjan and Liem Bian Kie of the Centre of Strategic and International Studies (CSIS) persuaded the Australian Foreign Minister Andrew Peacock that Australia should not object if Indonesia had to use force to "restore peace" in East Timor.

In this invasion, hundreds of Timorese and Chinese were gunned down at random in the streets of Dili. The Indonesians believed, rightly or wrongly, that some Chinese communists who fled from Indonesia after the bloodbath that followed the September 30 coup in 1965 had established themselves in Portuguese Timor as a springboard for new adventures in the archipelago.

In one such incident, a large number of members of Apodeti (the party which was supposed to be pro-integration with Indonesia), who had just been released from internment by Fretilin, went out to greet their liberators but were machine-gunned in the street. A number of public executions were carried out by Indonesian troops, with some of the condemned selected at random. One of the most bizzare and gruesome of these atrocities occurred within 24 hours of the invasion and involved the killing of about 150 people.

The Chinese, who had been studiously neutral in the political conflicts, died by the hundreds in the aftermath of the invasion. In some cases, the men were separated from their families and shot.

The orgy of killing was reported to have continued for about a week. According to a Catholic priest who was in Dili after the invasion, as many as 2,000 citizens of the capital, some 700 of them Chinese, were killed in the first few days of the Indonesian invasion.

After the savagery of the first days of the invasion, tens of thousands of Timorese fled from their homes to the relative sanctuary of the mountainous regions behind Fretilin lines. They included thousands who had hitherto been supporters of UDI and Apodeti.

In July 1976, Indonesia formally annexed their acquired territory as the country's 27th province. This was described by many critics as a clear instance of Javanese imperialism.

In April 1978, the Indonesian troops staged another extensive operation involving 2,500 troops supported by helicopters, and resulted in the seizure of Fretilin's radio station and the capture of Fretilin's Minister of Information and the shooting of Lobato on 31 December the same year. By 1979, the Indonesian armed forces had broken the back of the Fretilin's main resistance. In 1981-82, the Indonesian armed forces made further major operations that greatly reduced Fretilin's strength. After Lobato's death, the leadership of Fretilin was taken over by Xanana Gusmao, who was the leader of the guerrillas.

By 1985, the Fretilin's strength was greatly depleted, but the Indonesians had not succeeded in wiping out the resistance movement. In 1986, as a consequence of military pressure and internal disputes, the Fretilin agreed to participate in talks initiated by the Catholic Church but no meaningful talks resulted. Abri continued its operation, with the 20 infantry battalions stationed in East Timor gradually whittling away the Fretilin forces. By December 1987, the Fretilin strength had reduced to about 500 and it decided to adopt a more politically-oriented strategy.

The political strategy culminated in the Dili massacre of 12 November 1991, because of the ineffective coordination between the operations and intelligence staffs at military headquarters. There was a tragic massacre of unarmed Timorese demonstrators at Santa Cruze cemetery. This massacre has also resulted in the arrest of Xanana Gusmao a year later.

As late as January 1995, another incident occurred in Liquica when six unarmed East Timorese suspected of being rebel sympathisers were summarily executed. This incident caught the attention of the international media. The International Human Rights Commission found that the six had been tortured and unlawfully killed.

The international support for the East Timorese cause is irritating to the Indonesians and also helps to maintain the morale of the resistance movement. Even the Indonesian military commander admitted that the Timorese problem would not be resolved until it was struck off the United Nation's agenda. The agenda included the necessary steps which should be taken to enable its people of that territory to attain the goal set forth in the charter of the United Nations and declaration (in the granting of independence to colonial countries and people).

According to reliable sources, the Fretilin now has about 180 guerrillas with 110 weapons and a number of sympathisers assist with supplies, information and other support. Other reports claim that guerrilla strength has increased to 700 armed Fretilins and 5,000 clandestine supporters.

Under Bishop Carlos Belo's leadership, the Christian church grew in strength in membership from 50 percent of the population to 80 percent in 1996. In the years following the invasion, thousands of Timorese embraced the church, largely because it offered the only protection against the excesses of the invaders. Bishop Belo, who is a Timorese, has continued to stand up for the rights of his people, winning him the respect of the international community, as well as the devotion of his flock. In February 1989, he wrote to the UN Secretary-General calling for a referendum on East Timor's future. He played a key role in exposing the true extent of killings in the Dili massacre of November 1991, and has kept up pressure on the Indonesian authorities to end human rights abuses. His courage won him the Nobel Peace Prize. He had helped to expose the dark side of the Suharto regime. Because of Bishop Belo's support, the Timorese are no longer alone: they have a devoted international following with committed support groups found in all parts of the world.

East Timor today remains broken, dominated and in fact virtually forgotten under the yoke of a new colonial power. There was international pressure on Indonesia to withdraw, but such pressure is also fading. The Indonesians are eager to show the world that life has returned to normal and that a new era of freedom has begun for East Timor. In Janunary 1989, after 15 years of occupation, Indonesia declares that the country is officially "opened".

But the Timorese, backed by Fretilin guerrillas, have not abandoned their effort toward independence and self-determination. According to a report by an Australian journalist who trekked into the mountains and interviewed Xanana Gusmao, about 90 percent of East Timorese were supporting the independence movement. But the 1,500 guerrilla fighters are pitted against Indonesia's 15,000 heavily-armed forces. The Indonesians have also planted a large number of police and spies described by the Timorese as "cats" in civilian attire.

The Timorese feel almost totally repressed. An atmosphere of benign terror permeates the land. There are 130 political detainees on the island of Atauro off the north coast who are suspected of having links with the guerrillas.

Who are the Timorese and what are their characteristics? There are about 1.85 million of them in both East and West Timor. In East Timor, there are about 680,000 in 1975 and 97 percent are Timorese on the eve of the Indonesian invasion.

Although Malays, Makassarese and Papuan-type people came to Timor and left traces of their presence, neither Hinduism nor Islam reached this remote island. Generally, the Proto-Malay type predominates, with most of the Timorese dark-skinned and light-built. There are 36 distinct ethno-linguistic groups in East Timor, and they can be divided into two dominant language families, the Malayo-Polynesian or Austronesian and the Papuan, or non-Austranesian. Although some words have been borrowed there are suprisingly few links between Bahasa Indonesia and the languages of East Timor.

In Dili, the Timorese are not allowed to speak either Portuguese or *Tetum* in public. And children described the Indonesian language as "the fucking language". In Dili, the Indonesian language is used for mass and catechism, but in the countryside, Tetum is still used despite the ban.

The East Timorese are predominantly Catholics (comprising 91 percent) and the remainder are Muslims, Protestants, Hindus, Buddhists and animists. The fact that the vast majority of the Indonesian soldiers are Muslims from Java, as well as the traditional fear and dislike of the Javanese, the East Timorese bear a deep resentment of their political domination by the Javanese. When the Indonesian soldiers invaded Timor, they were given to understand that they were there to fight communists, while others were given to understand that they were embarking on a *jihad* (holy war) against Timorese Christians. The language barrier presented a serious problem. The Indonesians spoke neither Portuguese nor Tetum and the Timorese had no knowldge of Bahasa Indonesia.

Although most Timorese are Catholics, they respect their tradition of animism. The farmer still spills blood before tilling the soil. The East Timorese are religious people and are enthusiastic about building churches even at the expense of depriving themselves of water canals which they badly need. The Indonesian authorities realised the power of the church and invited Pope John Paul II to visit Timor in October 1989 to give his blessing. The church is today torn between supporting the people or the government's program which benefits them.

How did the Portuguese discover East Timor? Their navigators first set foot on its soil a mere two decades after Christopher Columbus made his epic voyage across the Atlantic.

Before the Portuguese took over East Timor, head-hunting was a popular sport. However, when peace returned, the severed heads were returned to their owners' villages. The head-hunters belong to the Tetum tribe.

Another tribe called *atoni* is believed to be the aborigines of Timor. They were driven to the West by the *Atoni* and now predominate in West Timor. They too were divided into various small princedoms before the arrival of the Europeans. It is believed that they were strongly influenced by Hinduism, possibly as a result of Javanese traders who were Hindus and are still strong believers of spirits and ancestor worships.

In West Timor, the Atoni which is an old indigenous Melanesian race are the biggest group. The other groups are the *Beluese* and *Roinese* who arrived at a later date but pushed the Atoni into the eroded mountains of the interior.

The Atoni are short negroit types, with dark brown skin and frizzy hair like Papuans. The native atoni belong to 10 traditional princedoms (*swapraja*) and speak a number of different Malayo-Polynesian languages. They stay in hamlets along the ridges of hills and mountains. East hamlet usually consists of a church and school and houses. Traditional atoni houses are built with mud floors and bamboo frames, characteristically beehive shaped with high conical thatched roofs which extend downwards almost to the ground. The different parts of the house are arranged according to cosmological beliefs. On the top are animals, birds, or little people. Although the Indonesian authorities have been depolicising the native headmen (rajas), some of them are still powerful and have control over the allocation of village agricultural lands.

All ethnic groups in the Timor Archipelago chew *surih* (a kind of leaf with bitter taste) after meals and especially on ceremonial occasions. An adult chews 15 betel nut seeds a day and children also start to chew surih at the age of seven or eight.

Despite the fact that most West Timorese are Christians, they still follow traditional beliefs. They believe that after death, all human beings go back to their original professions and carry on with their worries and necessities of this earthly life. They worship the fertility god — the crocodiles. If one is killed in self-defence, he must be given the privilege of a human burial. Reports as late as the early 19th century claim that virgins were sacrificed to hungry crocodiles. Crocodiles are still used frequently in Timorese weaving motifs.

Portuguese navigators came to the eastern islands of the Lesser Sundas shortly after their conquest of Malacca in 1511. However, they were by no means the first to set foot on the islands. According to a Chinese chronicle, in the year 1436, the Chinese arrived here because of the "mountains of sandalwood trees" and they came to exploit the trade. As the Portuguese were interested in the sandalwood which could fetch high prices in Europe because of its aroma and medical values, they decided to colonise the country. Then in the mid-17th century, the Dutch occupied Kupang in West Timor, also because of the sandalwood trade. There was a conflict between the two Europeans countries, but finally an agreement was reached in 1913 resulting in Portuguese taking over East Timor and the Dutch West Timor.

Portuguese power in East Timor waned after the sandalwood trade fizzled out and the country fell into a depression after World War I. East Timor then depended on its high quality coffee.

On the eve of World War II, Dili was a town without electricity, no water supply, no paved roads, no telephone service and not even a wharf for cargo handling. In 1942, Japan attacked East Timor because they wanted to use it as a springboard to attack Australia. Several hundred Australian soldiers were sent to the island and carried out guerrilla warfare against the Japanese troops numbering 20,000, killing at least 1,500 of them. The Australian were victorious because they had the support of the East Timorese. During the war, all farms were abandoned resulting in starvation, while other Timorese were killed by the Allied bombing. By the end of the war, between 40,000 to 60,000 East Timorese had died.

After the war, the Portuguese resumed control. They rebuilt Dili, plantations were put back in shape, and the production of livestock and grain increased. But by the 1970s, there was little industry and no sign of valuable mineral resources and scant improvement in education.

Before the Portuguese colonised Timor, the country was divided into a number of kingdoms, or *rais* or *reinos* as Portuguese would call them. Each rais was under a king or *liurai*. The rais were made up of a number of *sucos*, or tribal groups, most of which were in turn broken up into *ahli matan* or clans or village units which the Portuguese called *povoacao* (settlements). This was the colonial system used for local administration in its indirect rule and was adapted as its control extended across the territory. In practise, the Portuguese system meant direct control at the provincial level with the administrators' presence having little direct impact on the population.

Dili's urban centres have always been small. In 1970, it had only 28,000 people. More than 80 percent of the population lived in the hundreds of small hamlets or povoacao, scattered across the country. The hamlet consisted of between three and a dozen or so houses, constructed mainly of timber, bamboo and palm leaves. The style of construction and the design varied remarkably from region to region. In the east, especially in the Lautermk-Tutuala area, intricately adorned houses on stilts were to be found. Rectagular houses were to be found along the northern coast. In the mountainous regions hamlets often adorned the tops of hills and peaks, a reminder of past needs for defence against surprise attack by traditional enemies. Most settlements were well away from the roads, but they were invariably interlinked by a maze of tracks, along which the Timorese moved at impressive speed.

The Timorese farmers live primarily by the cultivation of corn and root crops in patrilineally-inherited ancestral gardens; grow rice in elaborately sculpted and irrigated montain terraces; herd water buffalos, goats and pigs; raised chikens and fighting cocks; and weave cloths which, along with their crops and livestock, ancient swords, glass beads and a few gold amulets, comprise the totality of their exchangeable wealth.

Not far from Dili's thin facade of affluence, most of the Timorese continue to eke out a bare existence through subsistence agriculture, often based on the destructive *lalang* (grass) or slash-and-burn system, with maize as the principal crop. All the retail business in Dili is in the hands of the Chinese, who have also expanded their economic activities to the cultivation and export of coffee. The largest Chinese firm and the most dynamic business in the province was Sang Tai Hoo, which was owned by two brothers who had good contacts in Singapore, Hong Kong and Macau. There are about 400 Chinese businesses which control about 95 percent of the business activities in East Timor. They have also acted as middlemen in the purchase of grain and coffee from the Timorese.

According to the official census statistics of 1970, there were about 6,120 Chinese in East Timor, but the figure did not include the *mestico* (products of intermarriage between the Chinese and the Timorese) who make up an equal number. The Chinese were law-abiding and were totally uninterested in local politics or China-oriented politics such as being pro-Beijing or pro-Taiwan. They were interested only in their business. In a situation where the Chinese generally are discriminated against in Indonesia and Southeast Asia, East Timor becomes a pleasant haven although it is isolated and progress is slow in development.

However, in the eyes of the educated Timorese, the Chinese are aliens who care for nothing about the country except money. They regard the Chinese as exploiters of the country's resources "by devious means", who had come to monopolise its wealth and secretly trans-ferred such wealth to Singapore and Hong Kong. They feel strongly that the Chinese economic stronghold must be broken. Under such circumstances, the Chinese became the strongest supporters of a con-tinuation of Portuguese rule in East Timor.

Apart from the Chinese, there is a small Arab community of about 500 persons. Most of them are Muslims, and the Timorese are also suspicious of them. Among the Muslims are those from Surabaya and Makassar carrying on business in smaller shops and all of them speak Bahasa Indonesia. These were the people who supported East Timor's integration with Indonesia. For example, a leading member of Dili's Muslim community, Mari Alkatiri was Minister for Foreign Affairs for the short-lived Fretilin-controlled government after that party assumed power.

I visited Dili, the capital of East Timor, to see how the Timorese had fared under Indonesian rule. Dili is a lovely town with distinctive Mediterranean features. It has clean wide streets, shady squares and is always in a sleepy mood. The town has few scars of war, although there had been fierce fighting, a civil war and the Indonesian invasion.

There are old Portuguese buildings with terracotta roofs and white stucco walls overlooking the Dili Bay. The Indonesian authorities apparently have spent a lot of money building up new roads, schools, a library, a university, a stadium and a cathedral.

I saw *Merah Putih* (red and white Indonesian national flag) flattering on a pole in front of the governor's office. The Indonesians have retained all street names bearing the names of Portuguese governors, war heroes, explorers and Portuguese leaders. The dominance of Chinese businesses and shops are glaring. They are in all lines of businesses. The Chinese speak Mandarin and Indonesian and some Portuguese. Some of them are descendents of the early Chinese pioneers who came to Timor to look for sandalwood in the 1500s. The Chinese children attended Chinese schools where they studied Mandarin, Chinese history and Chinese culture based on the Taiwan syllabus. Few Chinese spoke Portuguese fluently, although many of them spoke Tetum, especially those living in small towns and villages who are in constant contact with the indigenous population.

The Chinese minority were mostly concentrated in Dili and in the larger towns such as Baucau, Ermera, Manutujto and Bobonam, but they were to be found wherever villages were large enough to attract retail outlets. Some of the wealthier Chinese possessed coffee plantations and rice fields but very few lived outside the precincts of the towns and larger villages.

In the capital and the larger towns, the Chinese communities maintained a closely knit social organisation, stayed clear of sensitive political issues, and rarely mixed with the Portuguese or the Timorese. In the villages, there were some intermarriages between Chinese men and Timorese women, who nevertheless had to endure an inferior status in the eyes of the community at large.

As in most Mediterranean towns, the workers, clerks and managers take a siesta of about four hours in the afternoon during which the town appeared dead.

I saw the largest Catholic cathedral, easily the largest in Southeast Asia, which was opened by Pope John Paul II in October 1989 when he visited the town. During the Pope's visit, villagers came from faraway villages, walking for miles with a hungry stomach. The Fretilin claimed that the place where the Pope held his mass was the site where Indonesian soldiers had massacred thousands of Timorese.

There are a number of momuments, some dedicated to Australians who died during World War II. Another monument was built to commemorate Ir. Arthur Canto De Resende, who died in a Japanese prisoner-of-war camp in Aloar in 1942.

I could not find any Timorese food in Dili. Most restaurants served Javanese and Sulawesi dishes such as *gado gado* or *soto Makassar* or *soto ayam*.

Everywhere I went, I was greeted by the Timorese with a smile or a wave particularly school children in neat uniform. I also saw many new immigrants who were non-Timorese from Java, Sumatra, Sulawesi and islands surrounding Timor. The new immigrants are more open but the Timorese seemed to keep their mouth shut and refused to talk to strangers although they were not hostile. There was an unmistakably alarming gap between the new-comers and the local Timorese. The Timorese seemed rather hostile to the new immigrants. The local Timorese are more naive in business and they do not bargain. They had not been trained by the Portuguese to read and write. Most of them were employed as domestic servants by civil servants and foreigners.

Economically speaking, the war had disrupted business and agriculture. There is a heavy dose of military monopoly in business under the Indonesian administration. The export of coffee and timber is in the hands of the army. All coffee has to be sold to the government cooperatives with its shadowy military connections at fixed official price. Coffee growers complain that they receive less for their product than growers in West Timor, and this is adding unrest to the province. Until recently, coffee is exported to a company run by Indonesian Chinese businessmen.

On 12 July, 1988, this sleepy town of Dili suddenly became alive again when 50,000 non-Timorese residents — Javanese and Bugis from South Sulawesi — fled Dili when rumours spread that a massive pro-independence rally would be held there. The Bugis was the target of attack because the Timorese did not like them.

The Timorese became livelier on 28 July, 1998, when they came out in full force to watch the pull-out of 400 Indonesian elite combat troops from Dili in a hastily scheduled troop reduction signifying the beginning of the end of more than 20 years of bloody conflict. As local military, civil and religious leaders watched, 398 soldiers from the Kapassus Special Forces and Kostrad Strategic Reserves commands piled into the waiting ship for a five-day journey to Jakarta. The troop reduction exercise was recorded for posterity by invited Indonesian and foreign reporters. About 400 Indonesian troops have withdrawn from East Timor which Indonesia had annexed 22 years ago. The Indonesian military authorities are leaving behind about 7,500 troops to maintain security and do community work among the 800,000 people, a fifth of which are East Timorese.

The withdrawal came barely a week after UN special envoy Jamsheed Marker called for a partial troop pull-out as a "confidence-building measure" and as a requisite for bringing together Jakarta, Lisbon and East Timorese factions in a dialogue under UN auspices.

Today, more than two decades after the invasion of Dili, international interest on the Timorese issue is astonishingly greater than ever. One of the reasons was the fall of Suharto from power. Second, the collapse of the Soviet Union which led to the liberation of the Baltic states brought into focus the atrocities perpetrated in Bosnia that has shocked the international community and therefore the same effect is felt for the captive nation status of the people of East Timor. And of course, the increasingly popular passive resistance involving almost the entire Timorese population and the strong stand of Bishop Belo, the Nobel Peace Prize winner on the referendum issue.

If UN allows a referendum to be conducted in East Timor to decide what the people want, it is clear that the people would want to break away from Indonesian rule. This would be the first crack in Indonesia's territorial integrity.

Indonesia may let go of the troubled territory of East Timor if Jakarta's latest offer of wide-ranging autonomy is rejected by the majority of the population there. This was announced by Indonesia's Foreign Minister Ali Alatas confirming for the Indonesian Government after a cabinet meeting on 28 January 1999. He said, "If autonomy is rejected or results in a deadlock, it is only fair and wise and even democratic and constitutional to suggest to the upcoming elected people's representatives to allow East Timor to separate from Indonesia in a dignified and good manner." He however, added that "we have not reached that point because we are still proposing a comprehensive solution on the problem of East Timor and we will continue to discuss the extended autonomy." He said a referendum after five or even ten years was not the best way because it would lead to conflict or civil war.

In Dili, the capital of East Timor, pro-independence leaders were stunned by the news of independence and rushed into the streets in the late evening and joyfully embracing each other and shaking hands as they went. However, several pro-Indonesian activists felt rather worried and unhappy. The representatives of 13 districts met on 28 January and decided to ask the Indonesian to arm them "to protect ourselves".

The United States described the Indonesian's move as a "positive development" and welcomed any agreement on the future status of East Timor. The United Nation's Secretary-General welcomed the offer and announced that he was happy to hear that East Timor leader Xanana Gusmao would be transferred from gaol to house arrest. Portugal voiced caution, saying any immediate official reaction would be "premature". A spokesman of the Portuguese Foreign Ministry said that Lisbon was determined to "find out whether there is a new Indonesian policy or a new way of formulating the same policy". Australia, one of the few nations to recognise Indonesia's sovereignty applauded Indonesia's new stand. The Foreign Minister Alexander Downer said was a significant step forward when compared to the former government. The East Timorese Nobel Peace Prize winner Jose Ramos Horta, who lives in self-imposed exile in Australia, said the move was a sham aimed at the diplomatic community. He said, "We are sick and tired of promises, statements coming out of Jakarta which are in contrast with the reality in East Timor, where people are being slaughtered, where women are still raped, torture is rampant, and there are more than 20,000 troops there."

9
THE CHINESE
Target of Economic Jealousy

The Chinese in Indonesia numbering about 6.5 million are mostly Indonesian citizens, but they are the ethnic minority most discriminated against. They have been ostracised from the mainstream of Indonesian society and deprived of their political power and even the right to study their own language. The reason is that the *pribumis* (indigenous people) find it difficult to believe and swallow the fact that the Chinese, who constitute only three percent of Indonesia's population, control more than 70 percent of the country's private domestic capital. In a vast country like Indonesia where 80 million Indonesians are living below the poverty line, the Chinese, who are comparatively well-off, stick out like a sore-thumb and become a torn in the flesh of the Indonesian society. The Chinese succeed in all fields, as businessmen, bankers, professionals, traders, shop-keepers, plantation owners and overseers, mechanics, salesmen, tour guides as well as workers, all except as politicians and civil servants because they are barred from such professions. They are often described as the "Jews" of Southeast Asia.

Most of the young Chinese, who have forgotten their own mother tongue or any Chinese dialect, speak only Bahasa Indonesia. They have changed their names into Indonesian names, relinquished all Chinese customs and traditions and do not even celebrate Chinese New Year.

Many of them grow moustaches to look like Indonesians. Some married Indonesian girls and allowed themselves to be assimilated. And yet, when the student riots erupted in Jakarta in May 1998, they became the target of attacks; their shops looted, their properties smashed and burnt, many lost their lives and 70,000 Indonesian Chinese left the country in an exodus reluctantly. The Chinese lost altogether US$217 million worth of property damage and they took away with them US$369 million equivalent in capital.

It was the worst anti-Chinese riot ever staged in the history of Indonesia. At the height of the riots, more than 100 ethnic Chinese women and girls were raped and some thrown into the fire that burnt their houses. The gang rapes took on a disturbingly similar pattern throughout Jakarta on May 14 as rioters attacked Chinese houses, raped the younger women, and burnt the houses in succession. One woman killed herself by drinking insecticide after she was raped in front of her husband and children in the Chinatown district of North Jakarta. Even Indonesia's Minister of Women's Affair Tuti Allawiyah, said after the incident that rapes were "very inhuman". Activist groups said the rapes were done in "frighteningly systematic fashion, targetting women among Indonesian's ethnic Chinese minority". One source estimated that at least 1,000 Chinese women were raped in the whole of Indonesia. It could be the last straw for the Chinese, and a large number who had the means migrated elsewhere. This riot has shattered the confidence of the ethnic Chinese population. Despite frequent assurances and undertakings from the Indonesian Government that there would be no more anti-Chinese sentiments, most Chinese hesitate to return. Even if the older generation want to return, the younger generation who are Western educated would not take the risk of their daughters being molested in future.

What were the Armed Forces on duty doing during the burning of the Chinese houses and the raping of women? Why did they not intervene? Where was the law and order which they were supposed to maintain? Did the Armed Forces deliberately take no action in order to punish the Chinese? Or, was it an organised move by some elements with ulterior motives? These are some of the questions asked after the May riots. Someone well-versed in Indonesian politics told me that Suharto's divide-and-rule tactics which he had applied to the intelligence network had misfired. One group of intelligence personnel who have a grudge against another group would not listen to the information provided and thus no action was taken during the riots. Whether this is true or not, nobody knows.

There was no doubt in my mind that the May riots of 1998 were targetted at ethnic Chinese. On 20 July 1998, about two months after the riots, angry mobs in Indonesia's East Java began attacking shops and homes owned by Javanese Muslims just because these Muslims had protected ethnic Chinese during the recent riots. In the past few weeks, ethnic Chinese-owned shops in strongly Islamic districts have suffered attack and Chinese traders had sought help from local Muslim leaders. The hooligans attacking the Muslim leaders shouted, "You preachers should be defending Islamic followers but you instead defended the Chinese."

Anti-Chinese sentiments are not new. It first erupted in 1740 in Jakarta instigated by the Dutch because of their fear of Chinese competition and thousands of Chinese were massacred. Their bodies were thrown into the Jakarta Kali river *Tjiliwung* and the river turned red. It was known as the Red River Massacre. There was not a single Chinese left in Jakarta. Tanah Abang (which means "Red Earth" in English) the name of a district, still stands as a black memory. Even Chinese outside Jakarta were sought to be killed. The Dutch Government offered "two crowns for every Chinese head".

After the massacre, the Chinese were forcibly relocated in Glodok, Jakarta's Chinatown in Jalan Pintu Besar (the Street of Big Gate) outside the city walls. Here, the Dutch architecture contrasted strikingly with Chinese buildings with their curved red-tiled roofs and balconies. Jalan Gajah Mada houses the former home of the Chinese "capitan" called *Candra Naya*, who administered Batavia's Chinese community. There is a superstitious belief in the nearby Wall Street of Jakarta, known as Pintu Kechil (Xiao Nan Men) or Little Southern Gate, the centre of Chinese banking and trade, that anti-Chinese violence erupts in Indonesia once every eight years. Still fresh in the minds of most middle-aged and older generation Chinese are the incidents which took place at intervals of eight years since 1949. In 1949, many Chinese were murdered and their houses and cars burnt when the indigenous Indonesian went for them because many Chinese sided with the Dutch colonials against the Indonesian revolution. Eight years later, in 1957, Sukarno took drastic action against the Chinese by banning them from all retail trade throughout the country. In 1965, eight years later, a large number of Chinese were killed for their involvement in the Gestapu coup. The victims were mainly those Chinese who sympathised with the Baperki (Consultative Council of Indonesian citizenship) and the Communist Party of Indonesia (PKI) and their affiliated unions and farmers' association. In 1973, owing to the greedy manipulations of Chinese cukongs (rich Chinese who manipulated Indonesian military personnel from behind the scene) riots broke out in Bandung and Jakarta. Then one year later in 1974, another anti-Chinese riot took place during the visit of Japan's Prime Minister Kakuei Tanaka when rioters burnt down Chinese-owned cars and houses. The riot was engineered to show Indonesian displeasure of the Japanese choice of their business partners. They were angry that the Japanese had chosen the Chinese as their business partners instead of the pribumis (indigenous Indonesians).

In December 1980, an anti-Chinese riot in Solo damaged 400 vehicles, 500 scooters and four houses were burnt. It was one of the most serious riots that ever occurred. Since then, there had been a repetition of anti-Chinese riots and the worst was the recent riots which brought the downfall of Suharto.

Unlike the Jews who had settled down in the Middle East only after World War II, the Chinese arrived at the shores of Java as early as the 5th century. In fact, the famous Chinese Muslim eunuch, Admiral Cheng Ho, led "63 treasure ships" to the South seas including Java in the 15th century during the Ming dynasty. There is even a theory that it was Cheng Ho who introduced Islam to Java. The Sampo Beo (temple of Sampo — the honorific name of Cheng Ho) was built in the city of Semarang on the northern coast of Central

Java to commemorate Admiral Cheng Ho. This temple is known to Javanese as *Kelenteng Sampo*.

I visited the Sampo Beo a number of times before and after I became Ambassador to Indonesia. The temple resembles any other Chinese Buddhist or Taoist temple with oriental pagoda-type eaves and tall red pillars surrounding an open porch where incense holders made of brass are placed on a wooden altar. When I visited the temple, it was terribly crowded and the air was heavily polluted by thick smoke from the burning of joss-sticks. There was a long queue waiting to kneel before the altar of Sampo Kong (the spiritual name of Admiral Cheng Ho) in the inner chamber. The dark chamber was cramped with worshippers, each clutching smoking joss-sticks. I almost choked on the irritating, smelly smoke. However, strange as it may seem, nobody uttered a word. Each worshipper diligently shook a container of bamboo sticks, causing the harsh, hollow sounds to break the silence of the temple. Eventually, one bamboo stick would pop out of the container and fall to the floor. This would be brought to the counter in exchange for a yellow piece of paper called the *chiam-si* or fortune script.

The thing that struck me was the person who was looking after the chiam-si counter in the Kelenteng Sampo. He was not a Buddhist priest with shaven head and yellow robes. He wore a *songkok* (a black velvet cap worn mainly by Muslims) and claimed to be a Muslim. Another interesting aspect was that the chiam-si was written in the Indonesian language with detailed interpretation of the Chinese stories. The majority of those who now visit the Kelenteng Sampo are descendents of the early Chinese migrants in Indonesia and who do not speak any Chinese dialects. They are known as *Peranakan* which means literally 'born locally". Even the *tokoh* or *sin keh* (the term given to those Chinese who arrived from China comparatively recently) can read and write Bahasa Indonesia, the national language.

Next to the main temple is another smaller temple under a giant fig tree. It has three compartments: the one on the left displays a huge ancient anchor, the remains of one of the ships of Admiral Cheng Ho's fleet; the compartment in the centre contains a picture of the famous Chinese sage, Confucius and the one on the right has a plaque to commemorate the hundreds of unknown sailors who lost their lives during the long sea voyages to Java. The rusty anchor has become a pusaka, and people pray to it because they believe it holds magical powers. A root from the giant fig tree nearby has shot up from the ground behind where the anchor is placed. The snake-like root meanders up through the branches of the tree like a rope linking the anchor to the main tree trunk. The place where the anchor stands, I was told, was where a ship had anchored. Apparently, hundreds of years ago, the whole vicinity was covered by the sea.

The altar of Confucius in the Sampo temple has only helped to complicate matters further. How did the founders of the temple get Confucius mixed up in the whole affair? I asked the old Javanese Muslim caretaker, who replied, "I know Confucius. His spirit has been here since the temple was built."

The Sampo Beo has the characteristics of three religions combined into one. The Buddhist feature is the form of the temple, the Taoist is mysticism in making the anchor a pusaka, and the Confucianist features are the portrait of Confucius as well as the plaque honouring the souls of the hundreds of sailors, representing Confucius' teaching of ancestor worship.

When Admiral Cheng Ho arrived at Java, his treasure ships were loaded with silk, porcelains and camphors which they traded in exchange for products such as jade, elephant trunks, rhinoceros horns, spices, and precious stones.

During the Ming dynasty, about 500 years ago, there was already considerable migration from China to Java. There were those who were descendents of Chinese fugitives who escaped the scourge of the Mongols after the fall of the Southern Sung dynasty. The second groups of Chinese migrants to Indonesia consisted mainly of pirates, smugglers, criminals and those who were without the means of earning a living. There was another group consisting of those who fled or went overseas for various reasons and who served as officials of foreign countries.

After the Batavia Red River massacre in 1740, when Emperor Chien Lung heard about the Dutch cruelty, he said, "...they (the victims) deserted their ancestral tombs and sought benefits overseas and the court is not interested in them...."

The Ming and Ching emperors made no attempt to protect overseas Chinese as they were considered criminals and faced the risk of being beheaded when captured.

The Chinese were the first foreigners to set foot on Java. When Admiral Cheng Ho arrived in Java, he found in Gersik (a port in West Java) ethnic Chinese who were given the title of "syahbander" (meaning head) who were playing important roles in Java's political economic fields. When the Dutch conquered Indonesia, they discovered a small Chinese "kingdom" in Pontianak, Kalimantan run by a miner named Lo Fangbo, a Hakka, who had his own police force, own prison and own judges. Later on, the Dutch honoured him with the title of 'capitan' but took away all his powers through a military exercise.

At the end of the 16th century when the Dutch appeared on the Indonesian scene, they observed that small Chinese pedlars were already going to the hinterland to buy pepper and selling them for export. When the powerful Dutch trade monopoly of VOC (United East India Company) moved in, they relegated the Chinese to the position of collectors of indigenous agricultural commodities and distributors of imported Dutch manufactured goods and also Asian products such as opium, which was solely imported by the Dutch. One of the richest Chinese then was Oei Tiong Ham (1865-1924), born in Semarang whose company called Kian Gwan held the profitable opium monopoly in both central and east Java and made him a fortune. Some observers maintained that he was able to succeed because of his modern management. When he died, his property was worth about 200 milion guilders which was enormous in those days.

From the 17th century to the 20th century, the Dutch pressed ahead with their more systematic exploitation of the Indonesia economy and they needed the Chinese as middlemen to deal with the indigenous people. Jan Pieterszoon Coen, the greatest of all Governor-Generals of the Dutch who established the foundation of Dutch colonisation said, "We need the Chinese to build this country. They are diligent and hardworking people of various trades and crafts and lovers of peace and honesty." They farmed out to the Chinese several avenues of profits such as pawning, market, village, toll and other revenues and created a rich elite among the generally petty interme diate traders.

As the Dutch were using the Chinese, they were afraid of increasing Chinese power and influence and tried to curtail and minimise their various crafts and trades. In their attempt to defend their human rights and justice, a revolt against the Dutch rule took place in 1740. This resulted in the infamous Chinse massacre of Tjiliwung in Batavia, the worst act of human violence by the Dutch and a black mark in Dutch colonial history.

During the Dutch colonial days, the people of Indonesia were divided into various groupings: the white-faced Europeans — the Dutch who were the masters; the yellow man with his slit-eyes and the merchant class — the Chinese; and the dark-coloured natives — the Indonesian indigenous people who were peasants and coolies. In other words, the Dutch were the first class, the Chinese the second class and the Indonesians the third class. The Chinese somehow looked down on the pribumi. Even the Chinese mee-seller would make the pribumi carry the stall and he would hit the "tok tok" (a percussion block that makes the sound) alerting people that a mee-seller was coming.

That is the root of the long-hidden hatred of the Indonesians towards the Chinese. Then came the Indonesian revolution when a large number of Chinese sided with the Dutch, though some joined the Indonesian revolution. That further aggravated the hatred. Then, the disparity of wealth between the Chinese and the pribumi was the third factor causing the jealousy and hatred.

At the beginning of this century, Indonesian-born Chinese (Peranakan) had become culturally more Indonesian than Chinese, to the extent that most of them did not read or speak Chinese. A Tionghua Hwee Kuan (Chinese Association — THK) was founded in 1900 to stop the further erosion of Chinese culture among the

Peranakans. The formation of the Tionghua Hwee Kuan came about when Dr Sun Yat-sen's anti-Manchu revolutionary movement spread to Indonesia and he was propagandising that the Chinese should not forget their own language and culture.

Then, leaders of the Peranakan group founded the Baperki (Consultative Council of Indonesian citizenship) which began to spread the awareness of the political identity of the Indonesian Chinese. Out of the estimated one and half million Peranakan Chinese, about 300,000 were members of the Baperki.

Baperki was well regarded by the Chinese minority. It successfully protected the economic position of the Chinese and it owed its influence to two political power factors: President Sukarno and the Indonesian Communist Party (PKI) and its mass organisation. Baperki supported Sukarno's "guided democracy" and became closely associated wih the PKI. At that time, Sukarno's relations with the People's Republic of China was good.

The important activity of Baperki was in the field of education. It set up Chinese schools throughout the archipelago and in the early 1960s collected money to build a university. The university of Baperki opened its branches in Semarang and Surabaya. In its heydays in the first half of 1965, the university had in Jakarta more than 6,000 students or about 10,000, taking in those from the branches.

Never before in Indonesia had a university grown so swiftly. President Sukarno, enraptured by its speedy growth and early vigour, gave it a new name *Res Publicka*. It had opened wide its doors to the indigenous students but only a few of them had ever been admitted because indigenous students could easily get admission to the state universities.

During the Sukarno regime, all Indonesian citizens including the Chinese were treated equally as citizens. Sukarno had even appointed two ethnic Chinese as Ministers in the Cabinet. One of them was Oei Tjoe Tat, a lawyer. He never had an Indonesian name. He was Minister of State without portfolio attached to the Cabinet Presidium of Sukarno in December 1963. He was arrested after the Gestapu coup, detained for 10 years and released in 1977.

Although Sukarno was fair to the Chinese, he was under pressure in the early 1960s to curtail the retail business of the Chinese. Disclosing the reason to me when I met him in Singapore after his release, Oei Tjoe Tat, who was a confidant of Sukarno said pribumi had pressurised him to give them economic priority over the Chinese and he had to give in. The second reason was that the Muslim bodies were worried that the Chinese would subvert the country through their retail shops.

When the pribumi took over the retail business, they could not run them and their businesses flopped. Sukarno then again allowed the Chinese to resume retail business.

On the Indonesian authorities compelling the Chinese to change their names, Oei Tjoe Tat said he once asked Sukarno whether it was necessary to change names and Sukarno said, "Why should you change your name. It was given by your father and you should respect your father." He said Sukarno had always felt that the Chinese should be treated as one of the minorities with equal rights as citizens.

Oei Tjoe Tat was offered repatriation to the Netherlands and he refused. He said, "When I was detained in the same cell as Subandrio (former Foreign Minister under Sukarno), I felt that I was one of them. I am an Indonesian. I do not speak a word of Chinese and I am loyal to this country. I do not want to betray the lots of Chinese Indonesians who felt the same way as I do to Indonesia."

"They have kept me in as an Indonesian and I cannot leave the country for the sake of my own comfort. My roots are in Indonesia. My family has lived here for five generations."

There are hundreds of thousands of Indonesian Chinese who are like Oei Tjoe Tat. They do not speak any Chinese dialect, are almost completely assimilated by Indonesian culture and are loyal to Indonesia. There is no place for them in China for they do not speak Chinese and have no known relatives there.

However, there were many *totoks* who were educated in Chinese and who were loyal to China, having been taught by teachers from China. Some were pro-Beijing and others pro-Taipei. During the decade from 1948 to 1958, they played foreign politics on Indonesian soil and it became a great concern to the Indonesian authorities. There was a bitter struggle between the Communist and the Kuomintang. The Kuomintang associations bearing the colours of blue and white on their signboards clashed with the red and yellow pro-Communist associations. Pro-Taipei and pro-Beijing newspapers fought it out in the open. This struggle permeated the whole of the Chinese community, from the schools down to the clubs and associations. During the Sukarno regime, the pro-Beijing associations had the upper hand because Sukarno was flirting with the Jakarta-Peking axis and was friendly with the Chinese embassy. Therefore the pro-Taipei organisations were handicapped. In 1958, Taipei aided the rebellions which broke out in Sumatra and the Celebes. This provoked the Indonesian authorities to crack down on Kuomintang organisations. All Kuomintang organisations were banned and eventually schools and businesses with Kuomintang connections were closed. Then came the Gestapu coup of 1965 when the Chinese embassy was alleged to be involved with the PKI assassination of the six generals and a soldier. Pro-Beijing associations, including Baperki, were closed, their leaders arrested and detained and some killed.

After the abortive coup of September 30, 1965, the Baperki became the target of attack by the Indonesian armed forces which massacred 200,000 Communists. Thousands of Chinese who were officials of Baperki were killed. The Baperki was to have been the capitalist "cukong" (a phrase coined to discredit the Chinese who were the financial supporters of Indonesian communist party).

The Baperki was outlawed. All members of the board of its central committee were blacklisted and their bank accounts were frozen. All Chinese associations in the country were disbanded and its club houses taken over by the army. All Chinese schools were closed. The authorities banned the *Hsin Pao* (Sin Po) — a pro-Beijing Chinese daily. And in early 1966, Res Publicka University was taken over by the authorities which turned it into the *Tri Sakti*.

With the downfall of Baperki, the economic position of the Chinese became imperilled. During a racial riot, no distinction was made between members of the hated organisation and non-members, the chief target of the pogrom was the whole Chinese population.

In early 1960, an exodus of Chinese took place when many banished and others migrated to China because they were unhappy with the discriminatory measures against the Chinese. One reliable estimate puts the total number of those who returned to China between 1949 and 1966 at 100,000. They were looking forward to return to a new China under Communism and thought that life would be rosier there. Many returned with high hopes and expectations of Communist transformation of society. Most of them were disillusioned especially after the cultural revolution in the mid 1960s.

With the fall of Sukarno, the 20 years of "Old Order" was replaced by the New Order under the Suharto regime. Under the New Order, there was a rumour purporting that ethnic Chinese Indonesians were required to change their Chinese names into Indonesian names. There was no government decree as such nor official proclamation. However, there was an official announcement in the newspapers that the government had fixed a period in which the procedures of changing Chinese names would be made easy and that any Chinese who wished to avail themselves of the opportunity should do so.

The Suharto regime closed down all Chinese schools, banned all Chinese newspapers and did not even allow any Chinese characters to be displayed in Indonesia. I wrote a book entitled "Indonesia between Myth and Reality" which introduces the cultures of the Indonesian people. Not a word was critical of Indonesia or the Indonesians but it was still banned in Indonesia. It was written in Chinese.

I remember when I first visited Jakarta and Bandung in 1955 during the Afro-Asian Conference that there were still Chinese signboards everywhere. Chinese newspapers fought out their Chinese ideological war on Indonesian soil and Chinese schools could be seen in every village. When I visited Indonesia again in 1960 with Prime Minister Lee Kuan Yew to see President Sukarno, there were still Chinese newspapers and Chinese schools and Chinese signboards. But when I went to Indonesia to present credentials to President Suharto, there were no more Chinese signboards nor any Chinese associations or schools or newspapers. Not only was the Chinese language considered "harmful", but even Chinese religion and customs were regarded as undesirable. I was told that in 1967 a Presidential instruction stated that Chinese religion, beliefs and customs originated from their ancestral land and their various manifestations might generate unnatural influence on the psychology, mentality and morality of Indonesian citizens and therefore impede natural prosperity. It was ordered that Chinese religion be observed only in recognised circles. But later in 1969, the government officially recognised two minority religions, Buddhism and Confucianism. Law No. 5 of 1969 (UU No. 5/1969) stipulates that these two religions and four others (Islam, Protestantism, Catholicism and Hindu-Bali) were officially recognised by the government. Since the Indonesian state ideology, the Pancasila, included "Belief in God" as the first principle, every person in Indonesia was expected to have a religion of some kind.

The New Order hoped to completely assimilate the Chinese citizens into what is considered as "real Indonesians". The clearest manifestation of the New Order assimilation policy in the cultural field was the name-changing regulation issued in December 1966. Previously, a law (UU No. 4/1964) had given all Indonesian citizens of foreign descent the opportunity to change their names to Indonesian (or Indonesian sounding) names. The applicants were required to obtain letters of recommendations from governors or local regents and local police chiefs. But, the government did not publicise the law and did not actively encourage it. In December 1966, the Suharto Government simplified the procedure in order to encourage name-changing among Indonesian citizens of foreign descent. They could simply submit their applications to the local authorities (usually governors, regents or mayors). A small fee would be charged and the applications would be passed on to the Department of Justice. In 1980, the Suharto Government further simplified its procedure for Chinese to be naturalised. He issued two decrees, the first, known as the Presidential Instruction No. 2/1980, was signed on 31 January 1980 and the second, the Presidential Decision No. 13/1980, was signed on 11 February 1980.

The simplification of the procedures for naturalisation of non-citizen Chinese into Indonesian citizens was one of the steps the Suharto Government had taken to ensure that when Indonesia normalised relations with Beijing, the problems of the Chinese would be minimised. The authorities wanted to be sure that the Chinese are properly assimilated before embarking on normalising relations with Beijing.

What is meant by properly assimilated? This was what General Sumitro, one time strongman in Indonesia who was the Head of Kopkamtib (Security) had to say when I had a game of golf with him in April 1971, "I would like to see all Chinese in Indonesia forget their own culture and tradition and be assimilated completely into the Indonesian society. The Chinese should not continue to stick to their old customs and traditions or identify themselves either with Beijing or Taiwan."

I think many Indonesian leaders share his views and that was why the Indonesian authorities were taking steps to assimilate the Chinese.

Will anti-Chinese riots disappear once all the Chinese in Indonesia are completely assmilated? As far as I can see, most of the younger generation Chinese, the Peranakan, do not speak any Chinese dialect, not to mention reading or writing Chinese. I met one young Indonesian whose name is Kintamani who came from Jakarta and who was educated in England. I asked him which village his ancestors came from in China. He said even his father would not know. "What is your Chinese surname?". He said, "Kintamani." I laughed and he laughed too. Many young Indonesians are in a similar frame of mind. I would consider young ethnic Chinese of this nature completely assimilated. They do not celebrate Chinese auspicious days or practise traditional customs such as making "tsang" (rice wrapped in bamboo leaves) for the "dragon-boat festival" or the "mooncake festival". They are afraid to perform ancestor worship or to keep ancestral altars. They are even afraid to celebrate the Lunar New Year. Some of them grow moustaches to look like Indonesians. In years to come, they will definitely lose their roots.

The feeling of the Chinese in Indonesia was best described by an Indonesian-born Chinese who returned to China, took part in the 1911 revolution, got disillusioned and returned to Indonesia. He was Thung Liang Lee (deceased) who was secretary to Wang Ching Wei, one of the leading Chinese revolutionaries who collaborated with the Japanese during the occupation and who was considered a "traitor". Writing in March 1954 in an article entitled "The unreality of Chinese nationalism in Indonesia — an apologia and a reorientation", Thung said,

> "The Chinese loathe to assimilate themselves with the native population especially since owing to Dutch colonial policy, assimilation did not mean equalisation of rights with the Indonesians. They succumbed to the Dutch view of regarding the Indonesians as a somewhat inferior race. There were few intermarriages. Racially, linguistically and psychologically, they are much closer even than the China Chinese. But they not only persisted in their refusal to assimilate themselves with their natural brothers and sisters; they even refused to regard the country of their birth and upbringing as their own, true country. Yet, disregarding the facts of history and of ethnology, they tried to become as Chinese-Chinese as possible.
>
> Chinese nationalism became an obsession which hampered their outlook and hindered their political advancement at every step. It enmeshed them in a mess of contradictions, causing friction and suspicion everywhere."

Thung Liang Lee felt that the early immigrants prior to and during the early days of the East Indies Company were completely assimilated by the native population, which acquired a certain strain in their blood. He added,

> "Some of the well-known Princely Houses and aristocratic families of Indonesia like the Sultan of Palembang, Bantam, Cirebon and the regents of Tjiamis and Sumedang have had Chinese ancestors and are proud to acknowledge the fact.

Lacking in historical perspective, unversed in international affairs, devoid of political realism, the 20th century Indonesian Chinese could only dream of a new China which, once arisen to the position of a Great Power, would automatically secure for them the same privileged status which Japan had, as a special case, secured for their handful of nationals.

China had become a panacea for all their woes and sufferings, real and imaginary. Thus, they started a movement to repudiate the *juis soli* element in the Netherlands Indies National Law and demanded the right for the Indonesian Chinese to owe political allegiance to the Chinese Republic. In this way, they formally announced their intention of seeking redress of their grievances ouside the framework of the existing political system. They were completely oblivious of the fact that what would be conceded as a special case to a handful of people would be intolerable if applied to a considerable and unassimilable minority group amounting to over a million people. (The Chinese population was then one million.) They could not realise that no country in the world could possibly tolerate, even at the risk of provoking an international war, the formation of what in effect would be a state within a state."

Commenting on the granting of citizenship to Chinese by the Indonesian authorities, Thung said:

"The grant by the Republic of Indonesia was a measure of goodwill of an unprecedented nature. It was a declaration on the part of the republic that we are wanted. It makes us all formally and legally Sino-Indonesians. It did not compel us, however, to accept the gift. But it put us in a far more favourable position than the Indo-European who had to make a special petition to acquire that status.

The warga negara status must be made into a reality by a proper response on our part. And this response must consist in the realisation that our salvation depends on our realising the unreality of Chinese nationalism and our renouncing all political and sentimental ties with the country that in fact had never wanted us.

We must never again fall under the delusion of China being our Fatherland, of being our true own country which loves and protects us and is therefore entitled to our allegiance and loyalty.

"Our true Fatherland is this country of Indonesia, the country of our mothers, our grandmothers, great-grandmothers and great-great-grandmothers. Our loyalty belongs to the Republic of Indonesia, and it must be one and undivided. Our efforts should be directed to making out of this archipelago the kind of commonwealth as we find in the United States of America — only without the racial discrimination that has become a blot on the American scene and a disgrace to modern civilisation.

A change of heart, more even than a reorientation of policy is required. For only with this change of heart can we devote our best efforts and energy to the construction of our new Fatherland, as statesmanship no less than self-interest demands."

Thung emphasised: "As the Republic of Indonesia needs us, so do we need the R.I. We require fair treatment and protection from the R.I. and the abolition of the last vestiges of the racial discrimination inherited from the old colonial regime. In return, we must give the R.I. not only our bodies but also our souls."

What Thung had said 40 years ago was right. It was a warning to the Indonesian Chinese to be more practical. Events have proved that hundreds of thousands of Indonesian Chinese were unrealistic. They could not realise the "unreality" of Chinese nationalism and they did not denounce their political and sentimental ties with China which in fact had never wanted them. In the early 1960s, hundreds of thousands of Indonesian Chinese fled to China and refused to take up Indonesian citizenship. They had expected China to protect them and to love them. But, nearly all of them were frustrated and disillusioned when the Chinese cultural revolution broke out in 1966 and they were denounced as "rightwing reactionaries", "spies" for foreign countries and were persecuted. Thung was right that China had never wanted them. They escaped to Hong Kong and are now stranded, never allowed to return to their "homeland" — Indonesia.

During May 1998 when the worst anti-Chinese riots occurred in Jakarta, there was a Chinese Embassy in Jakarta for Indonesia had established diplomatic relations with Beijing. However, what could the embassy do? It did not even raise a voice in protest against the riots.

But, Thung never expected that despite the loyalty the Indonesian Chinese who became warga negara (citizens) and did their best for the country, there was no fair treatment given to them and they were not protected. A series of anti-Chinese riots have broken out since Thung left this earth and the worst anti-Chinese riot in the history of Indonesia took place in May 1998.

What is the real cause of the frequent anti-Chinse riots in Indonesia? One of the fundamental reasons is the disparity of wealth between the indigenous Indonesians and the Indonesian Chinese. Although not all Chinese are rich and in fact the majority are poor, the bad image created by the minority cukongs could affect the well-being of the majority of innocent Chinese.

When the Indonesian revolution ousted the Dutch colonial masters from the country, the Dutch pulled out the entire administrative infrastructure, from the Governor down to the ordinary clerks and typists, leaving behind not a skeleton staff to man the administrative machinery. Sukarno's nationalist anti-West fervour had brought with it drastic measures of nationalisation of all US and European dominated oil industry and the confiscation of Dutch estates. These measures frightened away all western capitalists.

In Sukarno's 17-year rule, he was more interested in slogans and the revolution. He had no time to tap the natural resources of the country. He failed to utilise the capital and know-how of the Chinese to develop the country. In fact, he curtailed the retail business of the Chinese in the rural areas causing many Chinese to flee the country.

When Suharto took over, he realised that after the Dutch left, the Chinese was the only group in the country which had the capital and know-how to develop the country. Moreover, the Chinese had once worked with the Dutch in exploiting the country and knew the country well. During the days of the Dutch East Indies Company, many prominent Chinese were made Bupati (district officers and village chiefs) or Regents for reasons of expediency, because of their economic power and efficiency. The efficient Chinese organised the link between the islands and the Northern Java Coast from where the agricultural produce had to be shipped to the Netherlands. The Dutch found the pribumis incapable of filling this gap because of their easygoing habits.

When Suharto came to power, he consolidated the system of "cukongism" — co-operation and collaboration between the Chinese business tycoons and military officers in business deals. The words "cu" means "master" or "boss" and "kong" means "grandfather" or "Godfather". Although previously used, it became popular after Suharto took over power. The cukong collaborates with license holders who are indigenous Indonesians. The cukong made unofficial arrangements with indigenous license holders, the former providing capital and know-how as well as running the business and split the profit with the latter.

When I first arrived in Indonesia in June 1970, the *Nusantara*, a newspaper run by an Indonesian friend of mine, Dr Hafas, came out to attack the cukongs. It published an article naming the 20 persons who had "wide holdings ranging from airlines and banks to flour mills, import-export companies, tourist corporations, shipping companies, rice mills, timber concessions and a variety of other enterprises. The article also identified the generals who were connected with the cukongs.

The article shook Jakarta and other newspapers picked up the story and went to town with them. Some Members of Parliament began to question the government on the matter. The government denied the charges. Dr Hafas was prosecuted for his campaign against cukongism and later sentenced to two years' imprisonment pending appeal. The government's action against the anti-cukong campaign was interpreted by some foreign observers as a measure to reassure the Chinese that they could safely continue investing in Indonesia.

One of the biggest cukongs was Liem Sioe Liong (Salim is the Indonesian name of the ethnic Chinese family). He came to befriend Suharto when he was still a major in the army. He helped the Suharto family and got to know the family well. When the September 30 coup took place, Suharto's relation with Liem was so close that he reportedly called Liem for tactical advice and Liem became his personal banker.

Politically insecure, the most clever Chinese Indonesians had learnt how to make friends with the powers that be. No one did it better than Liem. He made sure that the Suharto family was in on many of the big deals. The Suharto Government showered favours on Liem's businesses which developed into Indonesia's biggest conglomerate. A clove importing monopoly came first (through Suharto's son Tommy who later became the "clove king"). Then a flour milling monopoly and government wheat subsidies for Liem's noodle-making company. Suharto also gave government contracts to Liem and other loyal Chinese entrepreneurs in exchange for payments to his *yayasans* (charity organisations) for his pet projects such as image burnishing hospitals, mini-Indonesia and other social affairs projects.

Today, Liem is a doddering old patriarch of 81 recuperating from eye surgery in California. When Suharto was in power, he helped finance a steel plant in 1984 when it needed funds. Liem opened his wallet when Suharto's family bank was going down the tubes in 1990, covering its losses of half a billion dollars. His empire of cement and chemicals, property developments and banking flourished under the Suharto regime. Liem lets Suharto's children in on his best deals. Until the end of May 1998, Suharto's son Sigit and daughter Tutut owned 25 percent of Liem's now failing Bank Central Asia. Suharto's cousin, Sudwitkatmono has a share in Liem's flour milling, petro-chemical and cement operations.

It was therefore no surprise that Liem was the main target of the May 13, 1998 student riots. Hundreds of vandals burned Liem's three cars, smashed Chinese vases, slashed Liem's personal portrait and finally set fire to the house where he has been staying.

Suharto had used the Chinese to run the economy because they could never threaten his political position. The Chinese were totally dependent on the Suharto's Government for political protection and patronage.

As Liem and the other Chinese cukongs mastered the art of vulnerabilty and made huge profits from their enterprises, the pribumi businessmen were complaining about the privileges the Chinese enjoyed. There are about 100 Chinese conglomerates in Indonesia according to figures published in 1995. Next to Liem Sioe Liong was Eka Tjitpa Widjaja of the Sinar Mas group. Then the Barito Pacific Group run by Prajogo Pangestu. There is also Lim Tek Siong of the Gajah Tunggal Group which deals with the cable industry, finance and property, the Kian Seng (Bob Hassan) group of Pasopati/Nusamba who deal with timber and the Lippo Group run by Lie Mo Tie (Mochtar Riady), to mention only a few.

Some of the cukongs have become too greedy. They do not confine their activities to exploiting the country's natural resources, but begin meddling with land grab which affects the livelihood of the common people. For example, in an attempt to get rich quick, a number of land speculators scrambled for land around Jakarta occupied by thousands of squatters. They used the military to evict the squatters forcefully. Since these squatters do not hold land titles, they were paid the minimum compensation, hardly sufficient for them to find alternative accommodation. When they refused to vacate the land, soldiers in military uniform arrived with bulldozers to tear down the houses.

The cukongs either developed the vacated land into housing projects reaping handsome profits, or sold them to developers at very high prices.

Such actions by some Chinese cukongs have infuriated the *pribumis* of the lower strata of society and they were only waiting for a chance to take their revenge. They hated the Suharto regime because they sided with the cukongs. They hated the cukongs more because, in their opinion, they were looting the country and exploiting the poorer classes. So, in May 1998, when they went for Suharto, they also went for the Chinese, not distinguishing who were ordinary Chinese and who were cukongs. Just because of the indiscreet acts of the minority cukongs, the majority of Chinese suffered.

The May 13 anti-Chinese riots of 1998 have shaken the confidence of many Chinese who now hesitate to go back to Indonesia. What will happen to Indonesia, if the rich Chinese who have fled the country do not return to the country? Will Indonesia survive economically without the Chinese entrepreneurs and their capital? Who will replace them? Evidence has shown that the countries which are anti-Chinese are always economically handicapped.

The first thing the new President Habibie did when he took over the reign was to visit Chinatown and to assure the Chinese that they would not be discriminated. He has forgotten what he had said in Tokyo in March 1998 when he went there to negotiate the rescheduling of Indonesian debt. Speaking to the *Nihon Keizei Shimbun*, he said, "It is absurd that the ethnic Chinese, who make up 3 percent of the population are controlling 90 percent of the economy. I would like to give opportunities to the pribumi, who make up the majority of the population, and build them up." That was said when Habibie was Vice-President. Now that he has become the President of Indonesia, he began to realise that, without the Chinese, Indonesia's economy will be in the doldrums. As President he will have to do a lot to recapture the confidence of the Chinese and to ensure, not by words but by action that there would be no more discrimination against them. After all, the Chinese are citizens of Indonesia and are loyal to the country.

President Habibie had changed his tune. He even attempted to include a prominent Chinese economist, Kwik Kian Gie, who has been a Suharto critic, in his Cabinet, but the offer was declined.

By 19 July, 1998, Habibie again changed his attitude towards the Chinese. In an interview with the foreign press, he said Indonesia could survive without the Chinese. He said if the Chinese who fled did not return, their businesses would be replaced by others. I think he had in mind Orang Padang from Minangkabau and the Arabs who had always been jealous and competitive vis-à-vis the Chinese in Indonesia.

The situation for the ethnic Chinese has changed after the fall of Suharto. They have re-emerged politically. On June 5, 1998, a group of young Chinese Indonesians led by Lieus Sungkharisma (alias Li Xuexiong) announced the establishment of the Partai Reformasi Tinghoa Indonesia (Indonesian Chinese Reform Party).

Lieus, 39, and his friends have been actively involved in the Young Buddhist Association. He is also the treasurer of the Komite Nasional Pemuda Indonesia (National Committee of Indonesian Youth, KNPI) and an indigenous\ dominated organisation linked to Golkar.

It is noteworthy that Lieus, who had changed his name to Indonesian, insisted on establishing an ethnic Chinese party while Kwik Kian Gie, who retains his Chinese name, is the champion of Indonesian nationalism.

Many ethnic Chinese prefer not to form political parties but to work with associations and pressure groups to fight against discrimination. They have worked with like-minded indigenous Indonesian pribumi to carry on the task of bringing justice to the Chinese.

A group of prominent Chinese is preparing to form an association to improve the position of ethnic Chinese. This group includes Dr Christianto Wibisono, a leading Chinese Indonesian intellectual.

However, the Chinese are divided in their approach to the problem of discrimination against the Chinese by the authorities. Some want to form a Chinese political party whilst others feel there is no necessity.

Professor Iskandar Alisyahbana, the Vice-Chancellor of Bandung Institute of Technology, has this to say about the Chinese political party, "There is no prohibition against establishing a Chinese party, but in my view, it is not right."

The largest Indonesian newspaper, *Kompas*, while recognising the importance of political participation for ethnic Chinese, said that it is not sure whether ethnic Chinese parties are the proper format.

The most critical attack came from a writer, Surya Paloh, who said: "Chinese parties are similar to snakes which look for people to hit them."

Professor Emil Salim, who nearly became the Vice-President, has been quoted as having said, "Chinese Indonesians should be accepted wholeheartedly; indigenous Indonesians should not use double standards and all discriminatory laws against the Chinese should be abolished." Indonesian intellectuals have echoed Professor Emil Salim's view.

The Habibie Government, however, has allowed the establishment of Indonesian ethnic Chinese parties.

What will happen to the Chinese? Is it wise to form a political party when the Chinese population is only 3 percent? Will the party be more of a hindrance than a benefit to the Chinese? These are the questions the ethnic Chinese will have to consider seriously.

The lastest I read in the newspapers is that the Indonesian Government will draft new laws to erase the distinctions between its indigenous and non-indigenous people and give all citizens equal rights. The Minister for State Enterprises Tanri Abeng said, "The priority now is to convince the ethnic Chinese that they are Indonesians and they should be coming back and doing their usual business."

Ethnic Chinese Indonesians have for a long time said that codes on identity cards lead to discrimination against them in many areas, such as in getting jobs or places at state universities. Very few Chinese make it into the civil service or the military. This refers to the controversial coding system used when identity cards are issued to the Chinese. In Jakarta, for instance, the identity cards numbers of Chinese Indonesians were marked with a zero before the serial number. This was to identify the pribumi from the non-pribumi. It has caused a lot of unhappiness in the Chinese community. As early as 1979, many Chinese Indonesians protested against this practice. On 19 February, 1979, *Kompas*, a leading Indonesian newspaper, quoted the then Governor of Jakarta, General Tjokropranolo, as saying that the ID for Jakarta residents would be standardised. It was not done despite his assurance. Apparently, he was not aware of the difference in ID held by pribumi and non-pribumi.

According to the Indonesian constitution of 1945 which was against racial discrimination among the citizens, it was stipulated that only an *asli* (meaning pribumi) can be the president of Indonesia. Apart from that, the constitution guarantees that all citizens have equal rights and obligations. Nevertheless, in practice, the government continues to differentiate between the two groups, forcing the Chinese Indonesians to be aware that they are not yet full Indonesians.

When will the Indonesian Chinese be treated equally? A younger-generation leader, Siswono Yudohusodo, one-time Minister of State on People's Housing, once said that the Chinese in Indonesia were too exclusive and economically powerful. He felt that they were disliked by the indigenous population for these two reasons. He suggested that the Chinese should become Muslims because Islam is the religion of the majority population. There was in fact an unofficial move by the Suharto Government to persuade the *cukongs* to become Muslims but with little success.

Ocassionally, some Indonesian leaders have advocated the abolition of the division between indigenous and non-indigenous population. For instance, the Indonesian Chamber of Commerce and Industry (Kadin) which is dominated by pribumi, suggested that there should not be a division between pribumi and non-pribumi business. However, the suggestion was not pursued precisely because of the contradiction between the social reality and the dream of creating a multi-racial Indonesian nation.

The Dean of the Faculty of International Relations, Dr Juwono Sudarsono, advocated the idea of not differentiating pribumi and non-pribumi "since they are already part of the Indonesian nation". But his remains a minority view.

When will the Chinese in Indonesia who are Indonesian citizens be treated equally with the pribumi and receive similar protection of their lives and properties? This is the fundamental question facing the present government if it is serious in wanting the Chinese to return to the country to help revive the economy.

Let me end this chapter by quoting the words of a Peranakan Chinese who had helped Suharto to power during his student days. He was later a leader of the Centre of Strategic and International Studies in Indonesia, which was a think-tank of Suharto. He is Jusuf Wanandi, whose Chinese name was Lim Bien Kie, an old friend of mine when I was Ambassador to Indonesia. Writing in the commentary analysis of *The Straits Times* under the title of "Whither place of Chinese Indonesians", he said that "the guilty must be punished, thus assuring the Chinese Indonesians and others that such abuses would not recur." He added,

> "The strategy of Chinese assimilation was started by former president Suharto in 1967. Though it appears to have failed, the fault may be that he never implemented this strategy consistently, never stood up for the ideal or bothered to educate the people on nation-building. Instead, he gave his personal protection to a group of Chinese Indonesian businesses that he used and exploited for his own interest.
>
> "He was not interested in bringing the Chinese Indonesians into politics, the civil service or public life. He treated them like concubines to be enjoyed but not recognised. This arrangement worked for him and was perhaps accepted by the majority of Chinese Indonesians, who may have felt that they could at least do well in business, if not in the other parts of Indonesian life. The May riots have put an end to this."

Jusuf said, "a new era is beginning. The immediate reaction on the part of Chinese Indonesians is to fight for their rights as citizens of Indonesia." Jusuf's statement quite accurately reflects the feelings of the Chinese Indonesians.

Yet, anti-Chinese riots continue to break out from time to time including the worst riot in history — the May 13 riots of 1998.

The first President of Indonesia, Sukarno, taken at Bogor Palace, 1966. (Photo courtesy of Pananews)

President Sukarno welcoming Prime Minister Lee Kuan Yew's delegation to Indonesia in 1960 at Istana Negara, Jakarta.

President Sukarno, handing over power to Suharto to maintain security in Indonesia in 1966. (Photo courtesy of Pananews)

Some 2,000 strong anti-Chinese demonstrators affiliated to Indonesian youth fronts stormed the Communist Chinese embassy in Jakarta in 1967.

Author presenting credentials to President Suharto, as Singapore's Ambassador, at Istana Negara in 1970.

Prime Minister Lee Kuan Yew's delegation being received by President Suharto at Kemajoran airport in May 1973.

Lee Kuan Yew and President Suharto before their first golf game in Jakarta in 1973.

Lee Kuan Yew sprinkling flowers on the graves of two Indonesian marines who were hanged in Singapore after their conviction for sabotage in killing three Singaporeans.

Suharto and Lee Kuan Yew walking towards the banquet.

Banquet given by President Suharto in honour of Prime Minister Lee Kuan Yew's delegation in Jakarta.

Lee Kuan Yew and Suharto exchanging gifts at Presidential Palace, Singapore in 1974.

President Suharto with Singapore President Benjamin Shears at the international airport when he visited Singapore in 1974.

Lee Kuan Yew and B.J. Habibie at Batam Islands in 1974.

Suharto announces his resignation before military officials after 32 years in power and handed over power to Habibie at Presidential Palace in Jakarta on 21 May, 1998.

Riots in Jakarta on 13 May, 1998.

Collision between government troops and students in Jakarta on 13 May, 1998.

Angry Indonesian mobs burn cars and Chinese shops as they plundered shops in Jakarta on 14 May, the third day of violence. (Photo courtesy of AFP)

A boy on a bicycle passes by a burning motorcycle set alight by rioters in Senen shopping district in central Jakarta on 14 November, 1998 as thousands take to the streets to protest against the government. (Photo courtesy of AFP)

The NU leader, Abdurrahman Wahid, popularly known as Gus Dur, now head of the National Awakening Party, with 30 million supporters is one of the strong candidates for the Presidency.

Indonesian Muslim leader Amien Rais, head of the 28-million-strong Muhammadiyah Islamic movement and now chairman of the new National Mandate Party, is running for the post of President of Indonesia.

Ms Megawati, daughter of former President Sukarno, leader of the People's Democratic Party for Struggle (PDI – Perjuangan) is also a Presidential candidate for the coming elections. (Photo courtesy of AFP)

Gus Dur and the NU masses in Jakarta.

Indonesian Co-ordinating Minister for Economics, Ginandjar Kartasasmita, talking to World Bank representative Hubert Neist in Jakarta (1998).

Suharto dressed in traditional Javanese costume at his sister's wedding held in Jakarta in accordance with Muslim traditions.

Mochtar Lubis, editor of the leading daily newspaper "Indonesian Raya", who advised the author to study Javanese mysticism. Picture taken in May 1966, soon after his release from prison after being detained by President Sukarno for a few years.

The inauguration of Sri Sultan Hamengkubuwono in Jogjakarta in March 1940.

A procession towards the Grand Mosque in Jogjakarta.

A royal procession in central Java.

A Javanese gamelan orchestra.

The Tangkuban Perahu volcano in West Java.

Lee Kuan Yew's delegation visiting Borobudur in 1960.

Madura bull races in its capital Pamekasan — a bird's eye view.

Almost at the winning point, the two bulls are making their last effort.

Each pair of bulls is perched in colourful, tasselled parasol or flag and had a large bell dangling from its yoke.

The bull-racing fans dodging the bulls after the race.

Author having a group picture with three Balinese friends in front of Gunung Agung in Bali.

Author with a 93-year-old Javanese Chinese who believe in *Sam Kow* — the merger of Confucianism, Taoism and Buddhism in Bali.

A Singapore cultural delegation to Indonesia in 1974, being received by Ibu Tien Suharto in Jakarta.

The Singapore cultural delegation had a group picture taken at a Bali temple after the lion dance performance.

A Singapore parliamentary delegation led by the Speaker Prof. Yeoh Ghim Seng visited Indonesia and had viewed a Balinese performance in Denpasar.

The Balinese barong dancing on the stage of a Balinese temple.

Two Singapore lions dancing in a Balinese temple.

The legong dance when the dancers pierce the body with their kris.

The kecak (monkey) dance in Bali.

A group of East Timorese who are in favour of integrating Timor with Indonesia.

East Timorese separatist leader, Xanana Gusmao, speaking to journalists during a press conference at his detention house in Jakarta on 2 March, 1999. (Photo courtesy of AFP)

The *sampo beo* in Semarang built in honour of Admiral Cheng Ho who led 63 treasure ships to the Southseas during the Ming dynasty.

Author and his staff visiting Minangkabau and had a full view of the "buffalo-horn" houses there.

The *tari lilin* (candle) dance.

Prime Minister Lee Kuan Yew visiting the Batak Land soon after Singapore made a breakthrough in diplomatic relations with Indonesia in 1974. Picture shows Lee's delegation arriving at Medan airport.

Batak dancers paying their respect to the honoured guest Lee Kuan Yew and his delegation on the island of Samosir.

The Governor's wife greeting the author in Brastagi, West Sumatra during his visit in 1972.

She also honoured Mrs Lee Khoon Choy with the same *ulos*.

Dr Goh Keng Swee and the author being welcomed by the then Defence Minister Panggabean and the Batak community in Samosir.

A welcome reception for Dr Goh Keng Swee on Pulau Samosir in 1973.

The Singapore delegation was honoured by the Batak host with *ulos* (colourful and long clothes of traditional scarf) over their shoulders.

Author and his old friend Adam Malik, the former Foreign Minister of Indonesia who is a Batak.

Author talking with former Minister for Information Mr Mashuri in 1972.

General Ibnu Sutowo, President of Pertamina, welcoming a Singapore golf delegation to Palembang to play golf.

The man wearing batik shirt is General Ali Murtopo, once the right-hand man of Suharto.

The Mayor of Makassar Pakempto, presenting the key of freedom to the author when he visited the city in 1972.

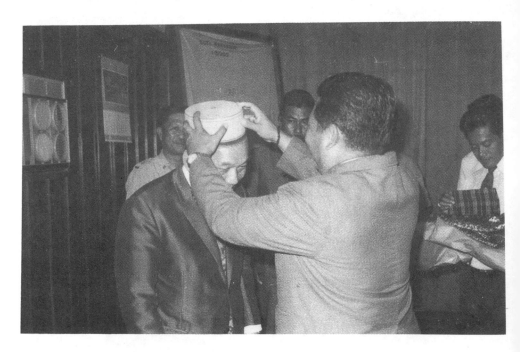

The Mayor of Makassar putting a Bugis songkok on the author.

The Makassar mayor also presented the traditional dress to the author.

A Bugis dress is being worn by the author.

A good chat with the Makassar Mayor.

A typical Bugis house in the village of Makassar.

Visiting Toraja, the land of the kings (author and wife).

The traditional Torajan houses with sweeping roofs.

Author and a Torajan headman in front of his house with hanging bull horns.

Author and his wife chatting with a group of Torajans in front of a traditional Torajan house.

Author and wife having a group picture with Torajan boys and girls.

A Torajan village.

The Torajans carrying long bamboo rods containing bull's blood to be cooked into a delicacy called *papiong*.

Torajan boys and girls taking a rest after a long journey.

The rock-cliffs of the Torajans' burial grounds in Rantepao.

An albino bull in Toraja, the most precious animal.

A Torajan woman with her hat.

The Torajan warrior dancers.

A bird's eye view of Ambon from the hotel where I was staying in 1998.

Statue of Kapitan Pattimura, an Ambonese hero stands in the centre of the city.

Des Alwi, showing the author's family the reading room of Sutan Sjahrir, first Prime Minister of Indonesia.

Lunching with Des Alwi at his hotel in the open air. On author's left is Mrs Lee.

Dr Mohammed Hatta, who was under house arrest in Banda Island.

Indigenous Dayak men parade through the village of Tebas in Kalimantan, atop a pickup truck displaying the severed heads of Madurese men decapitated earlier in the day on 20 March, 1999. Kalimantan has seen a renewal of long-standing violence between the Dayak tribe and migrants from the island of Madura which has left over 70 people dead during the recent clash. (Photo courtesy of AFP)

Tribesmen from the island of Kalimantan held up the decapitated head of a Madurese settler who was beheaded one day earlier in the village of Sambas on 21 March, 1999. (Photo courtesy of AFP)

Ambassadors arriving at the airport in Irian Jaya.

Foreign diplomats talking to the Dhanis.

The more civilised Irianese in Biak.

Irianese men wearing *kotekas*.

Irianese women at the marketplace.

10

THE MINANGKABAU

The Shrewd Gypsies of Indonesia

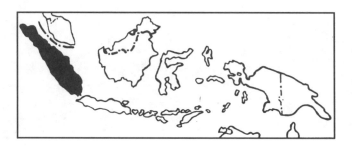

When I first visited Padang, the capital of West Sumatra, I was captivated by the magnificent architecture of the Minangkabau houses. They have peaked, swooping roofs shaped like buffalo horns which normally attracts the attention of visitors. I also noticed that Minangkabau women wore ceremonial headdresses with similarly curved horns of the revered water buffalo. They call themselves Minangkabau and at about 3.3 million comprise about a quarter of Sumatra's population and are Indonesia's fourth largest ethnic group.

The Minangkabau, known by their compatriots as "the gypsies of Indonesia", are easygoing, peaceful, self-confident, hardworking and well-known for their shrewdness in business — the only ethnic group that can compete successfully with the Chinese in Jakarta. They have a reputation for adaptability and intelligence and are one of the most educated and vigorous peoples in the whole of Indonesia. Many of the nation's intellectuals, political leaders and authors are Minangkabau. One of them was Sutan Sjahrir, the first Prime Minister of Indonesia, and Dr Mohammad Hatta, the Vice-President of Indonesia.

How did the name of Minangkabau come about? There are several legends about the origin. One of them was that about 600 years ago, one of the Javanese kings wanted to conquer Western Sumatra and sent a messenger to the land of Minangkabau to ask them to surrender. The Minangkabaus were not prepared to surrender without a fight. The shrewd West Sumatrans suggested a bullfight between a Javanese bull and a Sumatran bull. The Javanese dispatched a huge bull with strong muscles and the Sumatran sent a tiny calf which apparently was no match for the Javanese mighty bull.

The Minangkabau cunningly starved the tiny calf for 10 days, separating it from the mother and attached sharp metal spears to its horn. When the fight began, the calf rushed straight into the Javanese giant bull's belly searching for milk, thinking that it was its mother. The bull let out a bellow of pain and took to its heels with blood pouring from its stomach and the calf running after it. When the bull finally dropped dead, the West Sumatran shouted: "Minang" (meaning win) and "kabau" (bull), in other words: "The buffalo wins, the buffalo wins".

The West Sumatrans got the inspiration from the buffalo fight and built their houses in the shape of buffalo horns and designed their women's headdresses in similar style.

Although the victory of the Minangkabau calf against the Javanese bull is only a legend, it is significant that the Sumatrans have never liked Javanese domination, even in modern times. Sometime in 1950, they staged a rebellion against their Javanese supreme leader Sukarno. The military colonels who controlled the *major administration* in West Sumatra and Barlian in South Sumatra had different grievances with Jakarta, which became more intense as the influence of Sukarno and the communists grew in the mid-1950s. They deplored Sukarno's anti-Western megalomania and economic mismanagement. They feared the godless militancy and "Javaneseness" of the Communists and also resisted General A.H. Nasution, then Chief of Staff of the Indonesian Army, attempts to centralise the military structure, and central government's attempts to gain a bigger share of Sumatra's great wealth in export products. With the help of their civilian allies in Masyumi and the small Socialist Party led by Dr Sumitro Djojohadikusumo, they declared a Revolutionary Government of the Republic of Indonesia (PRRI) on 15 February, 1958, with its headquarters in Bukittinggi.

The rebellious colonels had expected Western countries like Europe and America to support them and thought that Dr Hatta, who later became Vice-President of Indonesia, would accept premiership of the rebel government.

Just before the outbreak of civil war, two men, the rebel Prime Minister Sjafruddin Prawiranegara and Mohammed Nasir, the leader of the anti-Sukarno Masjumi Party, slipped out of Java with their families. Sjafruddin had brought several suitcases full of bank notes from the vaults of the National Bank, of which he was a director.

If Dr Hatta had accepted the premiership of the rebel government, as Simbolon, a Sumatran colonel, and others had hoped, Sjafruddin would probably have taken over the Ministry of Finance. But Hatta had washed his hands off the rebellion, so Sjafruddin had been thrust into the premiership of the rebel government overnight. When asked by journalists for comments about the rebellion, Sjafruddin said, "there can be no compromise with Sukarno any more. He is a wicked, godless man. He must be eliminated, swept away. It is our sacred duty to Indonesia." He said he was expecting more material and moral support from Britain and America. He added, "this is a fight against communism which is also an enemy of Britain and America and which Sukarno has invited to trample over the people of Java. We need more arms, more understanding. It is time for the West to recognise my government as a *legitimate entity*."

At that time, the tireless Dr Sumitro, who was operating as the rebel's treasurer, flew to Washington D.C. from time to time to convince Washington that it was Bukittinggi and not Jakarta that spoke with the true voice of Indonesia's seventy-eight million inhabitants. Dr Sumitro had his headquarters in Singapore and I met him on several occasions.

The Americans had already supplied arms and equipment to them by various roundabout means. The British and Australians had been in regular touch with the rebels through Dr Sumitro in Singapore.

But, when the chips were down, none of the Western countries held their hands. They did not give any help while the military situation hung in the balance. The caution of the West puzzled and disappointed the rebel leaders.

During the height of the rebellion, Padang, the capital of Minangkabau, was hardly recognisable. Half of the population had gone to stay with relatives in the villages leaving their homes shuttered and desolate. The other half stayed indoors. The streets near the port had been evacuated and in some of the houses student volunteers were blocking doors and windows with the heavier pieces of furniture. The rebels had sunk a merchant ship in the harbour so that it would block the entrance.

The rebellion was finally suppressed by the stronger Javanese troops under the command of General Djatikusumo who later became Indonesia's first Ambassador to Singapore. Dr Sumitro later became a prominent economic minister under the Suharto's regime and his son General Prabowo married Suharto's daughter. General Prabowo is now under investigation for involvment in the May 1998 riots.

That was the friction between Padang and Jakarta in modern history.

The word Minangkabau has other origins. One theory is that Minangkabau is a combination of two words — *minanga*, a river in that region, and *kerbau* meaning buffalo. Another version is that it comes from the archaic expression *pinang Kahbhu* meaning "origin home".

Traditional houses with buffalo horns are, however, disappearing in modern times. It has become too expensive to build the thatch-roof "rumah adat" (customary house) and they were now being replaced by brick and iron-roofed structures.

In Padang, there are Rumah Dadang "big houses" where the traditional Minangkabau live. Each cluster of houses in a village is often the locale of one matrilineage with a communal *surau* (mosque) nearby where the men and boys hang out. Bedrooms are set aside for daughters of the household and their husbands. There is a long common room for living and dining. The back half of the house is divided into small rooms where the married and marriageable women sleep.

An annex to the house would mean a daughter has come of age and a separate room has to be built. One can always tell how many husbands and children a family's daughters have by the number of "horn" extensions to the rumah dagang, curving skyward and adorned with swinging ridepoles.

In front of the rumah gadang (room for general purpose) is a long veranda used for dining, meetings and a sleeping place for children, elders and guests. It is often raised to about three metres off the ground on wooden pillars. Beneath are kept small livestock like chickens.

In Padang, I saw lovely old houses along wide, tree-lined streets in Pandang Baru. There were also a few Chinese temples in kampong Cina, Padang's little Chinatown.

On Padang's sea front, we saw the sea aquarium which has plenty of rainbow fish. We also saw a beautiful sunset scene with the background of many Minangkabau men and women promenading along the old harbour of Muara.

The Minangkabau are famous for their matriarchal society and the matrilineal system of inheritance. Minangkabau queens are still celebrated in many old legends such as *Kaba Chinda Mata*, the narrations of which would take 17 evenings. They also believe that in the afterlife, "Heaven is below the sole of mother's foot", and that one would not go to heaven if one ill-treats one's mother. All properties, titles and family names are handed down through the female line from generation to generation. The grandmother is the grand matriarch and relatives from the mother's side carry weight in family politics. Houses are very much the domain of women. Daughters usually inherit the property which is *shared equally* and they own the shops.

In Minangkabau society, all children bear the clan name of their mother. The right to use land and the right to be given a clan's title is transferred by the mother or grandmother's brother. The family consists of a *sapunruik* (people of the same womb) which means the mother's offsprings and their brothers. Each clan has a chief, called

Penghulu datuk, who is chosen among the brothers of certain families. The Penghulu settles all clan disputes and quarrels before they are brought to civil courts. When a Penghulu dies or retires because of age, the title is passed on to his first nephew or one of his brothers.

In a marriage proposal, the father has no say and it is decided by the mother's family group. The bride does not leave her home and the husband moves in to stay with her. After the wedding, the bridegroom is escorted to the home of the bride together with all his possessions to prove that he is a man of substance. After marriage, the man will spend most of his time at his sister's house, working and eating there, and returning to his wife's house only at night.

However, times have changed and nowadays men assume more responsibility for their own family. In big towns, married couples spend a symbolic few nights at the mother's house and then go out to live on their own.

Because of the matriarchal tradition in Minangkabau with women holding bigger power than men, there is a tendency to encourage men "to go abroad" to seek fortune. The Minangkabau call it *"merantau"* meaning to go to the "outer reaches or frontiers"; in other words, the outer world. It has become a Minangkabau custom that men must go out to the world to look for fortune. Men who stayed behind at home are considered lacking in courage and drive.

How did the Minangkabau matriarchal system come about? According to one source, it was the Acehnese women leaders who had brought the matriarchal system to Minangkabau after they had lost power in Aceh. After the *uleebalang* (the male district leaders) had ousted them out of power, the frustrated women leaders move south to Minangkabau with their traditional social system.

The central area of Minangkabau is a group of fertile valleys surrounding three imposing volcanoes, Gunung Merapi, Gunung Sago and Gunung Singgalang. This central area is known as *darek*. Because of the rapid expansion of the population, there is little space left for development and the men had to go outside the *darek*. The move is called rantau, meaning going beyond the darek.

From time immemorial, Minangkabau men had to do *rantau* to do business, for further education and to look for greener pastures. There is not much to keep a man down at his farm except to wait politely for a girl to ask for his hand in marriage. There is also not much fun to be under the scrutiny of his brother-in-law and to tolerate the matriarchal system. As there is not much industrial development going on in the village, half of the Minangkabau males are driven from the darek to Java. In the past, a Minangkabau would leave the village for a year and come back to the village with tales of their fame, fortune and adventure and feel proud of his achievements.

The migration of Minangkabau men to Jakarta is so great that there are more Minangkabaus in Jakarta than in Padang. There are also many Minangkabau men in Malaysia, especially Negri Sembilan, where most of the Malays are descendents of the Minangkabau. At Pangkalam Kempas in Negri Sembilan, there are a few columns which resembles the pillars of Guguk (Puar Datar) in Negri Sembilan. These pillars are adorned with volutes, and conventional figures of animals such as birds, horses and dragons, just like those found in Minangkabau. The similarity is by no means an accident. There are also Minangkabau in Singapore and other countries in Southeast Asia. Many of them establish restaurants famous for their Padang *rendang* and Padang curry. In Jakarta, the Minangkabau are also known as "Orang Padang", and are the only Indonesians who can match the Chinese in business.

Legend has it that the Minangkabau descended from the wandering Macedonian tyrant, Alexander the Great. According to the legend, the ancestors of the Minangkabau arrived in Sumatra under the leadership of King Maharo Dirajo, the youngest son of Alexander, more commonly known in Indonesia as Iskandar Zulkarnain. Others, however, attribute Minangkabau's origin to Adam's youngest son who married a nymph from paradise who *gave birth to* Iskandar Zulkarnain. His third son, Maharaj Diraja, sailed to Gunung Merapi when the rest of Sumatra was still submerged in water. There, he started the first matriarchal clan. As the water receded, the people spread out into what is now the interior of West Sumatra.

It is believed that the Minangkabau arrived in Indonesia between 1000 and 2000 B.C. The early Melayu kingdom was established there and, after the demise of the Srivijaya Empire, extended to include what is now West Sumatra. Minangkabau is also known as the cradle of the Malay civilisation. The Hindu-Malay kingdom of Minangkabau rose in the 12th to 14th centuries after the decay of the Srivijaya Empire to the east, when Indian influences began to spread into the highlands. The imprint of Brahmanic Indian civilisation is still evident with a multitude of Hindi loans words, agricultural skills, methods of political organisation and even remains of Hindu-Buddhist monuments.

By the 14th century, Islam began to penetrate the region, which split into small Muslim states ruled by sultans. They gradually pushed further inland the Minangkabau kingdom, which started disintegrating when the Europeans arrived. It continued to survive until the early 19th century when a group of Muslim fanatics known as the "men of Padri" used force to convert the Minangkabau into Muslims. The Padri resorted to killing and enslaving anyone who resisted them. Bitter struggles between the Minangkabau and the Padri lasted from 1820 to 1837 and finally, backed by the Dutch and non-Muslim Bataks, the adat leaders overcame the Padri strongholds. Today, a curious mixture of traditional beliefs and Islam is practised in Minangkabau.

Today, the Minangkabau ardently embrace both Islam and their female-oriented adat system of customary lane. Being Islamic and matriarchal may seem contradictory, but it is this blend that makes the culture interesting and intriguing. Although according to Islam, a husband is allowed to take four wives, it is rare that a Minangkabau man will marry more than one. And even though women have a strong voice in the house, they remain modestly dressed and are humble.

Minangkabau food, also known as padang food, and Minangkabau dances are famous in the world. When I was in the Ministry of Culture, Chinese and Malay cultural troupes used to perform the *tari piring* or "dish dance" with dancers holding plates, and the *tari lilin* (candles), with dancers deftly twisting and turning the candles without extinguishing the flames. There was also the *tari payung* with dancers holding umbrellas. These dances often enthralled the Singapore crowd when they were first performed at the *Aneka Ragam Rakyat* (Peoples' concert) which I organised to introduce to Singaporeans the different types of dancing, music and drama of Indonesia.

Minangkabau is also well-known for its *pencak silat* (martial arts). It is customary for Minang youth to spend a lot of their time practising pencak silat. They use the legs more than the hands and when they attack, it is very swift and violent. The *Harimau silat* is the most aggressive and dangerous style of Minang martial art, which originated in the Painana district of West Sumatra. *Harimau* means tiger, and the steps imitate a tiger stalking and killing its prey. With their bodies as close to the ground as possible, the two fighters circle around menacingly, springing at each other from time to time.

The Minangkabau combine martial arts with dance. They created a dance called *randai* which is a unique dance-drama performed at weddings, harvest festivals and other celebrations. The randai combines the movements of pencak silat with literature, sport, song and drama. In every village of West Sumatra, there is at least one randai group. In the randai performance, both the female and male roles are played by men wearing traditional *gelambuk* trousers and black dress. The traditional version tells the story of a wicked woman driven out of her village before she causes a disaster to the community. The drama is backed by gamelan music. The percussion instruments used to accompany the dances are similar to those of Javanese gamelan and are collectively called the *telempong* in West Sumatra.

Speaking of Padang's rendang (a dish of dried beef mixed with coconut gravy), I always remember the most delicious rendang I had ever tasted in Bukittinggi, served at the Government resthouse where I stayed when I was the guest of the Governor. It was the centre for the Minangkabau people. Bukittinggi, meaning "high hill", is nestled in the mountains just south of the equator. It is cool and sunny. This small university town has the country's oldest teachers' college and other educational institutions. There are musical taxis, pompadoured for streetsweepers, veiled schoolgirls, regal women walking sedately under parasols, good restaurants, plenty of flowers and a wide selection of hotels. It even has comfortable sidewalks.

We visited the shops, which invariably are owned by women but run by men.

The 90-km drive from Padang to Bukittinggi was really beautiful. We saw peaceful rice paddies, Minangkabau houses, glimpses of the sea and views of the towering Singgalang and Merapi volcanoes — each almost 3,000 metres high.

When we reached Bukittinggi, the first thing that struck me was the clock tower situated in the centre of the town overlooking the market. It was constructed by the Dutch in 1827 and known as the "Big Ben" of Bukittinggi. It embodies a Dutch idea and Minangkabau design. It reminds the villagers that they have to be punctual.

I also visited a cattle market called *Pasar Ternak*, a short walk from Bukittinggi on the road to Sungai Tanang. We found cattle being sold the traditional way with the buyer and seller bargaining over the prices under a cloth using their fingers instead of words. Minangkabaus are gentlemen. If no agreement is reached, they part happily with no bad feelings.

The next interesting place was the zoo which is situated at the highest point of the town. We were there one Sunday and we had a good glimpse of the parade of Minang apparel with their horn-shaped headdresses and colourful traditional dresses. The zoo specialises in Sumatran wildlife and is especially strong on birds with at least 150 different species.

In the centre of the park in the city is a traditional Minangkabau building built sometime in 1844. It was flanked by two rice barns with fine woodcarving. It houses the museum which was opened in 1945 and became the oldest museum in West Sumatra. It specialises in local history and culture and houses resplendent with traditional wedding costumes, headdresses, musical instruments, architectural models and old firearms.

We went to see Ngarai Canyon, known as "Buffalo Hole", which borders Bukittinggi in the south and west and separated from the foothills of Gunung Singgalang. This is the pride of West Sumatra for it resembles America's "Grand Canyon" and is known as the Grand Canyon of Indonesia. Viewed from Panorama Park, it is really beautiful, particularly in the morning when a veil of mist hangs over the valley and Gunung Singgalang, about 2,877 metres high, rises above it in the background.

When I was in Padang, I also took the opportunity to see a *bouraq* festival at a seaside town called Pariaman, about 36 km north of Padang. Bouraq is a winged horse-like creature with the head of a woman. The villagers constructed effigies of bouraqs which they painted in vibrant reds, blues, greens and yellows and adorn with gold necklaces and other paraphernalia. They carried the effigies through the streets with excitement and merriment accompanied by dancing and music. We saw two bouraq groups crossed paths and the procession staged a mock fight. One group praising their own bouraq and insulting the opponent. After the mocking, they threw the effigies into the sea. Spectators and participants dived into the sea to salvage the remains of the bouraq, the most valuable memento being the gold necklaces. It was real fun. It drew quite a large number of tourists.

In Padang, there are also bullfights known as *adu kerbau*. It is quite different from the Spanish bullfight because there is no blood in the Minang bullfight. The bulls are ordinary water buffaloes and they do not get hurt. They lock horns on a trial of strength. Once the horns are locked, the fight continues until the losing animal gets tired and runs off, pursed by the winner.

There is also horse racing. It is nothing like the horse racing in Western countries. The horses are ridden bareback and the jockeys are dressed in the traditional costume of the region and village that they come from. The purpose of horse racing is to gain prestige for the district where the horse is bred and raised. However, watching Minang horse racing was fun for the spectators made a lot of noise and the atmosphere was exciting.

11

THE BATAKS
Ferocity and Cannibalism

The word "batak" was in use in the 17th century. It was originally a derogatory Old Malay term for "robber" or "pig eater" as translated by others. Another theory insists that the word originated from Bataha, the name of a Karen village in Myanmar on the Thai border where the Batak people originated. According to Batak legend, all Bataks were descendents from Si Radja Batak, a person born of supernatural parentage on Bukit Pusuk, a mountain on the western edge of Danau Toba.

According to anthropologists, the Bataks are a pro-Malay people descended from Neolithic mountain tribes in northern Thailand and Burma who were driven out by migrating Mongoloid and Siamese tribes. When they arrived in Sumatra, they did not remain in the coastal areas but trekked their way inland and finally settled down in the Lake Toba area. The surrounding mountains provided a natural barrier and they lived in isolation. These rice-growing people live in fertile mountainous valleys extending up to 200 km north and 300 km south of Lake Toba.

The Bataks, who number about 1.5 million, are shorter and heavier than the Minangkabau. They have kept their racial stock pure because they live inland and have developed an early reputation for ferocity and cannibalism. They are sometimes described as "workers and not thinkers".

Bataks are by nature quite aggressive, direct and flamboyant, especially the Toba Bataks which number more than a million. As they are brave and dynamic, they developed a war-like tradition providing Indonesia with a number of highly regarded military generals. One of them was Panggabean, the former Minister of Defence, who was our host when I first accompanied Dr Goh Keng Swee, then Singapore's Deputy Prime Minister, and later Prime Minister Lee Kuan Yew to Lake Toba and the Batak land.

Bataks have the good habit of saving money for their younger generation to go to Jakarta and Medan for further studies. Thus, many Bataks are well-placed in the government, universities and business circles. Bataks are also good singers, musicians and have many popular bands singing songs for tourists visiting Lake Toba. A barefooted peasant once stalemated a match at the *Dutch World Championship for Chess* held in Medan in 1939, a major event in the history of the Batak.

Bataks are polynesians and are cousins of such tribes as the Igorots of the Philippines, the Dayaks of Kalimantan, the Torajans of South Sulawesi, the Kaosan hill tribes in Taiwan and the Hawaiians.

The Bataks retained their own way of life in isolation right up to the 19th century, when the Dutch and German missionaries discovered and converted them. They had long being squeezed by the Kato Batak (Christian Bataks) who were constantly at odds with the Islamic Acehnese to the north and who tried several times to conquer and convert them into Islam. It was strange that, after resisting Islam for so many years years, they were eventually subdued by the Germans and Dutch who brought Christianity to them. The majority of Bataks in the north today are protestant Christians. In the south, however, Islam has gained some inroads.

The Bataks were first converted to Christianity by a fearless German missionary, Nommernsen, who arrived in the Lake Toba area in 1861 with only a Bible and a violin. Because of German influence, many Bataks today still carry German names such as Luther, Bismarck and Wihelm. However, a large number of Bataks are still animists who believe in the spirits of dead ancestors, sacred trees, stones and places.

Their last king, Sisingamangaraja, died in a battle against the Dutch in 1907. Samosir Island was the last bastion of the Toba Batak. It was eventually discovered by tourists and became famous.

The Bataks were the "head-hunters" of Sumatra and were known for indulging in cannibalism. Herodotus, the Greek philosopher, was the first to write about Batak cannibalism, followed by Marco Polo in 1292 who reported that the Batak ate their own parents when they became too old to work. Then in 1783, Marsden wrote the first accurate account of cannibalism. When it was published, it shocked the civilised world. Raffles reported in the 19th century that in certain crimes a criminal would be eaten alive. He said, "The flesh was sometimes eaten raw, or grilled and eaten with lime, salt, pepper and a little rice." Raffles said human blood was drunk out of bamboo container. The palms, hands and soles of the feet were delicacies to the Batak epicures. After they were Christianised, cannibalism ceased. However, from time to time, we have heard of cannibalistic incidents.

When I was in Indonesia sometime in 1973, it was reported in the newspapers that one tribe had eaten a would-be bride of another tribe because she offended their honour.

The first time I visited Lake Toba was sometime in 1970, after presenting my credentials to President Suharto. When I arrived at Prapat, the first thing I heard was "Horas, Horas", a Batak greeting for visitors. Prapat is a cosy town at the edge of Lake Toba, the largest lake in Southeast Asia and also the highest above sea level.

Horas is the word used by the Bataks to welcome a guest and it is often followed by the throwing of rice and flowers on visitors of special importance. Horas was the first word I learnt when I visited the home of the world-famous "Sing Sing So", a song which is now popularly sung in many languages throughout the world. I did not know that "Sing Sing So" had a Batak origin until I visited Lake Toba.

Where did the word horas come from? I asked many Batak friends but few could give me a satisfactory answer. The word kept ringing in my ears until much later when its significance suddenly dawned on me. Of course, it was the god Horas whom I have read about in

Egyptian mythology. But how could there be any connection between the word horas which the Bataks use as a greeting and the god Horas in Egyptian mythology? Had the Egyptians been to Batak land in ancient times and left behind traces of their culture?

Whatever the explanation, the resemblance in certain aspects of the two cultures is striking. Egyptian mythology tells of how man is admitted to heaven by first passing a stern test to prove his worth and honesty. For this test, one had to face the Goddess of Truth who would place the heart of the deceased on one side of the scales and the magical feather which was her sacred emblem on the other. In attendence was the dog-headed god who would record the result of the test on his papyrus scroll. If the heart and feather balanced exactly, then the jury of the forty-two assessors would allow the person to pass into the next world. The god Horas was the one who would then step forward to welcome the person and usher him to the gate of heaven. Is it not interesting to note that the Bataks of Sumatra use the word horas to welcome guests?

The god Horas in Egyptian mythology was half-falcon half-man. In Batak mythology, there are also stories of half-man and half-animal creatures walking in hell on their hands instead of on their feet. Batak *lontar* (ancient writings on palm leaves) tell the story of Si Aji Sambola, a half-man-half-animal who was on his way from hell to heaven when he saw men doing the reverse of what they did when they were alive — they were walking on their hands instead of their feet, a sign that they were sinners. Some of these people were also balancing *kerbau* (buffalo), pigs, chickens, dogs or other things which they had stolen during their lifetime. Others were walking upside-down with long tongues hanging from their mouths right down to the ground. The god Horas would not welcome such people who had sinned.

The Bataks could not have found a more appropriate word than horas to welcome visitors to Lake Toba, which can easily be considered the gateway to heaven with its beauty, refreshingly cool climate and atmosphere of tranquillty. The lake, a picture of serenity, is situated at the top of a volcano far way from the hustle and bustle of city life. If the ancient Egyptians had reached the shores of the lake, they would have exclaimed, "How beautiful the water is." The Egyptian word for "beauty" is *toi* and for "water" *ba;* thus the exclamation would have sounded *toiba.* Can it be that the Egyptians did come to Lake Toba and that the exclamation *toiba* gradually became Toba? Whether the origin of the name Lake Toba has any Egyptian connection or not remains a subject of historical, anthropological and etymological studies.

The words horas and toba are not the only traces of possible Egyptian influence in the Batak land. When we crossed the lake, we came to the island of Samosir, which incidentally sounds like *mesir,* the Arabic word for "Egypt". Like other tourists, we were taken to the burial ground of Raja Sida Buta, the King of Samosir, who is said to have died about 400 years ago. It was a less than five-minutes walk from the shores of the lake. The moment I set eyes on the tombstone, I noticed its striking resemblance to the sarcophagi of Egyptian Pharaohs which I had seen in the Cairo Museum. It was customary for the ancient Eygtians to carve an image of the Pharaoh on the top of his coffin. Similarly, King Sida Buta had his own image carved on the stone coffin in which he was buried.

King Sida Buta had a pair of melancholic eyes which were mysteriously penetrating and he wore his hair long — like present-day hippies. Below the King's image was a carving of a determined-looking, bare-chested man. Our tourist guide, who claimed to be a descendent of King Sida Buta, explained to us that the man, Tengku Mohammed Syed, was the King's *panglima besar* (military commander-in-chief) and also his personal bodyguard. As a brave general, Syed had helped the King to defeat all his enemies. Although the King was an animist, he trusted and loved the Muslim general so much that he ordered Syed's image to be carved on his coffin before he died. Syed's image was also meant to provide continued protection to the King in the next world.

The lady carved on the back of the coffin was the King's sweetheart, Anteng Melila Senaga, who was the loveliest maiden in Samosir. The romance between Sida Buta and Melila lasted ten years. When the King eventually asked for her hand in marriage, Melila refused. It is said that she was charmed by the black magic of another suitor who was a rival king living nearby. Sida Buta became so angry that he, in turn, used black magic to turn Melila into a mad girl, whereupon she ran aimlessly into the jungle, never to appear again. Till the time of his death, Raja Sida Buta was in love with Melila and so he ordered her image to be carved on his coffin too. Spattered over the carved tombstone was a red liquid — not red paint, I was told, but human blood. It is said that in the days of tribal battles, the Bataks used to commemorate Raja Sida Buta's death by killing prisoners from rival tribes. The blood was thrown over the King's coffin and the hearts of the enemies were devoured during a feast lasting a week. Animists believed that the heart was sacred and that by eating the heart of an enemy one became brave and the enemy's soul would be destroyed.

The resemblance of Raja Sida Buta's stone coffin to those of the Egyptian Pharaohs further strengthens my belief that Egyptian influence must have crept into the Batak culture. But how did this come about? I kept asking myself. I finally got a clue from an Indonesian book *Sejarah Kebudayaan Suku-Suku Di Sumatrera Utara* (*History of the Tribes in North Sumatra*) written by Data Meuraxa. Quoting research sources, the book claims that more than 2,000 years ago, the Arabs had come to trade with the Bataks. They came for *kapur barus*, a sort of camphor which was necessary for mummifying the dead. I am more inclined to believe that the traders who came to Lake Toba were Egyptians who brought with them ancient customs and traditions such as carving images on stone coffins.

Whenever I visited the tomb of Raja Sida Buta and pondered over the strange similarity between Batak and Egyptian customs, my attention was always drawn to the gigantic banyan tree that provided permanent shade over the tomb. Tourist guides usually explain that the tree is as old as the coffin because the king's mourners were said to have planted it. A combination of beauty and mystery surrounds every branch that hangs down and takes root again in the earth. Because of its spiritual significance, the banyan tree, or *warringin*, is generally treated with reverence and respect by Indonesians. To the Bataks, the banyan tree is the origin of life.

According to Batak mythology, in the beginning there was a god called *Umpung Tuan Bubi na Bolon*, the only God. God Umpung, meaning "great grandparent", is omnipresent and omnipotent. He makes the rain, creates the waves and determines favourable or unfavourable harvests. As he leaned against a huge banyan tree, a decaying branch broke and fell into the sea. From his branch came fishes and all living creatures of the vast oceans. Not long afterwards, a decaying branch fell to the ground and from this originated crickets, caterpillars, centipedes, scorpions and insects. A third branch crumbled over the plains and turned into *kerbau* (buffalos), horses, goats, pigs and all other domestic animals. The marriage of two of the newly created birds, *Patiaraja* (the male) and *Manduangmandoing* (the female) bore eggs from which human beings were brought forth into the world during a violent earthquake. This is how Batak mythology explains the origin of all living creatures.

The banyan tree is considered the tree of life in more ways than one. In every Batak home you will find a family tree in the form of a diagram of the banyan tree. The family hierarchy is represented by the branches moving downward showing close and distant relations often dating back several generations. Whenever Bataks meet, conversation invariably leads to comparison of their positions of seniority in the family hierarchy and each would assume his place and behave in a manner appropriate to his status.

As the banyan tree is considered the tree of life, it is not surprising that much Batak philosophy and culture revolve around it. I have chosen to relate the legends explaining the origin of two Batak customs and will illustrate how the tree is still very much a part of the culture of Bataks today. The legends concerned *Si Gale Gale*, a puppet, and the *tunggal panaluan*, a walking stick — both objects traditionally carved from the wood of the banyan tree.

Si Gale Gale is a puppet show with a difference. It is a dance — a one-man show — and is quite unlike the Javanese puppet shows or the Chinese puppet-shows I have seen in Singapore, Malaysia or China. It is purely of Batak origin, untainted by any foreign influence. Carved from the wood of the banyan tree, the man-sized puppet is a replica of a Batak youth in traditional costume. He wears a red turban, a loose pyjamas-type shirt and a blue sarong. From his shoulders hangs a red *ulos*, a cloth traditionally used to wrap around new-born babies and also used to place around the shoulders of a bride and bridegroom to bless them with harmony, unity and fertility.

The prelude to the dance is a musical introduction by a flute, a wooden gamelan orchestra and drums. Then the dalang manipulates Si Gale Gale to roll his eyes and raises his hands to display long gracious fingernails. The puppet continues to dance to the sound of rather monotonous but rhythmic music, sometimes standing, sometimes sitting, as directed by the dalang from behind. Manipulating several strings at a time, the skilful dalang guides every movement of Si Gale Gale. In some more elaborate performances, Si Gale Gale can be made to shed tears or even smoke a cigarette.

But what is the origin of the puppet show of Si Gale Gale? One source says that once upon a time, there lived on Pulau Samosir a very loving couple who had no children. When the husband suddenly died, his wife felt very lonely. So, she made a wooden puppet in her husband's image. Whenever she felt lonely, the widow would employ a dalang to make the puppet dance and a dukun to communicate with the soul of the husband through the puppet. The ritual of communicating with a soul in this way soon became part of the Batak culture. Si Gale Gale was therefore performed at funeral ceremonies to revive the souls of the dead and to communicate with them.

Another source explains the origin of Si Gale Gale with the following legend. Once upon a time, in a moment of inspiration, a skilful wood-carver fashioned a statue of an unusually beautiful maiden from a banyan tree trunk. She looked so real and charming that she captivated a dress pedlar who offered to dress her up in beautiful clothing. A passing dukun suggested that she be given herbs. Naturally the wood-carver was overjoyed with his masterpiece and hurried home to show the statue to his wife. Imagine their surprise when the maiden suddenly came alive. As they had no children, the couple named the girl Nai Mangale and raised her like a daughter.

Word quickly spread that Nai Mangale was not only a rare beauty but also a talented dancer. It was not long before both the dress pedlar and the dukun came to claim Mangale for their own because of their contributions towards her beauty and existence. The ensuing dispute was settled by a wise chief who suggested that the carver remain as the girl's father, the dukun her godfather, and the dress pedlar her brother.

Soon, a prominent young man, Datu Partiktik, came to ask for Nai Mangale's hand in marriage. As she refused, she was forced by black magic to marry him. Many years passed, but no child was born. One day, Mangale became ill and died. Her dying request was that a wooden replica of herself be made so that she could return to her original source.

The Si Gale Gale puppet dance became popular long before the advent of Islam and Christianity to the Batak land. It reflects the ancient Batak animistic belief in the existence of souls and spirits in nature such as in trees, rivers and mountains. Like other races in Indonesia, Bataks believe that the souls of their ancestors survive after death and that they can be contacted to give continued guidance and advice to those who are still living. Whatever the origin of the Si Gale Gale dance, the puppets provide a means for the Bataks to communicate with the souls of the dead.

Like the Balinese who often spend their fortunes on cremation ceremonies, the Bataks who die rich but childless often spend all their accumulated wealth on Si Gale Gale ceremonies which can sometimes last seven days and seven nights. As the Bataks believe that many children bring prosperity, a childless marriage is often construed as a curse. The Si Gale Gale myth is perhaps a reflection of the fear of being childless and the desire to have many children. To ensure many children, the Bataks in the past practised polygamy; one Batak king, Raja Simalungun, had fourteen wives and seventy-two children.

During a Si Gale Gale funeral ceremony, all personal possessions of the deceased will be used to decocrate the puppet. To the accompaniment of music, the dukun will invite the deceased's soul to enter the wooden puppet as it dances on top of the grave. At the end of the dance, the villagers hurl spears and arrows at the puppet while the dukun performs a ceremony to drive away evil spirits. Several days later, the dukun will return to perform another ceremony, sometimes lasting 24 hours, to chase away evil spirits again.

However, with the growing influence of Christianity, the Si Gale Gale funeral ceremony is gradually disappearing. Nowadays, Si Gale Gale is mostly performed simply as a puppet show but the vertical hand-waving movements of the puppet to the accompaniment of music has become a part of a Batak dance performed during wedding ceremonies and other functions.

When I first visited Lake Toba in 1970, I was struck by the peculiar style of Batak architecture. Traditional Batak houses are built on stilts a metre to two metres from the ground. The houses are originally made of wood slotted together without nails and roofed with sugar palm fibre. However, more often these days, they are slotted together with rusting corrugated iron. The interesting thing about a Batak house is the roof, which has a concave, saddleback bend with each end rising in a sharp point and from certain angles look like a buffalo's horns. The gables are usually embellished with mosaics and carvings of serpents, spirals, lizards and monster heads complete with bulbous eyes.

The Batak houses resemble Dayak houses except that the former is divided into three levels. The lower floor is meant for rearing chickens, cows, pigs and goats. Animal excretion is conveniently used as fertiliser. The middle floor is for human habitation and is reached by wooden steps supported by bamboo poles. It is usually an unpartitioned community sleeping hall. Privacy is nobody's privilege. The roof which has no ceiling represents the highest level. A traditional Batak village is made up of a number of such houses, similar to the villages of the Toraja people of central Sulawesi.

One of the biggest Batak longhouses that I visited was once used by Raja Simalungun to accommodate his fourteen wives. A longhouse is a dwelling to accommodate the members of a family, long in shape and has many rooms. It is now preserved as a museum. It was actually part of the King's residential complex. The longhouse is flanked by the court-house, a VIP guest house and another complex for pounding paddy. With the support of a thick bamboo pole, I climbed up the seven steep steps leading to the King's hall. It was bleak and dark inside. Not a ray of sun could penetrate the mysterious, unventilated chamber. On the pillars facing the entrance hung a glorious display of bulls' horns representing the changes of dynasties. My guide showed me to a small dark room situated near the entrance of the huge sleeping chamber for the fourteen wives. It was the King's private room which was deliberately made dark. The fourteen wives slept in the larger adjoining chamber in two rows of seven, each with her own cooking stove and utensils. The King's hobby was to organise cooking contests for the wives once year for he was a gourmet. King Simalungun was the last descendent of a line of thirteen kings. When the Japanese came, the villagers took the opportunity to kill him because he collaborated with the Dutch and work against the interests of the people. Nobody knows what became of his wives and children.

The Bataks also built special houses to preserve the ashes of the dead of each clan. These houses called *tugu* also have three levels. The upper level is meant for the ancestors, the middle level is reserved for the present adult generation, and the lower level is for their children. A dead person is first buried in the ground until the body decomposes. Then it is exhumed and burnt so that the ashes can be stored in the family *tugu*. All members of a clan must contribute to a tugu fund and rich clans build bigger tugus. Once a year, there is communal worshipping of ancestors, somewhat similar to the annual Chinese *Cheng Beng*, a traditional festival to worship ancestors.

The trinity concept extends even further into the lives of present-day Bataks. To a Batak, life itself is divided into three stages — childhood, puberty and manhood. An interesting Batak custom is the teeth-filing ceremony when a child reaches puberty. Like the Balinese, the Bataks believe that if one's teeth are not properly levelled by filing, it would be difficut for one to enter the kingdom of heaven. In olden days, it was difficult for one to get a marriage partner if the teeth were not filed. There were special *Tukang* (artisans) who file teeth and they are supported by a dukun who gave his blessing. The teeth-filing feast was one of the joys for the family for it meant that one's offspring had grown up and had learnt the Batak *adat* (customs).

Another important aspect of the trinity concept is what the Bataks called *Dalihan Natolu*, a sort of clan system stipulating the hierarchy of inter-family relations. *Dalihan* is an earthen burner used for cooking. *Natolu* means three-legged. The dalihan used to be a vital cooking utensil — an item of survival in ancient days. It had three legs so that it could stand firmly on the ground. The philosophy of survival and stability of the Batak society evolves from the earthen tripod burner. Each of the three legs has a name: one leg is called *dongan sabutuha* (*dogan* means "friend" and *sabutuha* means "stomach") referring to friends and relatives; the second leg is scalled *hula-hula*, representing the family of the bride; and the third is called *boru*, representing the groom's family to which the bride is given. Hula-hula has a higher status than boru because it is the family that gives away the bride. The bridegroom's family or boru is considered inferior in status. This is the way the Bataks fix the hierarchy of the inter-family status even today. Wealth and power are not the criteria in determining family status in society. However rich and powerful a Batak family may be, it has to pay due respect to the hula-hula, the bride's family, however poor or humble it may be. When a couple marries and the ulos is placed around their shoulders, parents and elders utter the word, "May you have sixteen sons and seventeen daughters." Like olden Chinese, Bataks believe that the more children you have, the luckier you are and the happier you will be.

To the Bataks, the Dalihan Natolu is a triangle-democracy according to the law of nature. Thus, although Batak society is a patriarchal one, the birth of a girl is never regretted for it gives the family a chance to be hula-hula. This may be interpreted as the matriarchal aspect of a patriarchal society. The principle of triangle-democracy is applied in all family functions relating to birth, marriage and death. The triangle shows the interdependence of each hierarchy of Bataks in their relationships which does not allow one group to dominate the other. Thus, it is considered democratic.

The Bataks also have the tradition of honouring important visitors by presenting them with a walking stick, called *tunggal panaluan*, a symbol of great honour. The tunggal panaluan is an alat (instrument) of authority which is said to possess mystical powers. When Lee Kuan Yew visited Lake Toba as Singapore's Prime Minister after a successful trip to Jakarta at the end of May 1973, the Bataks regarded the visit as a rare honour and presented him with the walking stick. On the walking stick is carved three men, a pair of twins, a dog and a serpent. Lee Kuan Yew was treated as a "Rajah" (king) of Batak.

The ceremony took place at the Prapat Town Hall. There a Batak Chief and an Indonesian official placed a cloth head-dress on the Prime Minister. It was the highest award that the Batak people of Lake Toba could offer. The Indonesian Minister of Defence, Panggabean, the Chief Security Officer to President Suharto General Tjokropranolo, and Governor of Sumatra General Marah Halim were all present. In their presence, the royal staff tunggal panaluan was presented to Prime Minister Lee. The ceremony was simple and solemn.

It just happened that the royal staff presented to Lee Kuan Yew had been borrowed from someone and that person demanded it back. It came out in the newspapers and this embarrassed the governor. When I told Lee about this, he arranged for the royal staff to be returned to the owner. Meanwhile, Marah Halim, the governor, settled the matter with the owner by giving him a certain sum of money as he did not want to lose face.

Lee Kuan Yew's mission also toured the isle of Samosir, the largest island on Lake Toba just off the mainland. The first time I visited Samosir, the protocol officer pointed at the island and said to me smilingly: "The whole of Singapore can sink into that island." He was trying to indicate how small Singapore was.

Lake Toba is easily the largest lake in Southeast Asia (1,707 square km) and one of the deepest (450 metres) in the world. The mythical homeland of all the Bataks, Lake Toba was formed as a result of a gigantic volcanic explosion. The island has a spell-binding setting as it sits right in the middle of an area surrounded on all sides by pine-covered beaches, steep mountain, slopes and cliffs.

I loved its serenity and cool mountain air. It always gave me a feeling of contentment and peace of mind. The legend related to Lake Toba is interesting:

Once upon a time, there lived a farmer at the foot of Dolok Rihit, a huge mountain that once towered over Samosir Island. The farmer liked to fish in a stream nearby. One sunny morning, he caught such a heavy fish that it took all his might to land it. To his surprise, his catch turned out to be a beautiful maiden. The farmer fell in love with the beautiful girl, who was called Saniang, and asked for her hand in marriage. She agreed to marry him provided that he swore never to disclose her identity to anyone. She warned him that there would be great calamity if he ever broke his promise. He happily agreed and married her.

It was not long before Saniang gave birth to a son. One evening, when the farmer returned from the fields, he discovered that his son, who was then a growing boy, had eaten all the dinner, leaving nothing for him. The father, impulsive and hot-tempered by nature, scolded his son loudly, "You uneducated son of a fish." On hearing this, Saniang was furious and angrily accused her husband, "You have broken your promise and now all is ruined." Almost immediately, a volcano erupted causing Mount Rihit to tremble. A violent storm followed which flooded the whole valley and turned it into a lake. All that was left of Dolok Rihit was the mountain top which is now known as the island of Samosir. Saniang returned to the water, never to be reunited with her husband and son again. Since then, whenever a storm threatens Lake Toba, the local folk would remember Saniang, the Dragon Queen, who they believed was expressing her displeasure by disturbing the calm waters of the lake.

Lee Kuan Yew was also impressed by Lake Toba. When he returned to Singapore after his Indonesian trip, he announced that the Singapore Tourist Promotion Board (STPB) would send a mission to the Lake Toba district to see how it could help develop the tourist industry there. The STPB team surveyed the lake and arranged for package tours to Lake Toba which has now become a popular holiday resort for Singaporeans.

12
THE ACEHNESE
The Eastern Gateway to Mecca

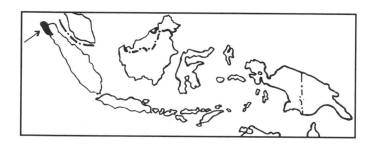

Aceh, Indonesia's gateway to Mecca, suddenly attracted world attention again in the middle of January 1999 when Acehnese religious extremists, pursuing an Aceh independence movement started killing Indonesian Armed Forces stationed there. The military found the body of a Sergeant with a gun-shot wound. He was lured from his house and a group of 50 people outside the mosque kidnapped him and threw away his dead body. The military says Aceh Merdeka, a group which has been fighting for independence in the province since the mid 1970s, was responsible for the violence. But the Aceh leader Mustafa Abubakar said, "Recent riots, looting and the murder of Abri troops were an expression of the local people's anger, which has lots to do with Abri's past oppression and its inability to resolve cases of military atrocities." Analysts suggest that the discovery of seven badly maimed bodies of soldiers in the province in December 1998, prompted some 50 soldiers to torture and kill civilians. The soldiers had been searching for separatist rebel, Ahmad Kandang, who, according to the military, killed seven soldiers and abducted two others in December.

For ten years, Aceh has been under a special military operation status which was lifted in August 1998. The ending of military operations followed accusations of army atrocities in Aceh after the fall of Suharto. When Abri ended its special status, Indonesian combat troops were withdrawn from Aceh.

The Defence Minister and Commander-in-Chief of the Armed Forces, General Wiranto, visited north Sumatra on 7 August, 1998 to investigate reports of torture and killings during the past decade of crackdowns against separatist insurgencies. He announced that the armed forces' troops would be withdrawn over the next month.

General Wiranto said, "On behalf of Indonesia's armed forces, I apologise to the people of Aceh if, during military operations, the armed forces have made you suffer."

The Legal Aid Foundation in Banda Aceh said 10 mass graves had been found at three sites in the province, where the armed forces suppressed a separatist insurgency that peaked in the early 90s. The graves are believed to contain the bodies of hundreds of people killed by soldiers during operation "Red Net" which was carried out mainly between 1991 and 1993 to smash the insurgency and scatter its leaders.

General Wiranto said that given the present situation in Aceh, there was no justification for maintaining military operations there. Both Aceh's governor and a parliamentary fact-finding group last week called for an end to military operations there.

Since the ouster of former President Suharto on 21 May, 1998, Aceh residents have spoken out about human rights abuses during the military operations with details of abductions, rapes, tortures and mass killings.

During his visit, General Wiranto held talks with human-rights groups over their plans to exhume suspected mass graves of the victims of military abuses in the region to look for physical evidence of rights violations.

Since independence, separatists in the province have been fighting for an independent Islamic state.

In recent weeks, Indonesia has pulled hundreds of troops out of East Timor, where it has also been facing a separatist insurgency, as part of efforts to reach a settlement on the territory's future.

The Acehnese have reputations of being religious extremists and they have, till today, been pursuing an Aceh independence movement to achieve "Aceh Merdeka" (freedom for Aceh). As Aceh was the first part of the archipelago to be converted to Islam, it is the bedrock of the Islamic religion and the Islamic faith is practised with unusual intensity and severity in this part of Indonesia. It is the only place in Indonesia where a visitor can see women wearing full veils in the kampong (village). A man was caught stealing an old tape recorder and as a punishment, his hand was cut off in public. It is the same kind of Islamic law practised in Saudi Arabia and other orthodox Muslim countries.

There are 3 million Acehnese divided into the earlier pro-Malay hill people, the Gayo, the Alas and the more recent lowland coastal people who are a product of centuries of inter-racial breeding with the Batak, Dravidians, North Indians, Javanese, Arabs, Chinese and Nisans. The heterogeneous coastal Acehnese are taller, more stout and darker than most other Sumatrans because they are of Arabian, Indian, and Portuguese descent.

The Acehnese are real fighters. They are a people who seldom speak loudly and rarely point fingers at others. Despite the area's reputation for aggressiveness, most of them speak softly, always accompanied by gentle gestures. The younger generation show respect for the older generation and always address the elders as "bapa" (father) or "ibu" (mother). Laughter is part of the Acehnese life for Acehnese love the sound of laughter. The region is known for its frequent festivals which include the water festival which is similar to that of the Burmese.

Apart from their hostility towards foreigners, especially the Dutch, the Acehnese are generally rather warm hearted.

Today, the Acehnese hold two main types of festivities: those marking family, community, or social events and those relating to religious observances which express reverence for Allah and the Islamic faith.

Marriage is an important event in an Acehnese's life. An Acehnese will count the calendar days with the words "peace", "prosperity" "meeting" and "death" when choosing a favourable date to make a marriage proposal. Dates that fall on the first and last terms are not chosen. After a partner is chosen, he prepares for the wedding. Sometimes the wedding celebration is expanded into a festival that involves the entire village if he is rich. The bride and groom perform the traditional *gacha* ceremony in which henna is applied to the hands and feet of the bride. The henna is derived from the leaves of the *lawsonia inermis* which are boiled, ground into a paste and then smeared onto the skin or applied carefully to form patterns.

On the morning of the wedding, the *andan* or hair-shaving ceremony is performed on the bride. The hairline of the bride is shaved back about 1 centimetre. This shaving must be done before midday as the ceremony is only considered blessed if it takes place while the sun is still rising. After the shaving is done, a bit of glutinous rice dyed yellow with tumeric root is applied behind the ears for protection.

The bride is then dressed in her ceremonial wedding costume — a richly embroidered velvet jacket matched with a pair of silk trousers. She wraps around her waist a *songket* sash. She also decorates her hair with *gold filigree* flowers and wears a crown-like ornament. Jewellery adorns her ears, neck, wrist, ankles and fingers. The groom is also dressed in ceremonial garb. This includes an embroidered jacket, a pair of silk trousers with a *songket* sarong wraped over it and a ceremonial dagger tucked into the waistband. He also puts on a stylished crown made of cloth.

As Aceh is a matriarchal society, the groom always move out of his village to live in the kampong of the bride, just like the Minangkabau. On the wedding day, both bride and groom sit on an elaborate dais laid with embroidered satin cushions. Pretty coloured umbrellas decorated with gold-leaf fringes line the steps of the dais.

During the harvest season, the Acehnese celebrate the padi offering ceremony to ensure the continued fertility of the fields. There is also the fishermen ceremony and the pepper plant ceremony to ensure continued good harvests.

Although Aceh is highly Islamic, a system of animist beliefs still exists throughout the region. The Acehnese attribute human characteristics and abilities to a number of common animals while many types of flora are renowned for their healing properties. For example, more than 50 spices and herbs are used in traditional Acehnese medicines. Some plants, such as toadstool, are believed to possess magical powers to enable one to cast and take away spells. The tallest hardwood trees in Aceh are thought to be haunted while hanas supposedly can protect one from evil spirits.

The Acehnese also believe that tigers are often seen around graveyards and are thus thought to represent the spirits of saints. They also believe that white buffaloes will bring good luck, although they are also sought after for their horns to make dagger sheaths. Ape spirits are said to roam the forests of Aceh and a pregnant woman is warned not to look at monkeys because her unborn child might resemble them in appearance. This belief is somewhat similar to Chinese belief.

Another tribe in Aceh is the Gayo who have less tendency to fight. The Gayo and Alas are the dominant ethnic groups of the isolated lake plains and river valleys of the Central Aceh district. Isolated from contact with Westerners until the early 20th century, they live in a mountainous range with some peaks over 3,000 metres high, bounded on the west, east and north by the Acehnese and to the south by Batak highlanders. Having been converted to Islam at a later date than the coastal Acehnese, the Gayo and Alas have their own patrilineal culture, language and traditional arts. In 1904, the ruthless Dutch General Van Dalen first penetrated the upland regions to subdue these tribes. They wiped out whole villages as they mercilessly massacred the Gayos.

Aceh is historically and culturally distinct from the rest of Indonesia. Lying almost 1,700 km northwest of Jakarta, it is physically isolated from Indonesia's other provinces. For over 1,000 years, Aceh has been trading with Malaysia, China, India, Sri Lanka and the Middle East countries. It had been an independent kingdom but the target of numerous Western colonisers. The Chinese Liang dynasty records mention a state of Poli in northern Sumatra. Descriptions tell of a Buddhist society with 136 villages in which rice was harvested twice a year.

In the court annals of the Chinese Han emperor (1-23 A.D.) there is a record of China sending a mission to Huangtche (the Chinese name for the region — meaning Aceh) to acquire a rhinoceros for the Imperial Zoological Gardens.

Aceh's direct link with Arabic traders was a natural impetus for the expansion of Islam. While Islamisation of Indonesia dates back to the early 17th century, the waves through Southeast Asia from the 9th to the 13th century spread their beliefs as they travelled. Since northern Sumatra was the first point in Indonesia where these traders touched down, Aceh is considered the archipelago's "cradle of Islam" and remains one of the country's religious strongholds.

In the 1500s, a line of shrewd and powerful sultans succeeded to the throne and soon turned Aceh's economy into one of the strongest in Southeast Asia. The first ruler of the new era was Sultan Ali Mughayat Shah (1514-30) known as the "pirate king" who brought Banda Aceh into the contest for international trade. Malacca was then the major rival of Aceh for both mercantile and religious prestige until 1511, when the port was captured by the Portuguese.

Historically speaking, the Acehnese and the Bataks were enemies. In 1539, relations between the two countries were strained because an Acehnese tyrant had proposed that a Batak King's son marry his daughter if they were all converted to Islam. The Batak king refused and the Acehnese tyrant declared war on the Bataks. The Acehnese lost the war because the Bataks were more superior militarily. The Bataks besieged the Acehnese soldiers for 23 days. The Acehnese camp was ravaged by disease and, with his army running short of supplies, the tyrant agreed to terminate the hostilities and signed a peace treaty that required the Acehnese to make reparations of five taels of gold.

However, the Bataks agreed to give his oldest son in marriage to the sister of the Acehnese tyrant.

The year 1604, during Sultan Iskandar Muda Merukuta Alam's reign, was considered Aceh's "golden age", with the country extending its dominance east to the states of Perak, Pahang and Kedah on the Malay peninsula and west to the island of Nias. Under his rule, Aceh became a centre for education attracting famed writers and Aceh grew into a major religious power for Islam. It became known throughout Asia as "the eastern gateway to Mecca".

Although Aceh was an Islamic country, it had four queens who successfully rose to the throne. The First was Tajul al-alam Shfiasuddin Shah (literally meaning Crown of the World, Purity of the Faith), the daughter of Iskandar Muda, who inherited her position of power and reigned from 1641 to 1675.

Owing to the reign by female leaders, the Acehnese have remained a strongly matriarchal society despite its deep Islamic background. Even in the modern Acehnese society, it is the daughter who inherits property and it is the bridegroom who must move to his wife's village after marriage. However, during the 1600s, the stresses of warfare, rival traders and internal uprisings caused the power of the queen to decline. The uleebalang or male district leaders took over power and displaced the queen and greatly restricted the authority of women in Aceh.

Perhaps out of frustration, the female leaders left the province and moved south to form Sumatra's matriarchal Minangkabau culture.

In the 15th century, Admiral Cheng Ho visited Aceh and presented a giant cast-iron Chinese bell, now known as Cakra Donya, which sits in front of the Rumah Aceh, a model of a home of an Acehnese. Admiral Cheng Ho heard that Aceh was famous for Islam teaching and, being a Muslim himself took an interest in Aceh. Inscriptions on the bell tell the story of his visit to Aceh.

During the 16th and 17th centuries, the capital Banda Aceh was a major international trading centre that attracted settlements of Indians, Chinese, Arabs, Persians and Turks. In the 17th century, under the rule of the great Sultan Iskandar Muda, Aceh reached the peak of its political power. It had a representative in Istanbul and engaged in diplomacy with London through the English sea captain, James Lancaster. Aceh even had a trade agreement with England which lasted until the 19th century. In a letter which the Sultan wrote to Queen Elizabeth I of England, he said,

> "I am the ruler of the Regions below the wind who holds sway over the land of Aceh and over the land of Sumatra and over all the lands tributary to Aceh, which stretch from sunrise to the sunset."

It shows the extent of Aceh's sphere of influence as a trading nation as well as providing a colourful assessment of Aceh's importance.

Aceh was Malacca's chief competitor for trade before Malacca fell to the Portuguese. Rivalry between them was intensified by religious hostility as Aceh was one of the earliest centres of Islam in the archipelago. Religious differences and the harsh Portuguese rule spurred many traders of different nationalities — Islamic scholars, Egyptians and Arabians, craftspeople from India and goldsmiths from China — into abandoning Malacca and setting themselves up in Aceh.

Aceh's power began to decline towards the end of the 17th century but it remained independent of Dutch rule for a long time. The first Dutch expeditionary force of 7000 retreated when its commander General Kohler was killed. The Acehnese were great fighters and went all out to defend the country. They fought the Dutch for 30 years and the fight was known as the Aceh War, Indonesia's bloodiest fight as well as the longest running battle in the Netherlands' history.

From this war emerged many heroes and heroines who have gained recognition throughout the archipelago. One such figure was Teuku Umar, the leader and war chief of the village of Datar, whose expertise in strategy during the war led him to become one of Aceh's most honoured heroes. When Teuku Umar was ambushed and killed, his wife Cut Nyak Dhien joined the fight for Aceh's freedom in 1873. She was exiled to Sumedang in West Java where she died in November 1908.

The Dutch finally sent a new army contingent which was twice as large and finally succeeded in taking the capital, the central mosque and the sultan's palace. However, the war went on for 35 years before the last of the Sultans, Tuanku Muhamat Dawot, surrendered.

During the Second World War, the Japanese were at first welcomed by the Acehnese but resistance soon sprang up when the Japanese disrespected Aceh's local institutions and religion. The Acehnese did not like the Japanese because they were asked to bow to the East (that was where the "Teno Haika", the Japanese emperor lived) whereas as Muslims they got used to bowing to the West (where Mecca is situated). This Japanese insensitivity made the Acehnese hate the Japanese more than the Dutch.

Then in 1939, the Islamic party emerged as a political force under the leadership of Daud Beureueh. He appointed himself military governor during the revolution but lost his post after the revolution and was downgraded to a residency of North Sumatra in August 1950. A complex political and social struggle ensued in the course of which Daud withdrew to the interior and prepared a rebellion. In September 1953, he declared Aceh part of the Islamic State of Indonesia under the leadership of Kartosuwiryo, leader of the Darul Islam revolt which was centred in West Java.

When Sukarno declared independence for Indonesia, the Darul Islam revolt movement based in West Java attempted to establish a theocratic state in Indonesia. The Achenese joined the rebellion and it took them many years (from 1953 to 1961) to come to terms with the central government who realised that Aceh was a political and not a military problem and made concessions to Aceh, including the reestablishment of the province of Aceh in December 1956, granting of special status in mid-1959, agreeing to the application of Islamic law in Aceh in 1962 and offering an amnesty to Acehnese rebels. Today it is still a very sensitive area politically. Jakarta wisely treats the Acehnese with kid gloves and has declared Aceh a "special autonomous territory" (Daerah Istimewa) where Islamic law applies.

In December 1976, Tengku Hasan di Tiro, one of the Acehnese leaders of the Aceh Independence Movement (*Gerakan Aceh Merdeka*

— GAM) under Daud Beureueh's returned from the United States. Hasan di Tiro had been the self-appointed ambassador for the movement in the US and had on several occasions claimed the US had proffered support for the Aceh rebels. This, however, never materialised.

Hasan's new movement, however, failed to ignite the support of the Indonesian Muslims as it was aimed to secure independence for Aceh and possible union with the Federation of Malaysia. When it became known that Daud Beureueh had signed a proclamation in May 1977 calling for a holy war of independence from Indonesia, he was exiled to Jakarta. The GAM movement was crushed by 1978 and Hasan di Tior went into self-imposed exile in Sweden and continued to lead the movement from there.

In 1980, Acehnese youths began to receive military training in Libya. It was planned that 800 youths would be sent to Libya for training but ultimately only 49 were sent.

Everything was quiet until 1988 when an Indonesian territorial military commander was shot in the Pidie district. When in September 1989 a military post there was attacked and 20 weapons seized, the Indonesians realised that rebellion was reignited. The rebels portrayed themselves as revolutionaries who wanted to establish an independent Islamic republic of Aceh. They highlighted the social gap between non-Acehnese big business employees, and the ordinary Acehnese peasants. The non-Acehnese indulged in oil, paper and fertiliser projects, and the central government had failed to return a fair share of oil royalties to the Acehnese.

The rebellion was crushed and one rebel military commander was sentenced to death in absentia in September 1993 for burning a military headquarters, stealing 20 weapons, killing a number of Arabic personnel and evicting Javanese from transmigration sites.

In that suppression of the Aceh rebellion, President Suharto sent 6,000 reinforcement troops including special forces, marines and air support with orders to wipe out the rebellions. The suppression produced quick results forcing the rebels to leave the villages and break into small guerrilla bands which became increasingly isolated from the population. Due to that operation, Abri had killed at least 2,000 unarmed civilians in Aceh by 1993. Hasan di Tiro remained safely in exile in Sweden but his local representative was shot dead in December 1992 and the rebels' military commander fled overseas.

There are still Acehnese clamouring for an independent Aceh. Recently a large number of Acehnese refugees sought political asylum in Malaysia in a widely publicised move.

I went to Aceh some years ago with an investor who was looking for limestone as there are many limestone hills in Aceh. We went to Banda Aceh, the capital of Aceh, which is situated on the northern tip of Sumatra. Banda is a beautiful and quiet city with the Sungei Aceh river flowing through the city with a backdrop of huge mountains behind. According to Chinese *feng sui* (geomancy), its location is good because it has both water and earth. Government offices along the river intermingled with shop houses which were noisy and busy. The centre of the town is dominated by a massive five-domed mosque facing Simpang Lima, the hub of the traffic. As Islamic laws are severely enforced, there is less danger of being victimised by robbers or thiefs. It was quite safe to walk alone at night in the streets. The people are better dressed than in other Sumatran cities and respectful towards foreigners. Although Aceh is strictly Islamic, we saw very few veiled women. Times have changed. Today we saw girls in Levis jeans riding motor scooters and couples walking affectionately in the streets, though not holding hands as in Western countries. There is a feeling of calmness when walking in the streets because we do not see large crowd such as in big cities like Tokyo. The city got its first traffic light only in 1971.

We visited the Dutch churchyard called Kher Khoff, a well-maintained Dutch cemetery in the city where 2,200 Dutch soldiers were buried. These soldiers had died during the Acehnese resistance movement. We came across the first grave bearing the name of General Kohler, the first senior officer killed while storming the mosque in the very first expedition against Aceh in 1873. We also saw gravestones of Germans and Indonesian mercenaries, mostly Ambonese, who were used by the Dutch to suppress rebellions in Indonesia. There were also graves of Acehnese who were considered "traitors" as they had worked for the Dutch colonisers.

We also visited th Rumah Aceh which is a model of a home of an Acehnese uleebalang built in 1914 in Semarang. Uleebalang is a word for traditional chieftains. During the war between the Dutch and the Acehnese, an Islamic scholar Snouck Hurgronge, advised the Dutch to use the strength of uleebalang to neutralise the authority of the ulamas (religious chiefs). As a result of this advice, the Dutch succeeded in maintaining an uneasy peace in the province.

Near the Kher Khoff are some Islamic graves of Acehnese rulers including that of Sultan Iskandar Muda, and another group of royal tombs dating from the 15th to the 16th centuries.

We also visited an unusual mosque with a marble interior called Mesjid Baturrachman which was built in 1879 by the Dutch to appease the Acehnese. Its white-washed walls gleamed by the sun or moonlight are in striking contrast to its coal-black ironwood shingles while its thick timber towers rise above the city to watch over its people and call them to prayer. Today, the Mesjid Baturrachman stands as a representation of the independent Acehnese *umma* that is linked to the international Islamic community. The construction of the mosque failed to secure peace, for more Dutchmen were killed after the mosque was built. Today, the mosque is a beehive of activities for Acehnese Muslims. The elaborate multi-arched facade is a mixture of different styles from Arabia, India, and Malaysia. Behind the mosque is the minaret, higher than the highest dome. In front of the mosque is a garden and pathways.

Along the river are also some historical sites. One of them is the "Walking Palace" which was built by the Sultan for a Malay princess. It was meant for the princess to walk along the river in her leisure, for in those days women were not allowed to walk in the streets.

In Aceh, we also saw some Acehnese dances. I was impressed by an all-male dance accompanied by drums in which 28 men marched single file onto the stage chanting as the leader said a prayer. The dancers acted in rhythm as they moved their arms, patted their knees and shook their heads in time with the chanting. They moved faster as the chanting went faster. When they reached top speed and their words were no longer intelligible, they abruptly stopped.

Acehnese music is robust and has a multicultural flavour. Although one can easily detect traces of Indian, Chinese and Middle Eastern themes, yet haunting notes that still ebb within the soul of the music embrace the heart of Acehnese culture. The sound of the Acehnese *siruene kale*, a recorder-like woodwind, is fascinating. The reed is double, like that of an oboe, made of the leaf of a lontar palm and rumbia tree and surrounded by a curved piece of coconut shell that fits over the mouth. It also sounds like an oboe. It is played with a drum to accompany Acehnese dancers.

We also visited the gleaming, white Gunungan (mountain) which is an architectural enigma in Aceh. It was constructed by Sultan Iskandar Muda as the centrepiece in his gardens which served as a playground for his daughter and his wife. Often referred to as the "pleasure tower", the Gunungan's many rounded domes, steep steps and narrow inner tunnels form a maze that still fascinates children today.

Aceh is one of Indonesia's most productive and prosperous regions exporting rubber, palm oil, pepper, cloves, timber and coffee. In olden times, it monopolised the pepper trade. In 1873, the United India Company sent an expedition to try to break the pepper monopoly and the Acehnese drove them into the sea. The Dutch declared war on Aceh and a bitter war (*perang sabil*) broke out. As the Dutch had an army comprised of troops of 10,000 and all the available commanders they could muster, the Acehnese were outnumbered and the kraton of Aceh fell in 1878. It had cost 107,000 lives.

During the war of independence, the Acehnese had always remained loyal to the Indonesian revolutionaries but they found that their loyalty was not appreciated and not rewarded. The Acehnese fought against the Dutch in Medan. During the civil war in North Sumatra, Kalimantan and North Sulawesi, Aceh remained neutral and did not fight against the central government. Even during the uprisings of the Sumatrans in 1965, Aceh continued to side with Jakarta.

The Acehnese were angry with the central government because recently when they wanted to commemorate their protracted struggle against the Dutch in a special ceremony, the Javanese military commander turned down their application for fear that it might rekindle the flame of regionalism. And today, Jakarta insisted that all the religious ulamas in Aceh must become members of the *Majelis Alim Ulama*, a kind of religious trade union to control all religious activities.

All these are changing after the fall of Suharto and the declining influence of Golkar in Aceh.

Acehnese are complaining that they have contributed more to the central government than they have received. The Javanese do not really understand the Acehnese and there has been very little understanding and development of relationships between the two peoples historically, politically, economically, socially and geographically. At times, the Javanese leaders have an arrogant attitude towards the Acehnese and say, "Why should we cultivate the savages?". As a result of this, there is a hidden consciousness among the Acehnese that the Javanese are taking them for granted and that they have been treated rather unfairly. This resulted in the emergence of an Acehnese independence movement. The Indonesian troops have mounted military forays on the Acehnese and there have been sustained counter-attacks. The *Aceh Merdeka's* back was broken by early 1980 with the death of five of the movement's ten "cabinet members".

The Indonesian authorities are now treating the Acehnese more sensitively and using consensus and consultation when dealing with the Acehnese. Although the Acehnese have agreed to stay within Indonesia, what they felt inside was no longer the same. They felt hurt that Jakarta had taken the wealth, such as natural gas, away from Aceh but had ploughed very little back to the province. They felt that ten tankers of gas from Aceh could set up new tertiary educational institutes in the province. Aceh's US$400 million natural gas project at Arun is the biggest in all of Asia and is expected to net Jakarta US$10 billion over the next 20 years. Aceh was formerly the archipelago's main producer of rubber but its output has been affected by the production of synthetic rubber during the last 20 years. They even have a privately owned gold mine located on the west coast at Tutut. About 70% of the region consists of forests, very little of which has been logged.

Aceh has a surplus of rice and meat and possesses large quantities of fish caught off its coast. An Indonesian Chinese classmate of mine, Adil Nurimba, has set up modern cold storage facilities in Aceh to catch and export fish to Japan.

Aceh's per capita income (not including oil or natural gas which belongs to the central government) is above the national average.

Aceh, therefore, can be economically independent without the help of the Central Government. Therefore, they feel that they have every right to be independent. In fact, the rulers of Jakarta do not dare to install a Javanese governor in Aceh for fear of hurting their feelings.

Aceh is the only province that was able to defeat the army-backed Golkar in the 1987 parliamentary elections. The Acehnese are still very parochial. Now that there is no strong military leadership in the Indonesian armed forces, nobody knows what the Acehnese will do to press on with their independence movement.

The Acehnese have five dialects related to Bahasa Indonesia. They borrow Arabic words a lot and some words are similar to the Cham language spoken in Cambodia. An Acehnese name such as Cut Nyak Dhien have obvious Vietnamese origin. Until recently, there was no written Acehnese language. Now, Acehnese is written in Latin script. The Acehnese give their children three years of education in the Aceh language and then make them study Bahasa Indonesia when they attend school. Most Acehnese read and write Arabic and they pray in Arabic when they attend mosque. It can be said that the Acehnese are the most Arabic-oriented people in Indonesia.

In Aceh, the natives are socially conservative but religiously radical. Rich men are not respected unless they contribute towards Islamic causes and charity. The Acehnese resist westernisation and especially dislike attempts by the West to Christianise them. They have prohibited the Bible from being translated into the Acehnese language and Bible cassette tapes cannot be sold in Aceh. However, they have allowed a Catholic Church to be built in Banda Aceh, with an Italian priest.

The Acehnese are going through traumatic changes as western influence seeps in and westernised young people return to their villages with new ideas. The influx of foreign investments and the transmigration of Javanese workers to Aceh have created problems and frictions in the Acehnese society. A general gap is fast developing within the Acehnese family. The youth nowadays listen to contemporary music, watch rock-and-roll videos, watch western movies, exchange views with foreigners and start to imitate western behaviour. All this has become heartbreaking for the older generation. The appearance of unversity students with modern approaches and thinking will accelerate the split within the society.

Can Aceh withstand the onslaught of western civilisation? Will the Acehnese continue with their struggle for independence and take advantage of the fluid situation in Indonesia following the downfall of Suharto which has left the country without a strong leader? Is the Indonesian armed forces strong enough to deal with any future Aceh independence movement? These are the questions uppermost in the minds of those interested in the future of Aceh.

13

THE ORANG MELAYU (THE MALAYS)
Phoenicians of the East

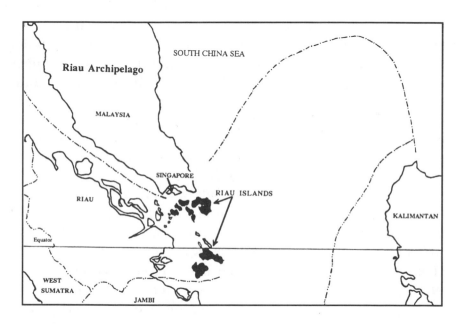

When we talk about the Orang Melayu, we always identify them as a race associated to the prominent race in Malaysia. But, in fact, the Malay race is a minority race of Indonesia who inhabit the Riau Islands, Palembang and some in Minangkabau. They had once established the greatest Buddhist Srivijaya Empire in the region. It has even been stated that the Malays derived their origin from Java and the Javan word *Malayu* means runaway. They were said to be the runaways and outcasts of Java.

The Orang Melayu comprise 7.5 percent of Indonesia's population. They are the descendents of the original deutero-Malay race. As authentic a race as the Bataks, Minangkabau and other Sumatran peoples, the Melayu on both sides of the Straits separating Sumatra and Malaysia share the same ethnicity, though it is not known for sure which arrived in Indonesia first.

The Orang Melayu first established the mighty Srivijaya Empire sometime in 683 A.D. and included the Malay peninsula. In the 8th century, Srivijaya sent an army to Cambodia where the king of Cambodia was taken prisoner and beheaded. After that, every morning, the kings of Cambodia would bow to the west in prayer as a tribute to the Maharaja of Srivijaya. In the ninth and eleventh centuries, Srivijaya had monasteries in Bengal and South India. The capital Palembang was a great flourishing town with more than a thousand Buddhist monks. Pilgrims from China, including the famous I Tsing, lingered there for a long time in order to learn Sanskrit and to become inbued with the teachings of Buddhism.

In those days, Srivijaya was a Buddhist state. Archeologists found a huge granite image of Buddha. Another bronze Buddha head with a twisted bandeau with rosettes was found in Kedukan Bukit where a well-known inscription of 683 A.D. was found. It announced that a king had set sail in order to attain magic power (*siddhayaatra*). The king left Menanga Tambang with an army of 20,000 men and had come and founded the city of Srivijaya on a place formerly called Malayu. The present inhabitants of Palembang still know that the rivulet Tatang, not far from there, was formerly called Malayu. A district Tanah Malayu lies up-stream on the Musi River.

It is hard to believe that the Malays who were behind the mighty Buddhist Srivijaya Empire have now become so Islamic.

For 500 years up to the 13th century, Palembang was one of the world's principal ports. The city flourished in pepper and tin and grew rich on oil. Palembang was then the capital of the Srivijaya Empire and scholars have described it as "The Phoenicians of the East". In early 600 A.D. Mahayana Buddhism reached Palembang and traces of the religion have been found in the inscription of Candi Kalasan in

Central Java. There are not many inscriptions in Palembang because the ancient fields had been plundered for centuries by the inhabitants. It is also possible that the rulers of Srivijaya had less inclination to build temples than their contemporaries in Java and Cambodia.

According to the Chinese annals, in 671 A.D., a Chinese Buddhist pilgrim, I Tsing, arrived at the university of Palembang and stayed there for four years, writing memoirs and handing down a valuable description of the city. He described the city as a huge marketplace where Tamil, Persian, Arabic, Cambodian, Siamese, Chinese, and Burmese were spoken. A thousand ships had laid anchor at the harbour of Palembang. Thousands of monks learned Buddhist teachings and translated Sanskrit texts there.

The city reached its height of fame in the beginning of the 11th century. Then in 1025 A.D., a jealous Chola King from India brutally attacked the city and devastated it. Palembang never recovered from that attack. By the end of the 14th century, Srivijaya split into eight small princedoms, the largest of which was Melayu which became part of Jambi, a powerful maritime state. With the rise of the Islamic Kingdom of Malacca, Palembang became a remote backwater. Islam has taken over from Buddhism and all the Orang Melayu who were previously Buddhists became Muslims.

With the emergence of the Kingdom of Malacca, Riau Orang Melayu concentrated their effort in developing the Riau islands as a rising Islamic power.

I have visited Palembang several times, the first was for a golf game organised by General Ibnu Sutowo who was then President Director of Pertamina. Palembang produces one-third of the total oil used in Indonesia. Pertamina has donated to the city a large sports stadium, a TV station, a town clock and a handsome minaret for its mosque. This Islamic city has its own dances, songs, customs and cuisines. I was very much impressed by the special type of fish from the Musi River which was delicious. We visited the Musi River which divides the city into two sections: the southern half called the *Ulu* and the northern half called the *Ilir*. The great attraction of the city is the Ampera Bridge built in the 1960s.

According to a Chinese chronicle: "In the year 1225, in order to protect the capital from attacks, there was formerly an iron chain stretched over the Musi River. This chain could be raised or lowered by an ingenious device. Later, after many years of peace, when the chain was no longer necessary, it was deposited on the river bank where for a long time it was an object of veneration among the natives."

In the 17th century, a great cannon was also worshipped in Palembang. It was wrapped in red silk, strewn with flowers and perfumed with incense. The Palembang residents, most of them Orang Melayu, believed in the magic power of metal. Although Islam has come to Palembang, the old Buddist influence still lingered on.

The Musi River reminds me of the disastrous air crash that took place sometime in September 1997 when a Singapore Silk Air plane crashed into the Musi River. The plane carrying 104 passengers exploded in the air and plunged into the Musi River. No corpse was found Where had the bodies gone? Today, there is a special burial ground erected by the Singapore Government for the deceased passengers to commemorate their misfortune as not even one body had been found. A special memorial was also built in Singapore.

Could they have been eaten by the crocodiles which are numerous in the Musi River? According to a legend, an Indian came to Palembang and claimed that he could charm the crocodiles. The King was fond of throwing convicts who were condemned to death into the Musi River to feed the crocodiles. When the Indian used mantras to charm the crocodiles, the victim who was thrown into the river was not eaten. The next day after this happened, the king asked the Indian to repeat the performance. When the Indian succeeded in putting the crocodiles under a spell, the king beheaded the Indian for obstructing his desire to throw convicts into the river. According to a chronicle, since the beheading of the Indian, crocodiles in the Musi River have become harmless.

Throughout Sumatra, the people believe that there can be a sort of friendship between human beings and crocodiles. They believe that every man has a special crocodile which takes him on its back to distant places and protects him from possible dangers. During the annual rowing contests which are held on the Queen of Sumatra's birthday, some Malays beseech their guardian crocodile to give speed to their boats.

Beside the Ampera Bridge is Palembang's unique attraction: the river where 10,000 ton ships lie amidst small, bobbing rowboats, sailboats and motorised *perahu*. Boat-houses are moored along the river-bank, functioning as houses above the water and as floating *warungs* (shops). It was this river that gave Palembang the nickname "The Venice of the East". Down the river we came to the floating market of Palembang, which was similar to the floating markets on the *klongs* of Bangkok, selling everything from vegetables to soap.

We also visited a Chinese temple called *Kelenteng Kwa Sam Yo* near the city which has a remarkable collection of hundreds of fascinating murals and wall paintings depicting the story of the great Kublai Khan and other Mongolian heroes. According to Chinese chronicles, Marco Polo visited Palembang in 1292. The Mongolian collection could have been influenced by his visit.

Sometime in 1407 when Admiral Cheng Ho led his 63 treasure ships to the "south seas", he also visited Palembang. According to the Ming dynasty chronicles, in Palembang, Cheng Ho's expedition encountered the famous and treacherous pirate called Chan Chor Ee. His pirate ships had plundered all passing cargo ships and became a well-known terror. It was Cheng Ho's first expedition and he ordered his sailors, numbering 27,800, to seize the Chinese pirate. After a fierce battle during which his men managed to kill 5,000 of Chan's men, burn 10 of his ships and detain another seven, he arrested Chan and brought him back to China for execution. Cheng Ho's victory over the pirates brought him fame and glory and piracy disappeared from the Palembang seas.

When Cheng Ho arrived in Palembang, the country had already been converted to Islam. Java's Majapahit empire had fallen and Islam made inroads into Sumatra through Aceh. Islam also spread to the kingdom of Malacca and the Riau islands whose fates were interlinked.

Admiral Cheng Ho also left behind his imprints. There is a Chinese temple on Pulau Kemarau downriver at the junction of the Musi, Komering and Ogan rivers. This temple also has Malay worshippers because the Malays regard that temple as a *kramat* (holy place) to Muslims. It is known as the "double sanctuaries". This reminds me of the *Sampo Beo* in Semarang built to commemorate Cheng Ho where Muslims wearing *songkok* (hat) are in charge of the temple. This could be a temple built to commemorate Admiral Cheng Ho.

After Admiral Cheng Ho's seven expeditions, the Europeans came to Southeast Asia with their "gunboat" diplomacy, The Portuguese were the first to appear. They seized power in Bintan in 1526 but lost it by 1539. Their departure marked the beginning of Riau's Golden Era: from about 1530 to nearly the end of the 18th century, the Riau archipelago became the centre of the Malay civilisation.

Beginning from the 17th century, Riau had blossomed into a famous trading centre. In 1687, Thomas Slicher, the Governor of Malacca, wrote:

> "The number of ships going to Riau (then the capital of Johore) is so great that the river is scarcely navigable as a result of the many trading vessels... Here the tin traders are paid half in cash and half in cloth; whereas in Malacca they are given whatever cloth available and not the newest styles as in Riau."

In 1685, the Sultan of Riau Mahmud Syah II was forced to sign a cooperative agreement with the increasingly powerful Dutch. Over the following century, the Raja's authority was greatly eroded. From 1784 onwards, the Dutch had complete control over the Riau archipelago with the Rajas having a say only on matters relating to the adat law.

By the early 1800s, the Sultan of Tanjung Pinang, Hussein, once again held power over Johore, the southern islands of Kep. Lingga and even as far as Tembilahan on Sumatra. Learning the use of gunpowder, he reigned by virtue of a powerful fleet. It was from Hussein that Sir Stamford Raffles obtained his license to establish a trading post on Singapore island in 1819.

The Orang Melayu in the Riau islands were not too happy with the Dutch and their opposition went underground in the early 1900s. Under the leadership of the last Malay Sultan Abdurrachman Muazan Syah (1883-1911) they formed the Rusydiah Club which secretly liaised with the famous nationalist organisation, Sarikat Islam, and assisted its effort to rid Indonesia of Dutch control and achieve Indonesian independence.

The main population of the Riau islands is of pure Malay stock. There are also several indigenous population groupings including the Orang Laut, who are like gypsies from the Natuna island and Sulawesi, as well as the *akit* tribes of the Bengkalis District, the Mantang people of Pulau Penuba and Penang Kelumu and the Baruk people of Sungeibuluh. Riau comprises 1,176,530 square km of vast expanses of sea bordered on the north by Singapore, on the west by mainland Sumatra, and on the east by Borneo. Of its 3,214 large and small islands, about 1,000 of them are occupied but only 743 have names.

The early history of the Riau archipelago suggests a wave of immigration of Austronesian tribes from Southern India in the years 2500-1500 B.C. Around 1000 A.D., a separate kingdom was founded in Pulau Bintan and it was further enlarged by a propitious marriage of a Riau princess to the son of Palembang. A capital was built in Temasik (which is now Singapore) and the principality named Bintan Temasik Singapura.

By 1500, the Islamic kingdom of Malacca had conquered the Riau Islands of Kundur, Jemaja, Bungujran, Tambelan, Lingga and Bintan. Later, the archipelago came under the control of Hang Tuah who became a Malay hero in Malay history. The Portuguese ruled Riau for a brief period following the conquest of the Kingdom of Malacca. After their withdrawal, from 1530 to the end of the 18th century, Riau became the centre of Malay civilisation.

The Riau islands were the heart of Malay civilisation about 300 years ago, but strangely little evidence of this remains today. The biggest contribution which the Orang Melayu has made to Indonesia is its Melayu language which has been adopted as Bahasa Indonesia.

The Melayu language is so simple and easy to learn that Sukarno has chosen it as the national language of Indonesia instead of the Javanese language, a difficult language — which after all is spoken by 60 percent of Indonesians. In that sense, the Malays should be proud that their language was chosen as the national language of the people. Because of this, there is a misconception that Indonesia is dominated by the Malay race when in fact, the Orang Melayu is only a minority of a multi-racial, multi-lingual and multi-cultural society.

In fact, the creation of a British and Dutch sphere of influence started after the signing of the Anglo-Dutch Treaty in 1824. This was the result of a five-year war between the two countries resulting in British having a foothold on the present-day Malay dominated Malaysia. The Malays therefore came to be ruled on the one side by the British and on the other side by the Dutch.

After World War II, there was a move by some radical Malay leaders in Malaya but with Indonesian origin to include Malaya as part of the Indonesian struggle for independence. During the Japanese occupation, they initially planned to "Japanise" the Malays in order to help their war effort. To achieve their objective, they aimed at destroying the Malay elite and sultan to a position of inconsequence and encouraged the radical Malays who were excluded from the British establishment. The radical Malays who had formed the *Kesatuan Melayu Muda* (The Malay Youth organisation) were encouraged to adopt an uncompromising attitude towards the British. Hence, in mid-1945 *Kesatuan Rakyat Istimewa* (KRIS) was born which was an attempt to create a resistance group ready to oppose the return of the British. The war, however, ended suddenly and the radical Malays who had allied themselves with the Japanese were placed in a position where they were seen as persons disloyal to the British. Since retreat was no longer possible, the only course open to them was to sustain their anti-colonial struggle. The radical leftwing leaders such as Ibrahim Yacob, Dr Burhanuddin Al-Helmi, Ahmad Moestaman were striving to achieve independence of Malaya through a merger with Indonesia. Some of the radical Malays even used an Indonesian term to describe their political party such as *Partai Kebangsaan Melayu Malaya* or *Partai Rakyat,* and they were against UMNO, which they thought only looked after the interest of the sultans.

Such parties carried the platform of "to unite Malayan races, to instill the spirit of nationalism in the hearts of the Malays and its aim at uniting Malaya within the larger family, i.e., the Republic of Greater Indonesia" and "to support the movement of the people of Indonesia in their struggle to seize independence". Ibrahim Yacob was one of them leading this movement. I met him after I became Ambassador to Indonesia and he told me that during the Japanese occupation, Sukarno had visited Taiping to negotiate with them on how to bring Malaya into the orbit of Indonesia. Ibrahim later became a member of the Indonesian Parliament after the war.

After Malaya gained self-government with Tengku Abdul Rahman as Chief Minister, the Malays in Indonesia and Malaya became separated and the drive to bring Malaya into Indonesia died off, although Sukarno had not given up hope in taking over Malay dominated countries such as Malaya as well as the Philippines into his scheme of Greater Indonesia.

Since the radical Malays fail to bring Malaya into Indonesian arms, the Malays in Indonesia have become a minority race and those in Malaysia have become a majority race. The Riau islands is the main centre of Indonesian Malays. It is a quiet and peaceful, and fantastic paradise for explorers. The seas around Riau are generally shallow and *kelong* (fishing huts) can be seen all over the islands. Scattered across the South China sea like confetti, the Riau islands comprise some 3,000 islands (many uninhabited curving south-east from Sumatra to Kalimantan and north to Malaysia). The islands can be divided into two groups: one bunched closely to the coast of Sumatra and the other nearer to Singapore. The main islands in the first group consist of Bengkalis, Rupat, Padang, Tebingtinggi, Rangasang, Lalang, Mendok, Penyalai, Serapang, Muda, Kijang, Pucung and Kateman. The second can be broken down into the Karimun islands, the Lingga-Singkep, the Tambelan, Anambas, North and South Natuna groups.

Riau is one of the richest parts of Indonesia. There is oil in Bintan, granite in Karimun, tin in Bangka, Singkep and Kundur. Indonesia is today the world's fourth-largest producer of tin, which is second only to petroleum as a foreign-currency-earning mineral.

Riau's capital is Pekanbaru which has a population of 210,000, a large proportion of whom are Chinese. Pekanbaru is a modern, clean and well laid-out town on the Siak River. It is the gateway to Southeast Asia's largest and richest oilfields. Pekanbaru means "New Market". It was founded in 1784 on the upstream of Siak River where the water is deep enough for bigger ships to navigate.

In Pekanbaru, the name of Hang Tuah, a legendary hero in Malay history, is remembered. Hang Tuah is believed to have led guerrilla warfare against the Dutch and raided the Dutch outposts on the Siak and in the Straits of Melaka during colonial times. He used a swift little sailboat to attack the Dutch and always managed to elude his enemy. A street and many shops are named after Hang Tuah.

In Pekanbaru, we had a glimpse of Riau's traditional architecture. The shape of the roofs resemble hairpin and they are called *rumah lipat kijang* meaning hairpin. Even modern buildings are copying this style of traditional architecture. The houses are usually adorned with carvings of flowers, birds and bees. The flowers symbolise prosperity and happiness, the birds symbolise the one true God and the bees reflect the desire for mutual understanding. Riau houses also normally have four pillars symbolising their ability to live in the four corners of the universe.

The main attraction in Riau is the Festival of the Sea which is held on Pulau Sarasan during the second month of the Islamic calendar. During the celebration, the islanders hang packets of sticky rice on trees near the beach. Then they cut logs from the forest and cart them down to the beach where they are loaded onto canoes and dropped into the deep water to appease the gods of the ocean. This was also supposed to protect swimmers from drowning. Apart from the celebration, the Riau islanders also observe the principal festivals in the Islamic calender.

Riau's most popular dances are the *joget* (a fun Malay dance), the *zaping* and the *dabus* which have religious significance. The Malay theatre of Pulau Mantang (just south of Bintan) is known throughout

Indonesia and still popular in the island of Singkep. I have danced the joget many times whenever there was a function organised by Malaysian leaders in honour of Singapore leaders. It is a simple and graceful dance accompanied by *ronggeng* (a Malay style of dancing) music.

The Malays are by nature easy going, friendly and humble people. They prefer a more leisurely pace of life and would like fishing or farming than toiling under the sun. As they are predominantly Muslims, they are influenced by the Islamic teaching and depend entirely on God's desire meaning 'Inshaallah' (meaning if God wishes) and when they succeed, 'Alhamdulilah' (Thank God for the help). As Muslims, most of them pray five times a day and their whole life is centred on the mosque.

There is a slight difference between the Malays in Malaysia and those in Indonesia. In Malaysia, one can hardly find a Malay who is not a Muslim, whereas in Indonesia, it is easy to find a Malay who is a Christian, a Buddhist or even a Hindu. The Malays in Indonesia are more tolerant to religion. A Malay girl could marry a Christian or Buddhist without insisting that the partner become a Muslim and vice versa.

The Malays are by nature, a peaceful and contented race. They are contented with what nature has given them and prefer to lead a leisurely life. They are quite religious and most of them are orthodox Muslims. There is a difference between the Malays in Indonesia and those in Malaysia in that the former is more relaxed, less orthodox and the latter more rigid in their religious belief. It is also significant that in Malaysia, there is not a single Malay who is not a Muslim, whereas the Malays in Indonesia are free to choose their religion other than Islam. There are more intermarriages among the Malays in Indonesia.

At the end of the Japanese occupation, the Japanese used the Allied prisoners of war to build a rail link between Pekanbaru and Muara in an attempt to get coal from West Sumatra to the east coast. 15,000 men, mostly prisoners of war, died in the process. The train started running just days before World War II ended.

Before Riau became the centre of the oil industry in 1930, it was a major exporter of rubber, gold, tin, cloves and indigo from Central Sumatra and imported cloth, machinery, foodstuff and other items.

We visited Istana Asserayah, about 160 km east of Pekanbaru. It was an impressive building which housed the royal family. Built in 1889 by Sultan Assaidi Ssyarif Hasim Abdul Jalil Saifuddin, the 11th Siak sultan who controlled the region from Langkat (North Sumatra) nearly all the way to Jambi, it is reminiscent of the Versailles. His son, Sultan Syarief Kasim II, who was educated in Amsterdam, lost power in 1946 when the sultanate was taken over by the Indonesian Republican Government. Unlike other sultans who resisted the Indonesian revolutionaries, he openly sided with the republicans and was much admired for his courage.

After the Indonesian revolution, the Istana was abandoned and, not being properly maintained, began to fall apart. Caltex contributed towards the reconstruction and renovation of the Istana but the government is still paying for the upkeep. Some members of the royal family are still alive.

A small museum inside the palace contains many of the sultan's possessions: old furniture, china and other ceramic pieces, odd historical objects, a 19th century gramophone which was still working, and the sultan's gold-plated throne. On the grounds are a mosque, the burial complex for the Siak royal family, and the High Court building in which criminal cases and other lawsuits were tried.

About 130 km west of Pekanbaru, we saw ruins of a Buddhist complex, one of which is a topless *candi* (temple) called *Candi Maligai*, one of the few stupas ever recovered in Indonesia. This stupa dates from the 12th century. There is a legend that the Bataks attacked the Buddhist complex.

Another major town in Riau is Tanjung Pinang, a small Malay-Chinese trading centre about 80 south and four hours by launch from Singapore. The town serves as an important commercial shopping centre for such cities like Medan, Jambi, Jakarta, Palembang, and Padang. A lot of goods can be found. Almost every house has a TV set. The residents can select channels from Malaysian, Singapore and Indonesia stations.

Bintan is the largest island in the Riau archipelago. During the past few years, Singapore investors have poured in a great deal of investments into the island to make it into a holiday resort. Situated on important commercial sea lanes, Bintan has always been of strategic importance.

I am very familiar with the Malays for I stayed in a Malay kampong in Butterworth during my youth. I had many Malay friends when I was young and became more acquainted with Malay political leaders when I joined the People's Action Party. But, I did not realise that the ancestors of Orang Melayu were in fact the founders of the strongest empire, the Srivijaya, who once controlled the whole of Southeast Asia.

14

THE BUGIS AND MAKASSARESE
Cape of the Infamous Ones

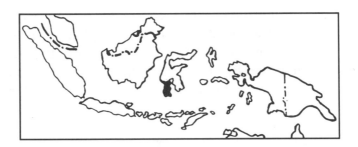

The word "Bugis" is very familiar to the ears of Singaporeans as there is a Bugis Street in Singapore where we could find *pondants* (transvestites or men dressed up like women and behaving like women) catering for sex with men. Although this trade was banned by the Singapore authorities, the area is still known as Bugis Street and now there is a shopping complex known as Bugis Junction. It is significant that Bugis street is famous for pondants for the Bugis have a traditional name for pondants and they are called *calabai*, who serve a useful purpose at Bugis wedding.

The fiercely Islamic Bugis and Makassarese together with the animist Christian Torajans, live in a peculiarly shaped island called Sulawesi which has an area of 172,000 square km and a population of 6.5 million. I say peculiar because Sulawesi looks like an open-jawed crocodile.

The population of Sulawesi is 6.5 million, of which four million are Bugis, two million Makassarese and around 500,000 Torajans. The

Bugis and Makassarese are the main groups on the coast. The Makassarese are concentrated in the southern tip, centred on the port of Makassar now known as Ujung Pandang. Bugis and Makassarese have similar cultures. Both are seafaring people and therefore good sailors and shipbuilders.

The Bugis are known for their fierce character and sense of honour, which sometimes result in violence. Yet they are among the most hospitable and amiable of peoples and the most steadfast in their friendship, for they talk of *siri*, a concept very much similar to that of the Chinese *yigi* (faithfulness). Although the cohesiveness of their society is based largely on the existence of a system of pervasive and interlocking clienteles, most of them still have a strong sense of their individuality. Bugis society is one of the most complex and rigidly hierarchical. They are strongly motivated to attain high office and wealth ranks.

Something rather interesting in Bugis society is the existence of the *calabai* (homosexual person), some of whom are impotent but others do get married. Such calabai have a special role to perform in the Bugis society. They are employed to take charge of practical matters such as the decoration of the house during a wedding. They do the cooking, the make-up and dressing of the bride and bridegroom and hire the ornaments and accessories for the couple and their retinue. Often they also conduct the traditional ritual ceremonies. For most calabai, these activities represent their main source of income and some become fairly well off. This prospect may explain why parents do not object if a young boy shows a propensity to adopt feminine behaviour like playing girls' games or dressing up as a girl. In the 16th century, calabai convicted of sexual intercourse with women were put to death by boiling.

While the Bugis were at the zenith of their power in the late 1700s, many Bugis merchants came to Singapore in their *sampan panjang* (literally meaning "long boats") with red or green bows and based themselves in Kampong Glam (the Malay quarter of Singapore) which was soon to become the busy street known as Bugis Street. One historian described the Bugis as "nondescript traders".

The Bugis seem to have conflicting tendencies — to be hierarchical and to be egalitarian; to compete and to compromise. Their sense of individual honour and solidarity with their fellow Bugis, combined with such valued qualities as bravery, cleverness, religious belief and business acumen, has been a consistent driving force in their development. These qualities will ensure their enduring future as a dynamic and strongly individualistic people.

The coexistence of these conflicting traits is perhaps what makes the Bugis so adaptable, and is at the root of another of their characteristic, namely their propensity to migrate. They can be found from Malaysia to western New Guinea, from southern Philippines and north Borneo to the Lesser Sunda islands. Their most valuable assets are their versatility and adaptality which have enabled them to survive over the centuries, always changing and yet always preserving their traditional character.

Around 4000 B.C., the migration of Austronesian-speaking people with a basically Mongoloid genetic make-up moved southwards from Taiwan through the Philippines and settled down in Sulawesi. Trade may have led to the early settlement of both sides of the Makassar Straits by proto-South Sulawesi people.

Anthropologists have discovered in Makassar a Neolithic settlement and pre-historic remains — 4,000-year-old hollow-based stone arrow-heads known as Maros points. They have also found images of Buddha at Sampaga on the southwest coast of Sulawesi belonging to the Indian Amarawati school of art, an art form which once flourished in the 2nd century. The famous bronze "Sulawesi Buddha" now exhibited at the Jakarta National Museum, shows many stylistic similiarities with Indian sculpture. Mysterious megaliths, sarcophagi and other pre-historic artifacts can be seen in the remote Bensoa and Bada of Central Sulawesi. Finds of Buddhist images at several places on the Sulawesi coast point to the possibility of early visits from Sumatran Buddhists connected by commercial, religious and diplomatic links with Tamils from south-east India and Sri Lanka. Other indications of possible contacts with Sumatran Buddhism are offered by certain aspects of the pre-Islamic Bugis priests, the *Bissu* which is similar to the Sanskrit word *bhiksu* used for a Buddhist monk.

In the ancient Bugis world, commoners with their red blood were considered fundamentally different from the "white-blooded" nobility through whom some of the divine essense had come down to Earth. There is a myth accounting for the origin of the Bugis which says that, in the beginning, water covered the Earth. Then, a few pieces of land emerged which were to become Mt. Latimojong (west of Luwu), Mt. Bawalaraneng (north of Bantaeng), the hill of Tombolo in Kajang and the hill of Gojeng in Sinjai. According to the legend man sprang up on top of these heights and then came downhill to people the plains. The Bugis believe that it is through marriage and childbearing that the "white blood" received from the gods is kept pure and perpetuated on Earth.

In early Bugis history, the Bugis practised head-hunting which was part of the ritual related to agriculture and fertility. They generally buried their dead by disposing of bodies by immersion (in the sea or lakes) or by putting them in trees. The ancient megalithic sites bear witness to their practise of disposing dead bodies. Their religion was dominated by the worship of ancestors and spirits to whom offerings were made through specialist intermediaries.

For centuries, Sulawesi had been a refuge for pirates. The pirates hid themselves in its deserted coastal mangrove swamps and Bugis' most famous pirate was Arung Singkang, a descendent of the royal family of Wajo in South Sulawesi. In 1726, he conquered Pasir, then Kitai, and in 1733 his forces made an unsuccessful attempt on Banjarmasin.

Before Islam came to Sulawesi, there were four Bugis kingdoms: the Luwu, Pammana, Soppeng, and Sidenreng. By the end of the 15th century, Luwu was still the dominant power in most of the Bugis country including the banks of the Great Lake. The period between about 1500 and 1530 saw the end of the Luwu's supremacy in South Sulawesi after years of unceasing turmoil. In 1509, Luwu attacked the Bugis state of Bone, one of Sulawesi's major states, but Bone's proved to be superior militarily and took over the sacred red umbrella of Luwu, the very emblem of its paramount overlord.

For nearly 20 years, there was competition between Goa, a state consisting of Makassarese and Bone, a state comprising (the Bugis) for hegemony on the Sulawesi which finally led to war. The Portuguese were Makassar's main provider of firearms and gunpowder. They also provided Western technology on fort building, artillery, mathematics, astronomy, geography and cartograpy. With these, Makassarese invaded Bugis territories. They took more than 30,000 Bugis prisoners including the Bugis ruler, La Ma'daremmeng. The defeated Bugis took their revenge with the help of the Dutch and attacked Sulawesi. In 1666, a joint Dutch-Bugis force with the help of troops from Ternate, Ambon and Button besieged Makassar — the Dutch from the sea and the Bugis from land. After a fierce and protracted battle the Makassarese were forced to dismantle most of their fortifications, give up their trade in spices and expel the Portuguese. In 1669, Sultan Hasanuddin of Goa abdicated.

The people of Sulawesi were among the very last to be converted to Islam. In 1605, the Muslim kings of West Java came to Sulawesi to covert the Bugis and the Makassarese into Muslims. When Islam eventually came to Sulawesi, indigenous people like the Torajans moved into the hinterland and settled down, quite isolated from civilisation. When Christian missionaries came to convert the people of Sulawesi, they found the Torajans and converted most of them.

Although the Bugis and the Makassarese are mainly Muslims, they still practise certain rituals which are un-Islamic. Some of them still believe in genies and angels. Muslim saints and local miracle workers are considered intermediaries with God. Some traditional houses have in their attics miniature houses and beds, complete with small mattresses, pillows and bed-curtains. These are provided as temporary residences for spiritual beings who are summoned in the course of certain rites and to whom offerings are made. Outside the house, other places where offerings are made include the seashore, river banks and certain boulders, trees, cliffs or hilltops where spiritual beings are said to inhabit, or where points of access to Heaven are located. They also worship graves of important leaders of the past. A number of these graves are, however, not real ones, but are covers for those who wish to maintain formal respect for Muslim orthodoxy to visit in pilgrimage without appearing to be indulging in spirit worship.

According to a view widespread among the Bugis, the main difference between traditional Bugis rites and Islamic rites is that the former address the divinity through offerings and the latter through prayers. These are seen as two means that can be used concurrently to obtain the same results.

Being good sailors, shrewd businessmen and skilled in shipbuilding, the Bugis and the Makassarese started to migrate in the 17th and 18th centuries and expanded their influence to Kutai, Johore and Selangor. They almost controlled the region.

The Bugis and Makassarese also have a 500-year history of trading and cultural links with the aborigines of northern Australia. British explorer Mathew Flinders encountered 60 Indonesian sailing ships at Melville Bay in 1803, and today many more are making the risky journey to the reefs off the north Australian coast to fish.

The Bugis and the Makassarese were masters of the sea in the region until the bloodthirsty Portuguese arrived soon after their conquest of Malacca in 1511. They called Sulawasi "Ponto dos Celebres" (Cape of the Infamous Ones), the name for the cape north of Minahasa which had caused so many Portuguese shipwrecks. The Portuguese came to Sulawesi for gold, copper and lead which could be found in the Toraja mountains. Gold from North Sulawesi seemed to have been under the control of the Makassar people. In 1544, some Portuguese visitors to Suppa were impressed by a procession of thirty noblemen wearing many gold bracelets.

One new commodity in the sixteenth century was slaves. These were prisoners of war, which could mean anyone taken in a conquered place — man, woman or child. Portuguese accounts say that many of them were trained as galley slaves from childhood. A slave could fetch 1,000 rials, a good bargain for the Portuguese. The slave trade in South Sulawesi was prompted by demand in America and Europe from the fifteen century onwards and it persisted for centuries.

When the English came, they called these islands the Celebes. In the 16th century, the Portuguese began colonising northern Sulawesi from their base in the Philippines and Macau. From the 17th century onwards, the Dutch drove away the Portuguese. They gained complete control over the docile Minahasans in the north but experienced much bloody resistance from the Bugis in the south. The rebellious Bugis and Makassarese were finally subjugated by a Dutch fleet in 1666-67. Although the Dutch imposed a maritime monopoly on the spice trade in the southern part of the island, wars between the Dutch and the Islamic states of Goa and Bone continued throughout the 19th century. It was not until 1905-06 that the Dutch finally achieved complete political control over Sulawesi.

The Japanese occupied the island for three-and-a-half years from 1942 and were more preoccupied with extracting mineral resources necessary for their war efforts. After the Japanese surrendered, the North Sulawesi-born Dr Ratulangi was appointed by the new republican government led by Sukarno and Hatta as Governor of all Sulawesi and he took up his post in Makassar on 19 August, 1945. In September, however, Allied troops arrived on the island, and in contrast to other places in Java and Sumatra where they met resistance from Japanese-trained guerrilla fighters, there was no resistance in Sulawesi. The Allies brought with them Dutch officers of the Netherlands Indies Civil Administration (NICA) who compelled Dr Ratulangi to stand down as Governor and established their own local government. The troops of the Royal Netherlands East Indies Army (KNIL) later took over the military role from the Allies. Dr Ratulangi received the support of most Bugis rulers to cooperate with the Java-based Indonesian republic. The pro-Indonesia factions formed guerrilla groups and were brought together in a federated organisation called the Sulawesi Revolutionary Fighters (LAPRIS). The guerrillas had skirmishes with the KNIL troops but, due to lack of weapons, they were defeated by the KNIL and Dr Ratulangi and his supporters were arrested. They were detained in the Dutch controlled prison in Jakarta.

Meanwhile, a number of young anti-colonial Bugis radicals organised themselves into a resistance movement and fought alongside the Javanese guerrillas against the Dutch. One of them was Kahar Muzakkar, a young man from Luwu who organised infiltrations into Sulawesi with local boats of arms, ammunition and trained fighters. Among them were two youngsters Andi Mattalata and Yusuf who later became prominent generals of Indonesia. I came to know General Yusuf who later became Minister of Defence under Suharto and Vice-President of Indonesia. Kahar formed a resistance group called the Indonesian Republican Army for the preparation of the Liberation of Sulawesi (TRIPS). General Yusuf was a soft-spoken Bugis, very polite, considerate and brave. When he was Minister of Defence, he was ingenious and aggressive. He toured the country inspecting his troops. He was also an incorruptible general.

In order to suppress the resistance movement, the Dutch sent the notorious Dutch captain, Westerlin, who was cruel and aggressive. He committed atrocities like executing hostages and carried out mass killings to terrorise the villagers. Within a very short time, he succeeded in suppressing the resistance movement and took over the LAPRIS (Sulawesi Revolutionary Fighters for the Indonesian Republic) head-quarters. The Dutch created a federated state of East Indonesia in January 1947 which included Moluccas, the Lesser Sunda Islands, Bali and Sulawesi in a bid to isolate the Indonesian Republic. This puppet state had the support of a large proportion of the conservative South Sulawesi aristocracy while those of a more progressive cast of mind supported the incorporation of their lands into a unitary Indonesian Republic.

Meanwhile, Kahar Muzakkar, who had escaped Dutch capture from Sulawesi when they attacked TRIPS headquarters, went to Java and continued his resistance against the Dutch. He was promoted to the rank of lieutenant-colonel and made deputy commander of the Sixteenth Brigade of the Indonesian National Army. In August 1949, he was put in charge of coordinating the guerrilla units in all the "outer islands" as part of the endeavour to form a Union of South Sulawesi Guerrillas (KGSS). In December 1949, the Dutch recognised Indonesian independence but only within the framework of a federal constitution and a Dutch-Indonesian union.

At that time, the state of East Indonesia was the largest of the constituent states of the new United States of Indonesia outside Java. It retained a very conservative attitude such as allowing the local aristocrats, the traditional rulers, to have a big say in administration. The South Sulawesi guerrillas, which did not disband, was officially in charge of maintaining law and order and they were suspicious of the new Jakarta-based central government. Meanwhile with the support of the National Indonesian Army they were also fighting the KNIL units controlled by the Dutch. Fighting between pro-Dutch and pro-Indonesia forces broke out on several occasions and for several months causing hundreds of casualties in Makassar city. In these clashes, the guerrillas gave significance support to the National Army. The pro-Dutch forces were finally defeated and Indonesia became a unitary state on 17 August, 1947.

After Indonesia became independent, the biggest problem which the central government faced was how to handle the 15,000 Sulawesi guerrillas. Most of the guerrillas wanted to be incorporated into the Indonesian Army as members of a separate "Hasanuddin Brigade". Kahar Muzakkar, who, even before the dissolution of the State of East Indonesia, had been asked by the central army command to help settle the issue, supported this idea. But the Minahasan Colonel Kawilarang, the territorial commander for East Indonesia appointed by the Jakarta government, rejected the proposal and issued a decree liquidating the KGSS. Incensed by Kawilarang's decision, Kahar joined the guerrillas and began obstructing South Sulawesi's main roads of the guerrillas bases. There were military skirmishes amidst attempts at mediation and negotiations. In March 1951, a provisional agreement was reached stipulating that former guerrillas were to join the National Reserve Corps made up of five battalions pending selection of those men who would be taken into the regular army and the rest to be demobilised and "returned to society".

When the time came to carry out the agreement on 17 August, 1951, Kahar and his troops failed to turn up. They had retreated to the jungle. Kahar said the army had not kept its promises to the former guerrillas. The Jakarta government launched several campaigns to suppress the dissidents but met with little success. On the contrary, the rebellion took root in all of South and South-East Sulawesi. The rebellion was encouraged by other rebellions taking place in other parts of Indonesia including West Java where the so-called Darul Islam (DI) rebellion occurred.

In 1952, Kahar accepted the offer made by the leader of Darul Islam in West Java, Sekar Madji Kartosuwiryo, to join forces against the Jakarta Government. He took the title of Commander of the Fourth (Hasanujdin) Division of the Islamic Army of Indonesia (TII). In fact, he continued to act quite independently although his rebel organisation took on an increasingly Islamic orientation. In 1953, it began collecting taxes in the name of the Islamic Republican State of Indonesia and implemented strict Islamic rules in the area of South Sulawesi it controlled, namely Makassar, Bugis, Ma'senrempulu and Mandar countryside.

Kahar called his Islamic reforms the "Makalua charter", named after his constituency stronghold in Ma'senrempulu. This charter was a kind of Islamic socialism including a moderate degree of land reform and the suppression of social inequality. The Charter also determined the way the people should dress such as prohibiting ostentatious dress and behaviour and wearing of gold, jewels or silks and sumptuous feasting at weddings. It spelled out the eradication of all traces of feudalism such as traditional political offices and aristocratic titles and paganism. It also prohibited people from making pilgrimages to sacred places and the performance of pre-Islamic rituals. One significant Islamic reform was the implementation of the *shari'a* courts which has very strict punishments for offenders such as stoning for adulterers and the amputation of a hand for thieves. The new regime even prohibited people from smoking foreign branded cigarettes or eating "delicacies" originating from the cities. A kind of anti-city orientation similar to that of the Khmer Rouge was growing among the rebel force. As a token of their asceticism, the rebels left their hair uncut. This would immediately single out any of them who yielded to the lure of a short visit to the city and its temptations.

Kahar's tactics were rather brutal. They would burn down the houses of those who did not support Darul Islam and branded them as stooges of the Indonesian National Army (TNI). Some were even thrown into gaol. Many residents faced the dilemma of whether to support the TNI or the DI. Those who refused to cooperate with the DI became refugees and migrated to Central Sulawesi, East Kalimantan or South Sumatra. The strict measures of Kahar created a division among the rebels. Some factions of the rebels defected to the TNI. For instance, the rebels in Pare split away from Kahar's army to form an independent rebel army resulting in a three-corner fight.

By 1960, the rebellion was much weakened and significant resistance was restricted to a few strongholds in the northern mountains around Mt. Matimojong in Luwu and in Southeast Sulawesi around Kolaka. My friend General M. Yusuf, a Bugis who later became military commander in Makassar, did a lot to strengthen the forces of TNI and get support from the Bugis soldiers who had worked for Kahar. He even tried to strike a deal with Kahar while hostility was continuing. But finally in February 1965, the remnants of Kahar's troops were forced to retreat to Southeast Sulawesi when Kahar was killed.

Both the Bugis and the Makassarese are known in Indonesian history as Sea Gypsies. They were extraordinary shipbuilders, sailors, merchants, slave runners, warriors and adventurers. The Bugis were once the most feared pirates of the Java Sea, their ships armed with bronze bow rammers shaped like dragons' gullets.

In the 14th century, the Bugis were a formidable naval power. During the 17th and 18th centuries, they established a kingdom in South Sulawesi known as the Kingdom of Makassar which dominated Borneo, Sumatra and even maintained colonies as far away as Singapore. The kingdom traded with New Guinea, the Philippines, Burma, Cambodia, China and India. Its prosperity persisted until the Dutch conquest when the kings of Makassar were treated by the Dutch as vassals.

To the Bugis-Makassar people, the most basic element is *siri* (self-respect and dignity). They are ready to sacrifice even their own lives if their siri is stained by someone. Siri plays an important part in human relations, especially in marriage. If the siri of a girl is offended when a man refuses to marry her after engaging in romance, then the insulted party has the right to kill the culprit in order to restore the family's honour. Siri involves not only individual feelings but also extends to group feelings and solidarity. The spirit of siri played an important part when the Bugis chose to back Kahar's rebellion.

The Bugis believe in the wise sayings of ancient sages, which are featured in the few Bugis books printed since the 1960s. The book *La Toa* describes how things should be — how rulers should behave towards people, and how the people should behave among themselves in a state based on *ade* (custom), *rapang* (civil law), *wari* (the rules of inherited hierarchy), *bicara* (the deliberations of knowledgeable persons, constructing jurisprudence) and *sara* (Islamic law).

The Bugis pay particular attention to kinship which is inextricably interlinked to various aspects of society such as marriage, social hierarchy, power and personal influence. They have a bilateral organic kinship system. This means that a person's kindred is reckoned through both the father's and mother's side. They pay attention to "lineage" where descent is acknowledged from the mother's as well as the father's side.

To the Bugis, a marriage means *siala* which means "to take each other". Marriage is the best way of making a non-kin into a kin and to differentiate from *tennia tau laeng* (not other people). When two friends or business partners want a closer relationship, they marry their offspring to each other. In Bugis society, it is common to see cousins marrying one another especially in the noble families because both are considered to have white blood.

Wedding ceremonies take place in two stages: first the wedding proper (*ma'pabotting*) which is organised at the bride's house and which the groom's parents do not attend. This is later followed sometimes several days later by the *ma'parola* (having the bride going to the house of her parents-in-law), which the bride's parents do not attend. On the wedding day, there is a *sampa* (obstacle) when the groom has to overcome a number of symbolic obstacles, such as staged resistance by horsemen or demonstrations of martial arts, and has to gain his way through by dispensing small gifts to the obstructors. For the nobility, a special ritual called *ma'lawolo* is observed, involving a dialogue between the bridegroom's party and a *bissu* (medium) representing the bride's party. Speaking from an elevated platform of the house, the bissu would ask the bridegroom's party whether the bridegroom really was a descendent of the nobility who by their pure white blood "are nearest to god". During the ensuing dialogue, the bissu and the bridegroom would hold one end of the *lawolo*, a braid made from a *patola* cloth and a white cloth twisted together, symbolising the rainbow.

When the nobles married, a cut in one finger had to be made to demonstrate that the blood which dripped out was really white.

In a Bugis wedding, the groom has to be patient for he has to go through many procedures to get the bride's acceptance to sleep with him. The lengthy process sometimes takes months before a marriage is consummated. Sometimes, a bride persists in refusing consummation, in which case the mariage has to be dissolved by divorce. Even today, the process may take some weeks and if unsuccessful, can still end in a divorce.

In Bugis society, the woman's domain is around the house and the man's domain reaches "the border of the sky". The man's main duty is to be the income provider and the wife takes care of the children, pounds rice, cooks, washes, tends vegetables and makes purchases for the family.

In the early days, the Bugis did not use compasses or sextants when they sailed as they claimed that they could smell coral reefs and a coming tsunami. There was no distinction between the captain and the crew. Their *perahu* (boat) were usually forward tilting, square-bowed, with great oar-like rudders and seven sails ballooning from very high masts. In a strong wind, the *perahu* had to drop their sails to avoid capsizing. There were no bunks for they were considered unnecessary. The Bugis sailors slept and ate on deck in all weather. They cruised in their fully loaded ocean-going two-master with seven sails and could sail from Makassar to Jakarta in five days. Bugis *perahu* were used extensively during the revolutionary war against the Dutch.

Their flotillas are still being used as part of the Indonesian naval force.

Originating from Sulawesi, the Bugis were a seafaring race and their maritime power dominated the Malay states of Johore, Selangor and Kuala Linggi. The Malay states found it difficult to keep the Bugis permanently out of the local political jostling which frequently occurred. The Bugis entrenched themselves in the affairs of several Malay states and by the mid-eighteenth century, a Bugis prince, Raja Lumu, succeeded in becoming the *de facto* ruler of Selangor.

In Johore where the Bugis helped to defeat Raja Kecil, one of the sultans, the very foundation of the state rested on their shoulders. Nominally, succeeding members of the Bugis elite occupied the office of *Yang Di-Pertuan Muda*, a position second only to the ruler, but they retained the real power until the end of the nineteenth century. In fact, the last ruler of the emasculated Johore Sultanate — concentrated in Riau-Lingga since the Anglo-Dutch Treaty of 1824 — was a Bugis, Raja Muhammad Yusuf, the son of the 10th Yamtuan Muda.

The Bugis were so strong that they successfully installed a new sultan in Selangor in 1766. Till the opening years of the nineteenth century, all the four leading *orang besar* (literally means Big Men or Men of Power) in Johore were held by members of the Bugis royal family. But, by 1784, the might of the Bugis had been shattered so much by the Dutch that there was no clear controlling power in Johore by the time Sultan Mahmud died in 1809. After their fall in power, most Bugis were assimilated into the Johore Malay society.

Today, there are Bugis descendents among the Malay population. One of them was Tun Razak, the former Prime Minister of Malaysia. When he was alive, he paid an official visit to his ancestral land in Sulawesi and was well received, much like the return of a Bugis prince.

After World War II, the Dutch were determined to reoccupy Sulawesi but fierce resistance movement by Japanese-trained Bugis and Makassarese resisted them. The Dutch committed many atrocities including the notorious Westerling atrocities led by a Dutch captain known as "Turk", where it was claimed that over 40,000 local people were massacred. That atrocity ended the resistance and the Dutch ruled the province with an iron fist until 1965.

Nowadays, the Bugis and the Makassarese are predominantly farmers. Their crops include sugarcane, cotton, corn, coconuts, coffee and rubber. Sulawesi is able to support herds of cattle and is Indonesia's second largest exporter of cattle. Copper and oil deposits have also been discovered. Seventy percent of the people make their living from agriculture. Others work in fishing, industry and mining, government service, commerce and tourism. The province has about 22,000 isolated tribes that have not yet been "assimilated". Not all cultures have been documented but there are over 30 languages with more than 80 dialects. Each group has his own culture and linguistic identity. One of the tribes, called the Tona Towa, shuns cilivisation like the Baduis.

The majority of Bugis and Makassarese continue living as rice farmers but they remain Indonesia's premier seafaring people. Their ships carry goods between Java, Kalimantan and Sulawesi and comprise the biggest sailing fleet in the world today.

Today, southern Sulawesi is a fervent Muslim stronghold. Both the Bugis and Makassarese are staunch Muslims. The Islamic influence was so strong that some Muslim leaders gave support to the Darul Islam insurgency based in West Java headed by Sekar Madji Kartosuwiryo which tried to set up an Islamic State of Indonesia.

The capital of Sulawesi is Ujung Pandang, formerly known as Makassar and now the sixth largest city in Indonesia. For centuries, Makassar has been the gateway to eastern Indonesia and the spice islands of Maluku. During the war against the Ambonese rebels, the Indonesian armed forces used Ujung Pandang as their base.

I visited the city several times, once to see a flour mill run by a Singaporean. Ujung Pandang was a bustling commercial, shipping and government centre, easily the largest and busiest mercantile centre in all of eastern Indonesia. It has been so for the last 500 years. The city has one of the best preserved examples of Dutch architecture in Indonesia.

The city's surrounding area was once known as Jumpandang or Pandan Point because it has many *pandan* (screw pine) trees. We saw the old fort built by an early sultan of Goa to protect the strategic harbour from piracy. The old fort was reconstructed by the Portuguese and later by the Dutch and renamed Fort Rotterdam. The name of Makassar was changed to Ujung Pandang in 1971 which is closer to the original name of Jumpandang. We saw many Bugis wearing their *lipa* (a kind of Sulawesi sarong) which is rather loose, reaching half-way down the calf of the leg.

We attended a wedding and was impressed by the magnificent gold anklets, bracelets, and necklaces worn by the ladies. Some wore colourful, transparent blouse characteristic of South Sulawesi. In the olden days, certain colours for blouses were restricted to certain groups of people: green was the colour of the nobility, white of the noble children's wet-nurses and yellow that of ritual practitioners. The traditional colour code for the various life stages is still followed: pink for unmarried girls, light red for young married women, deep red for women who have had their first child, brown for older women with a married child and black for the elderly.

Today, Ujung Pandang is colourful. It has beautiful sunset scenes with sailing perahu in the background, particularly in the Makassar Bay. We saw the Clara Bundt's which has a collection of 200 varieties of seashells and clams and a 50-year-old orchid nursery. We also saw a 350-year-old Chinese temple which contained paintings, stone and woodcarvings, the Dutch Governor's mansion and a new university called Universitas '45' opened in 1987 in Panaikang on the edge of the city. The main attraction was the old fortress overlooking the harbour right in the heart of the city. The fort contains 13 buildings, 11 built by the Dutch and two by the Japanese during the war.

We also visited a small cemetery on Jalan Diponegoro to com-memorate the Indonesian hero Diponegoro, the first nationalist hero who skillfully fought the Dutch on Java for five years (1830-35) until he was tricked into negotiations and arrested, then exiled to Ujung Pandang for the remaining years of his life.

Ujung Pandang has many Chinese who run most of the businesses and restaurants. Most of the Chinese have become Indonesian citizens.

There are also some interesting antique Chinese porcelains in the Cony Karya shopping centres.

We also visited the tomb of Sultan Hasanuddin and tombs of other kings of Goa. Hasanuddin (1629-70) was the 12th and most famous of the Goa kings and regarded as a national hero because he waged a long and vigorous war against the Dutch.

We visited the Sukarno Harbour and saw a row of sailing ships unloading foodstuff, consumer goods, rattan and other things for Banjarmasin, Surabaya, Kendiri and other Indonesian ports. At the Paotare Harbour in the northwest end of the town, we saw handsome Bugis sailing ships (*pinisi*) whose designs had not changed since the days of Genghis Khan. We saw some tourists water skiing and nearby, fisherman were spreading their nets to dry.

Off the tip of the southwestern peninsula of Sulawesi and inhabited by the Bugis and the Makassarese is a long, narrow island called Pulau Selayar. In the chief town of Benteng is a repository of flotsam from nearby shipping lanes. A few kilometres south of Benteng, a 2,000-year-old Vietnamese Dongson drum was unearthed more than 300 years ago. How did the Vietnamese drum come to Benteng? One explanation is that the residents of Selayar had traded with Vietnam about 2,000 years ago and had brought back the drum from Vietnam. It is interesting to note that the Dongson drum is very similar to the drum found on the *tongkonan* (traditional Torajan house) in Tanatoraja. This drum is now kept in the annex near the former Bontogangun Palace, a few kilometres south of Benteng. The Bugis, being seafarers, could have travelled to Vietnam in the olden days and there could have been exchange of trade between Sulawesi and Vietnam.

We also visited the Mampu Caves about 40 km north-west of Bone. The Mampu Caves resembled a river of stone. It required good imagination to follow the guide who tried to explain to us the significance of each piece of stone. There were some pieces of stone in the shape of a ship, a buffalo, a deer or a crocodile, which was by far the most convincing. There were also human figures such as a wedding party, eloping lovers, and a princess with her beloved dog.

According to a legend, these animal and human figures were formerly living in the Mampu Caves. They were all turned into stone because of a curse. The story goes that the princess fell into a hole and could not get out. She promised that she would marry whoever could rescue her. The princess was rescued by a dog, which demanded that the princess keep her promise. There was a struggle between the two. A volcano erupted and they were all turned into stone.

This legend resembles the *Tangkuban Perahu* of West Java which is known as *Sangkuriang* and which also tells of the romance between a woman and a dog.

Makassar Bay has beautiful fishing villages. We saw many brightly painted craft with their wide sails looking like flocks of butterflies. The Bugis and the Makassarese seem to like butterflies. True enough, the valley of the Bantimurung waterfall, some 41 km northeast of the city is famous for its swarms of colourful butterflies. The great naturalist Alfred Russell Wallace (1823-1913) collected specimens here in 1856. This museum of *kupu kupu* (butterflies) had a large collection of butterfly specimens and attracted quite a good crowd of visitors.

The most interesting thing I saw was in a village near Bulukumba. There were row of houses on stilts — typical traditional Bugis houses. They were very much like the old traditional Malay houses. In its basic form, it has a roof with two planes joined by a straight ridge, in contrast to the curved ridge of the Toraja, Batak and Minangkabau houses. The walls are light and the floor is raised about 2 metres or more above the ground, the space beneath usually being completely open. The frame is made of pieces fitted into each other without the use of either pegs or nails.

I also visited the boatbuilding and repair workshops in Bantgaeng, about 100 km from Ujung Pandang, which belonged to the Bugis. The whole community was involved in ship building. They were shipwrights, carpenters and other craftsman involved with perahu construction. The Bugis experts in perahu building do not use plans. They build from experience and knowledge. They work on a palm-shaded beach and the shipwrights have about eight tools between them: a giant wooden mallet and wooden planes. The only modern tools they use are metal augers and steel blades. With such simple tools, they manage to build hundreds of highly seaworthy vessels each year and at very competitive prices. They now have a fleet of thousands of perahu.

The shipyard builds different types of perahu. They produce perahu weighing 50-200 tons with two masts and smaller ones of 25-50 tons with one mast. They also build even smaller ones called *sande* which is only two or three tons and are fast and agile. They also build racing perahu which have one or two outriggers that can jump out of water for a few seconds. Under sail, they have the grace of a bird.

It is good to see the Bugis still maintaining their traditions and skills in shipbuilding.

15

THE TORAJANS
Land of the Kings

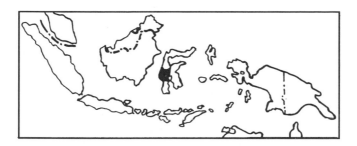

One of the more peaceful places in Indonesia today when the whole country is experiencing chaos and riots, tribal war and religious clashes is Toraja, about 400 kilometres north of Ujung Pandang, Sulawesi. There is no easy road to Toraja, the capital of South Sulawesi, often referred to as "Land of the Kings".

The Torajans and their culture had survived the constant threat from the Bugis, but in 1905 the Dutch decided to bring the Torajans under their control. The brave Torajans held out against the Dutch for two years, until the last substantial resistance was wiped out in the mountains of Pangala, north west of Rantepao.

The missionaries moved in on the heels of the Dutch army and by World War II many of the great Torajan ceremonies such as the remarkable funeral ceremonies were disappearing. Because of the onslaught of the missionaries, most Torajans have become Christians, with a few Muslims and "animists" among them. Physical isolation and the lack of a written language resulted in the Torajans having considerable variations in their beliefs, customs and mythology, although the ancestor cult is still very strong. Perhaps it is also because of the isolation that have kept the Torajans away from all the troubles in other parts of Indonesia.

There are about 500,000 Torajans in Sulawesi which has a population of 6.5 million.

The word "Toraja" is derived from the Bugis word *toraja* meaning "men of the mountains" or "people of the interior", but connotations of the word are something like "yokel" or "hillbilly" — rustic, unso-phisticated, oafish highlanders. In olden days, Bugis traded Indian cloth, Dutch coins and porcelain with the Torajans in return for their delicious and world famous coffee and slaves. The Bugis are even said to have introduced cock-fighting to the Torajans, who incorporated the sport into the death rituals of their noble class. In 1673 and 1674, the Bugis attacked the Torajans, but Islam never spread much further than the southern Toraja areas because, it is said the Torajans are fond of pork and *tuak* (palm wine).

The first time I visited Toraja was in 1972 when I was Ambassador to Indonesia. Accompanied by my wife and three friends, I hired a jeep which turned out to be a real bone-shaker. For eight hours, we rumbled along a rocky road, feeling most uncomfortable. In later years when I went back again, there was a beautiful road to Toraja and we could reach there in less than four hours. Although my first trip there was tiring, the scenery was indeed rewarding.

The green paddy fields on the way to Pare Pare were dotted here and there with tall Bugis houses on long stilts. Near Enrekang, the undulating hills made us feel as if we were riding the waves of a rough sea. It was late in the night when we eventually reached Rantepao, the spiritual centre of Toraja.

Toraja is a land of rocks. Rocks are seen not only along the banks of the rivers, but also scattered over the paddy fields. And the most fascinating feature of the Toraja landscape is that at Rantepao the rock-cliffs have "eyes". Near the top of Toraja's highest mountain, Mount Sesian, there is a place called Lokomata which literally means "the eyes of rocks". We inspected a massive rock which was as tall as coconut trees and as long as an ocean liner. There are square "eyes" all over it. These "eyes" are, in fact, large holes dug into the rock-cliffs. They are covered with wooden flaps painted and carved with beautiful Torajan designs. Inside are the corpses of royal families or prominent and wealthy Torajans buried there long ago. The "eyes" command a panoramic view of the orderly, sloping paddy fields and the breath-taking scenery of Rantepao below. Although Toraja means "Land of the Kings" I prefer to call it the "Land of the Eternal Souls". According to the Torajans, the souls of those who were interred into the rocks still mingle with them as they go about their daily activities. They help to keep an eye on the rice-fields and ward off evil spirits that might try to harm their people.

The Torajan tradition of burying the dead into rock-cliffs is unique to the religion of *Sa'adan Toraja* "the cult of the dead". It is only practised in Toraja, where the majority of the people still believe in animism, although a large number of them have been converted to Christianity and Islam. In many instances, even Christians bury their dead in rock-cliffs and perform the elaborate rites which are essential to ensure that the souls go to heaven, according to their traditional belief. A ceremonial burial is often a very expensive affair for it entails the slaughering of animals such as buffaloes and pigs for a continuous feast, sometimes lasting for a month.

Lokomata can be considered the highest and most exclusive place for rock-burials. It is about 30 km from Rantepao village. On rainy days, the roads are so bad that Lokomata can be reached only on foot. To carry a coffin 30 km through rugged mountains requires a strong will, courage and dedication. But, before a funeral can take place, a hole must be dug and the elaborate funeral rites properly performed. To chip a hole into hard rock sometimes takes one, two or even three years of manual labour. The task becomes even more difficult when the hole has to be dug at the top of a giant rock-cliff. So far, the use of drilling machines is still unknown to the Torajan rock artisans, whose work is dug out with sweat and blood. The process is therefore an expensive one, beyond the reach of the average Torajan. The expenditure includes the feeding of the whole family of the rock carver for the duration of his work plus a reward of three buffaloes when the work is completed.

In olden times, when the Torajan society was more feudalistic, only royal families and prominent, wealthy citizens were allowed to be buried in the rock-cliffs. In any case, the ordinary people could hardly afford such a luxury.

A stone's throw away from the Lokomata burial rock-cliff, we saw many tall rocks with their sharp peaks pointing skywards. The tallest one reminded me of *Cleopatra's Needle*, an obelisk which soars between the trees that line the Thames Embarkment. I used to admire Cleopatra's Needle when I strolled along the Thames on Sundays during my student days in London. The Torajan rock also reminded me of the obelisks which I saw in the Karnak Temple of Egypt. Although the obelisks which I saw in Toraja were pygmies compared to those which I have must mentioned, it is significant that the purpose of erecting an obelisk both in Egypt and Toraja was the same. In ancient Egypt, the Pharaohs erected the obelisk so that their achievements could be carved on the sides. In Toraja, it was a status symbol to have an obelisk erected after one's body was interred in the rocks, but there was no carving on the obelisk. Even without any carving, the erection of an obelisk was an expensive matter for it involved the search for a sharp-pointed rock, then its transportation by human effort to the desired place. A big feast was always arranged to celebrate the occasion.

On another burial rock-cliff, called Lemo, about 9 kilometres from Makale, a town near Rantepao in Toraja, we saw a row of well-clothed, wooden puppets perched high on a terraced rock-cliff, enjoying a bird's eye view of the surrounding scenery. These wooden puppets were actually the same as the Si Gale Gale puppets which I had seen on the island of Samosir in Lake Toba. In Batak land, the Si Gale Gale puppets perform dances, whereas in Toraja, they serve as replicas of the deceased and are placed on terraces near the rock-graves. Offerings are made to them from time to time and their clothing is changed as a sign of respect for the ancestors. The similarity between the wooden puppets of Samosir and Toraja is not a coincidence, for the

Bataks and the Torajans are, after all cousins. They belong to the same stock. The wooden puppets and the boat-shaped roofs of their houses remind the Bataks and the Torajans that they once shared the same civilisation.

Like the obelisks, carved wooden puppets were once restricted to royal families. It used to be the practise to assemble the wooden images of one family all together on one terrace. From afar, they look like humans looking out over the vast land below them. They serve as reminders to Torajans of the permanent presence of their ancestors' souls and they also exert a certain amount of psychic influence on the people.

The Lemo cliff appeared to me much steeper than that at Lokomata. It is difficult to imagine how the rock-carvers managed to dig holes into a sheer cliff-face using primitive hand-tools. It must have involved tremendous effort. I learnt that in ancient times, the Torajan feudal society divided the people into four categories: the rajas (kings), the relatives of the rajas, the free men and the slaves. Perhaps in those days, slaves were forced into the risky job of chipping graves out of rock-cliffs for the feudal lords. Toraja then was a heavily class-conscious society.

Since the cutting of rock-cliff graves is an expensive affair, one might wonder how less fortunate souls go to *Bambapuang*, the gate to heaven. But, nature has been kind to the poor by providing a natural cave in Rantepao. The huge limestone cave of Londa has become a public burial ground for those who cannot afford the expense of rock-cliff grave. When we visited Londa, a number of boys and girls were playing with human skulls scattered indiscriminately at the entrance of the gruesome cave. The skulls were placed on top of discarded wooden coffins. Over the entrance to the cave is the terrace where some wooden puppets, replicas of the deceased, seemed to be keeping an eye on visitors. The cheerful children, holding fire torches in their hands, showed us the way into the cave. A sense of eeriness pervades the air. At every corner of the cave are human skulls separated from their bodies. We passed deeper into the cave where thousands of skeletons and skulls were dumped together like victims of Hitler's concentration camps, or victims of Cambodians' Pol Pot mass massacre.

The cave is big enough to accommodate thousands and thousands more corpses — free of charge. The only requirement, according to custom, is the sacrificing of one or two pigs during the ceremony outside the cave to facilitate the passage of the deceased's soul through the gate of heaven. On our way out of the cave, we noticed, near the entrance, a new coffin containing a wrapped up corpse which could not have been there more than a week. To me, it was indeed a horrifying yet pitiful sight, but the children seemed to have got used to corpses. They even played games with skulls, sometimes using them as footballs. At least, playing with skulls are less gruesome than playing with newly decapitated human heads like the Dayak boys who were parading the streets with them during the recent tribal clash between the Dayaks and the Madurese.

Why do the Torajans bury their dead in rocks? When did it all started? These questions were uppermost in my mind as I toured Toraja. The custom of rock-burials is not new to me for I have seen similar practices in Egypt. The earlier rulers of Egypt regarded the pyramid as a kind of celestial step-ladder leading the dead kings upwards to their eternal homes in the sky. An early Egyptian text states clearly that "a staircase to heaven is laid for the Pharaoh so that he may ascend to heaven thereby". The pyramid of stone was considered holy. In ancient Egypt, the ordinary folk had a vested interest in keeping alive the memory of their ancient kings. The spiritual influence of a good Pharaoh continued even after his death.The King was as valuable an asset to his subjects when he was dead as when he was alive, continuing to be a source of psychic power. That was why the Egyptians buried their Pharaohs with such loving care and in such fantastic tombs as the pyramids. After the twelfth dynasty, kings and noblemen were no longer buried in pyramids but in cut-rock tombs such as those I saw in Beni Hasan. Later, the Theban autocrats of the New Kingdom decided to construct their cut-rock tombs in the celebrated Valley of the Kings to secure maximum secrecy as a precaution against tomb robberies.

I thought of the Egyptian pyramids and cut-rock graves of the Valley of the Kings when I saw the rock-cliff graves in Toraja. Could there be any connection between the two and if so, how did it come about? Not being an anthropologist, I tried to look for a quick answer. I talked to a few experts on Torajan culture, one of whom was Mr F.K. Salongalo, the Vice-Speaker of the Parliament of Toraja. I also tried to read whatever books I could lay my hands on. The literature on Torajan culture is, unfortunately, very scarce in the English language. Most of it is written in Dutch. So I only managed to get some clues to the origin of rock-cliff graves.

There is a Torajan legend which says that in olden times there was a staircase connecting heaven and earth. Once upon a time, there was a man called Pong Sumbung Sarepio (meaning the man with a loin-cloth made of patchwork) who climbed to heaven using the staircase and stole the gold flint belonging to the Lord of Heaven. He was so excited that he stumbled down the staircase, which suddenly turned into rock.

Another legend has it that Pong Maratintin climbed the staircase to heaven to seek the Lord's advice on whether a boy could marry his sister. The Lord split an areca nut to indicate that cousins too should not marry each other. A further split of the quarters was made and the lord explained that at this stage, marriage of distant relations was permissible. Pong Maratintin, however was so eager to contract the marriage with his sister, that when he returned to earth he deliberately told a lie, saying that the Lord had approved of his marriage. When the marriage took place, the earth sank into the ground and the staircase tumbled down and turned into scattered rocks.

The ancient Torajans obviously believed that there was a rock staircase connecting earth and heaven. The only link that now remains between earth and heaven is therefore the rocks which have tumbled down. Could it be that the Torajans chose to bury their dead in towering rocks so that the souls' passage to heaven would be easier?

It is interesting to note that both the Torajans and the Egyptians had similar beliefs concerning a staircase connecting earth and heaven. Both practised the cult of the dead by burying their deceased in rock-cliffs. Was there any connection between these people in the past? This question again cropped up in my mind just as it did during my trip to Pulau Samosir where I saw the stone tomb of King Sida Buta which closely resembled an Egyptian sarcophagus. Indonesian writers have written stories of Arabs who came to Lake Toba about 2,000 years ago. However, to my mind, they were not Arabs but Egyptians who came to Lake Toba, for Islam came only 1,000 years later. If the ancient Egyptians, who had built the pyramids, had reached Lake Toba, they could also have reached Toraja and brought with them certain aspects of their culture such as cut-rock graves.

While visiting Toraja, I met a Muslim Torajan businessman by the name of Sampe Tobing who has a keen interests in the history of Toraja and who has written an article called *Tanah Toraja* "The Land of Kings". During our conversation, he remarked that when he was a child, he used to roam about in the surrounding mountains, visiting the various rock-graves where ancient Torajans were buried. In a rock-cliff some four hours from Rantepao, he once found some skeletons which had exceptionally long limbs and huge skulls. He indicated that the ancestors of the Torajans might have been giants compared to the present population. I wondered about this and was therefore disappointed that I did not have the opportunity of examining the large skeletons myself. The mountain rock-graves had been neglected and the approaches to them were almost overgrown with thick jungle, so it was impossible for me to visit them. However, I was told that there were very few large skeletons left anyway, as they had mostly been removed for research by Western anthropologists. Nevertheless, I could not help wondering whether the large bones belonged to travellers from distant lands, such as sailors from ancient Egypt, where the people were in fact extraordinarily large. There is indeed a wealth of history and culture yet to be discovered in Toraja land. Is it not interesting to note that there is a village in Toraja called Kairo — a name sounding very much like Cairo, the capital of Egypt?

Another significant aspect is the similarity in shape between the roofs of Batak and Torajan houses and the ancient Egyptian papyrus boat. The Egyptian craft of ancient days had a low, curved prow and a high stern. The ends of both prow and stern were often curled into the form of a papyrus flower. The Egyptian ship also had a mast as long as the vessel itself, with a cross at the top, and usually located in the centre of the ship. The roof of a traditional Torajan house has a shape similar to that of the Egyptian papyrus ship. The only difference between the two is that the long mast which was used to carry the sail on the ship, is transformed into a long pillar, part of the foundation of the Torajan house. Again the cross at the top is retained, with a few more beams to support both sides of the curved roof. The Torajans themselves believe that in ancient days, Mount Sesian and other lofty mountains in Toraja were surrounded by sea, and the land of Toraja could only be reached by boat. Consequently, they believe that their ancestors arrived by boat. According to historians, the ancient Egyptian ventured out into the Atlantic beyond the Pillars of Hercules and may even have circumnavigated the African continent. Could it that they had also come to the East?

The traditional Torajan house, with its boat-shaped roof and tall pillars, is a masterpiece of architecture. It would surely puzzle Western architects, for the whole building, including the roof is like pieces of jig-saw puzzle, put together without using a single nail. A large part of the boat-shaped roof is made of bamboo knitted together. The other materials are hardwood for the pillars and timber for the walls. In almost every Torajan house, there are invariably three important symbols — the sun, the cock and the bull, beautifully decorated and painted on the front pyramid-shaped wall. The cock standing on the sun is usually at the top of the wall. According to Torajan culture, the sun represents the source of life and provides heat and energy for all living creatures. The cock is a symbol of strength, pride, patriotism and virility. In every Torajan house, there is at least one cock. The horns of a bull are a symbol of courage and bravery. They are either painted on the wall or the actual horns are mounted along the pillar that holds up the roof. The more bull horns the pillar bears, the richer and braver the owner of the house is. We saw on the pillars of a certain Torajan house, dozens of bull horns. It meant that the owner was so rich that he could afford to slaughter that many bulls for funeral ceremonies. It is interesting here to note that in ancient Egypt, the people worshipped the sun-god, Ra, and his gentle and much beloved wife, the goddess Hathor, who had the head of a cow.

The cock symbol may have evolved from Torajan mythology which considers the cock to have magical powers. According to a Torajan legend, there was once a beautiful lady who was pursued by strangers one evening as she was going through the woods. She tried to deter the strangers by distracting them with trinkets which she scattered along the way, but to no avail. She soon came against a huge tree blocking her path, so she climbed up the tree. But, the strangers chopped the tree down, causing the woman to fall to her death. At that moment, a cock came along, solemnly chanted some magic prayers and brought the women back to life. She then escaped to the moon. Nowadays, on the seventh day of the seventh moon each year, folks look to the moon to see the figure of a woman who spends her time weaving.

Strangely enough, this Torajan legend is very similar to a Chinese legend about a shepherd and a maiden who weaves on the moon. The Chinese celebrate a festival related to their legend and this celebration takes place on the seventh day of the seventh moon each year. It would be very interesting to discover the origin of both the Torajan and Chinese legends.

The traditional Torajan residential unit comprises a house for the whole family, a storage-hut known as *lumbong padi,* and a community house, known as *tongkonan.* The boat-shaped roof of the house always points from north to south and the main door must face east in order to ensure peace, security and prosperity. In the olden days, the Torajan house with a boat-shaped roof was built only for kings and noblemen. The houses are often built in a row, all the roofs pointing to the same direction. Torajans believe that their ancestors came from the south and moved towards the north. According to folklore, the ancestors sailed along the River Sa'adan from the sea and landed at Bamba Puang, north of Enrekang, which became the centre in those days.

The *lumbong padi* is a place where the Torajans store their rice. At harvest time, it is the custom to perform a small ceremony to ensure abundant harvest in future years. A rope is tied to the lumbong padi and stretched to the rice-fields. Four to six girls carrying torches then walk to the fields to sprinkle pig's blood over a few rice stalks heavy with grain. These few rice stalks are then cut, tied together into sheaves and taken to the lumbong for storing. They are not to be eaten. Torajans believe that these sheaves will then protect and preserve all the rice stored in the granary. The lumbong padi also serves as a community centre for villagers to hold meetings, to chat over coffee, or generally to entertain guests.

The third type of Torajan house called *tongkonan* is a sort of community house, the function of which is similar to that of Singapore's former Sago Lane's death houses. We visited one belonging to Sampe Tobing. The exterior is the same as the two other types of houses. The interior, however, is divided into three levels. The first compartment on the highest level is meant for praying, the second for sick persons who are receiving medical treatment, and the lowest for the dead. The patient is quite free to choose between treatment by a Westernised doctor or a medicine-man, either a Chinese *sinseh* or a Torajan dukun. When a patient dies, he is removed to the lowest compartment where he awaits burial. Thus, the tongkonan serves as a church, a mosque or a place of worship for any religion, a hospital and a "death house".

The Torajans make up a tightly-knit community because of their spirit of *gotong royong* (mutual help). Gotong royong is clearly manifested at burial ceremonies. Whenever a family has to conduct a funeral, not a single person in the village fails to turn up with a gift, which can be a bull, a pig, a chicken, a bamboo container filled with *tuak* (a sort of liquor made from palm seeds) or just some rice. A funeral ceremony can last one day or a month, depending on the family's financial resources. The biggest funeral ceremony even held the burial of Raja Sanglla, a prominent nobleman of Toraja, in October 1970. Funeral ceremonies, big or small, must be held only at harvest time, when everyone is free to take part. A funeral ceremony is not only to bury the dead, but also to appease the soul of the deceased so that he will ensure abundant harvests for his survivors and descendents.

To Torajans, it costs more to die than to live. A full funeral ceremony is not only expensive, but also extremely elaborate. In the case of a prominent person, it would mean slaughtering many full-grown buffaloes and pigs, and providing food and shelter for all those who turn up for a whole month. The average Torajan regards a perfect and proper funeral ceremony as the most important thing in life. He believes that without a proper funeral ceremony, his soul will not ascend to heaven. The Torajan concept of a human's spiritual nature is that a man has a *sanga* or life-force as well as *sumana* or consciousness present throughout his life on earth. A man also has a *bombo* or a personal spirit. The bombo can leave a man's physical body when he is still alive. A seer can actually see a person's bombo, can manipulate it and direct its action through black magic. It is believed that when a person dies, his bombo leaves the body of the dead person and it goes to the buffaloes or pigs that are slaughtered for him and takes away the spirits of these animals. They then wander round the village or gather under the tongkonan where the dead person awaits burial. The spirit of the dead person can proceed to the Land of the Souls only after the entire death ritual has been performed. Until then, the spirit will continue to roam about and feed on *kambola* fruits. A spirit can also manifest itself as ants which take a plant called fly-traps, known in the local dialect as duka bombo. When the ants die, they become clouds which later turn into rain to make rice grow.

The traditional belief in the necessity of having a complete burial site is so strong in Torajan society that even those who have been converted to Christianity or other religions continue to perform the ritual. Sometimes, the corpse of a person is kept in the house for a long period until sufficient funds are collected. When we were in Rantepao, we met a family who have cared for a corpse for twenty-five years. The body of their deceased father could not be interred in a rock-grave because of a dispute over the distribution of his property. During the twenty-five years, someone in the family had to touch the dead body of the father every day. This will continue until the funeral rite is performed.

The elaborate Torajan funeral ceremony starts when the *To Mebalam*, the expert who knows the secret of embalming corpses, is called in. He belongs to a class of slaves and usually wears a hat made of areca palm. As his main role in society is to prepare corpses, he is considered unclean and may never enter the houses of other people. In the past, like the Egyptians, the Torajan corpses were mummified. How it was done remains a secret. I was told that in Toraja, the roots of the *pinang* fruit tree are chopped off when the tree begins to flower. The roots are later pounded into a fine powder and applied all over the corpse. In certain cases, a minor operation is done on the dead body to allow the fluid of the intestine to flow through a bamboo pipe into a bucket. Toraja is a country with many limestone hills and we know that the Egyptians also used limestone for mummification of their corpses. Perhaps lime was also used by the Torajans.

Once the corpse is properly embalmed, it is wrapped in plain white cloth which may run into hundreds of yards, depending on the wealth of the deceased. Finally the body is wrapped in a beautifully designed red cloth. When completed, it looks like a huge, red tree trunk, ready to be transported to the chamber of the tongkonan. A pig is killed to mark the occasion.

Meanwhile, a wooden image of the deceased is placed in front of the tongkonan where the corpse is kept. A stage is then erected and decorated with colourful buntings, to be used to display all the gifts of food from relatives and friends who begin to gather outside the house. When a gong is sounded, the usher, who is usually an old man with a walking stick, would welcome the guests family by family, village by village. Strict protocol is observed in the procession of incoming guests. Those who bring the most expensive gifts of buffaloes lead the way, followed by those with pigs, then chickens and other gifts such as *tuak*, rice and other foodstuffs.

For the entertainment of the guests, a bull-fight and sometimes cockfight is arranged. In Toraja, a bull-fight takes place in the open paddy field. The bull fighter, often called *tukang bunoh* (one who kills) is usually a dukun who has a knife in his right hand. He catches the bull by the horn with his left hand, mumbles some chants as he looks up towards the sky and, in a single stroke, slashes the throat of the bull. The buffaloes must be killed with only one stroke, otherwise it is an omen of bad luck.

As soon as the bull falls to the ground bleeding from the throat, young men and children holding long bamboo rods with sharpened ends rush forward to thrust their rods into the throat of the bull to collect its blood. These blood-filled bamboo rods are often baked over a fire, sometimes with raw meat. The cooked dish, which is a delicacy for the Torajans, is called *papiong*.

After a sumptous evening feast, a gong is struck to signal that the guests may begin to sing hymns or *ma'badong* in praise of the dead. In the hymns, the names of Mount Bambapuang, Mount Kalesi, and Enrekang are often mentioned, for it is from these places that the great spirits usually ascend to heaven. Such hymns, which are sung into the early hours of the morning, are all in the Torajan language.

At dawn, it is time for the *Ma parempe* ceremony of bringing the body to the cut-rock grave. This is the turning point of the funeral when the solemn mood of mourning turns into gaiety and light-heartedness. After all, ought one not to be gay when a soul is about to ascend to heaven? When the corpse is placed onto a wooden stretcher, people push forward to give a helping hand. The journey to the cut-rock grave resembles that of a Balinese cremation procession with the difference that on top of the Torajan stretcher there is no pagoda-type structure or sacred cow, only the beautifully decorated red bundle containing the corpse. The bearers carry the stretcher all the way to the grave on their shoulders. They rock the corpse like a baby in a cradle as a sign of affection for the one who has departed. They wind through the mountains and cross rivers and streams, making merry all the way until they finally reach their destination. Then comes the last solemn moment when the corpse is about to be interred in its rock-grave. The family of the dead pay their last respects by weeping loudly as they caress the dead body.

In the evening of the same day, a final feast is laid out for the guests. All the buffaloes, pigs and any other livestock brought by the guests are slaughtered. The next morning, the guests take their leave and go back to their respective kampongs. Every gift, big or small, is recorded by the organising committee. Nothing is omitted for it is important to remember the gratitude one owes to everyone. The guests are always politely treated. They have to be received, provided with accommodation, and served with food and drinks. To organise a camp-in for thousands of guests for a week or, even worse, for a month, is not an easy task. Rarely does a villager fail to turn up for a funeral ceremony, for to do so without sufficient reason would mean self-isolation or ostracism from the community.

The funeral ceremony does not end when the corpse is interred in the rock-grave. Three days later at 2 a.m. a final ceremony is performed to guide the soul to heaven. In this ceremony only the womenfolk may participate. Led by a priest, the women walk silently in a row towards the forest. The eldest in the family, who leads the way, pretends to carry the soul of the dead on her shoulders. When they reach a certain distant spot in the forest, all of them utter the words "Ee, Ee" continuously to indicate to the soul that he should now leave the village to ascend to heaven. The womenfolk may not look back on their way home.

Throughout the funeral ceremony, the female members of the family wear a black band round their heads. When the last ritual is completed, a white thread is tied round their arms and a yellow band round their heads to indicate that the rituals are over. At the funeral, the closest relatives wear grey jute cloth similar to that worn by the Chinese or Vietnamese for a Taoist funeral. The eldest in the family holds a bamboo pole with a piece of jute cloth hanging from it. This practice is again similar to the Taoist tradition, but it is difficult to trace the origin of this custom to find out whether it was actually influenced by Taoism. There are many stories about mysticism and magic connected with Torajan funerals. I was told that during certain burials in the past, dukun with magical powers could jump and climb mountains and then finally retire into its cut-rock resting place. This was done by chanting magical formulae at a distance from the corpses. Is it not strange that the Taoists also had stories of frozen corpses rising from the coffin and jumping from place to place? Even today, Torajans still believe in the dukun's powers of black magic.

The Torajans also believe that God has bestowed on them a special breed of bull called *tedong* which is meant only for funeral rites. This type of bull, which is not found in any other part of Indonesia, has white skin with black spots and stripes. This very much sought after bull is worth at least half a million rupiahs (in those days) each, so that only the rich can afford it. The tedong belongs to an albino class which cannot be scientifically bred; it is the product of an accident of nature. The flesh is very tender and the horns are most valuable. Despite the large number of bulls slaughtered each year, there is no trade in bull's horns because the Torajans consider the bull's horn sacred and therefore keep them for display at home. Even though the owner of many horns may be poor, he would not part with them because of pride and also the superstition that selling the horns might bring bad luck.

Conducting all the proper rituals for a Torajan funeral ceremony means a great deal to the family of the deceased in terms of prestige. However, it has an adverse effect on the economy of the family, as well as the village as a whole. The younger generation, particularly those who have been converted to Christianity and Islam, are beginning to feel that grand funeral ceremonies take away the lives of too many buffaloes which are necessary for ploughing the paddy fields. In order to discourage indiscriminate slaughtering, the authorities have now imposed a tax on each bull that is killed.

The younger generation feels that something more should be done to restrict the number of bulls slaughtered for each funeral ceremony so that production of rice is not affected by the shortage of bulls. Here one finds an undercurrent of opposition resulting from the generation gap. The older generation feels that the performance of a full funeral is vital to ensure the blessing of their ancestors who will in turn give them good crops; therefore killing a few bulls is insignificant when compared to the abundant harvests the sacrificial offerings will bring. The younger generation, on the other hand, feels that it is the number of buffaloes ploughing the rice fields that proportionately decides the output. In most agricultural and rural societies, tradition dies hard. In Toraja, one can only hear personal grievances, but no one dares to organise a campaign to discourage expensive funeral rites for fear of being condemned as an offender against tradition. Social pressures at present are still on the side of the religion of *Sa'adan Toraja*.

In Toraja, just as the funeral rituals bind the community together, so do the rituals of a traditional marriage ceremony. A Torajan marriage is not a private matter between two persons in love. Before a marriage contract is signed by the bride and the bridegroom, there is a family meeting between the two parties. At the meeting, both parties solemnly pledged to God that should there be any separation, the sinner has to pay a certain number of buffaloes as compensation. In order to exert a moral obligation on the couple, a large number of buffloes, such as twelve or twenty four, is mentioned as the price for compensation. The interesting point is that not only the bride or bridegroom but every member of the family is responsible for the payment of the compensation. Thus, whenever a dispute or quarrel occurs between the couple, every member of the family makes an effort to put pressure on both parties to settle their differences amicably. They will generally keep an eye on the behaviour of the bridegroom and bride so that he or she does not commit adultery or go astray. This custom helps families to remain closely knit, but it is probably family pride and the fear of "losing face" in having to admit a mistake, as well as having to compensate, that enforces the custom. Thus, the divorce rate, I was told, is rather low in Toraja. There is however, traditionally, an escape route for the sinner if he or she is prepared to wash away his or her sins and if such a compromise is acceptable to the party who had been wronged. The sinner must sacrifice a cock, a bull and a pig and mix the blood of the three sacred animals in a porcelain plate. He should then dip his first finger in the blood and smear it on both his palms, his cheeks and his "third eye", the place between the eyebrows. This will clear him or her of all sins, and bygones will be bygones.

The Torajans are a proud race. They originally withdrew to the distant mountains because they refused to be converted to Islam when the Muslims invaded the southern part of Sulawesi and converted the Bugis and Makassarese. Long ago they guarded their religion so tenaciously that when the first Dutch priest came to preach Christianity, he was killed by Torajan animists. Later in 1913, however, the preaching of both Christianity and Islam was tolerated.

The Torajans are also brave people. They still remember their martyred hero Pong Tiku (1846-1907) who refuses to surrender to the Dutch in a gallant defence of Toraja land. They erected a monument to commemorate the hero on the site where he was killed. Pong Tiku was the leader of an underground movement which fought against the Dutch; he swore "never to surrender from the bottom of my feet to the top of my head". He was finally captured by the Dutch and shot. Today, Pong Tiku is somewhat a national hero to the Torajans.

When I was visiting the public market near the town of Rantepao, I met an old man who claimed that he was nearing 90. His face was heavily wrinkled. Despite the cold climate he wore a thin, torn shirt and shorts. With the help of a walking stick, he had come on foot from a village near Lokomata, the distance being easily more than 16 kilometres. I was curious about his age and wanted to know how he got his stamina. Through an interpreter, he told me his secret, "I get my strength and inspiration from Pong Tiku, our hero, who was also my friend and comrade." Relating stories of the struggle against invaders, the old man remembered the spears and the Dutch. He also remembered the buffalo-horn-shaped *songkok* or helmet which was used to protect the head. He also spoke of *tirik lada*, a sort of red pepper which was used to spray into the eyes of the enemy at close range. The name of Pong Tiku has become a legend. Some Torajan intellectuals are trying to persuade the Government to include Pong Tiku as one of the pahlawan (national heroes) of the Indonesian revolution.

In the Land of Toraja, there is a unique form of man-to-man combat call sesemba, an unarmed contest between two opponents. It is something like Thai boxing, but there is a ban on the use of hands.

The contestants use their legs to kick their opponent. The fights are held at the time of rice harvest or during funeral ceremony. One team from one village would challenge another village. The game is to instill courage and bravery to the young.

There is another kind of contest called the *sibamba* when wooden clubs are used to hit each other. They use bull-hide shields to fend off the blows.

Before the Dutch came, there were several groups of Torajans who were head-hunters. The head-hunting raids were basically an exercise to test young people of their manhood. Head-hunting was also necessary to find heads for a chief's death feast to provide slaves for his afterlife. In those days, if not enough enemies were captured in raids, then the chief's family would buy slaves and sacrifice them as servants for the master's afterlife. With the arrival of Christianity, such head-hunting habits have disappeared.

16

THE AMBONESE
The Black Dutch

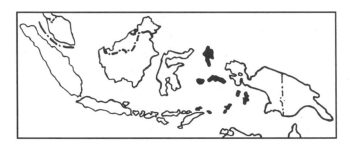

When I visited Ambon two years ago, the town was sleepy and dull. I heard music everywhere. Western taped music pulsated from shop fronts, guitars were played on street corners and porches. There was tranquility and peace. Nobody talks about politics. Ambon is one of the few places in Indonesia where you see drunkards on the street in broad daylight, especially on Sunday. I could never believe that 50 years ago, the Ambonese, known as the "black Dutch" had unsuccessfully declared Ambon and Maluku the "Republic of Maluku Selatan" (meaning south) and attempted to secede from Indonesia. They did this when the Javanese republican revolutionary forces came to replace the Dutch colonial army.

The Ambonese were called "black Dutch" because they were the Dutch-minded Indonesians trained by the Dutch colonialists to fight the Indonesian revolutionaries. Having failed to establish their own republic, hundreds of thousands of Ambonese have migrated to Amsterdam and other cities of Holland in the early 1950s and most of then got stranded.

Ambon is an island of the unexpected. I could never believe my eyes when I watched the news on television that on 20 January 1999, a three-day riot erupted in the quiet town of Ambon between the Christian dominated people and the Muslim population. It was a brutal and violent confrontation causing the death of more than 53 people. It was a clash between the Muslims and the Christians which took place om the first day of the Muslim Aidilfitri (New Year) celebration when three mosques and three churches were torched. Many cars were set on fire. Over 88 homes were burnt and more than 100 people injured. It was the most serious religious clash since 1955. Gangs of youths armed with machetes and iron rods roamed the street waiting to pick a fight with rival religious groups.

At the height of the riots, the flag of the separatist Republic of Maluku was raised by some supporters. The Ambon police Chief Colonel Karyono however denied this.

By 2 March, the security situation in Ambon became worse. Frightened residents were jostling to flee the riot-torn city which has already seen an exodus of more than 20,000 from the violence. Most of the residents who have fled since the riots first erupted on 20 January were Muslim migrant settlers from neigbouring Sulawesi province. The last ship to pull out of Ambon harbour at the end of February was packed with more than 5,000 families. The port had been jammed as about 1,300 people rushed in panic to flee the island after several days of waiting. They were carrying suitcases, furniture and kitchen utensils.

Since the start of the violence, 30,000 people have fled to safer areas. Some 20,000 people went to Central Sulawesi's Buton town, and about 10,000 to South Sulawesi's capital Ujung Pandang.

Sectarian violence in Ambon during the month of January and March has left at least 200 people dead and the city was reduced to rubble. Some estimated that at least 1,000 people had died. About 13,600 people whose houses were destroyed have sought refuge in churches, mosques and other public places, including military and police installations.

Ambon city has been turned into a virtual ghost town after the riots. Few people have been venturing out, and there is a heavy military presence. Reports said that thousands of residents were without drinking water because of damage to a municipal water plant and an attack on a building housing employees of the state water company. Unknown groups were reported to have staged petrol bomb attacks which were followed by the burning of homes and fighting among residents.

The military authorities recently arrested several members of Pemuda Pancasila, an organisation which is known to be supporting Suharto. The Pemuda Pancasila was set up in October 1959 by the then military commander general A.H. Nasution. The organisation forged an alliance with other mass organisations like HMI and Ansor to counterweigh the Communists who were strong in those days. It went into political oblivion temporarily after the emergence of other influential youth groups in the early 1970s. Then in 1978, with the backing of the government and the ruling Golkar, it was revived and branches throughout Indonesia's 27 province were established and it mushroomed.

The Pemuda Pancasila, usually referred to as Preman Pancasila or "Pancasila thugs" was reputedly the country's No. 1 hatchet man for the Suharto regime. Golkar had to a large extent depended on the Pemuda Pancasila as one of its main youth groups, to mobilise support for the party during the general elections. The Pemuda Pancasila had built Islamic boarding schools and held Quran recital competitions. In April 1997, 60 of its members were arrested for attacking five amusement centres in a Jakarta shopping complex. They claimed that they were taking action to wipe out gambling in the city.

It has often been said that there has been an "invisible hand" in much of Indonesia's recent rioting, sectarian violence, looting and mysterious killings in East Java last year, leaving behind a trail of untold deaths and mass destruction including what is happening in Ambon. Could it be that the Pemuda Pancasila which is a seven-million strong para-military outfit has a hand in these happenings?

One of the leaders of Pemuda Pancasila is Yorrys Rawayai, who is an admirer of Suharto and a close friend of Suharto's eldest son, Bambang Trihadmodjo. Yorrys is quoted by *The Sunday Times* as having said, "Suharto is Indonesia's Godfather. He is our true leader. He built the country into what It Is today and protected his people and followers. Without him, we have become a weak and divided society." To Yorrys, Suharto is his Godfather.

Respected Islamic scholar Abdurrahman Wahid, or Gus Dur believes that Suharto loyalists and pro-status quo elements within Golkar including the Pemuda Pancasila are responsible for recent riots. With the Godfather gunned down, his supporters are fighting back. Their aim? To cause sufficient problems in the country to signal the Former leader's continuing power and influence. There are already indications that people in rural and outlying areas are yearning for the Suharto past.

As the largest youth group in Indonesia, the Pemuda Pancasila still commands significant weight at grassroots level to affect political changes. It is also highly probable that it will do so again in the form of Golkar or newly formed pro-Suharto groups like the Indonesian National Party and the Republic Party.

One member of the Habibie cabinet even said that Pemuda Pancasila have been let loose to harass Islamic forces supporting Habibie because they see these forces as a threat to their survival. Gus Dur also hinted that the person who incited riots in Ambon live in Ciganjur, interpreted to mean Yorrys, who lives in that area in south Jakarta and by sheer coincidence, next to Gus Dur's house.

Meanwhile, in Jakarta, radical Islamic leaders have called for revenege against Muslim killings in Ambon as 2,000 students took to the streets demanding a holy war and accusing Christians and the military of "ethnic cleansing". Eggi Sudjana, head of the 600,000 strong Indonesian Trade Union of Muslim Brotherhood, vowed that there would be a "jihad" or holy war in Ambon in two weeks' time if Abri did not contain the rioting and protect Muslims. He told the press in an interview on 4 March:

"This is a warning to President Habibie and his government. If the military refuses to act in a fair and firm manner, we will have to call for a jihad. I hope it will not happen. I don't want a religious war. I love peace. Islam stands for peace. But, if our Muslim brothers are being slaughtered in Ambon, we will have to protect them with our blood."

If a jihad takes place in Ambon, there is nothing to prevent the jihad from spreading to other provinces where millions of non-Muslims are residing. If that happens, Indonesia will have a civil war.

The word "ambon" means "dew" in Indonesian. The island is almost always covered by fog or mist. That is what some people think "Ambon" is derived from. Another theory says the name comes from the word *apon*, which means plantation. In Ambon's long history of exploitation, commerce has always been handled by outsiders, beginning with the Chinese, then the Arabs followed by the Europeans, and now Indonesians.

Whatever the origin may be, Ambon has now become world famous because hundreds of thousands of Ambonese were repatriated to Holland after the pro-Dutch Ambonese failed in their attempt to establish a Republic of Maluku Selatan (RMS) and secede from Indonesia when the Javanese republican forces came to replace the Dutch colonial army. As a result of this repatriation, there are more Ambonese living in Holland than in Ambon.

The Ambonese, numbering about 100,000, occupy 777 square km of land together with Hanruki, Saparua and Nusa Laut in central Maluku. They live on this island which was at the crossroads of the colonial struggle for control of the Spice Islands and district capital since Dutch times. The Ambonese have mixed racially with the Portuguese, Alfuros, Malays, Javanese and Dutch creating a sort of creole Malukan culture. The mixed blood is most obvious in the lighter-skinned coastal villagers. The interior peoples have darker complexion and more pronounced Melanesian features. The urban population has stronger Melanesian elements as peoples from surrounding islands flock to Ambon for jobs. The Ambonese speak a dialect classified as belonging to the Ambon-Timor group of Malayo-Polynesian languages.

Most Ambonese believe that their ancestors either hail from West Seram or at least spent enough time here to adopt its language and customs. They are basically divided into two groups — the Patasiwa and the Patalima. All villagers fall into one of these groupings and the adat depends on the different circumstances in the founding of the villages. The two groups trace their origins to either east or west of the Mala River in Seram. *Pata* means "group" and *Siwa* means "nine", thus Patasiwa means group of nine (few knows the significance of the figure nine, whether it is a group of nine or the distance from the river). Similarly, Patalima means group of lima, meaning five.

The Ambonese did not seem to impress the early Western visitors. Travel accounts from the West heaped scorn on the native Christian Ambonese. A British naturalist, Sir Alfred Russell Wallace, in his mid-19th century account described the Ambonese as "dreadly lazy... half savage, and half civilised." But when the Dutch introduced Protestantism to Ambon, they began to groom the Ambonese for "useful" purpose, thereby bringing new status to the natives. In 1871 when the Dutch colonised Indonesia, they provided education to the Ambonese Christians who were hard to find in other parts of Indonesia, except the Javanese aristocracy and the Christians of Manado (north Sulawesi). As a result, the Ambonese threw in their lot with their colonials masters, even to the point of learning the Dutch language. They even imitated their Dutch masters in dress and conduct. They dubbed their first political organisation "Ambonese Wilhelmina Society" in honour of the Dutch Queen.

The Christian Ambonese were quite happy with the designation "Belanda Hitam" (meaning Black Dutch) even though their fellow countrymen meant it as a slur.

When I arrived at the horseshoe-shape island of Ambon, the quiet city did not give me the impression that the Ambonese wanted to be independent of the Javanese-control Republic of Indonesia. The main city which was called Amboina is now called Ambon. It has an excellent harbour which can accommodate large ships. The entire island is very mountainous, the highest point of Gunung Latua is about 900 metres and Gunung Horiel in Leitmor rises to nearly 580 metres. The highest point of Gunung Latua is nearly 915 metres. The first two mountains are volcanic in origin, although dormant. The island, however, is still subject to earthquakes from time to time.

The Ambonese were orginally slash-and-burn cultivators. They were first dominated by Islamic invaders from the Kingdom of Ternate to the north, which forcibly eradicated head-hunting and propagated Islam. Next came the Catholic Portuguese and then later the Dutch Protestant Calvinist who converted them to their faith.

Ambon entered the tumultuous spice trade quite late. In 1574, the Portuguese built a fortress on the magnificently sheltered Ambon Bay on the site of what is today Ambon City. Ambon became the Portuguese headquarters for the eastern islands replacing the fortresses on Ternate and Tidore. As a result of this Portuguese occupation, today the city has many Portuguese names for places. The entrance to the straits between the outer and inner bays of Ambon is called Boca and the narrow strip of land between the top of the bay and the ocean is called Passo.

The Dutch expelled the Portuguese in 1605 and started a campaign to convert the natives from Catholicism to Protestantism. The campaign was so successful that today it is difficult to find an Ambonese who is a direct descendent of the Portuguese. Ambon remained under Dutch colonial rule from 1605 to 1949, the longest and oldest directly governed Dutch territory in Indonesia. In the first 100 years of Dutch rule, one-third of Ambon's inhabitants were wiped out by either diseases or punitive expeditions. When the Dutch returned after the British interregnum in 1817, a rebellion broke out led by Thomas Matulesia. He took the Dutch fortress on the neighbouring island of Saparua and expelled the colonial forces. However, he was finally defeated and hanged in Ambon. The Ambonese eventually became the most loyal citizens of the Dutch.

From 1880 onwards, thousands among the cream of the educated Ambonese became soldiers, clerks and minor professionals, most of them working for the Duch administration. They enjoyed special privileges such as education for the family and medical care. Gradually a sophisticated elite emerged. By 1930, more than 10 percent of the Ambonese population had emigrated from their island for employment elswhere in Indonesia.

The most important segment of the Ambonese exodus, however, joined the Dutch colonial army which prior to World War II had integrated thousands of Ambonese soldiers. The Ambonese, like the "Ghurka" of the British Army who were from Nepal, were famous for their martial skills. They had fought with the Dutch as early as 1667 under Captain Jonkers and Admiral Speelman, and helped to defeat the forces of Makassar on Sulawesi. Ambonese also staffed the vicious *hongi* expeditions which enforced the spice monopoly and fought with the Dutch in the bloody 1675-1682 Java wars.

During the Dutch colonial period, the Ambonese were a class of their own. They were the "black Dutch" carrying out the orders of the Dutch to suppress rebellions within Indonesia. They made ideal soldiers: smart, brave, tough, obedient and respectful. During the early part of the 20th century, the Ambonese made up half of the colonial army and were crucial to the military expeditions that brought many semi-independent areas under Dutch control. Some of the Christian Ambonese identified so closely with the Dutch that they referred to their island as the 12th province of the Netherlands.

In spite of all the changes and influences pouring into the island, contemporary Ambon retains a strong sense of traditional beliefs. There is widespread reverence for the powers of ancestral spirits and an aura of magic power surrounds places like the *baileo*, the communal. The Ambonese have a complicated set of inner-village alliances called *peta* representing one of the strongest surviving features of Ambonese adat. This is the basis for Ambonese identity transcending religion and locality. The peta unites villages in West Seram, Ambon, Haruku, Saparua and Nusa Laut.

The origin of the peta probably goes back to the head-hunting days when a place of refuge, mutual protection and help between villages were essential for survival. Peta partners exchange a binding oath and drank each other's blood from a vessel into which weapons had been dipped. Intermarriage was considered incestuous between peta villages.

Through the centuries, the peta helped the villages face famine and other crisis, as well as providing shelter during the war, labour for community construction projects and security in a unified Ambonese society.

After assuming power over Ambon, the Indonesian authorities also respected the peta institution due to a lasting respect for adat tradition —perhaps partially for their supposed supernatural powers.

Although the peta influence is strong, it never prevented the Ambonese from being loyal to the Dutch and acted as "gurkha" for the Dutch. This was due to Dutch indoctrinated education of the Ambonese elite. The Ambonese soldiers assumed an ambiguous position in the Dutch-controlled East Indies society, isolated from their own local society as well as local host community. In their isolation, they developed, with official encouragement, an identity in which they saw themselves as superior to other peoples in the archipelago as partners of the Dutch. Although recruitment of Ambonese for the colonial army in significant numbers only began in the 1870s, Ambonese had served with the Dutch since the earliest days of the VOC (Dutch East Indies Company).

The development of the military identity not only served to reinforce the skills of the soldiers, but helped them become more loyal to the Dutch foreign power. Queen Wilhelmina became their *nene Mina* — royal patron, the Dutch flag their flag and so on. They strongly identified their interests with those of the Dutch. Ambonese soldiers came to envisage themselves in the light of their contribution to the Aceh War and other campaigns as the joint pacifiers of the archipelago and upholders of law and order. From 1890 onwards, Christian Ambonese became increasingly dependent on military service as a means to material welfare and status beyond what was possible in the community.

The Ambonese army was put in army barracks called the *tangsi*. Ambonese soldiers and their families spent their service lives in the tangsi, which was isolated from their own negeri village. Soldiers and their families in the tangsi were given good housing, food and a completely ordered work, leisure and sleep schedule. The Dutch set up special Ambonese schools for the children of the soldiers who were able to enjoy education facilities much higher than those outside the tangsi community.

In 1918, the Ambonese soldiers organised themselves and fought for equal pay and treatment as the European members of the Royal Netherlands East Indies Army. A special military commission was set up to investigate the matter. The Ambonese non-commissioned officers presented an appeal to the Queen of Holland with the following remarks:

> "Why must we be not equated with the European soldiers? Because we have made the Dutch culture our own and over the centuries taken over Dutch habits and traditions, it is doubly difficult for us to say farewell to the culture, habits and traditions which have become so beloved and therefore we must make this petition, so that our incomes would be equated with those of Europeans of the same rank.
>
> Following the principles of the Christian religion it is incumbent upon us to associate with the Netherlands, because we both follow the same religion."

The petition appealed to values cherished by the Ambonese and which they thought the Dutch shared. But, their appeal swayed neither the Queen nor the Military Salaries Commission.

At the beginning of the 20th century, Dutch power in the Indies was challenged by a growing independence movement led by Sukarno. The Dutch refused to discuss reforms that would allow the Indonesians any degree of self-rule. The situation changed drastically with the invasion of the Japanese in 1942. As the war turned against them, the Japanese began sponsoring meetings of independent leaders like Sukarno and Hatta to plan their strategy against Western colonialists. Sukarno and Hatta flew back to Indonesia after the Japanese surrender and proclaimed an independent Republic of Indonesia. At first the Dutch tried to deny the legitimacy of the new state, but the United States pressured Holland to recognise the Republic and to begin the process of decolonialisation. The United States threatened to cut off

Marshall Plan Aid provided by them and the Dutch was badly in need of such aid. So the Dutch at the Conference of Malino transformed their colony into a Federated States of Indonesia which included a semi-independent Negara Indonesia Timur.

Sukarno soon abandoned the federal structure and claimed all of the archipelago for the new Republic. However, the Ambonese and Moluccans refused to give up their territories despite the fact that Dutch soldiers had left. The elite military leaders and the Ambonese soldiers wanted to establish a Republic Maluku Selatan (RMS). There were attempts by the Indonesian leaders to persuade them to give up so as to avoid bloodshed on the island.

When all attempts had failed, the Indonesian army (TNI) landed in Namlea (Buru) on 13 July 1952. The Ambonese separatists led by Manusama and another leader Soumokil felt that the only survival was through international recognition of the new regime. They spoke to American and Australian representatives in Makassar about the RMS as they thought that by presenting RMS as an anti-Communist bastion, the West would support them. In a letter by Dr Soumokil who was Chief of the Department of Foreign Affairs of the Republic of South Moluccas to the Prime Minister of Australia R.G. Menzies in May 1950, he said:

> "An unequivocal stand against the communist danger was considered very advantageous for the success of this endeavour. In return for actual support from the Americans and Australians, both military and political, the government was willing to provide important military support (naval and air bases) to these countries, further, a special friendly relationship would be sought with the Netherlands."

Soumokil's letter was followed up with a telegram claiming to have found TNI documents detailing plans of communist infiltration with the purpose of annexing first Dutch New Guinea, then the Australian part. He also drew attention to the occupation of the islands of Timor, Tanimbar, Kei and Aru by the "communist" Abdullah battlement of the TNI. Soumokil suggested that if any more particulars were required "just send a plane to Ambon".

There were intense diplomatic efforts made by the Indonesians, the Netherlands governments and the United Nations, but it appeared that there were no initiatives taken by the RMS to reach a peaceful solution with the central government even when armed conflict seemed imminent. Later, under pressure even the Dutch betrayed them. They joined the Indonesians to persuade them to give up. They called on the RMS to return to their barracks and hand in their weapons. The Dutch warned that if the RMS would not give up, they would organise an evacuation of the Dutch community.

The RMS leaders were hoping that the Dutch would come to their aid, but the Dutch military instructions confronted the Ambonese soldiers with some of the consequences of their involvement with the RMS and that further disobedience would mean the end of a 350-year-old tradition of service to the Dutch.

In a highly emotional occasion, Sergeant-Major Tahapary, RMS Chief of Staff, delivered a speech on behalf of the soldiers. He said:

> "...We will remain here to defend our homeland against anybody who wants to dominate our homeland. To this end we have given up our membership of the Royal Netherlands East Indies Army (KNIL) and service to the Dutch Government. All the world knows that we Moluccan soldiers and our forebears for 350 years have maintained security in Indonesia as members of the Dutch army. We love the KNIL, but we love our homeland more and will defend it against all threats from outside. Because of this we Moluccan soldiers have decided to leave the KNIL with the sacrifice of our pay and our pension for the defence of our homeland. In a moment the tricolour will be taken down from the barracks and our green, blue, red and white flag will be raised in its place. If there are people who want to grab our flag, so be it, we are waiting. We are ready to sacrifice ourselves for the defence of our homeland to the last drop of blood. ...please convey to Queen Juliana

and Princess Wihelmina that we leave the KNIL not as enemies
but as comrades in arms. Thank you."

On 13 July 1950, troops from the Ambonese Pattimura battalion
landed in Namlea (Buru) and the first major clashes between the
Indonesian soldiers and RMS began.

During the fight, the Dutch Prime Minister W. Drees publicly
appealed to his Indonesian counterpart for a cessation of fighting and
a peaceful solution. This caused quite a commotion in Ambon. One
Ambonese leader Manuhutu was reported to have run out of the
bathroom, grabbed a weapon, and shot into the sky. Everybody else
with a weapon did likewise, with the loss of scarce ammunition. The
former Dutch promises to the RMS that they would send warship
disguised as sailing ship to help them became false expectations. The
Ambonese could not believe that the Dutch would ditch them in such
a way.

The war went on. It was in fact a civil war because the Muslim
Ambonese were on the side of the Indonesian army and fought hand
in hand with them against their own Ambonese brothers. The TNI
had expected the occupation of Ambon to take three or four days. But
it took two months before the entire island was under control. Initially
four battalions landed at Telehuad Hitu, but before the operation was
over at least ten battalions with air and navy support and various
units of auxiliary troops were deployed on Ambon island against a
defending force of about 1,500 partly former KNIL and "berets" and
partly volunteers. The RMS ran out of ammunition after a few days.

The results of the two-month war — an estimated casualty of 4,000
to 5,000 soldiers killed and 100 Ambonese soldiers and 400 volunteers
killed. The civilian population had a casualty of between 5,000 to
8,000.

All three of the RMS ministers, together with many of the soldiers,
managed to escape to Ceram at the beginning of December 1950.
During the following 12 years, the civilian and military rebel leaders
were either captured or made their way via New Guinea to the
Netherlands. In 1952, a combined military/political mission including

Manusama and Wairisal made its way to New Guinea. Manusama eventually established himself in the Netherlands, and since Soumokil's death has become the "President" in exile.

In 1955, 12 RMS civilian and military leaders were tried and sentenced to terms ranging from three to 15 years. Soumokil was captured in 1962 and executed in 1966. International recognition or intervention never materialised for the RMS leaders in Ceram.

Today, more than 40,000 Moluccans and Ambonese are now stranded in Holland. Caught in the middle of Indonesia's rocky transition from a Dutch colony to an independent republic, the story of the Ambonese and Moluccans is a poignant one. They were loyal soldiers of the Dutch colonial military forces, used by the Dutch to suppress those who aspired to free themselves from Dutch rule. They, their families and even their grandchildren enjoyed the hospitality of the Dutch and dreamed of an independent Republic of the South Moluccas.

They were the creation of the Dutch colonialists. The Dutch needed them and so fed them with food, comfort and education until they were completely Dutch-oriented, thinking that they were Dutch citizens or the "black Dutch" and were proud of the name. Because of their isolation, they found no common ground with the Indonesian struggle for independence and therefore regarded the Indonesians, especially the Javanese, as the new master who tried to control them. They fought alongside the Dutch and could not believe that they would finally be betrayed.

After the TNI occupied Ambon, the Ambonese soldiers refused to be demobilised in Ambon. After a long and complex process of negotiation and legal action, the Dutch authorities had no choice but to ship some 4,000 soldiers and their families to the Netherlands in early 1951 as a temporary measure. There, with very few exceptions, they have remained ever since.

The tangsi society of the Indies garrison towns was transplanted to the unfamiliar environment of provisional camps in the Netherlands surrounded by an isolated Dutch society. They live as a miserable minority in the Netherlands, born of a long-term commitment to the

Dutch psychologically and now a stranded lot at the mercy of the Dutch environment. Despite the increased frequency of family contact with Ambon over recent years, the community in Holland remains isolated from the majority and irrelevant to the metropolitan society. Perhaps, the exile community's greatest contribution is financial. The tradition of KNIL soldiers sending funds home for family support and community projects has been continued from Holland. Many splendid new churches in Christian community will testify to this financial support.

Whatever it may be, the Ambonese in Holland were a frustrated lot. The Dutch no longer treated them as they were treated in Ambon. The Dutch did not need them anymore now. The Ambonese were angry and twenty years of frustration erupted into violence. On the cold morning of December 2, 1975, a Moluccan boy pulled the safety brake of a commuter train which screeched to a halt near the north Holland village of Wijster. For the next 12 days, the passengers were held hostage by a group of young Moluccans.

On May 23, 1977, another train was stopped by Moluccans on the same track. Simultaneously, Moluccan terrorists took a primary school in Boven Smlde. The hostage were held for two weeks. The hijacking and the school takeover focussed international attention on the Moluccas' case in Holland. As a result, the Dutch Government finally began to take steps to heal a community wrecked by unemployment, drug addiction and broken dreams.

There were other problems facing the stranded Ambonese and Moluccans in Holland. They refused to pay taxes and protested that the Dutch had not kept their promise. What happened to the RMS? Who betrayed the soldiers? The protests began peacefully, but tension escalated in 1966 when the Indonesian Government executed RMS leader Soumokil. His followers in Holland angrily set fire to the Indonesian embassy in the Hague.

The Ambonese and the Moluccans now depend on Dutch doles for a living. Stripped of their former status, the ex-soldiers and their families had to survive on three guilders per adult a week and some clothing vouchers. Their only comfort was the knowledge that they would be sailing for their hometowns again in six months. Their living conditions were lousy. They ate heavy bland Dutch food all prepared in a central kitchen. To add insult to injury, the Dutch cut off their stipends. They were now supposed to fend for themselves in the unemployment and inflation wrecked job market of post-war Holland.

This stirred up racism, resentment and fierce trade union opposition. To many Ambonese and Moluccans, the final indignity came when they discovered that for the "privilege" of being taken from their native land, interned in concentration camps and thrust among the hostile populace, they were to pay 60 percent of what little income they could earn to the Dutch Government in taxes. They refused to pay.

Some Ambonese and Moluccans did return to their hometowns to meet their relatives whom they had not seen for 30 years. Young Dutch-born Ambonese who went "home" in search of their identities were confused. While they were considered "dole-drawing" people in Holland, once they reached home, they became wealthy Dutchmen. A lot of young Ambonese and Moluccans from Europe spent their holidays on the island, but very few remained behind.

That was the tragedy of a people who were deprived of learning about their own culture and adopted a foreign language and culture — those who were uprooted. They were the victims of Dutch manipulation. When the Dutch needed them, they were bestowed with the best food, comfort, prestige and honour. But, when they were no longer of use to the Dutch, they were dropped like a ripe apple through no fault of their own.

When I visited Ambon, I saw the statue of Kapitan Pattimura who fought against the Dutch which still stands. So does the statue of Martha Christiana Tiahahu built to commemorate the freedom fighter, as well as the former home of Prince Diponegoro who was banished by the Dutch to Ambon. Very few people still mention the RMS leaders who were either executed or exiled. They are now a forgotten people. Could it be that the fire of rebellion against Javanese domination amongst the Ambonese are still kindling? Or that some of the rebels who migrated to Holland and who are still living may have thought that the time was ripe for another attempt at secession?

The seed of hatred has already been sown as a result of the bloody clash. Ambon has again become a trouble spot.

17

THE BANDANESE
Victims of Nutmeg Massacre

The Banda Islands comprising nine volcanic islands are 160 km southeast of Ambon on the northeast fringe of the Banda Sea. These islands are insignificant to Indonesia today and they are very much off the beaten track. However, historically speaking, the Banda islands played a gigantic role because of the European scramble for nutmeg during the 17th to 19th centuries and they became world-famous because of the nutmeg trade. In 1619, the ruthless Dutch imperialists exterminated Banda's indigenous population — one of the blackest days of Dutch colonial history. Only few Bandanese had survived.

I have included the Bandanese as a separate chapter because this was also the isle of exiled Indonesian revolutionary leaders such as Sutan Sjahrir and Dr Mohammed Hatta, the co-founder of the Indonesian republic. These two Indonesian leaders helped to put Banda on the map of the Indonesian modern history.

I made a visit to Banda because the man who is responsible for the development of Banda happened to be my old friend Des Alwi, now 70, who was the adopted son of Sutan Sjahrir. I knew Des Alwi when we were both studying in London. Des Alwi was a close friend of Tun Razak, former chairman of the Malay Society of Great Britain and he was also close to the former Foreign Minister of Indonesia, Subandrio. I bumped into Des Alwi one day in Singapore and he invited me to visit Banda. Sometime in 1997, we met in Ambon and from there we took a six-seater mosquito plane flown by an American pilot to Banda. It took us about 45 minutes. Des Alwi accompanied my small party — my wife and my daughter Lily.

The first glimpse of the Banda archipelago from the small plane justified the effort of getting there. The nine Banda islands jut out of the depths of the Banda Sea in splendid isolation. Three of the islands, in close proximity, form a lovely lagoon and shelter one of Indonesia's finest harbours. When we were about to arrive, we saw Gunung Api's majestic slopes and crater topped by a thin stream of smoke.

On landing, we saw a few perahus (native launches) glide between the islands. Here and there were little rusting tin-roofed huts clinging to the shoreline, crowded by steep slopes. The only concentration of houses was in Banda Neira, the central island of the group and the only one with enough flat space to allow a small town to be established. There were also government offices, stores, and the wharf. The original population of Banda Neira before 1619 was about 15,000. But today, because of the Dutch atrocity, only 1,000 Bandanese have survived.

The Bandanese were the miserable lot in the history of Indonesia. Two-thirds of the original Bandanese were wiped out by the Dutch when the Bandanese refused to allow them to have a monopoly of the nutmeg trade and continued to trade with the British. The Dutch blockaded the islands in an attempt to starve the Bandanese into submission but the Bandanese resisted and expelled the Dutch from the island. Then a new Dutch commander, the ruthless Jan Pieterszoon Coen, invaded the island with 2,000 men from Batavia, razed all villages, burned boats, raped the women and looted whatever they found. Two-thirds of the population was massacred. Whoever survived were either sold into slavery or had to flee to the hills to die of exposure.

Most Bandanese are descendents of exiles and therefore it is known as "the isle of exiles". The islands of Banda are so secluded from mainland Indonesia that it is not possible for any exile to escape. In

1854, there were 6,000 people on the island and one-fifth were exiles. When nationalist leaders like Dr Hatta and former Prime Minister of Indonesia Sutan Sjahrir resisted the Dutch colonial masters, they were exiled to Banda. Des Alwi took us to visit the historical house where Dr Hatta and his godfather Sutan Sjahrir lived during their exile. We saw the bedroom, reading room and the tables and chairs where they taught the local children to study. Both Hatta and Sjahrir were free to move around on the island.

They lived in Banda for six years. While there, the two intellectuals befriended the grandchildren of Seyid Abdulah Baadilla, the patriarch of Banda's Arab community. They set up a school and tutored the children. Baadilla had earned a small fortune dealing in pearls from Aru Islands. Unfortunately, he lost all his investment in the 1920s when, after investing heavily in mother-of-pearl gathering operations, the invention of Bakelite as a substitute caused the price of mother-of-pearl to drop sharply.

Another host of ours was Kaneko, who owns a pearl farm in Banda under the name of Kaneko Pearls.

Both Dr Hatta and Sutan Sjahrir were allowed to return to Java in 1942 after the Japanese invaders were getting uncomfortably close to Indonesia. The two politicians were strongly anti-fascist and the Dutch had hoped that they could help turn the Javanese against the Japanese. When Hatta and Sjahrir went back to Java, they brought with them the children of Baadilla. An American Catalina seaplane flew Hatta and Sjahrir and the childen from Banda just an hour before the Japanese pursuit planes bombed Banda Neira. One of the Baadilla children, Des Alwi was kept behind by his mother. But, as soon as she consented, Des Alwi took a boat and went to Java to join his mentors. He was later to become an important force for change and improvement in the tiny archipelago.

As Des Alwi grew up, he became the companion and courier for both Dr Hatta and Sjahrir and got in touch with Sukarno, the man who led Indonesian into independence. He went to England for further studies and became close to Abdul Razak, who was studying law and who was the chairman of the Malay Society of Great Britain.

It was in London that I came to know Des Alwi. He was always with Razak and at the same time close to Subandrio, then Foreign Minister of Indonesia. Des Alwi played an active role in bringing about closer understanding between the Malayans and the Indonesians.

After Indonesia gained independence, Des Alwi joined the Indonesian diplomatic service. During the Permesta Rebellion in 1956 when Sumatra rebelled against the Sukarno Government, Alwi was the rebel's overseas spokesman. After Sukarno crushed the rebellion, Des Alwi, being close to Tun Razak who was then Deputy Prime Minister, was invited to stay in Kuala Lumpur. After the fall of Sukarno in 1967, Des Alwi played an important role in bringing an end to the confrontation between Indonesia and Malaysia. With powerful friends and acute economic skills, Des Alwi did well in the byzantine business world of Jakarta.

After an absence of 25 years, Des Alwi returned to his hometown of Banda and found it in a sorry condition. Banda was losing many of its nutmeg trees that made the island famous. They were replaced with subsistance crops during the Japanese occupation. He found the splendid old mansions stripped of their belongings. Because of government neglect and lack of funds, social services were poor. Lack of transport facility made the Islands of Banda, once famous in the world, the forgotten islands and few visitors from the outside world visited them.

Des Alwi did his best to change the image of the Banda islands. With the help of powerful friends in Jakarta, he started to reconstruct the island. He brought in a doctor, built an airstrip and provided a skeletal infrastructure for Banda. He also built a vacation home there and two cosy hotels near the sea and produced several documentary films on Banda. One of the films was about Gunung Api (Fire mountain).

Gunung Api rises 650 metres (2,100 ft) above the Banda Sea. Although normally dormant, Gunung Api is still very much alive. Between 1910 and 1977, 33 tremors of 5.0 or greater on the Richter scale were recorded, 20 of them within one year. In May 1988, Gunung Api's top blew with great violence, killing three and forcing a mass evacuation of the 2,000 people living on its slopes. During the eruption, Des Alwi was resting on the island. Relating his experience of the eruption, Des Alwi said:

"I was sleeping and in the middle of the night I heard some big noises. I got up and found that Gunung Api was angry again. I went out of the house and was told that lava was flowing out of the volcano. I immediately took my family in a plane and flew off. Of course, I didn't forget my video camera. When flying over the volcano, the sight was so captivating that I got the plane to circle round the volcano and started taking pictures. I thought it was a rare opportunity to take such exciting pictures."

That is Des Alwi, always friendly and adventurous.

In 1972, he brought Dr Hatta back to the island for the sake of old times. Sutan Sjahrir had since passed away and could not join them on the journey. He also showed me the picture of Dr Hatta's return to the island. He visited the gleaming Hatta-Sjahrir Mosque built to commemorate their stay on the island. He also visited his former home-in-exile which has been converted into a museum.

Since them, Des Alwi has invited many of his friends from Asia and the West to visit the island. Now, he visits the island from time to time. He has a comfortable house on the island with a nutmeg tree planted right outside.

The first thing we did when we arrived at Banda was to go by speedboat to a scuba diving location near the lava site beneath Gunung Api. My daughter Lily is fond of scuba diving and went with Des Alwi for the dive. The underwater scene of Banda Neira was really breathtaking. The reefs were a kaleidoscope of life with endlessly varied coral formations and bright tropical fishes. The lagoon provided safe diving and snorkeling. Before we went for scuba diving, we went to the hotel run by Des Alwi. We sat under shady trees which were at least 100 years old and enjoyed the view of the sea. We also had delicious *nasi champor* (rice mixed with vegetables and fish).

Banda Neira is the principal town in Banda. It is perched on the edge of a gigantic crater. This quiet, peaceful town has only a few short streets filled with Mediterranean-style houses and shops. It was the centre of Dutch administration for the whole region of Sulawesi. The town's dilapidated buildings, though, reflects its turbulent history as they have a mysterious air of decay about them. It has an old Dutch church, ancient Fort Nassau built in 1621 and some grand mansions of the *perkeniers* (contract farmers). Around the town, we saw some glorious colonial architecture but many of them were left to crumble into ruins.

We also visited the Governor's Palace which was once occupied by the Dutch controller of the island. It was built in 1820 with giant granite paving slabs, bright floor tiles, shiny marble, heavily carved beams, huge wooden doors and shutter-windows. Behind the building in the garden is a statue of the Dutch King Willem III which has an inscription by a 19th century French prisoner who scratched a lament on the wall.

We also saw the waterfront's grandest building, the Harmonie Club, which was the centre of Dutch social life in those days when *perkeniers* socialised with their fat wives in the cool of the evening, smoking cigars, drinking Bols gin and playing cards. There were often balls, bands, musicals or theatrical performances by travelling troupes. These were the golden days of Banda Neira when the Westerners came for its nutmeg. Today, the Harmonie Club is in ruin.

On a plateau above Banda Neira backed by a 240-metre high rock is massive Fort Bellgica. It was built in 1611 and has survived numerous earthquakes. Fort Bellgica is a pentagonal-shaped Dutch fort built on a 16th century Portuguese fort located about 500 metres from the harbour. Although overgrown, the structure is still standing in good condition. It was last restored in 1935. All cannons point out over Banda Neira's sleepy harbour. The main reason for building the fort was to protect the white population from an uprising of the slaves because Banda had a severe and inhuman system of punishing the slaves who were brought to work there.

After the massacre of the Bandanese population, the Dutch imported many Makassarese convicts, Javanese coolies and Papuan and Timorese slaves to work the nutmeg plantations. These were joined later by an influx of Europeans, Eurasians, Chinese, Bugis, Arab merchants, and other immigrants. The contract labourers in time earned their freedom and many of the present-day inhabitants of Bandas are descended from them. All these various races, languages and religions eventually produced today's homogenous, highly distinct and complex Bandanese people. In some of these islands, an archaic dialect is spoken which is not used anywhere else in Indonesia.

At night, we saw a dance peculiar to Banda Neira. It was called the *cakelele* dance, put on by Des Alwi. It has a distinctive Portuguese flavour. In this war dance, village men dance around a large bronze drum decorated with leaf offerings. In other Portuguese influenced dances, old costumes, blunderbusses, helmets and shields were worn.

The Bandanese are a stubborn race and would not kowtow to any foreigners. They are a proud people who like to be independent. When they traded with the Portuguese, they never allowed them to build a fort or permanent post in the islands, maintaining their spirit of independence. Ironically, it was because there were no Portuguese forts in Banda that the Dutch ships first came to trade in Banda.

It was the unsubmissiveness of the Bandanese that caused the Dutch to dislike them from the beginning when they came to trade in nutmeg. Holland's first merchants complained that the "natives" reneged on promises to deliver nutmeg and mace at the agreed price, juggled and cheated on weights, and mixed cheaper nutmegs with mace. An early Dutch captain writes of the Europeans' exasperation with the Bandanese: "these people are so crooked and brazen that it is almost unbelievable."

The lack of goodwill and good feelings was mutual. The Bandanese found the Dutch very stingy and unscrupulous. They found that the goods offered in exchange for nutmegs were unsuitable. Heavy Dutch woolens and unwanted manufactured goods could not substitute for the traditional items brought there by the Portuguese, Javanese, Arabs,

Indians and Chinese merchants. The Chinese even brought valuable porcelain, steel knives, copper and medicine.

Although the Dutch disliked dealing with the Bandanese, their profits were handsome. The spices and nutmeg sold in Amsterdam were 320 times the price they purchased from Banda. The phenomenal profits of the first expeditions awakened the greed of the Dutch merchants who financed the expeditions. As profits grew, the Dutch became ambitious and wanted to monopolise the trade.

In the early 17th century, the Bandanese society was ruled, as it had been for a long time, by a group of leading citizens called *orang kaya* literally meaning "rich men". Each of these was the political head of a district. The Dutch had lured some of the orang kaya into signing a treaty that granted Holland the monopoly on nutmeg and mace purchase.

The Bandanese did not understand the implication of what they had signed. But the Dutch later used the document as a legal basis for bringing in the troops to defend their monopoly. Even though not all the islands' leaders had signed the treaty, the Dutch meant for it to apply to everyone.

Even though the orang kaya got sick of the low prices which the Dutch paid them for their nutmeg, they were forced to sell only to them.

Then, in 1609, the Dutch reinforced Fort Nassau on Banda Neira Island. This was the last straw for the orang kaya who were tired of humouring the absurd barbarians. They lured a Dutch admiral and some 40 of his top men to a secluded spot under the pretext of negotiations. The orang kaya ambushed and murdered all of them. After that incident, they continued to trade with the Portuguese and the British.

Four years later, there was growing tension between the Dutch and the British resulting in the Dutch invading the Ai islands and the weaker British withdrawing. With the British out of the way, the Dutch sent a ruthless governor general Jan Pieterszoon Coen who sent 2,000 troops to Banda to massacre the orang kayas.

We visited a museum which showed the scene of the Dutch massacre. The Dutch had hired Japanese mercenaries who were good with long swords and we witnessed a scene where the Japanese samurais used their sword to behead 44 orang kayas. After the beheading, their heads were hung on bamboo spears for display. During the massacre, there was an exodus of Bandanese who became refugees in Keffing and Guli Guli in the Seram Laut chain.

After the massacre, Coen set about reviving the spice trade and brought in slaves to work on the farms because there were no Bandanese who could work. To ensure its 300 percent profit margin, the Dutch paid a price lower than the going price of nutmeg in Holland. The merchants who bore the expenses of the Banda War began to reap huge profits.

Towards the end of the 18th century, the Dutch could see ominous clouds on the horizon. French ships had smuggled out some nutmeg seedlings and planted them on Ile de France (now Mauritius). The Dutch Government was in the red and headed towards bankruptcy. In 1790s, the great monopoly finally fell, mortally wounded by graft, smuggling, bad management and world events. When it sank, the company was 12 million guilders in debt. The Dutch thought the Bandas were an unprofitable drain on their resources. Towards the end of the century, the economic importance of Banda faded. The slaves were freed in 1962 and they were replaced by convicts and cheap labour. Even then the nutmeg trade failed and soon disappeared.

Although nutmeg and mace are still the mainstay of the Bandanese economy, production of these spices has slipped drastically in recent years, especially compared with the pre-war days. Banda nutmeg is still ranked by many as the world's best in aroma, flavour and shape. During the late 1980s, the prices of nutmeg and mace took off again with the help of the Indonesian Nutmeg Association (ASPIN), which supplies 75 percent of the world's nutmeg and mace. It is Des Alwi's ambition to revive the nutmeg trade in Banda.

In Asian folk medicine, powdered nutmeg is recommended for overeating, as a carminative for swollen bellies, for stimulating appetite, as a tonic for indigestion and after childbirth, and for alleviating dysentery, rheumatism, malaria, sciatica and leprosy in its early stages. The spice can even be used as an aphrodisiac and a cure for madness. Powdered nutmeg has reportedly been used as a hallucinogen. This is perhaps due to the Bandanese predilection to grow mushrooms on heaps of rotting nutmeg fruit.

18

THE IRIANESE — DHANIS AND BIAKS
Living in the Stone Age

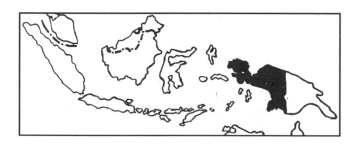

Morning star, greatest of all stars,
Come and be my herald and make me a hut of leaves
In the east, in the east of Judaca.

a koreri hymn

Irian Jaya hit the world headlines again in July 1998 when supporters of the separatist movement hoisted their flag of Independent Irian Jaya on a flagpole at the local Parliament in Wamena resulting in the Indonesian Armed Forces firing at them killing five people. Indonesian troops were sent in to disperse thousands of secessionist demonstrators. They lowered the separatist flag but later, demonstrators, some carrying traditional weapons such as spears and bows and arrows, raised another flag.

A day before the incident, the Irianese pro-separatists also raised a flag on Biak Island on the northern coast of Irian Jaya. Seven people were killed and over 100 wounded by the military in an operation involving some 200 marines, army and air force. More than 100 were arrested and 40 detained including the alleged ringleader, a local civil servant.

Mineral-rich Irian Jaya, which borders Papua New Guinea, was taken over by Indonesia in 1963, in a move recognised by the United Nations in 1969. Since 1960, the Free Papua Movement (OPM) has been waging a low-level separatist guerrilla campaign which peaked in the late 1970s with attacks on government outposts.

The recent upheaval took place soon after the fall of Suharto. The separatists had thought that the Indonesian armed forces have weakened and the country is beset by unsurmountable economic problems. They thought the time was ripe to push ahead with their secessionist movement.

On 8 July 1998 the Indonesian armed forces (Abri) chief General Wiranto labelled as "treachery" the hoisting of separatist flags in Irian Jaya. He said he would not tolerate such treacherous act.

Irian Jaya was colonised by the Dutch in 1848, but settled only in 1910 to lay political claim to the western half of the island — keeping it from the Germans who at the time controlled the land east of the border. The British, Spanish and Germans had tried to establish colonies in the territory, but most ended in disaster. It was not until 1938 that the Dutch succeeded in setting up a town called Hollandia (which is today's Jayapura) with a population of only 800 Indonesians, 400 Dutchmen and the indigenous negritos who had settled there about 30,000 years ago.

During World War II, General MacArthur had West Irian (then known as New Guinea) to prepare for the recapture of colonial territories lost to the Japanese. His purpose of using West Irian was to stage a campaign in Japanese-occupied Philippines. The American forces landed on the beach of Jayapura in the morning of April 1944 and met with little resistance. Over the coming months, Hollandia became a gigantic staging area and from there the American forces obliterated the coastal towns to flush out the Japanese.

After the surrender of the Japanese in 1945, West Irian was handed back to the Dutch who looked upon the colony as the last pearl in their empire in Indonesia, which has achieved independence. She encouraged the local Irianese to rule themselves and in fact trained them in the necessary administrative and technical skills. As Irianese nationalism made progress, the Dutch thought that an "independent" West Irian would be politically invaluable to them if the unstable Indonesian Republic should break up.

Indonesia was then facing rebellion from Sumatra, Sulawesi and Maluku, and the Dutch was hoping that an "independent" West Irian could be a base for them to reconquer Indonesia. The ambition was shrewdly used by Sukarno as a bogeyman to hold Indonesian masses together into a cohesive force in the new republic.

The Indonesian claim to West Irian was based on the historic half-truth that the territory once belonged to the sultan of Tidore in Maluku. They also claimed that the Dutch had promised to return the colony to them. He launched his first *confrontasi* (confrontation) campaign to oust the Dutch.

To lead the Irianese villagers in rebellion and sabotage the Dutch, more than 2,000 Indonesian soldiers parachuted into wild jungle and other places. Sukarno boasted that the Irianese had kept their Indonesian flags hidden in their homes, ready to be raised once the war of liberation began. But, few Irianese wished to welcome the new Indonesian conquerers, preferring an independent West Irian. The Indonesian forays into West Irian ended in catastrophe and hundreds of Indonesian soldiers were killed or captured. It was not so much the Indonesian soldiers that had helped Indonesia acquire the territory, but world opinion and power politics (including a meeting between US Senator Robert Kennedy and Sukarno) that had forced the Dutch out.

The so-called New York Agreement between the Netherlands and Indonesia in 1962 called for the Irianese to choose whether they would like to be independent or join the Indonesian Republic. In the year 1969 when the referendum was to be held, Indonesia waived the referendum and selected only 1,025 delegates to do the voting resulting in the creation of West Irian — a new name given by the Indonesians to mean "Victorious Irian".

The Irianese political struggle for a genuine act of free choice was taken up by the Irianese who had left with the Dutch and by their supporters abroad. They formed the Papuan Independence Organisation (*Organisasi Papua Merdeka* — OPM) in 1964 whose leaders were given refugee status in various countries. The OPM mounted operations of varying but generally low-level intensity since July 1965, initially capitalising on Irianese nationalism. The operations reached a peak in 1977-78 with widespread mass attacks against government administrative posts and troops. About 40 Indonesian soldiers were killed. Irianese casualties were unknown but it should number in the hundreds. Most of the Irianese were, however, armed only with primitive weapons and their numbers were small and presented no major threat to the Indonesians.

The OPM went through a period of reorganisation as some of their senior leaders were either arrested or coopted into the Indonesian army or sent into exile. In 1977, there was an uprising and the army used savage punishment against the rebels, thus generating widespread sympathy for the OPM and quickened the pace of Irianese nationalism. In 1984, another uprising arose, this time supported by 150 Irianese members of the Indonesian Armed Forces. During this uprising, 11,000 Irianese fled to Papua New Guinea, the other side of New Guinea which is now an independent state.

The ideal of having an independent West Irian seems reasonable since the province shares a long and rugged border with Papua New Guinea (PNG), a country populated by Melanesians. Why did the OPM failed either politically or militarily? The reason is simple: the Papua New Guinea government, like the previous Australian colonial administration, has given no moral or material support to the OPM. Both PNG and Australia have no desire to provoke Indonesia. In fact, PNG military leaders have demanded a more aggressive stance against OPM members inside PNG so as to deny Indonesia an excuse to launch cross-border operations.

At the beginning, there was some support for the OPM from the Papua New Guineans, but as refugees started to stream into PNG, they drain away the resources received from the international agencies and that stirred jealousy. Moreover, Irianese nationalism is a new and barely developed concept. The leadership remained fragmented and uncoordinated. The nominal political leader since 1983 was Moses Weror, an expatriate resident in Port Moresby, who had no public profile until a local OPM commander took hostage a group of foreigners in January 1996. His communications wih the OPM were sporadic and relied mainly on couriers.

One reason why the Indonesians had taken so long to quell Irian nationalism is that the occupying troops sent to West Irian were of poor calibre who went about looting, plundering and pillaging. There was no discipline: most offences were not investigated, let alone punished. The Indonesian troops behaved like occupying forces rather than security forces.

The chances of Irian nationalism succeeding is very remote.

I was one of the 30 foreign diplomats invited by Pertamina — the Indonesian oil company — to visit West Irian sometime in 1974. I do not know what was the intention of Pertamina inviting us to visit the territory. It could be an attempt by the Indonesian Government to convince foreign diplomats that everything was well in West Irian.

It is difficult to believe that a flight of only six hours from Jakarta to Irian Jaya via Makassar will bring us back to the stone age. Our Fokker Friendship 28 landed on a small airstrip in the village of Wamena, situated on a huge plateau 650 metres above sea level, in central Irian Jaya — the land of *cenderawasih* (birds of paradise).

It was a fine day, the weather was cool and refreshing when we arrivied at Wamena. We were quite taken aback by what we saw. Gathered along the barbed-wire fence at the perimeter of the airstrip was a group of wide-eyed but almost naked Dhani natives. The men wore only a rather strange horn-shaped covering over their penis. This covering, called *koteka* in Indonesian, or *holim* in the local Dhani dialect, juts out from the penis and held in place by a string tied one end to the tip of it and the other end around the waist. The womenfolk were equally naked with just a skirt of beads tied round their waists and dangling down over their bellies. Around the heads were long fish-net-like scarves hanging down to their buttocks. Characteristically, the Dhanis have curly hair, large mouths, and square jaws. Generally, they appeared strong-limbed and rugged.

The Dhanis, numbering over 200,000, live in the Grand Valley 72 km long by 16-32 km wide. They were like stone-age Neolithic warrior-farmers.

As we disembarked from the plane, we wondered whether the Dhanis had come to welcome us or were simply curious to see us. They probably considered us equally strange in our clothing. They made no gesture of welcome or protest, nor did they make any noise. Silent, with mouths agape, they stared blankly at the steel giant flying machine and the visitors. Until very recently, they regarded the rarely-seen planes as some fantastic, foreign animal. Being followers of the cargo cult, they worshipped whatever was new and strange to them. They believe that something will fall from heaven to make life easier for them and this is called the cargo cult. It was very difficult for them to understand how such a huge and heavy thing could fly like a bird without the aid of supernatural power. It must have been a divine creature to them. All these thoughts flashed through my mind as I looked at their charmingly innocent faces. While some of the foreign dignitaries avidly snapped photos, one of them turned to me and said, "It is unbelievable that in this modern age, there are still people living in the stone age. Am I walking in a dream? I just cannot believe it."

Believe it or not, the facts are there for everyone to see. The Dhani people, who live on the remote plateau of Wamena, have been isolated from the outside world for centuries. But what did the Dutch colonisers do to them or for them during the three centuries of colonial rule? It was the Dutch who kept the people of Irian Jaya in a state of colonial torpor. President Sukarno gave the order that 400,000 Papuans — those living in the jungle without outside contact — should be drawn from the wild. Lieutenant General Djatikusumo, who was then Ambassador to Malaya had visited the place and suggested enthusiastically that their level of life could be raised to that of "us all" within five years. In October 1962, Dr Subandrio wept when making a speech to a group of West Irianese visiting Jakarta after he was shown the film *The Sky Above, the Mud Below*. He was ashamed that his "own brothers' were being" put on show to the whole world as though they were half animals and half-humans. After watching the show, he made up his mind to liberate West Irian by any means.

Despite their primitive way of life, the Dhanis are a friendly and gentle people. They are soft-spoken and pleasant looking. Most of them speak a smattering of Bahasa Indonesia. They tried their best to please the visitors by posing for the photographers. Simply one word "*nayak*", meaning thank you in the Dhani language, was enough and they went away with a smile. Not a single native asked for a tip. Perhaps the materialistic values of modern civilisation have not caught up with them yet like tourists in Bali.

The valley of the Grand Valley was "discovered" by a wealthy American explorer during his botanical and zoological expeditions in 1938. He reported that this 1,600 metre-high valley appeared to be inhabited by a lost civilisation. The March 1941 issue of the *National Geographic* reported the discovery. The Grand Valley of the Baliem received worldwide attention in 1945 when a sightseeing plane out of wartime Hollandia crashed and its survivors had to be rescued in a daring glider operation. After that, missionaries started to settle there. In 1956, the Dutch established a settlement at Wamena and brought in schoolteachers, new breeds of livestock, modern clothing and metal tools. Wamena continued to be under Indonesian control until West New Guinea was wrested from the Dutch in 1962.

Although the Indonesians took over the valley in 1969, Wamena has not been completely Indonesianised, for even today, the people in the town still put on their koteka.

We were first taken to see the hamlets of the Dhani tribe in Wamena. The settlement was surrounded by cloud-wreathed mountain peaks. Wamena was a small town with rows upon rows of mission offices, schools and what seemed like hundreds of government offices, all sprawling across the flat Baliem Valley floor. The Wamena market, bustling with farmers selling produce, is the town's premier tourist attraction. It was a place to watch a mix of cultures and customs —

rugged Dhani tribesmen, tall stately Minangs, Western-attired Javanese,
and curly-haired Ambonese. Everywhere we could see naked Dhanis
with their kotekas.

Each Dhani hamlet is separated from the other about 300 metres
away and surrounded by a tall bamboo fence. Inside each hamlet, at
the far end of a long open space facing the entrance is the men's hut.
The hut is circular with a diameter of about 4 metres, and has a
domed, thatched roof. To the right of this are several women's huts —
the number of huts depending on the size of the family — and to the
left is the cooking area. Surrounding these living quarters is a garden
in the shape of a horseshoe.

We were invited to visit a male hut. As the entrance to the hut was
only waist high, we had to crawl in. It was almost pitch dark inside.
The daylight that managed to enter the doorless entrance enabled one
to see the fireplace in the centre of the hut. At night, a fire is
necessary to keep the hut warm. The smoke produced from burning
of wood helped to drive away the mosquitoes. How it is that the
occupants were not suffocated by the smoke remained a mystery as
there was not a single window or any other sort of ventilation on
either the ground floor or the upper floor which were separated by
a bamboo platform. All the occupants slept on the upper floor, which
could be reached by a ladder and groping one's way in the dark. We
noticed that on the ground floor were neither chairs nor tables. When
we visited the upper floor, one ambassador said, "What do the Dhanis
use for pillows?". But the Dhanis had never heard of a pillow. We also
noticed that there was no bathing area, because the Dhanis do not
bathe. At a height of 650 metres above sea level, the nights are often
extremely cold.

Designed originally as mini-fortresses, the Dhanis live in villages
with U-shaped courtyards very similar to the African *kraal*, guarded by
a swing door which can be easily defended. A typical Dhani settlement
is surrounded by a sturdy fence which keeps the village's pigs in and
the neighbouring villagers' pigs out. Straw-thatched, dome-roofed,
windowless round house, plus a long house for the women, are
grouped around the open space. Near the settlement are tobacco and

banana gardens. Dhani buildings are held together with only rattan vines or elephant grass. Roofs may be made of juniper tree bark or pandanus leaves which are interlocked like roof tiles, making the structures waterproof and wind-proof.

A village contains a tribal men's house called *iwool* which only initiated males can enter. The round grass men's house called *honnay* is used by males over the age of eight, or for sleeping naked at night. Women, children and p' ;s live in the long women's houses known as *weu uman*. Some of th' houses which are not insulated are freezing at night.

The Dhanis are often referred to as tribes living in the Baliem Valley but actually there are a number of other tribes such as the Lani to the east (with thicker koteka). The exact origin of the tribes is not known. All have negroid features and dark brown skin. Each tribe's language, customs and even physical appearance can be quite distinct. Nowadays, many younger Dhanis can read and write Indonesian.

The Dhanis spend most of their lives working their fields — cleaning, draining, pruning vines, weeding beds and scooping up the rich, dark soil to enrich their gardens.

Despite their nakedness, the Dhanis dr have a sense of modesty and moral standards. Their yardstick for modesty is in a way more conservative than Confucius teachings. Confucius only preached that a man and a woman should not get too close to each other if they are not married. In the case of the Dhanis, even married couples have to live apart. Privacy is a luxury. A husband and wife have to make appointments to meet, at an allocated time and they would meet near the fireplace in the woman's hut when no one else is around. After the wife has given birth, the couple will not have a rendezvous for the next three years. When asked why this should be so, the answer is that the ghost demanded it. In Wamena, polygamy is practiced only by those who are well off such as chiefs, witchdoctors or teachers.

The sequence of wives dictates their relative dominance. The first wife is the highest ranking and can expect help from the others.

Although the wives share a common kitchen, each woman has her own hearth, and prepares food for herself and her children. The women alternate in feeding the husband.

The custom of staying away from the wife has caused tremendous social problems. There are such things as rape, stealing of wives, and so on, which are considered immoral acts and which result in fights, and even in killings. Nature has not been kind to the Dhanis. Any additional birth means another mouth to feed. Produce from the land is limited because of the primitive tools still being used. Stone axes, bows and arrows and spears are the order of the day. Ropes are made by twisting bark fibres. Weaving is known but rarely practised. A number of fairly elaborate methods of plant netting and knitting are known and used in the manufacture of bags and armour. Pottery and basket making are unknown. Carving is worked only on arrows used for fighting. Because of the difficulty in making a living, a new child is often not welcome. Abortion is common. The woman would take a kind of leaf grown locally as medicine to bring on an abortion. It is often successful but if it should fail, then the aid of a medicine-man would be sought to perform the abortion with his bare hands.

The Dhanis eat only when they are hungry. They eat almost anything they can lay their hands on: roots, dragonfly larvae, mice, tadpoles frogs, caterpillars, spiny ant-eater and other marsupial entrails. No knives or forks and cooking vessels are used, just round water gourds.

The Dhani regard pigs as highly valued animals. They used pigs as "living currency". The Dhanis believe that pigs possess a soul similar to that of man. Pigs are raised as family members, called by ancestors' names, fed in the kitchen, take their rightful place around the hearth, and are stroked and fondled by their masters. Although raised by women, pigs are owned by the men. Each family cuts holes or notches on their pigs' ears so that they are immediately recognised. The name of a pig may not even be pronounced in the presence of women.

The Dhanis buried their dead and some of these corpses are dried like mummies for display. I saw one of the Dhani mummies in Akima. Like the Egyptians, the families and relatives of the dead, and in fact the whole village, mourn and wail. The women commonly smear their upper bodies and faces with yellow clay to show their grief. In olden days, female relatives of the dead, starting from 12 years of age had fingers amputated up to the second joint. The wound was usually dressed in banana leaves and husks, then bound with a mixture of clay and ashes. Such wounds were proudly displayed around the village to show their faithfulness to the dead and to show their pain. In the marketplace, we saw many women without two of their fingers.

The Dhanis like to fight. They conduct what the anthropologists call ritual warfare. They are divided into different clans and go to battle with one another. The fight is not over ideology, nor religion or annexation of land, but just to seek revenge for the ghosts of dead warriors or relatives. Frontline fighting seldom lasts for more than 10-15 minutes.

The *jao* could be used to purchase pigs, but nowadays is more commonly worn as jewellery. Bargaining is a problem for foreign visitors because Dhani hawkers are still unaccustomed to the various denominations of Indonesian currency. It is easier if the buyer has a hundred-rupiah piece. Otherwise, bargaining is a painful affair and usually the seller refuses to accept anything other than a hundred rupiah note. A middle-aged Dhani offered me a pair of pig's teeth for only 5 rupiahs. I thought he must have made a mistake and told him it was too little. He then increased the price to Rp500. I gave him Rp200 and the Dhani was very happy to part with the pig's teeth. A generous Ambassador paid Rp5,000 for a stone which was first offered to him for only Rp500.

At the marketplace, I saw an old woman selling vegetables, who had lost all her fingers except the thumb. Through an interpreter I asked what had happened to her fingers. She replied that she had chopped them off as a symbol of mourning for her husband who had died a long time ago. Another explanation which I got from an old Dhani nearby was that her fingers had been chopped off because she had stolen something when she was young.

The marketplace is an excellent place to study faces. There were two Dhani men who had their faces painted black from the eyes down to the mouth. They wore horns on their heads. I was told that they were brothers and that they were mourning for their mother who had just passed away. They looked stern and serious.

The most interesting character that I met during the trip was a short, limping, elderly Dhani called Joe, whose face looked like a chimpanzee's. He was one of the very few who was dressed in khaki uniform and he wore a hat. He spoke a little Bahasa Indonesia and followed our delegation from place to place. An Ambassador who was busy taking cine pictures discovered that Joe was a willing porter, and so asked him to carry a bunch of kotekas and other souvenirs he had bought. When the party reached the hotel, the Ambassador was still busy taking pictures when I saw Joe selling the kotekas to other Ambassadors for Rp1,000 each. When the time came to board the plane, the Ambassador asked Joe where his bunch of kotekas was. Joe replied that they were all in the plane. The Ambassador boarded the plane but found no trace of the kotekas. It was too late for him to get off the plane to question Joe. Meanwhile, Joe made a dash for the plane and was acting as if he wanted to hand over something to the Ambassador. When he was told to move back, he became furious and started to shout and quarrel with an officer on the airstrip. He then ran around the plane several times to see whether he could get in, but in vain. As the plane took off, through the little window I saw Joe looking very miserable and angry. The question which remains unanswered is why did Joe sell the kotekas when he was supposed to look after them? Did he try to make some money out of them? If that was the case, he could have just disappeared instead of waiting till the plane took off. In fact, when the Ambassador asked him, he said that the kotekas were in the plane. What did he try to explain? Was he trying to do the diplomats a favour by selling them the kotekas or was he showing off his salesmanship to the Ambassador who had entrusted him with the kotekas? Was he trying to return to the Ambassador the money he obtained for the kotekas when he tried to dash for the plane? The meaning of the whole melodrama remains a mystery.

The Pertamina plane took us back to Jayapura, the capital of West Irian, a small attractive town in an amphitheater-like setting with red-tiled roofs, inhabited by the Dutch civil servants. The provincial capital has a nice harbour surrounded by perpetually green hills. Most houses were built on the slopes, while the administrative centre was laid in a flat area between them. The town has all the worst features of a modern Indonesian city without any of the subtlety — noisy, dirty streets, too much polluting traffic, and garish blaring cassette-tape shops.

We saw a mixture of gentle Melanesians, immigrant merchants, Irianese labourers and Javanese bureaucrats. We also saw negritic tribesmen, vendors with Javanese-style *pikulan*, Minang shopowners, expatriates from the oil and timber companies, Bugis fishermen, sailors from Makassar, and a trickle of tourists. The residents there had a good nap in the afternoon for about two hours, and in the evening Jayapura's main streets pulsate again with life. Whilst in Jayapura, we saw no sign of tension between the Indonesians and the Irianese.

After Jayapura, we went to Biak, an island off the mainland and a resting terminal for oil-drillers and civil servants who work in Irian Jaya. The Biak people, who belong to one of the Papuan tribes, are comparatively more civilised than the Dhanis. Nearly every Biak Papuan is clothed. Most of the Biaks have become either Christians or Muslims, so that in Biak there are both churches and mosques. In order to provide entertainment for the oil company employees and civil servants, there are cinemas, restaurants, bars and nightclubs, a far cry in terms of modern materialistic civilisation from that of nearby Wamena.

However, the Biak people are still influenced by ancient Biak mythology. Many still believe in ancestor-worship and the cargo cult. A major element of Biak mythology concerns treasures and ceremonial valuables. In the past, Biak pirates went to the Moluccas to get their spoils, and valuables of foreign origin became an important element in Biak mythology. The emphasis on material goods is fully expressed in the myths and in the various movements termed cargo cult.

Biak is an island of wonderful and strange myths. There is the myth of Ori, the sun, and Paik, the moon, both of whom lived on the earth as brothers. Their father hid them in a cave and in the night Paik served as a light. One day Ori betrayed Paiks' hiding place to the humans. The people took him away, hung him on a tree and shot arrows at him. Slowly Paik rose into the sky until finally he stood still in the heaven. Ori and the people went after him but in vain for they could not reach him. I wonder what the Biak people have to say about this myth now that man has managed to reach the moon.

There is also a myth of an old, double-headed snake called Karubudawi, who lived in a cave and managed to entice a young pregnant woman to his lair. The snake brought up the woman's child as his grandson. Karubudawi was soon discovered by the real father who attacked him six times and finally succeeded in liberating his son. The old snake than changed his body into a canoe and set out to find his grandchild. He went to the nearby islands of Biak Roon, Numfor and Gebe, passing Salawati and Manokwari, until he was eventually recognised by his grandson. The real father also recognised old Karubudawi as his own father-in-law and decided to give him presents to make peace. He gave him a slave, cotton cloth, dishes, and bracelets made of steel and silver. After great rejoicing, the boy returned home with his parents, and everyone lived happily ever after.

The myth of the old, double-headed snake illustrates the Biak social organisation. The father was not entitled to his child until his wife's dowry had been paid to the old father-in-law. As soon as this was done, the father-in-law turned from being a rival to a feast-giver and tensions were soon eased.

Many Biak myths refer to the resurrection of the dead. Two of such myths tell of resurrection through the love of relatives, by singing a lament for the dead. The songs are called *kayob* (lament for the dead). The Biak people's belief in the resurrection of the dead was so strong that it developed into a sort of movement called *koreri*. Ko in Biak language means "we" and *reri* means "change" or "transform". They believe that some day a Messiah, called Manseren Manggundi, will appear and will bring with him eternal happiness and prosperity so that the people will not have to sweat and toil any more. The first reference to the messianic figure occurred in a publication in 1854 which speculated that Manseren Manggundi would return some day to establish an earthly kingdom of peace and plenty. The *koreri* movement began to grow and became a dynamic force in Biak and other neighbouring islands such as Numfor, Manshihan, and Wandamen. Supporters of the *koreri* movement would perform the ceremonial rites on moonlit nights. The men would get drunk on palm wine and dance in circles until they collapsed. They would sing the songs of lament which they believed would hasten the arrival of their saviour and resurrect their dead ancestors. The Biak people are talented singers and have a gift for creating songs of lament. One of the best known *kayob* goes something like this:

> *Morning star, greatest of all the stars,*
> *Come and be my herald and make me a hut of leaves*
> *In the east, in the east of Judaca*

The belief in koreri became so strong and widespread that, from time to time during the last century, many impostors tried to exploit the myth by claiming to be the saviour. Some even attempted to resurrect the dead. Most of these were medicine-men who indulged in black magic. The movement gathered momentum and even became a political weapon. The movement changed character sometime in 1938 when a woman by the name of Angganitha Menufaur was its leader. She was born in about 1905 and through her ancestress Inserensowek, was related to Manseren Manggundi. She tried to create a myth that she was the reincarnation of the Messiah, Manggundi, who was supposed to come one day to save the people.

Angganitha was married and had three children. She had a reputation as a poet and a composer, her songs being used mainly for dancing to invoke the return of the ancestors and better days. The koreri dance ceremonies gradually became more intense. Sometimes the gatherings turned into mass meetings of over 6,000 people. They would sing with excitement and would try to overcome their disappointments by increasingly drastic means such as magic, medicines and magic wands. Some fasted, whilst others drank palm-wine. They wanted to see visions and thus forced their tired bodies to perform the strangest exercises. In a frenzy, they would believe any rumour and would shout for the spirits of the deceased, reel over the graves and finally collapse.

It became an arduous task for the authorities to restrain the movement from getting out of hand, for sometimes the ceremonies led to fights and general disorder. In 1942, an Ambonese policeman was killed when he clashed with participants. When the Japanese took over West Irian, they tried to put a stop to the movement and had the leaders arrested. Consequently, the movement developed into an anti-Japanese and independence movement with the koreri army having its own blue, white and red flag. The supporters used *karbere* (club) and spears, hatchets and arrows as weapons against the Japanese. They also used magic powers said to be endowed upon them by their ancestors.

At one stage, Biak-Numfor armies tried to liberate the whole of New Guinea from the Japanese. It was a hopelessly vain attempt for the masses, who were inspired by the koreri beliefs that they were invulnerable and that Manermakeri, their god would turn their clubs into rifles and bullets of the enemy into water. The struggle for freedom became a holy war. However, in 1943, many leaders went over to the Japanese and one of them became a policeman. The remaining koreri disciples fled to Numfor.

When the American bombers came to attack the Japanese in Numfor, supporters of the koreri movement thought that Manermakeri was leading the Americans to liberate them. It must have been quite an experience for the koreri supporters when the bombs dropped on their land. The whole business of modern warfare must have appeared as an apocalyptic event to these simple-minded people. Could they be thinking that Manermakeri himself had descended in the light of the flames, the forerunner of a hell of fire and large-scale destruction? When the news came that the Americans were constructing a naval base in Biak and Meokwundi, the very island of the Messiah, the Biak people shouted themselves hoarse. The Americans generously distributed clothing and food to thousands of natives. To the Biak people, the koreri ideal had materialised. All that had been prophesised had been fulfilled — except the return of the dead.

Since then, the koreri myth has gradually died — perhaps because of the end of wars, the advance of modern civilisation and the introduction of Western technology. Most of the Biak population are now either Christians or Muslims. Yet songs of the koreri era can still be heard, though only as entertainment. As I sat in a seaside hotel in Biak admiring the sunset, I heard a boy and a girl singing a beautiful koreri tune, as they fished leisurely amongst the rocks. Indeed the sun had set for the koreri movement.

Although many of the Papuans in Wamena and Biak still live in the Stone Age, they can be considered somewhat civilised when compared to the head-hunters who still inhibit the jungles of southern and western Irian Jaya. One of the head-hunting tribes called Marind Anim, occupies a vast territory stretching along the coast in the Marukc district. They are one of the relatively few Papuan peoples who have a name of their own to denote their tribal identity. The word *anim* means "men" while *marind* is a distinctive native tribal name. The marind Anim is one of the head-hunting tribes in Irian Jaya of whom a study has been made.

It is not easy to get a guide to tour villages of head-hunters, for who could guarantee the safe return of the visitors, particularly when they are diplomats? According to stories derived from books and from indirect interviews, we have a rough idea of how, where and why head-hunting is still being practised in many parts of Irian Jaya.

To the Marind Anim, head-hunting is not just an act of warfare, self-defense or the human desire for conquest. The prime motive of the Marind Anim in organising head-hunting is to gather names for their children when the supply of names has been exhausted. To the Marind Anim, it is necessary to have a separate "head" name for each individual child. It is a sort of status symbol. Every child is named after a victim who has been beheaded. Before the victim's head is chopped off he is asked to spell out his name. Whether the name uttered is correct is immaterial so long as a sound is heard which resembles a name. Thus, when a child is born, the parents need to hunt for a head in order to inherit a name. Some renowned warriors have names saved up like a name bank. Sometimes they give them away to relatives as presents, or give their own children more than one name.

With the discovery of oil in Sorong on the eastern tip of Irian Jaya, modern technology has moved into an area which was inhabited by other groups of people whose development stagnated way back to the Stone Age. The sudden appearance of modern machines and equipment for the exploitation of the rich natural resources is bound to make an impact on a population who are handicapped by such a wide cultural gap. It is essential that development and industrialisation go hand in hand with an understanding and appreciation of the Papuans, if the reality of modern science is to avoid a clash with Stone Age myths and superstitions. The success of technological advancement depends a lot on the support and co-operation of the people being affected by the changes. In this respect, a great deal more is needed to be done in the field of anthropology and sociology.

As a nature lover, I went to Irian Jaya with a secret wish to see a *cenderawasih* (bird of paradise) for which Irian Jaya is famous. I also tried to see traces of Irianese nationalism. I did not see any. The noise of oil-drilling machines may have driven the birds deeper into the forest. Economic investment may have also discouraged Irianese nationalism. Instead of seeing signs of Irianese resistance, I saw the koteka, an instrument which the Dhanis used to protect the human bird. Will the koteka, too, disappear with the advance of modern civilisation?

19
THE DAYAKS
The Head-hunters

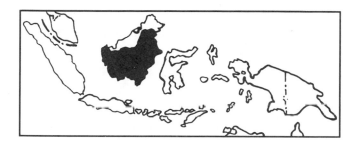

The Dayaks are the world's well-known head-hunters. In ancient days, they proudly displayed their spoils as "trophies" at the entrance of their houses. With the arrival of Christianity, such gruesome habits have disppeared. But, in March this year, the Dayaks have revived their old custom of head-hunting in the village of the Sambas district, some 50 km north-east of Singkawang, and this time they were assisted by the Malays. Their target: the Madurese from the eastern end of Java, about 120,000 of them have migrated to Kalimantan under Suharto's transmigration program. The indigenous Dayaks and Malays who comprise 35 to 40 percent of Kalimantan's population of four million have ganged up to chase the Madurese interlopers out.

On 20 March, 1999, in the village of Teras, near Singkawang, indigenous Dayaks and ethnic Malays waving freshly severed heads of Madurese paraded through the small town despite shoot-on-sight orders by the police. Crowds appeared on the dusty streets to cheer as the pickup trucks carrying the triumphant men waving three heads at them, shouting "Long Live the Malays" and brandishing spears, pitchforks and long knives. One of the three migrants from Madura island who was decapitated was rumoured to have been a local teacher. No military personnel was in sight to witness the grisly procession, but it was reported that the Chief Police had issued shoot-on-sight orders.

In the village of Sambas, about 50 km from Singkawang, the head-hunters did something very inhuman. They burned the body of a Madurese at the market place and offered passers-by with small shredded bits of the liver of the victim. Many accepted and ate the body parts in the local tribal tradition of eating parts of one's enemy. They believe that by eating the dead body, they also ate up the spirit of the person.

It is Dayak custom that when a transgressor refuses to accept the demands of Dayak adat or customary law concerning such a sin, usually a fine of about 11 million rupiahs to the family of the victim or his community turning himself in to the police, then tradition required the Dayak to perform a ritual that calls for the shedding of blood. The Dayak Chief explains that the killing of the Madurese was not for reasons of revenge, but rather the need to fulfill tradition obligations that have bound the Dayaks since time immemorial.

Shops in Singkawang had been shuttered and streets deserted. Security forces had set up road blocks at entry points into Singkawang and were frisking all who passed in and out of the city for concealed weapons.

The clash was triggered off in February when a Madurese mob attacked a Malay village over the beating of a Madurese thief, killing three people. This angered the Malays, who backed by the Dayaks started their head-hunting exercise.

Reports said up to 165 people had been killed. Three companies of Indonesian elite infantry were rushed there in the afternoon after the beheading exercise and were dragooning villagers to clear bodies from the area on makeshift stretches.

Thousands of Madurese, mostly the elderly, women and children have evacuated to Pontianak, a town near Singkawang which was comparatively free of violence. Many Madurese have gone back to their hometown of Madura.

Madurese are by nature very fierce. In 1866, a Dutchman Tadema Wop once wrote that "insult a Madurese and you will be answered with a knife". No Madurese would ever be seen without a spear or *kris* or a *tjaloq* — a kind of machete with a bent point. He uses such a *tjaloq* for almost everything. He cuts wood with it, cuts brush to clear a path and also uses it to cut off the arms, legs and the head of his enemies.

Perhaps it was a mistake for the Suharto Government to transmigrate Madurese to Kalimantan. Tens of thousands of Javanese, Bugis, Balinese and Madurese from all over Indonesia were brought in to settle down in Kalimantan. The Dayaks got along well with the Javanese, the Bugis and Balinese, but could not tolerate the aggressive behaviour of the Madurese. Two years ago, there was a serious clash between the Dayaks and Madurese resulting in a bloody tribal war when 300 were killed in months of unrest. Madurese women complained to their husbands that Dayaks had threatened them while the Dayak women also made similar complaints to their men.

A Dayak anthropologist, Stephanus Djuweng, said there was a serious cultural gap between the Dayaks and Madurese. He said, "the indigenous people of West Kalimantan don't want the Madurese." A confidential government report prepared last year tracing the bakground of the 1996-97 ethnic clash concluded that Jakarta had not only marginalised West Kalimantan's indigenous peoples economically and politically — only one of the provinces' six districts, the most remote, is headed by a Dayak — but also exacerbated the problem by transplanting the Muslim Madurese there.

The Madurese as a community, concedes a senior government official, are "sociologically unsuitable to harmonious living with the Dayaks" who consider Muslim beliefs and practices totally incompatible with their culture even though they can co-exist happily with the other main ethnic groups. The official said, "for a long time, the Dayaks have accumulated a lot of unhappiness against the government, and the Madurese are the victims of that unhappiness. It did not help that although most Madurese worked in urban areas as pedicab drivers, coolies and stevedores, some were able to acquire land in the coastal areas as small-time rice farmers under official scheme, taking them a notch above the dispossessed Dayaks."

The Dayaks live in Kalimantan which comprise roughly the southern three-quarters of Borneo, the third largest island in the world. Of the 12 million people in Borneo, about 9.8 million are mostly Dayaks living in Kalimantan. They settled down along its rivers.

Kalimantan is divided into four provinces, the East with Balikpapan as its capital has a population of 2.1 million, the West, with Pontianak as its capital, has 3.5 million, the Central has 1.4 million with Palangkarya as its capital, and the South with its capital at Banjarmasin known as the "Venice of the East", has a population of 2.8 million. Except for Pontianak which has a large population of Chinese making up 35 percent of the population, the other provinces are predominated by Dayaks.

As early as the Tang dynasty the Chinese had arrived at the coast and major waterways of Kalimantan. By 1000 A.D., Chinese trading posts had sprung up in Pontianak. Enterprising Chinese miners appeared on the south and west coast of Kalimantan to extract gold and diamond. In 1409, Admiral Cheng Ho, a Muslim eunuch of the Ming dynasty, led his 63 treasure ships and landed in Borneo, long before the arrival of the Europeans. Admiral Cheng Ho invited the king of Borneo, one Manajochiana to pay tribute to China. The King later led a 50-strong delegation to Beijing. He was then only 28 years old and went with his wife and four-year-old son. In Beijing, the King suddenly fell ill and died. A grand funeral was organised by the Ming emperor for the King. His son Hsia Wang took over the throne after his death.

That explains the existence of highly sophisticated late Chou style claypot, Chinese beads and other antiques brought in by Cheng Ho's expedition. All the porcelains bore the symbol of the dragon, which was typical of Chinese ornamental designs.

In the early days, there were also Indian traders travelling in merchant fleets of large, seagoing junks. Roman relics have been found in Kalimantan as well as Hindu-Javanese ones from around 400 A.D.. Hindu temple remains have been unearthed in southern Kalimantan near Amuntai and Negara and three are Sanskrit tablets in caves at Wahau, East Kalimantan.

Since 5000 B.C. Dayak tribes have lived in Kalimantan. They lived in places which are most difficult for outsiders to penetrate. But they were by no means uncivilised. In the Neolithic period (1800 to 500 B.C.) when Europeans were wearing deerskins and throwing spears, the Dayaks already had a highly advanced culture, fashioning polished stone tools, and making earthenware pottery, bone ornaments and cotton textiles. When the Malays migrated to Kalimantan in the coastal areas, the Dayaks retreated inland and refused to be converted to Islam because Islam prohibited eating pork and their favourite dish was pork. Their culture was gradually influenced by the introduction of Western culture and traditional culture began to decline.

The coastal ports of Kalimantan were Islamised during the 15th and 16th centuries with the onslaught of Islam. They developed into small independent sultanates at Smabas, Kutai and Banjarmasin, each had strong mercantile ties to the Islamic northern ports of Java.

The first fully documented European arrival occurred in 1521, when one of Magellan's ships pulled into the harbour of Brunei. The word "Borneo" in fact, is the anglicised word for Brunei, an ancient kingdom named after the *berunai* fruit. The Europeans had difficulty in controlling the Kalimantan ports which were hideouts for pirates. The Dutch found no commercial value in taking over the interior of Kalimantan. They however concluded treaties with the various small coastal states.

In the early 16th century, before the arrival of the Europeans, there was a well-known Chinese miner by the name of Loh Fang Per, who had his own little kingdom near Pontianak digging gold. He had his own police, judicial personnel and was almost the "king" in the mining area. The Dutch came along and pushed him out by force.

In 1838, the Dutch were however jolted by the arrival of an Englishman named James Brooke, a self-styled adventurer, who came to help the Brunei aristocrats who were facing rebellion from inland tribes. In gratitude for the assistance in quelling the rebellion, the Sultan gave power to James Brooke to administer Kuching (a town in Sarawak) in 1841. Brooke suppressed the inland tribe, abolished head-hunting, curbed piracy in the coastal area and established his own dynasty of white rajas. He ruled Sarawak for more than 100 years. His kingdom lasted until World War II.

The division of British-controlled North Borneo and Dutch-controlled Kalimantan resulted when Brooke handed over North Borneo to the British Government after World War II. It put Britain in a curious position of acquiring a new colony at the time when it was shedding other colonies. Sarawak remained under British control when Malaya gained independence in 1957. In 1963, Sarawak and Sabah joined with the Malay Peninsula and Singapore to form Malaysia. The Indonesian President Sukarno, suspicious of Britain's continued influence in Malaysia, challenged the newly independent state with military confrontations. Long after confrontation was abandoned, anti-Malaysian Chinese guerrillas of the Sarawak People's Guerrilla Troops, originally trained and armed by the Indonesians, remained in Kalimantan.

During World War II, the Japanese occupied the island from 1942 to 1945. Their ruthless suppression resulted in the deaths of 20,000 intellectuals, missionaries, businessmen, and aristocrats. During the occupation, the island provided Japan with almost half of its wartime requirement of fuel oil. When Indonesia declared independence, they changed the name of the island from Borneo to Kalimantan, which means "rivers of precious stones" which aptly describes the island which have rich deposits of gold, diamond, amethysts, agate, sapphire and emerald.

For many years, Kalimantan was a burden to the Dutch as well as the newly independent Indonesian nation. Then in 1950, oil, gas and timber were finally tapped and the island suddenly boomed. Today, East Kalimantan produces nearly 25 percent of Indonesia's total export earnings.

Kalimantan is rich in mineral resources. Coal, petroleum, and natural gas production have become big business here. Equally important is the timber industry, rubber, copra and gems. Gold and diamond mining and processing are also important sources of earnings. Kalimantan exports about 50 percent of Indonesia's timber. They are exploited by more than 100 overseas investors. In 1982-83, the largest forest fire in the history of Indonesia called "The Great Fire" broke out in East Kalimantan.

The word "Dayak" is a collective name for over 200 different tribes who live throughout the Borneo territory — both British Borneo and Kalimantan. Each *sukuh* (tribe) has its own tribal name and speaks its own dialect. The Dayak race is light-skinned, quite resembling the Chinese, with rounded, well-featured faces and slightly slanted eyes. The mountain Dayak tribes are physically taller and more imposing than most Asians. They are heavily muscled and weigh above 75 kg or more.

Some Indonesians call the Dayak villagers *orang bodoh* (stupid men) which is not a kind phrase. They were described as such because of the Dayak head-hunting habits and their animist customs. In fact, the Dayaks are more civilised than one can imagine. They have their own system of electing local government, maintaining their own political boundaries and even have a capital city called Palangkarya.

Head-hunting was once a Dayak custom in olden times. During the hunting season, men would be awakened by the spirit of courage, *Bali Akang*. After decapitating the enemies' heads, they would return for a big festival with the heads as trophies. They would extract the brain substance through the nostrils, then the heads were placed in plaited rattan nets and smoke-cured over a fire.

The Dayaks believed that a good head could save a village from plague, produce rain, ward off evil spirits or triple rice yields. They believed that dried skulls were the most powerful magic in the world. They could vitalise and transfuse energy for the whole village. Dayak people believed that a man's spirit continues to inhabit his head after death. These heads were offered food and cigarettes and surrounded by palm leaves, and their spirits would forgive and forget and feel welcome in the new environment. Such heads were hung in the house. The more heads a family has, the more prestigious will be its owners. These heads would impress sweethearts and were an initiation to manhood for the youths.

In some tribes, a head's power increased over time. The cherished ones were handed down from generation to generation. Villages without *ulu* (head) were considered spiritually weak and easy prey to their enemies.

Dayak tribes often use blowguns or blowpipes to hunt pigs and monkeys and in warfare against their enemies. Such blowpipes are called *sumpit*. The sumpit is a narrow tube about two to three metres long made of hardwood or bamboo fitted with iron sights, and shot darts. The Dayaks are very skilful with the sumpit and are very accurate for distances of 100 metres or more. The dart shaft falls away on impact and the deadly poisoned tip firmly embeds in the prey's flesh. Paralysis occurs instantly when one is hit by a blowpipe, and death occurs within three minutes.

Dayaks live in long houses called *lamin* or *betan*. Such long houses are always built along river banks. These ridge-roofed structures can be up to 180 metres long and 9-18 metres wide. Several long houses can accommodate 50 or more families and there are as many as 200 doors. This is the so-called Dayak village. It takes about a week to build and erect a new long house. All Dayak long houses are built on stilts. The space below can be used to raise chicken and pigs. The stilts are also as a protection against snakes, floods and enemies.

While I was in Pontianak, I visited some long houses. I was impressed by the Dayak architecture and craftsmanship. I admired the magnificently decorative teakwood railings carved into dragons, snakes, demons or bird, showing details down to scales and feathers. I even saw one carved with sexual designs. Such carvings also appeared in door frames, galleries and posts of the long houses.

A long house usually has a covered veranda which is a communal living area, running the full length of the building and always facing the river. The veranda is used for loafing, child care and for visitors as well as match-making.

I was told that if a girl falls in love with a visitor, he is invited to her sleeping room. If he blows off the lamp, it means he loves her.

And if he abandons her after having an affair with the girl, she will make sure that he is hunted down and leaves behind his head. She wants to remember him through the view of his head. In olden days, it was customary for the owner of the house to invite the visitor to sleep with his daughter. If he is too choosy, he will have to leave his head behind.

In most of the long houses, we saw the older generation Dayaks. The younger ones have gone down river to look for jobs. When we were visiting the long houses, we saw the village swarmed with hunting dogs, cats, hens, cocks and pigs under the long houses.

We saw Dayak women who had their ear lobes pierced and wearing heavy gold or brass rings stretching down to the shoulder. I was told that one ear was pierced by the mother and the other by a paternal kin.

In the long house, the women are the first to rise in the morning. They light up the cooking fires, fetch water, and bathe in the river. They can cook rice and if they have to work in the field, rice is wrapped in banana leaves to be brought to the field. The men got up later, then take a bath in the river, light up their cigarettes and then eat breakfast. In the evening, they sit around the hearth and eat with their fingers. Rice is heaped on tin plates which also come with fish, spices, vegetables and sauce. They eat pork only on special festive occasions. They like visitors. To them, our visit was an occasion that called for a festival.

The Indonesian Government is abolishing multi-family long houses and replacing them with modern, single-family dwellings. This has caused a drastic change in the Dayak's village life. Christianity has also helped to discourage the building of long houses.

In Pontianak, we saw many tattooed Dayak men and women. The tattooed designs of snakes, birds, dragons and plant motifs reveal their outstanding aesthetic sense in the incredibly refined art of tattooing. They first make woodcuts and then coloured them with charcoal. The woodcut designs are then stamped on the skin which is punctured with brass needles dipped in dye. An intricate tattoo may take months of hard work as well as torturing pain. The Dayaks regard tattoo not just as bodily ornaments and decorations, but also a sign of bravery and courage. The amount of tattoo on a person shows the extent of his courage.

Male tattoos were meant to beautify him when he goes to heaven. The Dayaks start to tattoo a boy when he reaches the age of 12. As he grows older, his journey, skirmishes and spiritual events are all recorded. At death, a historical and biological map of his whole life is tattooed on his shoulders, chest and legs. Tattoo may give away a woman's rank in society. In certain tribes, only wives and daughter of Chiefs are allowed to tattoo their thighs.

With the arrival of Christianity, and with government prohibition, the tattooing art is fast vanishing.

Many Dayak people still believe in their *wadian* or *dajung* (shamans) whom they believe can cure them of their illnesses and diseases. These dajungs are the dukuns of the Dayak society. Many sick people or those in ill fortune travel for days to see a famous dajung. She is a magician-healer who can seek out the cause of the sickness or ill-doing. She is also the mistress of many ceremonies performing rituals to bless a place or a company. She always wears uncoiled hair with huge jangling bracelets and performs her ritual dances in a trance. The Dayaks believe that she is the "door to the spiritual world". She yanks out toenails without anesthesia. When one of her clients suffers from fever, she would go into the jungle with a basket, imploring the devilish spirit to drop the wayward soul into the basket so that she can return it. In a village where there is no doctor, dajung is the only person the Dayaks can rely on. Even in Christianised villages, shamans are responsible for the mental, physical, and spiritual health of the Dayaks.

The Dayaks usually perform dances on festive occasions: the coming of age, marriage, death, banishing illness, fighting and finishing wars or during rice planting or harvesting seasons. Dayak dances are exciting spectacles for tourists who have not seen one. When we were in Pontianak, we attended some Dayak performances. The dancers wore animal skins and plumes of feathers. In mock battles, they screamed and danced to the tune of an instrument similar to gamelan. The

Dayaks are renowned for their solo sword dances. In the *ngejiak* show, a young Dayak demonstrated his skill of swordsmanship by using a sharp mandau. I was impressed by the mock fight which was called *kancet papatai* between two men, also wielding mandau. There was also a typical Dayak dance where the performers put on animal-like demon masks with fangs, big noses and bulging eyes.

I was captivated by an old Dayak musical instrument called *klendi* (a blowing instrument) which is like a mouth organ with six or eight narrow strips of bamboo protruding from a hollow oval gourd. Very few Dayaks nowadays know how to play the klendi. This instrument, strangely enough, was found in the bas-reliefs of 9th century Borobudur in central Java. Known since the Bronze Age, it is the only musical instrument which is still found in Kalimantan's interior. There must have been a great deal of trade between Java's Hindu empire of Majapahit and Kalimantan. The Dayak's goblet-shaped drums made from heavy, hollowed-out tree trunks also attracted my attention. I was told that in the northern region, magnificent dragon gongs are still being played.

Another musical instrument which also fascinated me was the *sampe*, a large flat lute with rattan strings which resonate over a painted wooden box.

The Dayaks were in fact not the original sons of the soil in Kalimantan. The real *bumis* were the Penan tribemen. With the successive waves of migration in Borneo, the Penan gradually moved inland from the coast and continued their primitive way of life. About 10,000 of them are left. They stay in isolated, scattered pockets in the upper Mahakam and in the Apo Kayan. The Government has made plans to settle the Penans in villages and encourages them to cultivate rice, but they are not interested. The Penans live off fruits, wild berries, wild boars, wild goats and other animals in the jungle. They hunt them with blowpipes and their hunting dogs. They live like nomads, moving from one place to another without proper settlement. They smoke like locomotives. One group of Penans still live a mesolithic existence in a stone cave.

There are many tribes among the Dayaks, but the major groups are the Kenyah and the Kayan. Outwardly, they are similar, but the Kenyahs and the Kayans speak different languages and have different customs. Both tribes possess a hierarchical social order of aristocrats and commoners. The Kenyah's hometown is the remote Apo Kayan of the upper Kayan River. Many of the Kenyahs have emigrated during the century, some establishing villages to the south of the Boh, Taban, Kelinjau and Kedang Kepala, all tributaries of the Mahakam River. Many have emigrated north to Sarawak which is now Malaysia. Almost all Kenyahs are Protestants.

The Kayan's hometown is the Apo Kayan, but most have now moved down the lower Kayan and its tributaries.

I visited the three major capitals: Pontianak of West Kalimantan, Balikpapan of East Kalimantan and Banjarmasin of South Kalimantan. I went first to Pontianak because that province has a large population of Chinese. Pontianak is also known as Kota Khatulistiwa ("Equator City") or the "Floating Town". The word "Pontianak" literally means "vampire ghosts of women who died in childbirth" and often refers to a baleful spirit who lures young men into the cemeteries. To many who understand Indonesian, the word "pontianak" is rather frightening.

Pontianak is Borneo's largest capital for rubber and plywood. We saw many Japanese and Koreans who were engaged by the giant international plywood companies. There were very few tourists. It was from here that we ventured into the interior Dayak villages. Pontianak felt the full brunt of the Japanese occupation (1942-45) perhaps because of the large Chinese population who were anti-Japanese. Between 1943 and July 1944, thousands of Indonesian intellectuals, especially ethnic Chinese and members of the Islamic aristocracy, were rounded up and executed. After the war, mass graves were uncovered, the largest at Mandor, containing at least 1,000 victims. Estimates of the total number of victims range from 3,000 to 20,000.

Starting from 1945, the Dayaks, Chinese and Malays formed guerrilla groups and started a resistance movement against the Japanese. Dayak warriors often attacked Japanese camps, taking away Japanese heads and hanging them on poles for all to see. When we saw Japanese expatriates stationed in Pontianak chatting happily with local Chinese and Dayaks, we knew that the deep scars of the war have been completely healed.

In this city, for the first time in Indonesia, we saw more churches than mosques. Everywhere, we saw ethnic Chinese who run businesses, restaurants, and shopkeepers and many others who were previously gold-miners. More than 60 percent of the population of Pontianak are Chinese. This was the only city in Indonesia where it is predominated by the Chinese. It is like a little pre-war Singapore except that there is not a single Chinese shop bearing Chinese signboard, for the Chinese language is banned in Indonesia. What attracted me most was the heavy presence of Indonesian soldiers in green uniform such as commandos, those working in helicopter companies, and small cruisers in the harbour. It is a bustling city with heavy traffic of automobiles, motorcycles, bicycles, trishaw, and pedestrians. The city has two large bridges spanning the river, a massive sports stadium, and a number of canals.

We visited the Pontianak harbour, which is the centre for both foreign and domestic trade. We saw ships transporting timber and rubber. In the evening, thousands of sparrows swarm along the waterfront.

There is a Chinese temple inside the city, but the Chinese and Dayaks are predominantly Christians.

Our next stop was Balikpapan, which is a sprawling city without any centre point. The city was a small village until the 1960s when oil was discovered in the coastal area and it started to boom. We saw expatriate Americans, Australians, and Europeans who work for oil companies and Indonesians who work for Pertamina. There is not much to see except Pertamina oil refinery, gas flares, pipes, tanks and girders and the building complexes of Western companies.

North of the Pertamina oil refinery is a village comprising houses on stilts connected by wooden walkways over a muddy estuary. Near the harbour is a row of houses where women are for sale as short-term "wives" for oilies and chippies. There is a highly organised brothel called "Lemah Harapan" (Valley of Hope) in an army camp.

There is also a row of white-washed houses where worn-out prostitutes from Surabaya came to earn their livelihood. The only recreation for expatriates is to watch women from a glass wall and picking the ones they like. There are also pool balls, pinballs and massage in the Blue Sky Hotel. There, Dayaks serve cocktails to expatriates in air-conditioned bars and nightclubs.

The last city we visited in Kalimantan was Banjarmasin, known as "Venice of the East". Banjarmasin is below sea level, and the water level rises and falls with the tides. It is situated on the banks of the Martapura River and enters the Barito River. Many houses are perched on stilts or ride the tides on hundles of floating logs. That is why it resembles a little Venice. It is the largest city in Kalimantan, with over 350,000 people (80 percent Muslims, 15 percent Christians, 5 percent Buddhists/Hindus). Banjarmasin, once populated by pirates, has now turned into a stronghold for Islamic conservatives. The Banjarese practice a more orthodox form of Islam than the other Muslims on Indonesia's western islands. Thousands leave the city for Mecca and are proud to be bestowed the title of *haji*. During the Ramadan, the piercing siren announces the beginning and end of the fasting hours.

Banjarmasin has a long history of intrigue and murder. It rose into prominence in 1526 when Pangeran Samujdera, a descendent of one of the Hindu kings, overthrew the ruler in Negara and moved the capital to Bandar Masih, the present site of Banjarmasin. The Dutch arrived first for the pepper and started trading with the Sultan of Banjarmasin. However, four years later when the Dutch East Indies Company sent their vessels to the port, they were attacked and all its crew massacred. The Dutch took punitive action and the sultan withdrew to Martapura. The Dutch were granted a monopoly on pepper in 1635, but disgruntled growers murdered all 64 residents of the Dutch trading post. The Banjarese also slaughtered 40 Dutch at Kota Waringin. After much fighting, the Dutch signed an agreement with the Sultan giving them monopoly for pepper in 1658.

Then the British came and started to compete with the Dutch. In 1701, trouble erupted when the British stationed a warship on Barito

River to guard their warehouses. The Banjarese revolted, and it took them six years to evict the foreigners.

The Dutch also felt the sting of Banjarese resistance after they placed an unpopular prince on the Banjarmasin throne in 1857. This led to the five-year (1859-63) Banjarmasin war when rural Islamic leaders led a courageous resistance against the Dutch, taxing Dutch financial and human resources. The Dutch regained control in 1860, but sporadic resistance continued until 1905.

We took a boat and arrived at Tamban, about four km from Banjarmasin. There we saw thousands of houses built on log floats, connected by an intricate system of canals. We visited the famous Kuin Market, a floating market where traders paddle their *jukung*, a kind of canoe simply dug out from a tree. Vendors wear the traditional *tangguji* hats made of straw to protect themselves from the hot tropical sun. River traders ply the waters of Banjarmasin, selling fish, vegetables, fruits, and household necessities door to door.

We went to the city centre where the massive mosque called Mesjid Raya Sabilal Muhtadin ("The road unto God's Blessing") is situated. The mosque is just opposite the Islamic university. It was built on the site of an old Dutch fort. The main minaret is 45 metres high, with four other smaller minarets of about 21 metres high. The shape of the mosque resembles an alien space vehicle with a copper-coloured dome. Nearby we found hundreds of brothels and a dozen cinemas. On Independence Day, the city puts on a *perahu dayung* (canoe) race to celebrate the occasion.

With the fall of Suharto and the weakening of the Abri, there is always a danger of a recurrence of racial conflict in Kalimantan. There will be no more military force strong enough to tackle the problem. In September 1998, two ethnic groups in Pontianak have formed private armies to protect their property from looters and found their effort backfired when they battled each other instead. During the month, hundreds of scared housewives in Pontianak had to flee from the market, when the Dayaks and Madurese groups — both trying to protect a rice merchant — turned on each other with knives and sickles. Colonel Erwin Sudono, the military commander of the town where stores and warehouses were attacked by mobs said he had to disband the private armies which were approved by him earlier.

The armed forces has been powerless to stop the looting, triggered by the soaring prices of rice.

Will there be peace in Kalimantan with such hostility between the two communities when even the armed forces failed to contain the conflicts?

INDEX

BIBLIOGRAPHY

Richard Chauvel, *Nationalists, Soldiers and Separatists*, KITLV Press, 1990

Des Alwi, *Turbulent Times Past in Ternate and Tidore*, Yayasan dan Budaya Banda Naira, 1990

James Dunn, *Timor — A People Betrayed*, ABC Book, 1996

Geoff Forrester and R.J. May, *The Fall of Suharto*, Select Books, 1999

Bruce Grant, *Indonesia*, Melbourne University Press, 1996

David Jenkins, *Suharto and His Generals — Indonesian Military Politics 1975-1983*, Cornell Modern Indonesia Project, 1997

Robert Lowry, *The Armed Forces of Indonesia*, Allen & Unwin, 1996

Paul Mojzes, *Yugoslavian Inferno*, Continuum Publishing Co., 1994

Kal Muller, *Spice Islands, the Moluccas*, Periplus Editions, 1991

Christian Pelras, *The Bugis*, Blackwell, 1996

Douglas E. Ramage, *Politics in Indonesia*, Routledge, 1996

F.M. Schnitger, *Forgotten Kingdoms in Sumatra*, Oxford University Press, Singapore, 1989

Adam Schwarz, *A Nation in Waiting*, Allen & Unwin, 1994

Bilveer Singh, *East Timor, Myths and Realities*, ADPR Consultant (M) Sdn Bhd, 1996

Holly S. Smith, *Aceh Art and Culture*, Oxford University Press, 1997

Leo Suryadinata, *Indonesia's Foreign Policy under Suharto*, Times Academic Press, 1996

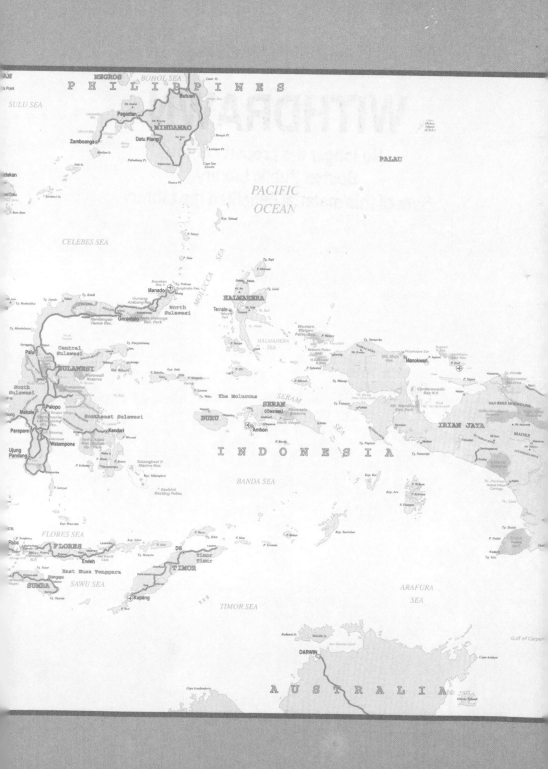